The B
Carthage, Missouri

The Battle of Carthage, Missouri

First Trans-Mississippi Conflict of the Civil War

KENNETH E. BURCHETT

McFarland & Company, Inc., Publishers

Jefferson, North Carolina, and London

ISBN 978-0-7864-6959-8
softcover : acid free paper ∞

LIBRARY OF CONGRESS CATALOGUING DATA ARE AVAILABLE

BRITISH LIBRARY CATALOGUING DATA ARE AVAILABLE

On the cover: Wood engraving of an imagining of
The Battle of Carthage, Missouri, 1861 (Library of Congress)

Manufactured in the United States of America

*McFarland & Company, Inc., Publishers
Box 611, Jefferson, North Carolina 28640
www.mcfarlandpub.com*

For Gena

Contents

AFTER THE BATTLE

Acknowledgments

The history of the Civil War is a hard history to unravel. It has been that way almost from the beginning. A few years after the war's end, an anonymous writer confessed his frustrations. He said, "At the close of the war, those who had engaged in the Southern side surrendered, and seemed to desire, and to endeavor to cast away from them the memories of all that had occurred in those four long years of war, and final failure; … they have, in great measure forgotten many incidents, and nearly all dates. Hence, perfect exactness and completeness have been found very nearly impossible."

Historians since have tried to piece together a fair history of the nation's most trying time, often with similar aggravation over the facts. This work will undoubtedly fall short in that respect as well. Although every effort went into rendering a true account of the Battle of Carthage and an accurate depiction of southwest Missouri, I take full responsibility for any errors of fact or omission.

I wish to thank the many authors both past and present whose work I used. Ward Schrantz was the first to write extensively about the Battle of Carthage. His work laid the foundation for this book in many important ways. The same is true of Marvin VanGilder who became steward of Mr. Schrantz's papers and added immeasurably to the understanding of the battle and the people of Carthage and Jasper County, Missouri. A special nod goes to David Hinze and Karen Farnham for their research and for their dedication to the preservation of the battleground.

I greatly appreciate the encouragement and support of Steve Weldon and Deborah Wood and the generosity of Maureen McGrath, a great-great-granddaughter of Colonel Joseph Kelly, and Richard K. Rains, Jr., a great-great-grandson of General James S. Rains. With apologies to anyone I may have missed, I wish to acknowledge the assistance of Kristopher L. Anstine, T. Juliette Arai, Carolyn Atkins, Heather D. Beattie, Christine M. Beauregard, Mike Bieker, Bill Boggess, Troy Branzhaf, Peter F. Brauer, Nancy Brewer, Jeff Bridges, Alan Chilton, Alex Choate, Stephanie O. Christensen, Sandy Clark, Amanda Claunch, Kyle Constant, Jonathan Eaker, Jake Ersland, Terry Foster, Renee Glass, Aryn Glazier, Michael Glenn, Marcia Goswick, William L. Graves, Michele Hansford, Douglas A. Harding, Irene Harvey, Philip Hinderberger, Michael Hoerman, Clyde B. Hood, III, Pam Hunter, Erica Kelly, Keith Kerr, Lisa Keys, Lauren Leeman, Barbara Leland, David Long, Kaye M.

Lundgren, Jim McGhee, Meredith McLemore, William A. McWhorter, Valerie Moore, Beverly Mosman, Daisy Njoku, Doug Para, L. Eileen Parris, Jeff Patrick, Linda R. Pine, Julie Potter, Sara Przybylski, Anita Roberts, John Rutherford, Kent Salomon, Daniel C. Schwartz, Donna Schwieder, Jennifer Seaton, Lola Shropshire, Ward W. Slack, Jason D. Stratman, Lynn Sullivan, and Ellen Thomasson.

Finally, thank you to the staffs of the many institutions and organizations that contributed to the research: Alabama Department of Archives and History, Arkansas Studies Institute, Barton County Library, Butt-Holdsworth Memorial Library, Carthage Public Library, Christian County Library, Cornell University Library, Dolph Briscoe Center for American History, Drury University Library, Greene County Archives and Records Center, Harvard-Smithsonian Center for Astrophysics, Hendrix College Library, Jasper County Records Center, Jefferson National Expansion Memorial, Leavenworth County Historical Society, Kansas State Historical Society, Library Center Springfield-Greene County, Library of Congress, Missouri History Museum, Missouri State Archives, Missouri State University Duane G. Meyer Library, Museum for Springfield–Greene County, National Anthropological Archives-Smithsonian, National Archives and Records Administration, National Archives at Kansas City, National Parks Service, New York Public Library Manuscripts and Special Collections, Oklahoma Historical Society, Pea Ridge National Military Park, Powers Museum–Carthage, Sarcoxie Public Library, Sedalia Public Library, Southern Memorial Association, State Historical Society of Missouri-Columbia, Texas Historical Commission, the Butler Center–Little Rock, the Carthage Press, Trails Regional Library–Lexington, U.S. Army Military History Institute, University of Arkansas at Little Rock Archives, University of Arkansas Press, University of California Libraries, University of Central Arkansas CFAC, University of Missouri Archives, Virginia Historical Society, W. Dale Clark Main Library, and Wilson's Creek National Battlefield.

Preface

The Battle of Carthage comprised six separate engagements in a day-long action that spread over several miles before Union troops withdrew under the cover of darkness. It was the largest full-scale land battle of the Civil War up to that time, occurring eleven days before the Battle of Bull Run. By any measure of importance, the Battle of Carthage was not as significant as Bull Run. It was, however, the heaviest engagement of the Civil War up to that point and the first all-out land campaign of the war. The *New York Times*, July 11, 1861, called it by far the most serious battle of the war and described it as the first major conflict between United States troops and the rebels. The battle had the largest number of casualties of any action since the firing on Fort Sumter and was the first clash of the Civil War designated as a battle in military records. What happened on that hot Friday afternoon of July 5, 1861, opened a tragic new chapter in American history, one of the very first clash of arms between federal and secessionist troops, and a prelude to so much carnage that followed.

There were no Confederate soldiers at the Battle of Carthage. Two armies from the same state met in the ultimate conflict over states' rights. An army of Missourians fought another army of Missourians, each strongly convinced of the rightness of their cause. The battle marked the first time that federal authority replaced a duly elected state government, sending immigrant nationals to fight native sons of Missouri in a state that had not seceded from the Union and was not part of the Confederacy. It is the only time a sitting governor took command of military forces in the field, and it marked the first time Congress ever expelled a United States congressional representative for hostile action against the federal government. Perhaps most important of all, the battle signaled an escalation in the hostilities between the North and South and lay bare the bitter partisanship of a deeply divided Missouri, a state critical to the prosecution of the Civil War.

Few people know about the Battle of Carthage. Overshadowed by the great battles of the war, it slipped from memory with hardly a page to recount its pivotal role in the fight to keep Missouri in the Union; and keeping Missouri in the Union was critical to the outcome of the Civil War. Had the result of the Battle of Carthage been different, ending in victory for federal forces instead of defeat, the war in the West arguably would have been over before it started. What happened on the prairie of Jasper County forever

1

changed Missouri, and in the process began the terrible journey that altered the future of America.

This book is about how the Civil War came to one small community in southwest Missouri. It comes from a lifelong curiosity about the war and about the people caught up in the tragedy and triumph of it. It is a patchwork of personal stories, many of them of an apocryphal nature, but it would not be a true history without some of those stories because they were part of the tapestry of the Civil War. The lifestyles of the people form an important backdrop to the narrative. Descriptions of scenes are in the context of the culture and geography of the region at the time of the battle. Place names are those in existence in 1861. Illustrations are of that era as much as possible. Imagined conversations closely follow the letters and documents produced by the speakers.

The task of getting the facts right required recognizing the pitfalls of sectional bias when trying to piece together the story. To be expected, the predominance of accounts of the battle comes from the victors and not the vanquished; more versions survive on the rebel side than the Union. None of the combatants retained a perfectly clear memory of what happened, either before, during, or after the battle. Hardly a single eyewitness account fully agreed with another. The old histories and accounts often contain prejudices supported by "facts" contradicted by the "facts" of the other side. William H. Matson, a veteran of the war, speaking on this point once said, "Your Yankee contributor is mistaken all the way through.... I am almost eighty years old and as long as I live, I won't read a Yankee history." Preference for the North or South still creeps into modern histories of the war, and perhaps no one can be entirely neutral. However, every effort was made in this book to write an account that Mr. Matson could read if he were alive, or anyone for that matter, and come away feeling that no point of view went unnoticed.

If any shall ask why I have entered into such details of engagements where the forces were comparatively so small, and the results so little affected the final issue of the war, the reply is that such heroism and self-sacrifice as these undisciplined, partially armed, unequipped men displayed against superior numbers, possessed of all appliances of the war, claims special notice as bearing evidence not only of the virtue of the men but the sanctity of the cause which could so inspire them.

JEFFERSON DAVIS

The Rise and Fall of the Confederate Government

1

Crisis in the Making

The consequences of a divided nation loomed large toward the middle of the 19th century. Postponement of a resolution to the slavery question was no longer possible. A growing distaste for it throughout the northern states gradually factionalized the fragile political harmony of the country. Division of the Union between North and South grew more and more apparent.

Missouri mirrored the politics of the nation. Southerners largely settled the state. They farmed the western counties and along the Missouri River in the Boonslick area of Little Dixie, and they controlled Missouri politics. The feeling on slavery in Missouri was either hard or soft, depending on one's point of view. The Boonslick hard Democrats were heavily proslavery, but they faced growing criticism from the soft Democrats concentrated mostly in St. Louis. There, corporate interests sought to balance cooperation with the agrarian slaveholding South and the industrial antislavery North. Talk of limiting slavery in Missouri freely circulated.[1]

As the frontier of the nation moved into the Great Plains, the Kansas and Nebraska Territories bordered Missouri and were next in succession for statehood. The U.S. Congress erased three decades of compromise between free and slave states when in 1854 it passed the Kansas-Nebraska Act, making the path to statehood a popular-sovereignty issue controlled not by the politics of the nation but by the powers within the sovereign territories of Kansas and Nebraska.[2]

Kansas was the first considered for statehood under the new act. The new law gave the right to decide the slavery issue to the residents of the Kansas Territory. A torrent of violence followed. The politics of the hard Democrats spilled out of Missouri across the border. Proslavery and antislavery forces struggled to control Kansas and with it the direction of slavery under the popular-sovereignty doctrine. Bloody confrontations erupted all along the Missouri-Kansas border. Partisans on both sides invaded Kansas to try to sway the vote on statehood. Prominent national figures such as John Brown, who was relentless and often brutal in his methods to abolish slavery, stirred the emotions of the nation while border politics pitted Slave State Missourians against Free State Kansans.[3]

The Dred Scott case pushed judicial reason past the edge of humanity in 1857 when a heavily proslavery U.S. Supreme Court found among other things in a far-reaching opinion that descendants of slaves had no rights as citizens. African Americans were, in the judgment of the court, "beings of an inferior order, and so far inferior that they had no rights which the white man was bound to respect." The court's opinion deepened the shadow over the national conscience.[4]

The following year, in the winter of 1858, John Brown left Bloody Kansas and took his fight to Harpers Ferry, Virginia. The slave revolt that he intended to start failed, but his capture and subsequent execution in Virginia galvanized the North, still filled with outrage over the Dred Scott case the year before.[5]

The election of Abraham Lincoln as president in 1860 further exacerbated sectional strife. Secession became the cry of the South. Even before Lincoln's inauguration, the Union began to fracture along the borders between North and South. A few states refrained from joining either side and reserved for themselves the designation Border States, Missouri being one of them.[6]

Missouri unwittingly elected a secessionist governor in the election of 1860. Claiborne Fox Jackson feigned support for presidential candidate Stephen A. Douglas and his platform of popular sovereignty. Jackson was a pro–South, pro–John C. Breckenridge hard Democrat by choice but ran on the Douglas ticket as a matter of political expediency. Missourians adhered to the middle course and went for Douglas — the only state in the Union to vote for him — thus sweeping Jackson into the governor's seat in the process.[7]

A state convention convened in Missouri to decide the secession question. After several meetings, the convention ended by rejecting secession in favor of neutrality. The decision of the convention did not satisfy the secessionist-minded, pro–South factions or the increasingly militant Governor Jackson. One journalist described the unease of the state. "Missouri might go anywhere at all," he said. "The only safe prediction was that it would produce a great deal of trouble for somebody."[8]

The fight for Missouri began to take shape.

One of the first acts of partisan hostility toward federal authority came on the night of April 20 when a band of about 200 renegade secessionists from Jackson County crossed the Missouri River at Sibley, six miles below Independence, and linked up with another group of rebels from Clay County on the north side of the river. They proceeded to the U.S. Arms Depot at Liberty, Missouri, seized the unguarded facility, ransacked it, and made off with a quantity of arms and munitions. The raid meant that the pro–South Missourians planned to resist federal military presence in the state.[9]

The prime military targets of the seceding states were the United States arsenals kept within the borders of the rebelling states. Both North and South saw the arsenal at St. Louis as critical to the future of Missouri. Who controlled it would control whether Missouri remained in the Union or joined the Confederacy; and command of Missouri meant command of traffic up and down the Mississippi and Missouri rivers, an essential strategy should there be war between the states.[10]

A little-known army captain by the name of Nathaniel Lyon left his post amid the Kansas upheaval to take command of federal property in St. Louis, specifically with orders to guard the St. Louis Arsenal against secessionist takeover. Fresh from the bitter confrontations between slave and free forces in Kansas, Captain Lyon came to St. Louis already convinced that armed conflict between North and South was unavoidable. He took over the defense of the St. Louis Arsenal amid dissension and growing political tensions.[11]

Prominent St. Louis politician Frank Blair — a U.S. congressman with connections in the Lincoln cabinet — lobbied Washington to increase federal military support against Missouri secessionists. The War Department responded cautiously for fear of upsetting the declared neutrality of the state.

Soon Blair met Lyon. Together they devised a political and military initiative to thwart a secessionist takeover of the St. Louis Arsenal. Lyon, whose orders were to guard the arsenal not command it, agitated for command that would give him access to the weapons kept at the arsenal and the authority to arm pro–Union supporters. Washington said no.[12]

In the absence of federal assistance to counter the growing separatist rebellion, paramilitary groups stepped up their organizational activity, especially in the wards of St. Louis. Men on both sides secretly drilled in preparation for military action.

President Lincoln called on the states for volunteers to help put down the rebellion. Governor Jackson rebuffed the president, pledging, "Not one man will the State of Missouri furnish to carry on any unholy crusade." Instead, Lyon and Blair requested and received authority to fill the Lincoln quota. Volunteers in St. Louis streamed into the Union ranks. Secessionists watched helplessly as hopes of taking the St. Louis Arsenal disappeared. Lincoln authorized an army of 10,000 Missourians, mostly German immigrants determined to fight to preserve the Union.[13]

The German population of St. Louis was staunchly Union and adamantly opposed to slavery. German newspapers ran stories on treatment of slaves in the city and agitated for a constitutional end to slavery. The heavily pro–Union *Anzeiger des Westens* drew the ire of South-leaning citizens when its editors rebuked the state's policy of armed neutrality. The German compulsion in St. Louis to save the Union went out across the state, bolstering the feelings of the pro–Union segment of the population, and stirring rebellion amid the heavily secessionist pockets of the state. The call to arms would surely follow.[14]

On May 6, 1861, Missouri state militia troops gathered on the outskirts of St. Louis after Governor Jackson ordered a supposed routine muster of state troops at an encampment named Camp Jackson in his honor. Captain Lyon suspected an attack on the arsenal and decided on military action to capture the state militia camp. On May 10, four days after the camp opened, Union volunteers marched on it in full force. The State militia surrendered, and Lyon decided to march the prisoners to the arsenal. An angry crowd of civilian spectators gathered along the route hurling insults at the German soldiers. Gunfire erupted between the Union soldiers and the civilian mob. Several innocent bystanders died as a result. Violence continued to flare up throughout St. Louis over the next few days, and many people left the city.[15]

Numerous Missouri citizens heretofore neutral in the conflict went over to the pro–South side because of Camp Jackson. In places such as Carroll County, Missouri, for instance, where sympathies had been about equally divided between North and South in the secession squabble, people suddenly turned against the Union. The *Carrollton Democrat*, then the only newspaper in Carroll County, had two editors, and, surprisingly enough, they stood divided in sentiment. One was a Union man, the other strong in his advocacy of Southern rights. In the same edition of the paper, one might find a bitter denunciation of Abe Lincoln and another article castigating the South Carolina traitors. Everything changed almost overnight. Within days after Camp Jackson, every township in Carroll County had one company of troops or more ready to defend the state against the national government. It went that way all across Missouri.[16]

An outraged Missouri General Assembly upon hearing news of the St. Louis massacre met at the State Capitol late at night and passed a sweeping military act to reorganize state military forces. Governor Jackson received near dictatorial authority to raise a Missouri

State Guard force to repel Union troops. Jackson appointed Mexican War hero Major General Sterling Price commanding general. Previously in favor of preserving the Union, the popular former governor Price took a decidedly antifederal position following Camp Jackson.[17]

Brigadier General William S. Harney, commander of all U.S. military affairs in Missouri, struck a truce with General Price promising not to use federal military force in Missouri if Price would agree to delay the buildup of the State Guard. Washington saw the offer as a capitulation to the rebellion, and, at the urging of Frank Blair, President Lincoln removed Harney from command and replaced him with Captain Nathaniel Lyon, promoting Lyon in the process from the rank of captain to brigadier general. General Lyon ignored the Price-Harney truce, and General Price turned his attention to forming the Missouri State Guard. Mark Twain, in a conversation many years after the war, reflected on the condition of affairs in Missouri. He said, "Out west there was a good deal of confusion in men's minds during the first months of the great trouble — a good deal of unsettledness, of leaning this way, then that, then the other way. It was hard for us to get our bearings." By the middle of May 1861, however, Missourians knew a crisis was at hand. The option to remain neutral was waning. All across the country, the race to war quickened apace. Passions ran about the land and only passion ruled.[18]

Union and Missouri leaders met on June 11, 1861, a Tuesday, at the St. Louis Planter's House hotel to try one last time to avert war. Frank Blair and Nathaniel Lyon represented the Union; Claiborne Jackson and Sterling Price represented the state. Lyon and Price faced off in a lengthy argument before an angry Lyon issued a declaration of war and stormed out of the meeting. General Price and Governor Jackson returned to the state capital, at Jefferson City, and began immediately to take steps to stop the Union army.[19]

General Lyon, meanwhile, devised a plan to drive Governor Jackson out of the capital and replace the elected state government with federal authority. Union troops under Lyon's command moved by boat up the Missouri River to Jefferson City, forcing the state government to flee. The occupation of the capital began a series of audacious actions aimed at nullifying the state government. Jefferson Davis, the Confederate States president, writing after the conclusion of the war still harbored a sense of outrage at Union acts that he thought justified rebellion in Missouri. On his list, "invasion with military force, expulsion of the lawful state authorities ... and the attempt to emancipate the slaves in violation of every law and constitutional principle." The latter act of freeing Missouri slaves came on the orders of Major General John C. Frémont, and even President Lincoln was compelled temporarily to roll it back as being in advance of the times. Keeping Missouri in the Union, Lincoln felt, now superseded any possible resolution to the slavery question.[20]

A protracted military conflict appeared imminent. Governor Jackson sent out a call for 50,000 volunteers to repel the invading federal army. His generals began to organize regiments across the state. Union partisans floated a rumor that before Governor Jackson abandoned the capital he first took the precaution to empty the state treasury and steal all the blankets from the state lunatic asylum at Fulton. Such was the acrimonious vilification heaped on the governor. What he did take with him from Jefferson City was the Great Seal of the State of Missouri.[21]

Moving rapidly by boat up the Missouri River, General Lyon chased Governor Jackson and most of the state government officers up the river to Boonville. General Price, meanwhile, went further upriver to Lexington, Missouri, where another large body of State Guard troops was gathering. Governor Jackson took command of the Guard at Boonville and,

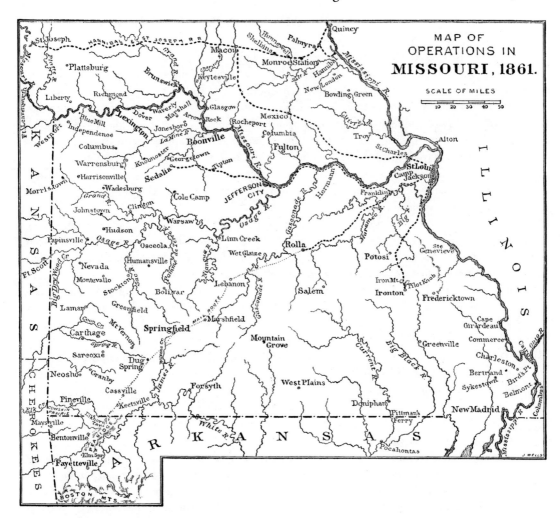

Missouri in 1861. Two columns of rebel Missouri State Guard troops started from Lexington and Boonville joining forces near Lamar, Missouri. At the same time, the Union Second Brigade from St. Louis came through Rolla down the Wire Road *("Mail Route" on the map)* to Springfield. After occupying Neosho, the brigade marched north to Carthage. The two forces met on the morning of July 5, 1861, nine miles north of Carthage on the open prairie just beyond Dry Fork Creek. (Based on an original map by Jacob Wells. Courtesy Springfield–Greene County Library.)

over objections from his military officers, ordered a stand against the Union advance. Lyon's troops easily routed the State Guard soldiers and overran their camp. Governor Jackson and his followers fled toward Tipton en route to southwest Missouri and sanctuary near the Confederate Arkansas border. Lyon triumphantly entered Boonville and confiscated war materials left in haste by the fleeing State Guard.[22]

The fight at Boonville, the least of skirmishes by later standards, was in fact a consequential victory for the federal government. Lyon deployed federal troops to all parts of the state to hold critical military points and to further his plan to trap state officials and defeat State Guard forces. His rapid occupation of key points along the Missouri River isolated secessionist support in the northern half of the state and allowed him to turn his full attention to his scheme to punish the rebel state government. He intended to block Governor Jackson's retreat and catch the governor in a pincer movement that included dispatching troops to southwest Missouri.[23]

The first wave of federal volunteers left St. Louis for Rolla, Missouri, on June 13, 1861. Their commander was an ambitious young volunteer colonel and German immigrant named Franz Sigel. He easily ousted secessionist sympathizers at Rolla and occupied the town. He turned it into a military outpost and a staging point for an overland march into southwest Missouri. His brigade represented the second wing of Lyon's strategy to block the Missouri State Guard from moving south to join Confederate troops encamped in northwest Arkansas. On the same day that Sigel left St. Louis, Union troops from Kansas under regular U.S. Army Major Samuel D. Sturgis moved to reinforce western Missouri at Kansas City. Sturgis then proceeded south to become the third arm of General Lyon's three-prong plan to capture the Missouri state government.[24]

While Governor Jackson and his contingent of the State Guard retreated from Boonville, more State Guard volunteers gathered at Lexington, Missouri. General Price placed the Lexington body under the command of Brigadier General James S. Rains, and then left for southwest Missouri to arrange a liaison with the Confederate army in Arkansas. Before he left, he ordered General Rains to follow him as soon as possible to prepare for an all-out resistance to federal occupation. The Lexington column planned to meet Governor Jackson's men coming down from Boonville somewhere in southwest Missouri before reaching General Price at the Missouri-Arkansas border.

Several miles to the south, a Union Home Guard regiment comprised of German immigrant farmers drilled at Cole Camp, Missouri, directly in the path of the State Guard exodus from Boonville. It was one of many semimilitary groups of volunteers organized on authority of the federal government to protect pro–Union communities from secessionist takeover. General Lyon sent orders for the regiment at Cole Camp to block Governor Jackson's troops now retreating south on the Boonville road.[25]

Hearing of the blockade at Cole Camp, secessionists at Warsaw, Missouri, quickly organized a force to go to the camp to clear a path for the governor's escape. Lieutenant Colonel Walter S. O'Kane led a surprise night attack on the sleeping Home Guard soldiers. Several men died on both sides before the German troops abandoned the fight. The Warsaw rebels secured the area, and Governor Jackson and his men continued their march.[26]

Within a matter of three days, the blood of Missourians was spilled twice in battle, first at Boonville and then at Cole Camp. The struggle for Missouri entered a new phase. The consequences of war settled tragically upon the citizens of a divided state. Slavery fell aside, no longer the engine that drove the conflict; expulsion of the federal invaders and restoration of the right of the state to determine its own destiny became the larger purpose.

The Missouri State Guard marched in two separate columns southward toward southwest Missouri: General Rains and his column from Lexington by the western route, Governor Jackson and the Boonville column traveling down from the center of the state. They expected to converge somewhere beyond the Osage River crossing. Colonel Sigel's Union brigade, meanwhile, hurried to intercept them, to reach southwest Missouri first, and to form the spider's web of General Lyon's three-prong pincer trap.

2

Trouble in Southwest Missouri

During the spring of 1861, everybody in Missouri was sure a fight was coming and went about the business of preparing for it. Those for and against secession readied for the clash. Throughout the state in every locality where the population was threatened either by Southern sympathizers or those loyal to the Union, it seemed like every arms-bearing male — and many who were not armed — enlisted in the federal service or joined fortunes with General Sterling Price and Governor Claiborne Jackson's Missouri State Guard. Secessionists listened expectantly to prominent leaders throughout Missouri, buoyed by frequent visits from authorities of the Confederate government who came from time to time and kept up a steady drumbeat of encouragement to pro–South factions.

When conflict between Missouri and federal troops appeared imminent, Governor Jackson ordered large quantities of gunpowder stockpiled throughout various counties in the state. James Harding, the quartermaster general of the Missouri State Guard, procured some 60 to 70 tons of powder for future use. Secessionist supporters hid large caches of it across Missouri in anticipation of a military confrontation. More than 12,000 kegs went out to various counties, approximately half to Governor Jackson's home county of Saline. He sent to Lafayette and Saline counties about 10,000 pounds of Lafin's and "Dupart's best," which was distributed among the friends of the Southern cause for safekeeping. It was common knowledge that the Missourians did not lack powder.[1]

They hauled black powder by stagecoach from Governor Jackson's cache at Linn Creek to Springfield, Missouri. From there, militants distributed it throughout the southwest counties. The part not used to arm the rebel Missouri State Guard troops, they secreted away for future use. They hid Springfield's share in Colonel Dick Campbell's barn, ready to find its way into the cartridge boxes and powder horns of the armed secessionists. Some of the less radical citizens prayed the time to use it would never come but they knew it would.[2]

The spotlight turned on southwest Missouri.

Anticipating little help from Washington, Union sympathizers in southwest Missouri took it upon themselves to counter the burgeoning State Guard organization with their own. Companies of Home Guards organized to protect local citizens. Several formed independently throughout southwest Missouri, in Greene, Christian, Stone, Webster, and surrounding counties. They procured a few arms from various sources, but their organizations existed mostly in name only because they had little in the way of weapons of war except the hunting rifles, shotguns, and a few revolvers they carried from home. In that respect, however, they were no worse off than their secessionist neighbors.[3]

One of the first showings of the hostile division between southwest Missourians happened on June 11, 1861, when Colonel Dick Campbell's company of State Guard Partisan Rangers and numerous other armed secessionists and their friends gathered for a barbecue at Fulbright spring west of Springfield. Union organizers got word of the gathering, and not wanting the secessionists to outdo them, all the Home Guard companies in the quarter contrived to meet on the same day and make a showing against the rebels. The Union companies chose for their meeting place the old Goose Pond on Kickapoo Prairie about two and a half miles south of Springfield.[4]

It was an oppressively hot day. Although a pleasant grove of trees ringed the pond, there was not enough shade for the throng of people who came bringing their guns, horses, and whatever else in the way of provisions they could add. An unexpectedly large crowd numbering in the hundreds showed up, carrying everything they needed to stay awhile. Despite the pleasant surroundings, a scarcity of water and the lack of shade for such a large assembly made it a miserable meeting. Congressman John Smith Phelps rode out to the place and seeing the unhappy congregation, invited the crowd to move over to his farm nearby where there was ample shade and water, plus corrals and grass for the horses. Soon all had organized and encamped on Phelps' pasturelands. Honoring his hospitality and esteemed government position as a congressional representative, they elected Phelps colonel of the regiment. Phelps at the time was in his ninth term as a United States congressman.[5]

The Phelps Home Guard regiment that met at Goose Pond organized on its own initiative without federal governmental authority strictly for the self-protection of Union-minded citizens. For that reason, it took the special name of the Phelps Independent Home Guard. Twelve companies totaling some 1,100 men made up the regiment, which chose Marcus Boyd as lieutenant colonel, and Pony Boyd and Sample Orr, majors. Several hundred of the regiment and others of the same Union sentiment attended the rally at Goose Pond. Ironically, the secessionists convened on state authority while the unionists had no federal authority at all.[6]

Feeling the invigorating adrenalin of military camaraderie, some of the more militant members wanted to go to Fulbright spring in the instant and clean out the seces-

John Smith Phelps, 1859. A United States Congressman from Missouri in his ninth term, Phelps spearheaded pro–Union sentiment in southwest Missouri. He organized Phelps Independent Home Guard in response to secessionist militants. (Library of Congress LC-DIG-ppmsca-26809.)

sionists. The fiery, redheaded Major Orr offered to lead them, but Colonel Phelps put a stop to the movement and ordered that nothing of the sort take place.

"There will be more than enough time," he said, "to receive your fill of battle and bloodshed without provoking unnecessary hostilities now." Orr objected but obeyed. Sample Orr embodied the conflicted political landscape of Missouri. Orr had run in opposition to Governor Claiborne Jackson in a close race in the last election, and he readily took up arms against the governor and his proslavery secessionists. Six months later, though, he fired off an audacious telegram to President Abraham Lincoln demanding that Lincoln write and enforce an order to round up all escaped slaves from southwest Missouri and have them returned to their rightful owners. Orr wished to stay in the Union and keep his slaves, too. Many Missourians like him never considered the war to be about slavery. It was about the politics of secession.[7]

While Colonel Phelps quieted the zeal of his Home Guards, the secessionist commanders gathering at nearby Fulbright spring were not as circumspect as the Union leadership. They planned a demonstration through the streets of Springfield culminating in the raising of a rebel flag over the courthouse. Couriers moved freely between the two camps, all the time passing news back and forth between them. The unionists learned from them that the secessionists were preparing for a demonstration in town. When the Home Guards learned of the secessionist plan tempers flared, and Union sympathizers threatened that the blood of relatives and neighbors would flow in the streets of Springfield if anyone hoisted a rebel flag. The Home Guards let the rebels know that any attempt to raise a secession flag over Springfield invited a collision that would spill blood as surely as night follows day.[8]

Colonel Campbell decided to go himself to the Union camp and talk to Colonel Phelps. He explained his desire to fly a rebel flag, to which Phelps reiterated that no such banner had a right to wave anywhere above Greene County. Phelps made it clear in his response that raising a secessionist flag over Springfield was an intolerable act of provocation.

"What about hoisting the State flag?" asked Campbell. Phelps thought no one could object to that and agreed as long as the national flag flew alongside and slightly above it. In this way, the secessionist supporters could rally to their flag while Unionists cheered theirs. The camps finally agreed that the secession party might hoist a state flag on the pole they had erected on the west side of the courthouse at the center of the public square, while the Unionists would march through town around the square and salute the Stars and Stripes that waved from the cupola of the courthouse. Both flags went up, and about the middle of the afternoon, the two camps marched into town. The hostile parties celebrated with their companies in the Springfield public square. The state flag turned out to be a nondescript affair pieced together by some Springfield women. One old Southerner said anyone could worship it with impunity since there was nothing like it either in heaven or on earth![9]

The sun went down, and the parties retired to their separate places around the city. The Home Guards held possession of the town that night. Very late, when all but two companies of the Union men had disappeared, a rumor circulated that the secessionists had slipped back into town and pulled down the Stars and Stripes, leaving the state flag fluttering alone in the breeze. Some of the Union extremists wanted to go out and whip the secessionists the next day, but the rumor about taking the national flag down proved to be false. Some fellow had climbed to the top of the cupola to tighten the guy ropes. Both flags stayed up. Colonel Campbell marched his men away and no blood flowed. Violence avoided for the time being, the Phelps Home Guards disbanded and each member returned to his home ready to respond to a call to arms at a moment's warning. Men on both sides soon learned to carry their guns wherever they went.[10]

The show of force by the rebel Missouri State Guard troops at Fulbright spring and the near confrontation alerted ardent unionists to the growing secessionist threat in the area. A delegation of pro–Union citizens from Springfield came together to seek help. Sometime around the middle of June, not long after the parties had paraded their organizations around the Springfield square, three prominent unionists decided to make a trip to St. Louis to apprise the federal military authorities there of the situation in southwest Missouri. L. A. D. Crenshaw, Dr. E. T. Robberson, and S. H. Boyd, all of Greene County, set out late one evening. The delegation departed for St. Louis in complete secrecy. No written messages accompanied them for fear of interception along the route, which would tip off their adversaries to the status of their concern.[11]

They waited until dark and then left by a narrow, obscure trail that led east through the woods. Each man rode a good gray horse. Dr. Robberson led the three-man party. Among the oldest settlers in the territory, Dr. Robberson knew every trail and road in the county and easily traveled the back paths by day or night. The trio met armed groups of men along the way, guns on their shoulders, passing mysteriously in the night, and slipping quietly by without asking if they were unionist or secessionist. Everyone proceeded silently and asked no questions. These mysterious movements of men taking place on a balmy June evening only heightened the urgency to quiet the stirring unrest now taking place around Springfield. After a hurried ride and the loss of a horse, the party safely reached Rolla just in time to witness its capture by the first wave of federal troops out of St. Louis under Colonel Franz Sigel.[12]

The three messengers arranged an audience with Colonel Sigel as soon as they could to brief him on the state of affairs in southwest Missouri. They wished to impress upon the authorities in St. Louis the importance of establishing a federal military presence in southwest Missouri to quell rebellion and hold the section for the Union. They feared the secessionists intended to drive all Union sympathizers out and permanently occupy the land for their own purposes.[13]

Sigel listened to the Greene County delegation with much interest. In a lengthy interview with him, the emissaries described the conditions in southwest Missouri and the need to restore and maintain the authority of the federal government in their part of the state. They stressed the importance of sending troops at once, along with arms and ammunition to the assistance of the good Union men wanting to resist the secessionists. More than a thousand Home Guards had mustered at Springfield under Colonel Phelps, they said, ready to cooperate with Union forces entering Greene County. Much to their relief, they learned from Sigel in return that he was on his way to do just that very thing. He told them he was on his way there to restore and maintain the authority of the federal government throughout southwest Missouri.[14]

Southwest Missouri waited, isolated from rapid military reprisals from the North or South. Only three railroads radiated from St. Louis; one toward the west in north-central Missouri ran parallel to the Missouri River about three-quarters of the way across the state, terminating at Sedalia, and the other two railroads scarcely reached halfway across the state. The one that angled toward the south stopped at Ironton, while the only one to the southwest ended at Rolla. No railroads connected to the south. Travel into the southwestern part of the state from any direction was still by horse and wagon in 1861.[15]

3

Federal Occupation of Springfield

Two days after Franz Sigel occupied Rolla, he pointed his Union army southwest and took up the line of march for Springfield. At the other end of the journey lay a place divided in its loyalty and teetering on the brink of open hostility. His trip from St. Louis to Rolla by train took about a day; a more arduous expedition to Springfield lay ahead.[1]

The Union column moved warily into unfamiliar territory. Sigel had with him his own regiment of Third Missouri Volunteers and a detachment of Reserve Corps Home Guards from St. Louis. The Fifth Missouri Volunteers under Colonel Charles E. Salomon trailed a few days behind, along with two artillery batteries.

The units comprised almost to a man German immigrants or men of German descent. Many of the volunteers went along reluctantly. Some were among the first Union men to volunteer in St. Louis following the Confederate bombardment of Fort Sumter at Charleston in April and the rise of secessionist activity within Missouri that followed. Their enlistment periods already nearly complete, a good many of these three-month recruits saw themselves solely as defenders of St. Louis.[2]

The German community wielded a contentious presence in the city of St. Louis. Their circumstance in the early days of the rebellion was of two kinds. They came to America in large numbers in the wake of the German Revolution, seeking to escape oppressive rule. They were also attracted by the words of German writer Gottfried Duden, who for three decades drew wave after wave of German refugees to Missouri with his idyllic descriptions of a land of promise altogether as fertile and abundant as the fatherland. Many who came found that Missouri did not live up to his descriptions. They found farming too difficult and migrated to St. Louis. Thus, farming communities of Germans developed across the state, each anchored to an ethnic and political base in St. Louis.[3]

The role of the Germans in putting down the rebellion had started in St. Louis in early January 1861, and escalated rapidly from that time. The first inkling of trouble came on January 7, when a group of secessionist St. Louis men met to form the Minute Men, a pro–Southern political faction that opposed the Wide Awakes, a so-called Black Republican organization made up primarily of abolitionists. A few days later, on January 11, the Wide Awakes — comprised mostly of men of German descent — met to widen the political appeal of their organization by changing the name from Wide Awakes to the Central Union Club.

Any Union man of good character could join regardless of political affiliation or standing on the slavery issue. The Union Club quickly evolved into the Home Guard as a paramilitary group to counter the Minute Men and the growing secessionist sentiment in St Louis. The Home Guard regiments, in turn, became the U.S. Missouri Volunteers, 10,000 federal troops authorized by President Lincoln. The Camp Jackson affair and St. Louis massacre of May 10 hastened the opposing political organizations toward armed military conflict, leading to the mission on which the Germans now found themselves in their march toward southwest Missouri.[4]

Almost all of them had participated in the capture of Camp Jackson. The German Union loyalists of St. Louis had promptly rallied to the support of the federal government. When the immediate danger of attack on the city passed, their force, which was of a local, temporary character, dissolved, and many returned to their normal jobs and civil pursuits. Those still stuck with time remaining on their enlistments and ordered to follow Sigel into southwest Missouri yearned to return to St. Louis. Guarding the city of St. Louis was one thing; protecting the wild prairies of southwest Missouri was an entirely different matter. Ahead lay not an easy train ride, like the one that brought them from St. Louis to Rolla, but a sustained march along the muddy roads and trails crisscrossing the hills, timberland, and untamed waterways of a politically and militarily divided Missouri frontier.[5]

Sigel and his men left Rolla traveling along the mail-route road — lately called the Wire Road, which connected Rolla to Springfield before it continued on to Fayetteville and Fort Smith, Arkansas. With no railroad beyond Rolla, the Wire Road — in places not much more than a trail — offered the only main route to southwest Missouri through a countryside not yet swallowed up by the elements of progress.[6]

Sigel's army felt its way cautiously along the road, marching slowly through hostile secessionist country. Detachments went out regularly on either side to reconnoiter against ambush attacks from secessionist rebels. The trio of informants — Boyd, Crenshaw, and Dr. Robberson — advised Sigel from time to time as they accompanied the column back to their homes in Greene County.[7]

It started to rain. The 120-mile trip from Rolla to Springfield usually required about three days by stage, longer on foot. Each mile opened a new vista to the city-dwelling soldiers of Sigel's Union regiment. The first 50 miles of road wound over and around the mountains of east-central Missouri before reaching the Gasconade River, one of the most beautiful mountain streams anywhere. Viewed from a place above the river, the picture of the Gasconade, contrasted with the landscape around it, is one of unforgettable tranquility and splendor. During the rainy season, however, it became a raging torrent. The rain-swept vista was small consolation to the reluctant German soldiers.[8]

The Union column passed through Waynesville on June 18 and through Lebanon on the 20th. Sigel established outposts at both towns but not before having to pause at Lebanon to deal with a group of disgruntled soldiers. Some in his column openly objected to the march to southwest Missouri and staged a rebellion at Lebanon. They said they had sworn into service upon the condition that they were not to perform duty outside of the county of St. Louis. They found themselves instead, they complained, pressed into Union service in the southwest Missouri campaign. They insisted at least on being paid and receiving new equipment. Colonel Sigel disarmed the mutineers, disbanded their company, sent them back to Rolla, and proceeded on to Springfield.[9]

The rains continued. The saturated ground fed runoff into the already flooded streams, causing them to rise even more. Moving wagons along the muddy road was all but impossible. Men worked constantly extracting wagons and animals from the mud, relieved intermittently by the struggle to ford a churning stream. The last few days of the march were through a driving rainstorm, leaving troops exhausted and in dreadful condition.

"We resembled a rabble more than soldiers," Private John T. Buegel wrote in his journal. "Each wore whatever clothes they chose to wear. They had become torn on the march. In place of trousers, they had slipped on flour sacks. Others had no shoes and were walking on uppers or going barefoot. Still others had no hats and used flour sacks for head coverings."[10]

Springfield, Missouri, was a growing city with a population of about 2,000, a bustling town that served Greene and nearby counties. It was the largest town in southwest Missouri and of considerable importance to the region, controlling the trade of a large territory surrounding it. Fast shedding itself of its frontier status, Springfield welcomed the Butterfield Mail Route in 1858, and the telegraph reached it from Jefferson City in 1860. These were the days, however, when towns without a railroad had to depend on the bullwhackers — the men who drove six yoke of oxen attached to gigantic wagons to the railheads to transport goods back to southwest Missouri. Such were the glory days of hardened drivers, in their broad-brimmed slouch hats, who formed the lifeline of a frontier city.[11]

Springfield was on balance a good Union town. It had a broad spectrum of businesses, ample hotels and fine entertainment establishments, many churches, and seven academies, which attested to the cultural sophistication of those who patronized the schools. The Germans found Springfield decidedly more cosmopolitan than Rolla.[12]

Several roads connecting to various outlying communities met at Springfield, such that the possession of the town controlled not only Springfield but also a vast section of the surrounding area. Going west out of Springfield was the Sarcoxie road leading to Mount Vernon and other towns in the predominantly pro–South, western counties, including the town of Carthage. General Nathaniel Lyon, the Union commander lately responsible for all federal forces in Missouri, saw the strategic importance of Springfield very early in the rebellion. He had ordered acting brigadier general Tom Sweeny to prepare an expedition to that part of the state as soon as possible. Colonel Franz Sigel now represented the vanguard of that expedition. Springfield was the military key to holding southwest Missouri.[13]

Sigel and his haggard men at last arrived at the outskirts of Springfield on Sunday, June 24, 1861, after a slow eight-day journey from Rolla. The rain had stopped. The citizens living on the east side of town looked out on the road that morning and saw the first Union troops coming leisurely along. A column of men stretched far into the distance, walking orderly behind their leaders on horseback. One of them shook out a banner and the wind unfurled it to reveal the Stars and Stripes. The band unlimbered its instruments and struck up a spirited tune. People came out to watch the army pass. No one had seen this many armed men in one place before. The whole entourage seemed like a foreign invasion, even to staunch Union supporters who welcomed their presence. Even the American flag they carried bore the German phrase "Lyon's *Fahnenwacht*" — Lyon's Color Guard, a reference to General Lyon's Third Missouri Volunteers. It was a handsome flag stitched together by the German women of St. Louis.[14]

Four-horse teams pulled wagons packed with baggage and provisions. Otherwise, it was mostly an army of foot soldiers. The officers and several members of a company of pioneers were mounted, but there were no cavalry. The plainly dressed Missouri soldiers of the Third Regiment marched steadily along in the summer heat. Amid much fanfare, Sigel and his army entered Springfield to the cheers of large numbers of its citizens. Word spread quickly throughout the city. "They are here! The Union soldiers are here!" some jubilantly announced. Those that had a different way of looking at it said more soberly, "The Yankee Dutch are here."[15]

Great excitement took hold of the children. They all raced forward, white and black alike, to see real soldiers parading along the hushed streets of their little town. The martial music of fife and drum stirred strange feelings in the hearts of people unaccustomed to the ritual of military pomp. The German volunteers tried hard to look warlike but impressed the townspeople as being not very soldierly. The children understood little of events surging around them, their youthful innocence shielded by protective parents not wanting to distress them with talk of war. They would know soon enough the meaning of North and South.[16]

Sigel sent ahead three advance scouts to reconnoiter the public square. Finding no imminent danger there, he marched his men down St. Louis Street four abreast, muskets with fixed bayonets at right shoulder shift, into the center of town. Sigel and his column reached the main part of town at around 11:30 A.M. The first order of business was to get rid of the state flag that flew on the west side of the courthouse. A squad of Germans chopped down the flagpole and ceremoniously reduced it to splinters. Sigel planted his batteries of brass cannon ranged with the muzzles west. He quickly and quietly gathered all known secessionist sympathizers at the courthouse as his prisoners. The courthouse soon filled with Southern sympathizers accused of being guilty of treason against the government

and illegally taking the property of law-abiding Union citizens. The old building bulged with prisoners. A new courthouse had been in the works since 1858 but lay unfinished as the cloud of war descended over Greene County.[17]

Local stories spread about the Union occupation. One story claimed that while Sigel busied himself with securing the public square, a detachment of his Germans marched swiftly to the nearby First Christian Church where the known secessionist clergyman Charles C. Carleton preached to the faithful and equally secession-minded congregation. Reverend Carleton had a full house in church that Sunday morning. The Germans surrounded the church with a cordon of soldiers and waited for the service to end.[18]

Louisa McKenny could not have been much more than 12 years old, seated in the congregation with her

Joseph Spiegelhalter, ca. 1862. Germans constituted the United States forces in southwest Missouri almost to a man. Spiegelhalter, German native and one-time Pennsylvania schoolteacher, left his studies at the Humboldt Medical Institute in St. Louis to fight in Franz Sigel's Second Brigade Missouri Volunteers. (WICR 11568 in the collection of Wilson's Creek National Battlefield. Image courtesy National Park Service.)

grandmother and young Will Campbell. Louisa's mother had died in childbirth and her father had moved to Texas, leaving her to the care of her grandmother, Lucy Campbell. The family regularly attended the Christian Church where Lucy was a member. On this day, a special protracted meeting brought out an especially large crowd because of the basket revival, so called because of the well-stocked hampers that accompanied the worshippers. Little Lou — everyone called Louisa Little Lou — and the other children looked forward to the picnicking in the grove next to the church after the services.[19]

In about a half hour, as Reverend Carleton concluded his sermon and the parishioners prepared to depart, the Union soldiers appeared. Little Lou remembered, "The morning service passed quietly, but during the afternoon there was suddenly a stir and excitement outside the church. Then, at the open doors and windows, we saw soldiers…. Two men of the congregation arose, and silently pointed out every man present who was a Southern sympathizer." Suddenly, men thought to be friends and neighbors became something else. For the first time, the sad, downcast face of her grandmother told Little Lou that the presence of the Union soldiers was a serious matter.[20]

A burly German major, medals dripping from his vest, stepped into the doorway and in broken English ordered everyone in the congregation to the courthouse as his prisoners. The tall officer stepped forward with a paper in his hand. "All Southern sympathizers," he read aloud, "are directed to come to the public square." To some people in Springfield, these were brave Union Germans who had come to protect the town from secessionist outrages; at the Christian Church that morning, however, they were the "damned Yankee Dutch."[21]

The men were placed under guard, and the women and children straggled along beside them, entire families herded rudely through the streets. When they reached the square, there began the slow business of processing the prisoners. Each adult was required individually to take an oath of allegiance, or stay a prisoner. Most refused, and it grew later and later. After several hours passed, the Union inquisitors allowed the women and children to go to their homes. "The ladies," they said, "may go home."

Darkness had settled over town when Little Lou and her grandmother reached the house. One of the servants came running to the gate to meet them.

"Mr. Sammy's gone," she cried. "Miss Lucy, Mr. Sammy's gone!"

Lucy Campbell showed no surprise. She asked no questions but went silently into the house and into her room and closed the door.[22]

Little Lou and Will wanted to know more. "He came running into the house and asked me to fix him a roll of his clothes," the eager messenger went on. "Then he ran to the stable and told Henry to saddle Telegraph." Sam Campbell

Louisa "Lucy" Terrell Cheairs Campbell, ca. 1860. Widow of the founder of Springfield, Missouri, Mrs. Campbell and her children were at church when Sigel's German troops took them into custody. Her sons joined the Missouri State Guard and then enlisted in the Confederate army. (Courtesy History Museum for Springfield–Greene County.)

had snatched his late father's old gun from the wall and galloped out of town as fast as Telegraph could carry him.

Lucy appeared at supper but no one spoke about Sam. The next morning, they saw
Tom Campbell start away from the house, headed out of town in the direction Sam had
gone, both looking to join the rebel forces of the Missouri State Guard. Lucy had lost
another son only last year in an accidental fall from a horse and now faced the dangerous
prospect of losing two more. Sam and Tom, though of distinctly different personalities,
shared a single desire, to chase the Yankee Dutch out of Springfield and out of Missouri.
The 16-year-old, daredevil, bred-in-the-bone rebel, Sam, was the first to take up the
cause; the studious and reserved Tom, two years his brother's senior, had a quiet nature
but no less fearless when it came to principle. Before the war ended, Lucy sent two more
of her sons to the Confederate army. Only young Will Campbell, aged nine, stayed
home, much to his disappointment. A Union officer once asked Lucy, "Madam, do you
have sons in the Confederacy?" Her grey eyes shone dark with trouble. She answered, "Four."
Then, with a flash of spirit, she added, "And I wish they were fifty and I were leading
them."[23]

The Union troops in Springfield seized secessionist's property and soon uncovered the
cache of gunpowder hidden in Colonel Campbell's barn. Campbell himself escaped impris-
onment only because no one could find him. Union pickets took up positions on all the
roads leading in and out of Springfield while scouting parties canvassed the countryside for
evidence of rebel activities. Local Home Guards went about helping Sigel round up secessionist supporters. Sigel brushed aside Mayor J. W. Mack and the other elected officials of
the town, instituting his own authority. From then on, the military governed the city; it
had no civil officers. The city of Springfield was indisputably under Union control. The
city belonged to the Union for the moment because Colonel Sigel's force occupied it. Possession of the state, however, remained up in the air.

Sigel's invasion of Greene County was the first step in making Springfield a military
depot to receive troops and serve as a Union supply route. It also won for the Wire Road
the additional title of Military Road during the war years. The federals wasted no time in
settling in.

Important visitors from Springfield soon showed up at Colonel Sigel's headquarters.
One was former Missouri secretary of state John M. Richardson, a strong Union supporter
and one of the few people in all of southwest Missouri who voted for Abraham Lincoln in
the 1860 election. As a delegate to the 1860 Republican convention, he had helped nominate
Lincoln for the presidency. A sometime newspaperman, Richardson started the short-lived
Missouri Tribune in 1856. Devoted to Union democracy, the paper's banner carried the
motto, "The people of Missouri love the Union and will maintain it at all hazards." Ironically,
Richardson served as secretary of state at the same time General Sterling Price was governor.
Richardson's newspaper obviously did not speak for Price, now commander of the rebellious
Missouri State Guard. Sigel welcomed Richardson into camp and readily accepted his offer
to ride along with the federal troops to scrutinize the loyalty of those seeking government
favor. Having spent most of his early years in nearby Jasper County, Richardson knew the
countryside and the residents as well as anyone. A former state representative from Jasper
County, Richardson still owned several sections of land in the county in 1861. He spent his
young adulthood on a farm near Bower's Mill on Spring River, studied law at Sarcoxie
while teaching school, and eventually set up a law practice at Springfield before going into
politics and the newspaper business. Although Virginia bred, his unquestioned devotion to

Lincoln put him squarely in the Union column. Sigel immediately recognized his potential value and named him brigade quartermaster.[24]

Sigel curried favor, too, with the Phelps Home Guard Regiment. Soon after the federal occupation of Springfield, Sigel mustered a company of them into federal service for three months to replace the company that had mutinied at Lebanon. He armed the 89 men with the muskets taken from the mutineers and assigned them to duties around Springfield. As a condition of its service to the government, however, the company insisted on remaining independent and not attached to any Union regiment or battalion.[25]

While in route from Rolla, Sigel had learned that the state forces of Governor Claiborne Jackson had broken through the Union blockade at Cole Camp and planned to join the Missouri State Guard troops of Brigadier General James Rains coming down from Lexington, rumored now to be somewhere north of Roup's Point in Barton County. Sigel decided not to wait for the rest of Sweeny's St. Louis brigade, as General Lyon had ordered. He instead determined on his own to take immediate steps to meet Governor Jackson's rebel force; if he moved fast enough he could attack and destroy them in their camp.[26]

He quickly readied his campaign to intercept the governor. He confiscated a number of horses and wagons from Springfield and elsewhere around the county, and prepared to move westward to find Jackson. He put together a train of ox wagons, horse wagons, stage-coaches, and family carriages and pressed animals and provisions into service until he had what he needed in a matter of about two days. On June 26, taking his Third Regiment and leaving Springfield under the protection of the Phelps Home Guard, he moved out on a hot summer morning headed westward out of town down the Mount Vernon road. His unique transportation train stretched three or four miles behind. He had with him a force of about 800 infantry and support troops. He left orders for Colonel Charles Salomon and his men coming down from Rolla to follow as soon as possible.[27]

The next day Salomon's detachment of eight companies of careworn and exhausted troops marched into Springfield. Salomon had about 650 soldiers, having left one company at Lebanon to guard the Wire Road and keep communication open between Springfield and Rolla. Salomon soon took up the march toward Mount Vernon with his fatigued force to catch up with Sigel. With Salomon's Fifth Missouri Regiment came Major Franz Back-hoff's artillery of eight pieces of 6- and 12-pounder cannon. Together, the southwest Missouri arm of General Lyon's pincer movement numbered about 1,500 Union soldiers.[28]

Meanwhile, General Sweeny, now on his way to Springfield, would augment the city's defenses when he arrived with the Third and Fourth Reserve Corps out of St. Louis in a day or two. Sweeny knew nothing of Sigel's plans to abandon Springfield in pursuit of Governor Jackson.

4

Rebel Rendezvous at Roup's Point

Brigadier General James Rains and the Lexington column of the Missouri State Guard reached the Marais des Cygnes River at Papinsville on June 28, 1861. The troops spent the day crossing the river on rafts constructed from parts of dismantled buildings lashed together by carpenters who had gone ahead to prepare the crossing. General Rains sent detachments up and down the river as he had at the Grand River, to destroy anything of use in crossing the river to slow Union troop pursuit, in case they came that way. That night the Missourians encamped on the low savannah along the river's edge.[1]

Rain poured down in torrents during the night. Tempers ran high. Fights broke out frequently, and one man shot and killed another and they buried him on the bank of the river.[2]

The column reached the Marmaton River the next day. Again, carpenters busily made rafts to ferry the column across the river, once a small stream now swollen to a mighty torrent. The troops lounged about while they waited, trying to keep dry from the frequent showers. Private Henry Martyn Cheavens spent the day sewing a tent. He had caught up with the Lexington column on his journey from Boone County in time to shoulder the hardships of the march. Cheavens had lost his Bowie knife somewhere along the way, and someone had stolen his only blanket. A lens from his spectacles popped out, adding to his personal misery. The misfortune compounded when Cheavens lost his spectacles completely as he poled a raft across the river.[3]

That evening as part of the army worked to ferry the wagons and swim the horses across the Marmaton, the other part bedded down without supper and slept on the bank in the mud. Swarms of summer insects descended on the waiting troops. One soldier in an expletive-laced diatribe counted nine varieties of Missouri pests, crowned by green-headed flies that kept both men and horses in constant agitation[4]

The typical state guardsman looked like a civilian, dressed in whatever clothing he brought from home or made himself. They dressed as farmers and laborers who quickly grew accustomed to the rejoinder, "You don't look much like a soldier." A few of the men, in the field since their release as Union prisoners at Camp Jackson, showed the wear and tear of the campaign. Many trudged on in boots utterly worn out, their pantaloons all one big hole, and hats actually falling to pieces. One fellow's hat had lost its crown, allowing

Missouri State Guard Soldiers, ca. 1861. S. W. Stone and Peter Stephens Alexander wear civilian clothing and carry a musket, pistol, shotgun, and large knife typical of State Guard equipage. A bouquet of flowers adorns Alexander's hat. The two were with General Mosby Parsons' Sixth Division. (WICR 30025 in the collection of Wilson's Creek National Battlefield. Image courtesy National Park Service.)

his hair, not cut for a season, to protrude, giving a picturesque finish to his appearance. Slouch hats in many styles were common, with a few plantation-style hats here and there. Patterned work shirts in a variety of checks and plaids, often punctuated with white porcelain buttons, reflected the wearer's occupation and standing in society.[5]

Despite the hot summer climate, many guardsmen wore civilian vests or the popular overshirt, an open-front, placket-style, wool shirt gathered at the waist and in colors from red to blue to gray. Butternut was the choice of cloth for trousers. Every farmer appeared clad in the homespun butternut jeans of those days. The dye of the local butternut or black walnut hulls gave the clothes their earthy shades. People called the State Guard soldiers the

Butternut Boys. They left their farms by the thousands, leaving vital farm work in the months of May and June to answer the call to defend the state. Most wore boots of various civilian styles. However, many showed up in common work shoes of the heavy brogan type fitting high on the ankle. Not a military button or buckle adorned any garment. Officers wore homemade patches of flannel or colored sashes to distinguish their rank.[6]

Kentucky-style hunting rifles, bird guns, and double-barrel shotguns, common to any Missouri homestead, constituted their arms. Guns came up often in conversations. Men sat around campfires in the evening talking guns. They made competitive shooting a camp pastime. Almost every rebel who had a gun carried an individual firearm brought from home. "What does she run?" someone would ask, admiring a fellow soldier's weapon. A rifle in those days was locally made to the specifications of its owner. Every town had a gun-smith who could make a good rifle. The smith measured a client for a new piece the way a tailor would measure for a good suit of clothes: length, size, and weight according to the size and strength of the individual. Each man had his own ideas about the length of a gun and the weight of the bullet it shot. Bullets went by the number to the pound. "I would not have a gun that run less than forty to the pound," one soldier might say, while another preferred shot sixty to the pound or some other number. The manufacture of ammunition for the plethora of individual rebel guns usually fell to the soldier. The central command furnished powder and lead, and the soldiers made their own bullets. Military-issue guns, where they existed, used a premanufactured standardized load that seemed always to be in low supply. Ammunition boxes of a military type did not exist. Each guardsman packed his cartridges in cloth bags or in his pockets. Hardly anything was made of leather. One private carried bullets in one vest pocket, percussion caps in another, and powder in a third. A homemade powder horn and shot pouch were common items. A few carried obsolete muskets, primarily of Mexican War surplus or earlier. At any given time, a sizeable number had no weapons at all. Those without a gun brought whatever could pass for a weapon. Pitchforks, axes, and scythe blades mixed with a plethora of clubs and homemade lances. A good many marched with a big Bowie knife tucked in his belt. Some of them carried a piece of brightly colored oilcloth, a suitable wrapping against wet weather. The mess kit consisted of a tin cup and a few utensils brought from home, if anything at all. Personal items they carried in a cloth bag tied at the waist or slung across the back, no military haversacks of any kind. If they had a canteen, it was the old wooden-drum type or a crude container fashioned from a gourd. The only exceptions to this description of the Missouri guardsman were the occasional Mexican War veterans who showed up in old uniforms with vintage military gear, standing out like peacocks in a chicken yard.[7]

They slept under the stars with a blanket as their only cover, that is, those who owned a blanket. A few lucky ones had tents. The vice of choice was tobacco. Just about every man used it. Out of ten men on either side, nine of them chewed tobacco. Cigars were a penny apiece, coarsely made but cheap.[8]

Finding enough for the Missouri army to eat was a daily chore. The men lived on bacon, beans, and an occasional ration of cornmeal. Southern sympathizers along the march kept them from going hungry, supplying fruits and vegetables from summer gardens. Now and then loaves of fresh baked bread and some churned butter added a special treat. Fresh meat came from the countryside, too. One St. Clair County farmer said he watched the soldiers pass all night with no damage to his place, except they ate one of his cows.[9]

As the Missouri State Guard column progressed southward, the population thinned and with it the resources. One soldier said, "The army reduced to two aims in life; to kill and get something to eat." Politicians traveling with the army took to writing out script for foragers to pay for what they took. The script, of course, turned out in due time to be completely worthless. Later on, they printed paper money with Governor Jackson's picture on it, and state defense bonds became known derisively as Jackson money; none had postwar value.[10]

Thirty miles beyond the Sac River crossing, Governor Jackson and his Boonville contingent, proceeding south on a separate path from the Lexington column, went into camp on Clear Creek near the village of Montevallo, in Vernon County, 15 miles north of Lamar. Jackson's rebel army now included the State Guard Sixth Division of Brigadier General Mosby Parsons coming down from Tipton. General Rains' State Guard troops coming from Lexington, having passed Papinsville, were a day's march behind them. The two would soon join forces and continue south toward the southwest corner of the state and contact with General Price and Ben McCulloch's Arkansas Confederates.[11]

Men came from all around to join Governor Jackson, some of them eager to attach

themselves to the governor's cause, others reluctantly out of a sense of duty to their homeland. There were many sad stories of separation. One story stands out. On the eve of departing for duty with the State Guard, John McPherson, a private in the Cedar County White Hare Company — that just ten days prior had elected its officers — got permission from his captain to go home and spend the night with his wife and baby. That evening, in a conversation with his sister, he talked of the war and the many sad things pertaining to it. He said, "Sister, I am not going into the war like many of the boys who seem to think it is only a little holiday sport and that it will soon be over and we will all be at home again. It is a very serious matter with me. Many of our boys' blood will run cold on the battlefield. I feel that I will be numbered with the slain."

His sister replied, "Brother, if I felt that way, I would not go."

"Yes, I will go. My country

Alexander Frank James, ca. 1865. Young Missourians of all lifestyles answered Governor Claiborne Jackson's call to resist federal takeover of the state. The future legendary outlaw Frank James of Clay County joined the rebel forces in May 1861, in General Parsons' Sixth Division. (State Historical Society of Missouri.)

calls, and duty demands it; but when I part with all of you tomorrow morning, I shall part as if in death and never expect to meet with any of you again in this life."

They sat up and talked until late bedtime. Rising early the next morning to a good breakfast, McPherson said goodbye. Putting his arms around his mother and kissing her tenderly, he said "Mother, take good care of Lizzie and the baby." He took his young wife, who was heartbroken, and their babe of ten months in his arms and hugged and kissed them repeatedly, and then turned to go, but came back and embraced his wife again. Then he walked briskly to the gate, mounted his horse, and rode away, never to return. He rode the ten miles to Montevallo and there rejoined his company to take up the march with Governor Jackson's Missouri State Guard, headed south toward Jasper County.[12]

Governor Jackson spent the first day of July resting his army at Montevallo, awaiting word of Brigadier General Rains and his column of Missourians coming down from Lexington. The Lexington troops would add another 2,000 volunteers to the growing State Guard force. While he waited, Governor Jackson received an answer to his urgent request for Confederate troops to come to his aid. He was furious when the Confederate secretary of war unceremoniously denied the request. Missouri was not in the Confederacy. Jackson gathered his men and proceeded on toward Lamar.[13]

The Confederate government's rejection of Governor Jackson's plea for help was consistent with an earlier decision by President Jefferson Davis not to become embroiled in Missouri politics. The South was not oblivious to the plight of Missouri, however; on June 28, interest stirred in Tennessee for mounting a major Confederate incursion into Missouri to help keep the state. Major General Gideon J. Pillow of Tennessee, writing to the Confederate secretary of war, L. P. Walker, expressed the concern of his state when he said, "There is great anxiety here to aid Missouri. I can gather for that purpose of Tennessee, Mississippi, and Arkansas troops 20,000 men, and with that force, I can place Missouri on her feet. It requires only the orders of the President." President Davis did not respond. Secretary Walker wrote back three days later to say that the Tennessee governor had changed his mind about using Tennessee troops to help keep Missouri. Again, a disinterested Confederate leadership rebuffed the idea of helping Missouri, and the Confederacy left the state to twist in the wind.[14]

Confederate support for Missouri never moved much beyond this in the early stages of the rebellion. Prewar events tempered Davis' decisions not to intervene. After the Price-Harney agreement and the meeting at the Planter's House in St. Louis, Davis had no use for what he saw as a duplicitous policy in Missouri politics that expressed a willingness to pursue the doctrine of armed neutrality, even against the South. Besides, Jefferson Davis and Sterling Price had a personal dislike for each other that dated back to their respective assignments in the Mexican War. The two argued back and forth over who would go where, and Price got his way. The experiences with Jackson and Price and Davis' dislike of any officer who was not a West Point graduate, which Price was not, caused him to hesitate when it came to Missouri.[15]

The Lexington column spent all day June 30 crossing the Marmaton River. Many men suffered from diarrhea, ill from eating meat and bread without salt. The horses had sore backs from saddles thrown over wet blankets. Once over the river, the Lexington army stopped about ten miles north of Nevada and pitched camp to rest for a while near Ball's Mill, or Ball Town—also known as Little Osage because of its river setting. Some of the Lexington men won a reprieve from misery on July 1 when the quartermaster issued an assortment of new clothing to replace garments worn out on the trip.[16]

General Rains and his Lexington troops passed Nevada on July 2 and arrived at Montevallo not long after Jackson's departure for Lamar. As the two armies closed, new recruits continued to flow out of southwest Missouri counties and into the rebel ranks. John Q. "Jack" Burbridge — a former prisoner in the Camp Jackson affair — brought a small contingent of ten men, but more importantly, he brought 150 extra rifles taken from a local Home Guard unit. Colonel James M. McCown added four companies of cavalry with his 250-man Independent Regiment made up of a mix of men from the Cedar County Company of Captain J. Johnson, Benjamin F. Walker's Stockton Grays, and several Johnson County boys. Other individual mounted volunteers coming into camp added to the regiment. Colonel McCown was brand new to the Guard, having only enlisted June 29, shortly after the Lexington column passed by his home in Johnson County. Meanwhile, Lieutenant Colonel Richard A. Boughan welcomed the State Guard to Vernon County, adding 200 men of the local Vernon County Battalion that he had organized at Ball Town as a militia company the year before in anticipation of the unrest that now gripped the region. The Vernon County troops were part of the old Missouri Militia Seventh Cavalry of D. M. Frost's Southwest Expedition. Originally organized to combat Border Ruffians, they saw little action at their Kansas border post on the Little Osage River. One soldier remembered, "We did a lot of drinking but not much fighting." They were still at Ball Town when sectional hostilities broke out the following April. As secessionist fever grew in southwest Missouri, so did the Vernon County company until it reached battalion size with more than 250 pro–South men. The South had its strongest allies in this part of Missouri. Not surprisingly, when the call to arms came, the border counties had rebel militia already formed and ready to join the fight.[17]

By July 2, the Lexington body altogether had grown rapidly in just a few days to a force of almost 3,000 men, which, though poorly equipped with fully one-third without arms, eased over the Ozark Divide and angled for Lamar to join Governor Jackson. The next day, a few miles north of Lamar, on the eve of Independence Day, the Lexington column caught up with Jackson's Boonville troops. The Lexington troops arrived later than expected, their progress slowed because of the high streams and having to cross men and baggage wagons over by ferry.[18]

The armies met about where W. Gil Roup's old settlement had been, at a place called Roup's Point on Muddy Creek, in Barton County. Just a place on the map to the soldiers, Roup's Point symbolized a less than noble history of the western frontier. Gil Roup had hunted down Indians in the territory with relentless and deadly pursuit. He left Muddy Creek for California where the race he persecuted and hated so much took its revenge and killed the entire Roup family, leaving as the lone family legacy Roup's Point in Missouri.[19]

The State Guard camp at Lamar lay along a bend in Muddy Creek spread across Muddy Bottoms, a flat piece of ground extending out from the creek's edge. The Muddy meanders 35 miles through Barton County as if trying to make up its mind to flow down the north slope of the Ozark Divide and send its waters to the Missouri River or take a southerly course into the watershed of the White River. It does the latter, emptying first into the North Fork branch of Spring River. A maze of creeks and streams cut through the rich alluvial soil of the Barton County bottoms: Horse Creek to the northeast, Little Dry Wood Creek north, and Big Dry Wood to the northwest. West Creek and Petty's Creek carved paths through the south-central part of the county, and Coon Creek snaked along the eastern half of Barton's southern boundary with Jasper County. The web of tributaries hindered the moving troops. The topography of southwest Missouri presented a far different military challenge to the rebel Missourians than the terrain of Lexington and the Missouri Valley.[20]

5

Lyon and the Great Comet

It had been just ten days since General Nathaniel Lyon embarked on his river campaign to unseat and capture Missouri Governor Claiborne Jackson; Major Samuel D. Sturgis stood prepared with Union troops in Kansas to push into Missouri; and the southwest Missouri campaign to intercept and stop Jackson was in full swing.

Acting brigadier general Tom Sweeny, still in St. Louis, ordered the final elements of the southwest column to move out. His orders from Lyon were to follow Colonel Sigel to Rolla, and then continue on to southwest Missouri to intercept the rebel Missouri army on its way to the Arkansas border, should it make it that far. Sweeny left St. Louis on June 23 with the Third and Fourth Reserve Corps Missouri Volunteers and arrived at Rolla the next day. He rolled into Rolla just as Sigel entered Springfield. Considerable distance now separated Sweeny from Sigel's vanguard and Colonel Salomon marching somewhere in between along the Wire Road, strung out because of bad weather and logistical problems. Sweeny found more supply problems in Rolla. The promised local transportation failed to meet him at the railhead. Nevertheless, he left Colonel Benjamin Gratz Brown and a contingent of reserves at Rolla, and, hesitating only long enough to organize his force, headed southwest toward Springfield, trailing Colonel Salomon's Fifth Regiment and Backhoff's artillery already four days out of Rolla. Passing through unfamiliar and potentially hostile territory, Sweeny took care to reinforce Union outposts along the route and to establish several others to keep his communications open.[1]

The Union troop movements in Missouri had General Lyon's usual stamp of pinpoint coordination. On the same day that Sigel arrived at Springfield and Sweeny at Rolla, on June 24, Major Sturgis left Kansas City in the west-central part of the state with a brigade of Union troops — the other arm of Lyon's pincer army on its way to southwest Missouri. Sturgis began his march with the First Kansas Regiment and a battalion of Regular U.S. Infantry. Two days later, the Second Kansas Regiment joined him. His command now included six companies of U.S. Regular Infantry and Dragoons; five companies of cavalry, including a company of Kansas Mounted Rangers; a four-gun artillery battery; and two companies of rifle recruits armed with muskets, altogether some 2,200 men. That number would double the size of the Union army then encamped at Boonville with General Lyon. Lyon expected Sturgis to join him somewhere around Clinton, in Henry County, Missouri,

Nathaniel Lyon, ca. 1861. Brigadier General Lyon took charge of federal troops in Missouri and engineered a military campaign to keep Missouri in the Union. His three-prong plan to trap the Missouri State Guard in southwest Missouri failed at the Battle of Carthage. (Library of Congress LC-DIG-cwpb-07025.)

before proceeding on to Springfield and a rendezvous with Sweeny and Sigel. He intended somewhere in the course of action to trap Governor Jackson and his rebel state government.[2]

The Union army now in motion, the public awaited the anticipated southwest Missouri expedition with great interest. The newspapers grandly described Lyon's Boonville force as an army of 3,000 men, carrying 37 days' rations — the assumed maximum time the campaign would last until the secessionist Missourians either fled or surrendered. Reports envisioned more than 150 wagons to transport the materials of war southwest, each wagon pulled by a grand team of from two to ten horses or mules. The higher officers and scouts required fine saddle horses, making overall an envisioned train of some 500 to 600 animals. They pictured the expedition carrying not only all this but forage, canteens, haversacks, and other articles associated with a military campaign. The Northern papers bragged that when Lyon sent out word of what he needed, he told the citizens if they came in peaceably, good — if not, he would take what he needed anyway. He supposedly offered to pay for what he took, and citizens allegedly came from everywhere to meet the Union demand, according to the Union papers.[3]

The actuality of the campaign, in fact, was quite different. Lyon's advance stalled after the rout of Governor Jackson's troops at Boonville. Short on wagons, horses, and the materials of war, attrition threatened his small army. His Home Guard volunteers — almost exclusively Germans — were a poorly clad and badly armed organization without proper pay because the currency of the state was subject to heavy discount and not on a par with the national currency used to pay the army regulars. The volunteers received less pay because people viewed any proposition for a permanent state military organization with distrust and suspicion, especially one paid by the Union. For a time the prospects of raising a Union force in Missouri outside St. Louis was not at all certain. Union organizers raised troops with difficulty and often under the most trying circumstances.

With Major Sturgis on the march from western Missouri and Colonel Sigel in place at Springfield ready to block the rebel retreat toward Arkansas, General Lyon contemplated his next move at Boonville. Lyon and his associates had easily secured the principal towns along the Missouri River. In a matter of two or three weeks, the Union occupation of strategic points up and down the Missouri River had cut communications between prosecessionists on both sides of the river. Everything progressed smoothly for the federals. Lyon secured the northern half of Missouri in no time and sent the state government hurrying into the jaws of a trap, or so he believed. Newspapermen covering the progress of his lightning campaign dashed off colorful reports to the Northern papers, hailing Lyon as the right man in the right place. He shrugged off publicity of his quick military successes. When one journalist asked him to list the most prominent events of his life for the benefit of the public, he refused to comply because he said he had no time for such things, and besides, he added, he had done nothing important that would interest the public. Only the future counted to him.[4]

"It is with the present we are dealing, and let us all devote ourselves to it," he urged, "rather than our cause fail before the unscrupulous villainy now at war upon it." The Northern press loved it.[5]

General Lyon waited at Boonville for more than two weeks. Heavy rains and logistical problems threatened to delay his scheduled June 26 departure. The federal troops busied themselves building a series of strong defenses around Boonville while they waited for the weather to clear. The First Iowa Regiment, sent into Missouri as reinforcements, camped impatiently at the Boonville fairgrounds and tried to settle into the routine of their new

St. Louis German compatriots. There were differences but many similarities. Like their German counterparts, the First Iowa consisted of three-month volunteers whose enlistments were to end in July, and none of the Iowans wanted to go home without a fight. Secretary of State William H. Seward had famously said the war would last only 90 days, and time was about up.[6]

The Iowans looked much like the rest of the Army of the West at this point in the conflict. No two companies of the First Iowa dressed alike; each company wore a different uniform and different colors. They were, however, a close-knit regiment, well trained and disciplined in military matters, with a smattering of personal attention to camp life that they found missing in most of the German camps. Each Iowan had the duty of carrying something of common use for his squad; one carried a razor, another a looking glass, or perhaps a deck of cards. A soldier need not carry one of everything in his knapsack, except for needles and sewing materials, which every soldier carried. They called it their "housewife" kit.

Charley Stypes would take out his accordion from a bag that he always carried over his shoulder and play. Charley was a favorite of the Iowa camp. A big, good-looking lad of even temper, he could play the accordion for days straight without stopping. He accompanied mocking birds, steamboat whistles, or a roll of thunder, any sound Charley Stypes could turn into a song.[7]

General Lyon waited for the weather to clear. It rained hard from sunrise to noon on June 28, and then cleared off in the afternoon. The rain started again in the evening and continued all night. Camp conditions turned miserable. Tents could not keep out the water. The men spent the night thoroughly drenched and finding any way they could to keep their ammunition dry. Soldiers had to pay for their carelessness under General Lyon's policy. He charged any loss of ammunition to their payroll. To add further annoyance, the mules that night insisted on braying precisely at midnight, rousting out those who had managed to find a reasonably dry place to sleep to investigate the cause of the agitation. It turned out to be nothing, only the first of several other midnight heehaws seemingly launched for no other purpose than to disturb the sleeping soldiers.[8]

The sun rose hot and intense on June 29, and it looked for a while as if the rains might let up. Some of the German companies put on drill exercises for the Boonville public. Their march seemed always to end somewhere close to the nearest beer tavern. Each German commander had his own style of drill. Major Peter Osterhaus proved to be especially entertaining. He had a voice like a trumpet; sometimes his orders were in English, sometimes in German, but usually a unique mix of both. Captain James Totten's battery always put on a good show, too. He had six 12-pounder brass smooth bores, each pulled by six horses. He always carried a canteen of brandy, and had a distinctive martial manner. His lurid commands echoed across the field and consistently ended in the same reprimand: "Forward that caisson, goddamn you, sir." "Swing that piece into line, goddamn you, sir."[9]

Colonel Frank Blair, the congressman from St. Louis largely responsible for the Union presence in Missouri, had a few command mannerisms too. For instance, he had a habit of using the phrase "Bejesus" to the extent that his men called him the Bejesus colonel. Few knew his reputation of forcing his point of view on an opponent at the end of a gun. Some of General Lyon's actions likewise framed an opinion of him. He never abandoned his old ways of military discipline. One day he ordered one of his Regulars "bucked and gagged"— tied to a wagon wheel and put out on the parade ground for all to see — just as he had done on countless other occasions at previous posts. Instead of serving as an example of military

The Great Comet of 1861. Seen in the summer of 1861, the Great Comet was interpreted by many people as an omen of the coming Civil War. (Weiss, *Bilderatlas der Sternenwelt*, John G. Wolbach Library, Harvard-Smithsonian Center for Astrophysics, Cambridge, MA.)

justice this time, however, the action offended the volunteers for its inhuman abuse of command authority. The Iowa volunteers thought it especially repugnant and disliked the Regulars for their harsh treatment of their own. The Iowans liked Blair but not Lyon. Unfortunately, Blair went back to Washington, and they were stuck with Lyon.[10]

Lyon seldom moderated his rude and overbearing behavior. It followed him from his earliest days as a young infantry lieutenant. He could punish a trooper by placing a barrel over the offender's shoulders, smearing honey in his hair, and marching him into the hot sun while the prairie flies bit the unfortunate boy's bare head. He perfected his cruel buck-and-gag technique from an incident 20 years earlier in which he had a private tied up with his feet drawn up behind him, gagged, and left face down in the road. A court-martial found young Lyon guilty of cruel and inappropriate discipline for that act, but that did little to temper his strict punishment of his men. So unorthodox were his methods that one biographer said that had he lived four centuries earlier, they would have burned him at the stake as a pestilent and altogether incorrigible person.[11]

On the night of July 1, 1861, a great comet appeared for the first time in the Missouri sky. It had not been there the night before because of cloud cover. The soldiers looked up in awe as the comet spread its effervescent tail across the northern sky. What did it signify, and why was it there just now? The sky cleared only long enough for the comet to assert its presence. The next day and during the night of July 2, a powerful thunderstorm rolled over the Union camp at Boonville. Rain poured and the wind blew a gale with such force that even the old timers at Boonville could not remember such a storm.

All kinds of bad signs pointed to war. The slaves of the Southern masters looked with special care for prophecy in signs and omens. There were hordes of ants in Florida the year before, and Harriet Gresham's mother said that was an omen of war. Liza Strickland experienced the worst Mississippi winter she had seen in a long time in 1860 to 1861. "The worst freeze that we had ever had," she said. "The limbs on the trees got so heavy with ice till they broke off. It sounded like guns firing." Then, there were the comets. "I saw the elements all red as blood," remembered Temple Wilson, "and I saw after that a great comet; and they said there was gonna be a war."[12]

It is an ancient superstition that comets foretell calamities, particularly wars. Donati's Comet was still fresh in the memory of those who saw it in 1858. Many connected it to Bloody Kansas and said it was a warning of the worst to come. First the comet of 1858, and now this one, coming in so timely a manner for the Civil War, surely confirmed the apprehensions of credulous minds.

There were not one but two comets in 1861. High in the northern sky, Thatcher's Comet brightened and was briefly visible beginning in late April 1861. Thatcher's Comet presented a fearful sight, ominous for its terrible beauty. Both head and tail remained visible simultaneously in broad daylight, a constant reminder of the evil omen of comets. People regarded it with fear, looking upon it as something terrible bringing in its train wars and desolation. More than a few religiously oriented citizens of Charleston, South Carolina, swore it was a sign of retribution for Fort Sumter. After a few weeks, it rounded the sun and disappeared in the twilight. As the days of June 1861 passed, the Great Comet appeared. It came into the earth's plane in late June, and by the end of the month, the plume of its broad tale stretched halfway across the heavens. Its dramatic appearance came as a foreboding surprise in the northern latitudes. An Australian sheep farmer had discovered it in mid–May. However, it did not appear in the northern hemisphere until June 29, before word of its discovery reached America. It was as if it had suddenly appeared from nowhere. By July 2, it lit up the northern sky, passing just west of due north. It showed even brighter the next night. From the outset, it outshone every star and planet except Venus, and grew ever brighter in the evening sky. Glowing as bright as the planet Saturn, its tail stretched for a hundred degrees across the black night sky. It loomed ever larger passing barely twelve million miles from the earth, very close by astronomical measure. Its brilliant nucleus at the horizon, its tail fanned out upward into a silvery light, covering at its zenith the entire northern sky. The comet was unusual for its extraordinarily dazzling tail and for its closeness to earth. Astronomers soon discovered that the tail actually touched the earth, its end sweeping over the planet. As the earth passed through its tail, a peculiar whitish light cast a diffused haze throughout the evening sky, deepening along the eastern horizon, and shining bright enough to cast a shadow. The unprecedented interaction with the earth caused the comet's tail and streams of material converging toward the nucleus at the horizon to be visible by day. It hung in the sky as an ominous visitor. For two days when the earth was actually within its tail, the comet's gas and dust spread a haze over the sun. Within six weeks of its discovery, the Great Comet brightened to become the most spectacular comet of the 19th century; and for three months, it performed its breathtaking show in the northern sky while opposing armies organized in the summer of 1861.[13]

It is true that many human disasters have happened without the accompaniment of a comet, but comets have been associated with many important incidents. History records momentous events, such as the conquest of England, linked to comets. There was the murder of Julius Caesar, the volcanic destruction of Pompeii, and the Great Fire and Plague of

London. Napoleon fought more than one of his many battles with a comet blazing overhead, including the disastrous Russian campaign. The Great Comet of 1811 appeared shortly before the war of 1812, and then there was the fall of the Alamo. The comet of 1858 preceded the Italian war of 1859, and now, barely three years later, two comets in 1861 foreshadowed the outbreak of the American Civil War.

6

Generals at Opposite Ends

July came and the rains did not let up. Lyon remained bogged down in Boonville. He had no doubt, however, that his troops in Springfield would make quick work of disposing of all secessionist opposition in southwest Missouri, clearing the way for him to unite with them and other Union forces and give battle to the Confederates in Arkansas. Lyon intended to capture or destroy the Missouri State Guard and go on to bigger things.[1]

The campaign to pursue the State Guard and capture Governor Jackson proceeded partly according to plan. The different commanders began their troop movements exactly as Lyon had scheduled, except for Lyon. He held up his pursuit, unable to piece together a supply train to support his operation. Availability of supplies was not a problem. Two boats a day landed at Boonville despite harassment by sharpshooters along the way. Plenty of provisions arrived daily. However, he had no transportation to carry the supplies into the interior. The State Guard had taken the best horses and wagons when it vacated Boonville, forcing Lyon's foragers deeper into the rain-drenched countryside to procure what they could in the way of conveyances. The task was further complicated by the same problems that Tom Sweeny had encountered in St. Louis when forming his supply line for the southwest column. Army Chief Quartermaster Justus McKinstry balked at Lyon's unorthodox procurement methods and repeatedly cancelled his acquisition arrangements. (The army later court-martialed McKinstry for his actions.)[2]

Beset by heavy rain and muddied roads, stranded and wanting for needed supplies, Lyon waited. The public grew impatient. The Union leaders in the state were convinced that the future of the state required the utmost diligence in carrying out military action with all possible dispatch. General Lyon suddenly had another reason to put his part of the southwest Missouri campaign in motion. Control of military actions in the state started to slip out of his grasp. Washington wanted a more experienced commander. A series of War Department reorganizations threatened to relegate the impetuous young general to a subordinate position. His orchestrations to gain command of the Army of the West threatened to be all for naught.[3]

Lyon could delay no longer. As soon as he gathered enough transportation for his army, he took up the chase of Governor Jackson. On July 3, the day Lincoln named Major General John C. Frémont to replace Lyon as commander of Union forces in Missouri and more than a week after Major Sturgis left Kansas City, Lyon departed the relative safety of Boonville destined for Springfield. It was but a feeble force with wholly inadequate provisions to enter the frontier of southwest Missouri, the stronghold of the rebellion in the state where a growing secessionist army awaited him. Down to a fraction of the 10,000 volunteers recruited in St. Louis in May, many of his men were nearing the end of their three-month enlistments.

The American public seemed unaware of the scale of the forces assembled in Missouri on July 3. One historian writing two decades afterward claimed there were 22,000 Confederates massed on the Arkansas-Missouri border ready to come to Missouri's aid when there was barely one-fourth of that number. He said Governor Jackson's force consisted of 10,000 mounted infantry, a figure nearly twice the actual number; and he put General Lyon's federal soldiers at 10,000. In fact, leaving Boonville on July 3, General Lyons' command consisted of 300 Regular troops, the First Regiment Missouri Volunteers, and the First Regiment Iowa Volunteers, about 2,400 men altogether.[4]

Politicians harbored the same naive attitude as the public. General William T. Sherman, who watched the unfolding of events in Missouri from his home in St. Louis, said he was shocked at the indifference of Washington to the western theater.

As Lyon turned his attention to southwest Missouri, the storm gathering there would be his biggest test yet, as opposing forces readied to engage in a violent struggle. When he marched his small army out of Boonville, Lyon was officially under the command of General Frémont and no longer in charge of military affairs in Missouri. However, he had already put events in motion that would set the stage for the beginning of the Civil War in the West. Neither Frémont on holiday in New York nor Lincoln in Washington ordered him to stop. Even though he was almost out of supplies, short of men, and short of wagons, Lyon gave the order to leave Boonville to pursue and punish the rebel Missourians. Before he left, not wanting to abandon the gains he had made in the center of the state, he placed Colonel John D. Stevenson and the Irish Seventh Missouri Volunteer Infantry in charge of holding the principal towns along the Missouri River from Kansas City to St. Louis and preventing any recruits for the State Guard army from crossing.[5]

Lyon marched out of Boonville with great fanfare, drums beating, and flags flying. Old men and handsome women and children walked alongside the soldiers to escort them out of town. The federal column aimed toward Sedalia and Green Ridge in route to Clinton, 100 miles south of Boonville. A giddy, nervous feeling rippled through the ranks; the Union volunteers were finally off to battle. A rumor circulated that 15,000 rebel troops had massed a hundred miles away. Bill Heustis, marching with the First Iowa, changed it to 100 troops at 15,000 miles, and there the rumor stayed.[6]

They had no sooner left Boonville than a 32-pounder howitzer broke through a bridge. It took eight horses to pull one of these heavy guns. Despite efforts to retrieve the crippled gun, it ended up in a ravine where it stayed. The column marched west five miles then turned southwest out onto the prairie upland. They came to the village of Pilot Grove. Already the companies spread out back along the road as far as the eye could see. Each man carried about 25 pounds of gear, including a nine-pound musket. They marched 15 miles through the mud the first day and went into camp. It started to rain again. The supply wagons were far behind. With the first day's journey behind them, the men went to sleep in the rain with no water and no food. It took seven wagonloads a day to feed the men. Provisions would have to be foraged along the way. Military supplies of any kind were in short supply. Each company had only one two-horse wagon for everything. To make matters worse, Charley Stypes accordion got wet and fell apart.[7]

The focus of the Union forces now shifted to southwest Missouri. Lyon led not 3,000 soldiers as the papers reported, but barely 2,400 poorly equipped men, many of whom would reach the end of their enlistment in a month. He faced an impossible task of supplying his army. When he left the Missouri River at Boonville, he left his supply line, which was precisely what the rebel leaders intended when they abandoned Lexington. Elements of the federal force were widely separated in the most unfriendly and dangerous parts of the state, none of which had either railroad or river transportation. Communication between the different Union commands of Lyon, Sturgis, Sweeny, and Sigel was practically nonexistent, and distances strained logistical support beyond sustainability.

A very large proportion of Missouri was in the undisputed possession of rebel forces. The whole state was more or less subject to the influence of either pro–South partisans or their sympathizers. The danger from secessionist attack loomed largest in southwest Missouri. Led by able generals, the rebels stood at convenient distances ready to combine forces not merely to assume the defensive, but stationed for the opportunity to strike Lyon and his army at the first opportune moment.

Ahead of Lyon's brigade, the first elements of Major Sturgis' federal command from Kansas City reached Clinton, in Henry County, on July 3, just as Lyon started out from Boonville. Sturgis arrived too late to intercept the rebel Missourians who had already passed. While Sturgis' troops waited for Lyon's column, they paused at Clinton long enough to express their devotion to the Union flag on July 4. A few amused themselves by taking over a deserted rebel printing office and issuing the *First Kansas*, a novel sheet filled with seasonings of patriotic fervor.[8]

July 4 started as just another day on the march for General Lyon's men. Up at 3:30 A.M., the soldiers continued south. Lyon's column did not always follow the road across the prairie. Scouts rode ahead to mark a route that best suited men and animals as they struggled through the deep, dense prairie grass, the mules straining to pull the heavy wagons over the soggy terrain. Some of the commanders detailed men to help the drivers as they urged their teams forward. Unable to do much to help, the men decided that their duties must be to assist the driver with profanity when he ran out of oaths trying to move the stubborn beasts. After the war ended, some said the Missouri mule helped save the Union. One craggy old veteran summed up the mule's contribution to the war effort when he said, "He would pull until he dropped; enjoyed profanity, liked a joke, and was a good judge of men."[9]

Lyon's army passed through Pleasant Green in Cooper County, and crossed over a prong of the La Mine River. The weather had mercifully changed. It was a dry and pleasant afternoon. The soldiers lifted their voices in song as they marched, pausing here and there to help themselves to the mulberries growing plentifully along the streams. They crossed into Pettis County, making good time but still two days' march from a rendezvous with Sturgis now waiting at Clinton.

The rebel Missourians, meanwhile, did not sit idly by. General Sterling Price made a beeline directly for General Ben McCulloch's headquarters in Arkansas when he left Lexington ahead of the State Guard troops. He hoped to secure the help of McCulloch's Confederate Regulars in the defense of Missouri against the Union. He barely avoided capture along the way. Not yet fully recovered from an illness that had sent him home to Keyesville to recuperate, he traveled by ambulance. His small entourage stayed over at the Bolton House in Warrensburg on June 18. A group of local Union sympathizers recognized him and chased him out of town all the way to the Henry County line before giving up the pursuit.[10]

All along the journey south, people heard Price was coming and reached out to him. Despite the urgency of his mission, the general took time to encourage State Guard recruits. On one occasion, he stopped briefly in Vernon County at the request of a company of volunteers there for a dress parade review. The company presented their shotguns and squirrel rifles amid loud cheers at the appearance of Price, who, in his dignified and correct military demeanor, reviewed the raw recruits as if they were the finest division on earth. The Vernon County boys had a band that consisted of a fiddle and a drum. The band beat off a rendition of "Dixie" as they accompanied General Price down and back in front of the company.[11]

By the time Price reached the extreme southwestern corner of the state, several hundred men had fallen in with him. Squads and companies of volunteers gathered as he progressed on his journey southward ready to fight; except few of them owned weapons. Price paused south of Neosho at Pool's Prairie to organize his new troops and await Governor Jackson and General Rains' State Guard regiments coming down from the north. Pool's Prairie was one of many large plots of prairieland that spread all across the region west of Springfield where the land flattens out and the prairies signal the beginning of the great American West. General Price chose the open prairie as a place to assemble and drill his small army of new State Guard recruits. After a few days at Pool's Prairie, he decided to move his men further south to Cowskin Prairie nearer the sanctuary of the Arkansas Confederacy. Upward of 1,200 volunteer Missourians followed him by now.[12]

Price soon learned that Brigadier General N. Bart Pearce, commander of Arkansas state militia troops, had encamped with an Arkansas brigade near Maysville, Arkansas, only a

few miles distant. The Confederate camp stood two miles from Maysville and about seven miles from the Missouri-Arkansas line. Confederate General Ben McCulloch, meanwhile, had left his headquarters at Fort Smith, Arkansas, and would reach Maysville in a day. McCulloch recently had been in Fort Smith to make an agreement with the Cherokee Nation pledging the intent of the Confederacy to respect their neutrality. The First Arkansas Mounted Rifles and the Third Louisiana Regiment accompanied him. He planned to reorganize these troops in northwestern Arkansas to maintain the border arrangement with the Indian Territory. The location at Maysville, just two miles from the Arkansas and Cherokee Nation border and seven miles

Sterling Price, ca. 1862. A former governor of Missouri, Major General Price presided over the state convention that rejected secession. Outraged by events at Camp Jackson, he took command of the Missouri State Guard's military resistance to the federal occupation of the state. (Library of Congress LC-DIG-cwpb-07527.)

below the Missouri line, put him in a position to watch the Indians on the west and the Missourians on the north.[13]

General Price left his small army in camp at Cowskin Prairie and taking a small escort proceeded to General Pearce's headquarters across the Arkansas line. Pearce and Price shared the same reservations about secession. Like Price, Pearce was a one-time career Union officer. He opposed secession but after Arkansas withdrew from the Union in May, he left his home at Osage Mills to accept a commission as commander of the state's Western Militia Division. Pearce said, "The question of secession was not a popular one in Arkansas where I was at the time. The people loved the Union." A large majority of the people of Arkansas rejected secession, and had it not been for Lincoln's call for 75,000 troops, of which the South was required to furnish its quota, both Arkansas and Missouri likely would have stayed loyal to the Union.[14]

Pearce received Price cordially. Price told him that a fighting force of the Missouri State Guard was gathering in Missouri to defend the state against invading federal troops, but that his men were poorly armed. Upon hearing of the plight of the Missourians, Pearce immediately agreed to loan price 650 muskets to help arm his men, not enough but more than he had before. When the State Guard soldiers showed up early the next day at Pearce's

camp to claim their weapons, it made a novel sight, these rough Missourians riding plough horses and armed with flintlock army muskets and bayonets. Pearce could hardly contain his amusement: "Well do I remember what a remarkable appearance this spirited body of men made in the bright morning light as they marched away from Camp Walker armed with the unusual cavalry weapon."[15]

Pearce suggested Price wait to meet General McCulloch who they expected to arrive at Camp Walker from Fort Smith the next day. Price did not wait for McCulloch but returned immediately to his camp at Cowskin Prairie with his cache of borrowed weapons and began to organize and drill his new recruits. Those he could arm he placed under Colonel Alexander E. Steen, a young Missourian who had recently resigned from the Union regular army.[16]

Ben McCulloch, ca. 1861. Confederate Brigadier General McCulloch volunteered to help the Missouri State Guard repel the Union incursion into southwest Missouri. He led the first Confederate troops into Missouri. (WICR 31541 in the collection of Wilson's Creek National Battlefield. Image courtesy National Park Service.)

General McCulloch arrived at Pearce's camp around 9 A.M., Sunday, June 30, with about 1,600 men. They moved on a few miles east and established a second encampment. There were two secessionist camps centered on Maysville, in Benton County, Arkansas. General Pearce set up a training facility for his Arkansas state troops at the edge of Beaty's Prairie, on an elevated point between Maysville and Harmony Springs, in extreme northwest Arkansas. The camp was directly west of the Harmonial Vegetarian Society lands, a large plot of land that once entertained a vegetarian society but which had recently been sold and the society disbanded. Pearce called his location Camp Walker. It became one of the rallying points for volunteers to the Southern cause. Meanwhile, when General McCulloch moved his headquarters from Fort Smith, he established his rendezvous point about three miles east-northeast of Maysville directly east of the large Harmony Springs mansion. He commandeered the lands for military exercises and named his encampment Camp Jackson in honor of the Missouri governor. The two camps together represented a formidable Confederate presence sitting on the doorstep of southwest Missouri.[17]

More Confederate troops were on their way and additional arms were due soon, including artillery expected to arrive in a day or two. Having started their march at moonrise, McCulloch's soldiers cooked a good breakfast and spent the day in good spirits practicing their best military drill on dress parade Sunday afternoon. They learned soon enough that General Sterling Price had been there and was only a few miles north of them with hundreds of Missourians ready to take on the federal Dutch now within striking distance of where the Confederates camped. Private Erasmus Stirman wrote home to his sister, "I think there will be a chance for a fight shortly." He looked forward to it.[18]

McCulloch broke camp on the morning of July 4, en route to Missouri. The bugle sounded and the orders came to take up arms for the march north. A shout went up from the camp as each soldier grabbed his gun and knapsack. Yet, there was an uneasiness in the ranks as they looked ahead to the next two or three days. "I shall be back if God is willing," wrote Ras Stirman. "If not, good bye my dear beloved Sister. I must quit [because] we start." With that, he put away his pen, and marched off.[19]

Fully aware of the situation in Missouri, General McCulloch headed north, riding in advance of his troops to meet Sterling Price. Behind him trailed the Confederate army, a force of well-trained infantry and cavalry. McCulloch soon reached General Price's headquarters at Cowskin Prairie. He at once agreed to help Price and his Missourians with his Confederate force. It was an uneasy liaison. The two men were of distinctly different character. The lofty McCulloch wore a black velvet suit with flowing swallowtails and rode a fine horse. Price, who often dressed plainly and rode an old horse, sized up McCulloch as a vain, flamboyant fellow. McCulloch at the same time thought Price and his rough, untrained Missourians unworthy of his disciplined Confederates. "There is no concert of action among them," McCulloch said, "and will not be until a competent military man is put in command of the entire force." Nonetheless, with General Pearce's Arkansans and McCulloch's Confederates, the Southern army was a sizable addition to General Price's State Guard volunteers and together they formed a substantial fighting force. Never before had there been an Independence Day in Missouri quite like this one.[20]

7

Union Blockade at Neosho

Colonel Franz Sigel's federal column camped outside Mount Vernon on June 27. The next day, leaving Captain August Hackmann and a company of infantry to garrison the town, Sigel continued toward Sarcoxie. The German soldiers led a trail of more than 40 wagons, many of them commandeered from Greene County citizens. They made an impression on the local population not accustomed to such a parade. Partisan secessionist spectators laconically dubbed the train the Yankee Dutchman's beer wagons.[1]

Four miles west of Mount Vernon, the federal column met a company of Lawrence County Home Guards, part of a larger force of a few hundred local citizen defenders. Sigel had accepted an offer from Captain William D. Gatton's company for scouting duties back on June 16. He now put the men to work guarding the supply train. Lawrence County was one of the few places in southwest Missouri with strong Union feeling. The first Home Guard raised in the interior of the state was David Murphy's Company A Rifle Battalion formed in Lawrence County on April 17, 1861. They opened General Lyon's campaign at Potosi and were at the capture of Camp Jackson in St. Louis; Captain Gatton's company had organized in May. There were initially six companies of the Lawrence County Union Guard Regiment averaging about 100 men each. They were local in nature formed in response to secessionist militant groups who ran the county at the time. It is uncertain how many if any of these companies besides Gatton's Company F accompanied Sigel beyond Lawrence County. However, the regiment later offered its entire Home Guard force to General Lyon prior to the Battle of Wilson's Creek, but he refused because they were not in uniform.[2]

Other volunteers rode in from neighboring counties and presented themselves for service as Sigel's federals marched along the Mount Vernon road. James Harvey Brady, for example, left his wife and two toddlers with his parents at Pleasant Hope; teamed up with a couple of Polk County Home Guard neighbors, James Alsup and his brother-in-law James Ross; and struck out to make contact with Sigel. Not one of these three would live to return home. Missouri-born Owen Smith Nichols, who lived in the Cave Springs-Bower's Mill area on the Jasper County line, strapped on his pistols, kissed his sweetheart Eliza Coats goodbye, mounted his best horse, and blissfully set out to join the Union troops. A mounted volunteer like the 22-year-old Nichols stood out from the German infantry. He liked to tell how Sigel handed him the regimental colors to bear and made him paymaster.[3]

From Mount Vernon, Sigel forded the upper Spring River, flowing deep from recent rains, and went past Gist's Mill and Gilbert's Post Office, before crossing from Lawrence County into Jasper County. Sigel arrived at Sarcoxie around five o'clock on Friday, the afternoon of June 28.

Sarcoxie — a town of about 400 — occupied a place of considerable political importance leading up to the war. When Thomas Benton ran for governor of Missouri, his speech at Sarcoxie drew one of the biggest crowds that had ever gathered in that part of the country. It was the oldest town in Jasper County and one of the oldest in southwest Missouri, tracing its beginning back to the 1830s. The stagecoach passed through daily connecting the town with the rest of the world, a service not extended to most southwest Missouri towns at that time. Sarcoxie's location made it a destination for both Northern and Southern troops during the course of the Civil War. Nearly every large body of soldiers in Missouri either stopped or passed through Sarcoxie. Like many of the neighboring towns, partisan raids left the town almost totally destroyed by the war's end.[4]

Sigel took little notice that Brigadier General James Rains of the Missouri State Guard lived at Sarcoxie. His plain but attractive colonial-revival home sat a few hundred feet north of the city limits across tiny Hasty Creek. A white, two-story, wood framed structure with a double portico façade, Rains called it home when not busy with politics and war. An arch-covered doorway opened from the second floor onto the upper porch where a relaxed Rains could survey graciously bending trees evenly spaced around an attractive lawn. A transom window above the front entrance illuminated spacious double archways in the interior. A short distance northwest a cool spring supplied water to the household. Far away to the north, General Rains could only imagine the state of affairs at home, as he guided the Lexington State Guard south into southwest Missouri.[5]

The appearance of the first federal troops in Sarcoxie caused great excitement. Unrest ran at a fever pitch. The town was a hotbed of proslavery and secessionist sentiment. A couple of years earlier, citizens had tarred and feathered a young abolitionist for his anti-slavery opinions. The Sarcoxie School employed a young teacher from Kansas in 1858 whose avid abolitionist views conflicted with the town's strong proslavery stance. His lessons included the reading of *Uncle Tom's Cabin* to his pupils. His outspoken lectures on the evils of slavery so incensed local patrons that when he refused to resign, a group of men called on him one evening and ordered him to leave. When he again refused, they took him to the woods, covered him with tar and feathers, and escorted him out of town.[6]

The first rebel flag in the state flew over Sarcoxie, hoisted before the news of the surrender of Fort Sumter. The flag had a length of 27 feet and flew atop a pole that one impressionable young trooper claimed must have been at least 100 feet in height. Sigel had his troops cut it down to the consternation of most residents of the town. They chopped down the pole and burned the flag.[7]

Sigel had barely arrived in Sarcoxie when a few local Union sympathizers quickly informed him that General Price with a force of several hundred men was camped at Pool's Prairie about six miles south of Neosho. As Sigel edged his troops further into hostile territory, rebel resistance was growing in southwest Missouri. Missouri volunteers hastened to come to the defense of the state in ever-increasing numbers. Besides Price's growing band on Pool's Prairie, Governor Jackson's body of the State Guard, now in Barton County, gathered more volunteers a few days' march north of Price's position. At the very moment Sigel was organizing federal troops at Sarcoxie, the rebel forces to the north were coming together in a determined effort to rendezvous with General Price and ultimately to link up with the regular Confederate army of General McCulloch on the Missouri-Arkansas border.[8]

It was Sigel's plan to move first against General Price at Pool's Prairie, then turn north to take on the forces of Jackson and his generals. Sigel's Union brigade would then meet up with the federal troops of Lyon and Sturgis coming south in pursuit of the renegade Missourians. Together, Union troops would crush the secessionist rebellion and chase the Southern sympathizers out of Missouri. Sigel did not know the positions of the other Union forces. He knew only that they were somewhere north of him. He believed General Lyon to be somewhere north of Nevada on the Little Osage River, where he was reportedly involved in a skirmish at Ball's Mill. Sigel did not know at the time that Lyon had not yet left Boonville. Nor did he know that the Lexington column of the Missouri State Guard, and not Lyon, bore southward only a day's ride from Ball's Mill. He sent several scouts to locate Lyon's position, but none returned except one who had nothing reliable to report. They were, after all, in a part of the state known for its deep resentment of the government and open hostility toward federal forces.[9]

The next morning, the Saturday morning of June 29, anticipating Sigel's intentions, General Price abandoned Pool's Prairie to reposition his troops at Elk Mills on Cowskin Prairie about 30 miles southwest of Neosho at the extreme southwest corner of the state. There they would be closer to the relative safety of the Confederate camp just across the Arkansas border. Price's plan was to unite the Missouri State Guard with the Southern regulars in a joint campaign to force the federals out of southwest Missouri, and push them back to St. Louis, if not completely out of the state.[10]

Just as Sigel was leaving Sarcoxie, he learned that General Price had broken camp at Pool's Prairie and was moving to consolidate his troops further south. Sigel felt good that he had compelled General Price to retreat. He learned, too, that for two days Governor Jackson and his State Guard had been in camp 15 miles north of Lamar at Montevallo. What he did not know was that Jackson had since left Montevallo and was approaching Lamar about to join forces with the Guard troops coming down from Lexington.[11]

Sigel abandoned his plan to pursue Price in the face of McCulloch's army. He had no desire, with his small brigade of volunteers, to engage the Confederate regulars so soon in the war. He instead decided to redirect his mission toward attacking the rebel forces assembled to the north. He believed that by a rapid and forceful engagement he could overcome Jackson's larger untrained force.

Sigel immediately sent instructions to Colonel Salomon, now on his way from Mount Vernon to Sarcoxie, to double-time his battalion to Neosho where Sigel would meet him. The occupation of Neosho would place the federals directly in the path of Governor Jackson's column trying to reach Price.[12]

Sigel arrived in the town of Neosho with the Third Regiment on Tuesday, July 2. They were in an uneasy situation, some 85 miles from Springfield in decidedly prosecessionist territory and without a supply line. Their headlong march toward the rebel Missourians had placed them squarely between two dangers. Barely 60 miles to the north was Governor Jackson's volunteer army moving into position to threaten to cut off Sigel's retreat back to Springfield. Meanwhile, little more than half that distance further to the southwest stood a seasoned force of 5,000 Arkansas volunteers and Confederate regulars encamped just across the Missouri border. Here Brigadier General Ben McCulloch, a decorated Texas Ranger and veteran of the War for Texas Independence, had assembled troops from Louisiana and Arkansas, along the Missouri line. They were ready to prosecute the Southern Cause in the border state of Missouri, and thus hold the South's strategic edge in the theatre of the West. General N. B. Pearce's Arkansas volunteers camped in the same vicinity, and close by stood General Price's Missourians. Sigel's little army found itself at the western front of the war in a perilous situation between two rebel forces, either of which greatly outnumbered his own. The situation grew more ominous when Governor Jackson advanced his growing army through Lamar on July 4, headed directly on a collision path with Sigel's army.[13]

Another sequence of events was unfolding back at Springfield. Brigadier General Sweeny and his column, hurrying down from Rolla, were within about two days of Springfield when they met some men from town upset that Sigel planned to leave the city unprotected to pursue Jackson. Surprised by the news, Sweeny rushed ahead. He marched into Springfield on July 1 to find that Sigel and Salomon were indeed gone. He set up his headquarters and contemplated his next move.[14]

Sweeny's appearance in Springfield resulted in untimely confusion as to who was in command. Military protocol determined that although Sigel wore the higher rank of colonel of U.S. Volunteers, Sweeny outranked him as a captain of the Regular Army because of the kinds of troops he commanded. His Regular Army commission entitled him to be commander of all federal troops then in southwest Missouri. Sweeny's rank as a brigadier general ostensibly came from his command of five regiments of the U.S. Reserve Corps in St. Louis who had supposedly elected him brigadier general, a post confirmed by General Harney back on May 20. Sweeny, however, in fact had neither election by his command nor confirmation from Washington. Nevertheless, his acting brigadier appointment gave him status before the volunteers who did not necessarily recognize his authority as a Regular Army captain, although brigadier general of volunteers had no warrant in law unless confirmed by Washington.[15]

It was a difficult situation from the beginning. Sweeny was Irish. Sigel was German. The German newspapers hailed Sigel as a military genius upon whose head a general's hat would fit best. In any event, General Lyon named Sweeny commander of the forces at Springfield. By the time Sweeny arrived, however, Sigel had taken command and already left without orders. Sweeny later claimed to be the one who ordered Sigel to advance to meet the rebel forces of Governor Jackson, but no such order ever surfaced. Sigel maintained that Sweeny never ordered him to engage the rebel army and that he went entirely on his own initiative. Sweeny, he said, had ordered Colonel Salomon to garrison Springfield and Sigel to take up a position farther west. Sigel decided instead to move ahead without Sweeny's knowledge, thinking that Sweeny could not know the circumstances of the rebel movements on the ground at the time. He further defended his decision to take both his and Salomon's force with him; else, Salomon faced possible attack by Governor Jackson, and Sigel by McCulloch and Price. Sweeny did not arrive in Springfield until July 1. By that time, Sigel was past Mount Vernon on his way to Neosho.[16]

Sigel's entry into Neosho was a silent one. General Price had come through a few days earlier to a rousing welcome, but the federals received no such reception. Citizens peered warily from behind curtains and closed shutters. If Sigel had not known before he knew now that many considered Neosho the strongest center of secession sentiment in southwest Missouri, if not the entire state. The whole region despised Lincoln. Out of more than 1,300 votes cast in the 1860 election in Newton County, where Neosho was the county seat, 22 went to Lincoln, and that was 22 more than he received in Stone, Taney, Vernon, and Christian counties where he did not receive a single vote. It was that way all up and down the state. In Chariton County, for example, in the heart of Little Dixie, he got one vote, which turned out later to be the result of a five-dollar bet. On a wager that Lincoln would not receive a single vote in the county, a challenger voted for Lincoln and won the bet. Lincoln managed to get 17 votes in Jasper County; one person in Barton County voted for him; and out of 50 Republicans in all of Greene County, only 42 voted for him. In a 14-county area of southwest Missouri, Lincoln garnered little more than 1½ percent of the vote.

One local pro–Southern fellow who had come to the Ozarks from back east said, "Much as I once liked New York, I never desire to see it again and would rather starve and die here than live and grow fat under Lincoln!"[17]

Lincoln's army was no more popular than the president was. Only three openly Union sympathizers came forward to meet Sigel at Neosho. They were R. V. Keller, T. P. Price, and Archibald M. Sevier, the editor of the Neosho *Herald*. As prominent citizens of the town, they helped to organize a company of Home Guards in January 1861 to defend the community on the condition that the protection favored neither Union nor pro–South forces. The local commander, Captain Henderson Jennings, and his 38 men remained quietly in the background offering neither resistance nor aid to Sigel's troops. All would later join Price and the Confederacy except two, one of those being

Thomas W. Sweeny, ca. 1861. Regular U.S. Army captain and acting brigadier general of Missouri Volunteers, Mexican War veteran Tom Sweeny commanded the Union incursion into southwest Missouri. Colonel Sigel ignored Sweeny's orders to hold off contact with rebel forces and advanced Union troops without Sweeny's knowledge. (WICR 32009 in the collection of Wilson's Creek National Battlefield. Image courtesy National Park Service.)

A. M. Sevier who enlisted with the Union. Sigel's appearance in town ended the *Herald*. It would be well after the war ended before Sevier returned to start up the Neosho *Times*.[18]

The federals ensconced themselves in the courthouse in Neosho. Amid the uneasy surroundings, Sigel blatantly drilled his men in the center of town. The offensive German commands reverberated through the streets. In their best broken English, the troops sang "John Brown's Body," a favorite battle ditty celebrating the German regard for the abolitionist martyr and dedication to saving the Yankee eagle. Hatred filled the air. Southern partisans considered Sigel and the Germans a foreign foe, at best foreign mercenaries sent to do the dirty work of the Yankee North. A group of Neosho men watched from the second floor of the Masonic Hall near the courthouse. The stately wood-frame, colonial-revival-style hall imparted a dignity not warranted by the scene playing out in the streets before it. The elegant arched windows with their double-hung, multipane glazing, and the fancy fanlights above the entry doors mocked the crude simplicity of the German drill. The men in the Masonic Hall exchanged glances and went downstairs.[19]

Sigel had no respect for the local insurrectionists, branding them as ignorant hill men and plainsmen farmers of weak morals and poor nutrition. Missourians had their own impression of Sigel, the little German with the arrogant expression. He wore

Franz Sigel, ca. 1862. An officer in the German Revolution and refugee to America, Sigel volunteered his military experience on behalf of the Union. A detachment of U.S. Missouri Volunteers under Colonel Sigel's command entered southwest Missouri to block rebel Missouri forces from joining Confederate troops in Arkansas. (Library of Congress LC-DIG-ppmsca-08359.)

spectacles and looked more like a student than a soldier. He was lean and slender with a pale complexion and a most impertinent face. He kept looking around like a weasel. The Americans never liked him but the Germans did. At 140 lbs., he stood five feet seven, and was smooth shaven with coal black hair, piercing black eyes, and stiff posture. A soldier in his regiment said after the war, "Sigel had military knowledge, but he was a very ambitious man, who was very vain and openly displayed his vanity." Nevertheless, he was an experienced officer. At 36 years of age, a native of Baden, Germany, Sigel graduated from military school at Carlsruhe. He was chief adjutant in the regular army of Baden in 1847 before his sympathies with the southern German faction in the first German revolution cost him his commission. He became general in chief at the start of the second revolution in 1848, but repeated battle losses forced him to flee Germany in 1850. He came to America and worked as a teacher and writer in St. Louis until the outbreak of the rebellion, then joined the U.S. Missouri Volunteers as colonel of the Third Regiment assigned to the southwest Missouri operation.[20]

Sigel remained two days at Neosho until Thursday, July 4, resting his troops amid the bucolic surroundings of this beautiful little town. The federals enjoyed the pastoral setting, ignored the people, and looked to the quartermaster for their next meal. Provisions were in short supply when marching. The army had no meat at all, but took time now to appropriate and slaughter a few head of beef, incurring additional enmity of the local population. Sigel had established a bakery at Springfield, and wagons soon arrived at Neosho with a hearty supply of fresh bread. It was a welcome treat to the foot-weary soldiers. Neosho proved to be a very good place for soldiers but not so much for horses because there was no forage for them — they had to be taken out in the brush to graze.[21]

Meanwhile, Colonel Charles Salomon's regiment, coming by forced march from Mount Vernon and Sarcoxie, caught up with General Sigel at Neosho. The little army now consisted of Sigel's Third Missouri, approximately 700 men under battalion commanders Major Henry Bischoff and Lieutenant Colonel Franz Hassendeubel; Colonel Salomon's Fifth Missouri of 400 men; and two batteries of artillery with eight cannons and 150 men. Together, the Union forces numbered approximately 1,350 men, including the transportation train. Most were German-Americans out of St. Louis, except for the attached local Home Guard volunteers.

Sigel fidgeted at Neosho waiting for the other arms of General Lyon's pincer maneuver to come into place. Of the three armies in the plan, Sigel's was the only one in proper position. In his headstrong drive to cut off General Price, he arrived early before the other wings of the movement could catch up. Growing impatient, he had exceeded his orders from Sweeny by not waiting for the arrival of Salomon at Springfield, instead marching his men to Neosho and countermanding Sweeny by directing Salomon to follow him. He received much criticism in his military career but never for tardiness. Never one to arrive after the first gun had been fired, his hurry-up-and-go tactics earned him the epithet of the Flying Dutchman. With his small army now intact with the addition of Colonel Salomon's men, Sigel prepared his troops for battle.[22]

The Great Comet grew more ominously visible in the first days of July. By July 3, the tail was of enormous length. Its fan-shaped train reached up to the Pole Star and passed across it, sweeping deep into the constellation Lyra. Its streaming jets etched across the sky, meeting at the nucleus like converging railway lines. A pale sliver of moon told of the ending lunar phase as people moved about the streets in the afterglow of the comet.

Sigel set up a delaying tactic to stall any effort General Price might make to send troops north to aid Jackson and at the same time to block the rebel Missourians from reaching Price. He sent two companies along with two pieces of artillery under captains John Cramer and Joseph Indest, one to Cedar Creek and the other to Grand Falls, to block the Military and Kansas Line Road. The road marked the edge of the frontier, stretching from Fort Scott to Fort Blair near Baxter Springs, Kansas. They were to keep their eyes and ears open for the disposition of the Missouri State Guard troops, and rejoin the main column once they determined that no Guard detachments were slipping past. It was an impossible assignment for Cramer and Indest to believe that their two companies could impede General Price or Governor Jackson should they decide to take that western route.[23]

Sigel's decision to send out detachments further cut the size of his already small force. Union generals had a proclivity for leaving garrisons to defend every Missouri town they went through, supposedly to protect the local citizenry. Garrisons were in place along the Wire Road between Rolla and Springfield, and Colonel Salomon's Fifth Missouri stood at less than half its normal strength because of detachments left at various outposts. There was no Company A of the Fifth Regiment. General Lyon originally had sent two companies of the Fifth to Washington County to quell disturbances around Potosi and De Soto, and Company A remained there, reducing the Fifth Regiment to 775 men. Then, in the march from Rolla to Neosho, another company remained at Lebanon, and Sigel had ordered two companies left with the garrison defense at Springfield. By the time Colonel Salomon reached Neosho, the Fifth Regiment was down to 400 men. Sigel initially posted another company under Captain August Hackmann to garrison Mount Vernon but now ordered it to position forward at Sarcoxie. Seeing that Sigel intended to abandon Neosho, the unionist delegation of Keller, Price, and Sevier approached him expressing concern about rebel looters. He decided to leave another occupying presence at Neosho and left Captain Joseph Conrad with a company of the Third Regiment and the instructions, "You are to protect the Union-loving people," he said, "against bands of secessionists."

"Yes, sir," replied Captain Conrad.

Sigel advised, "If necessary, retreat to Sarcoxie." He claimed years later that he left instructions for Conrad to follow him the next day.[24]

It is unclear why Sigel delayed two days in Neosho before he moved out to engage Governor Jackson's State Guard. Perhaps he hoped to give more time for General Lyon and his army to come. It was, after all, General Lyon who had sent an army to southwest Missouri in pursuit of the rebel Missourians in the first place. Maybe he felt conflicted by Sweeny's directive to stay where he was, which may also account for why he felt the need to leave a garrison at Neosho. Perhaps Sigel wanted to rest his own band of green recruits and prepare them for battle. Perhaps he felt miffed at Sweeny, having formed the expedition to overtake the rebels on his own initiative before Sweeny arrived and took credit for it. On the other hand, perhaps it was something else. In the gathering darkness of the waning moon, the Great Comet again announced its presence in the sky. The sky had an eerie golden hue to it, spreading a gossamer veil over the setting sun. As the soldiers gathered around their camp-fires and looked skyward, they wondered which side's fortunes lay with the coming proph-esied disaster. Sigel sent a courier to inform Sweeny in Springfield that he intended to move on Governor Jackson.[25]

8

Closing Forces

The Boonville and Lexington wings of the rebel Missouri State Guard met on July 3, 1861, during a violent thunderstorm. Artillery fired a few rounds to mark the liaison of the two forces. Men of the Lexington column arrived at Camp Lamar at various times throughout the day and into the evening. More bands of local men loyal to Governor Jackson began to appear at the camp even before the weather cleared off. George E. Ward, the founder of Lamar and publisher of the *Barton County Democrat*, rode out with his two sons and a small detachment of men. Their sympathies lay with the southland from which they came. A. R. Randall, a lawyer who worked out of the Lamar Hotel, brought in another group from Barton and Cedar counties, not armed, but welcomed; and around sundown, George Parker arrived with another gang, as more men poured into the encampment. A party from Lincoln and Warren counties arrived and fell in with the Jackson camp. Word reached Governor Jackson that a company of men on their way down from Callaway County was making an effort to join his forces. He sent enough overland coaches and horses back to them to ease their journey into camp. The Callaway Guards had organized back in April 1861. Like most of the State Guard companies that formed across Missouri, they comprised an odd lot made up of farmers' sons, young mechanics about town, and, in the case of the Callaway Guard, students from Westminster College at Fulton. Their captain was D. H. McIntyre, a senior student at the college. The Callaway Guards had two other distinctions: they were the only company in Governor Jackson's army that wore uniforms, and they carried the Enfield 1853 rifle-musket of British design capable of firing three rounds a minute.[1]

An air of frivolity gripped the camp. Some spent the evening chasing deer from the bottoms. New acquaintances lounged near smoky campfires, cooking rations, and exchanging rumors about General Lyon and the federals. No one knew that Lyon was still at Boonville, days from the State Guard position. The greater danger lay ahead in the advancing troops of Colonel Franz Sigel. Seventeen-year-old James T. Ward talked excitedly, and innocently ribbed his older brother about which one of them would get the first Dutchman.[2]

Feeding a large army without a reliable supply line continued to tax the Missourians to the limit. Food began to be scarce at Lamar. Foraging parties extended out in every direction, reaching further and further into the surrounding countryside. Ward's Mill at Lamar had already given up its supply of flour and grain. The settlements on Horse Creek and Dry

Wood Creek to the northeast and northwest, and those southeast at Golden Grove and along the banks of Muddy Creek, could provide only limited provisions. Foragers raided riverside mills and seized local stores and farm livestock. Some soldiers went west as far as the Kansas line looking for wild game, which although plentiful made itself scarce in the path of the army. Drummer Edward Dixon, a teenage Cole County lad in Brigadier General Parsons' division, took a party of foragers all the way to Bower's Mill on the Jasper-Lawrence County line, confiscated a wagonload of flour and grain, and hauled it back to the Lamar camp. Except for the Callaway County boys, the young State Guard army had little in the way of military equipment either. A few men carried the muskets taken in the fight at Cole Camp. Others carried arms taken from the U.S. depot at Liberty; most brought their hunting rifles and shotguns; many had no weapons at all. Those with military experience knew that for the Missourians the question of arms was a serious one. He who possessed a double-barrel shotgun was a happy soul, and a Colt revolver was a prize indeed. Many could only shoulder a squirrel rifle, but they knew how to use them effectively.[3]

The foray to Bower's Mill brought back one other item of interest. Bower's Mill was on Spring River in the Oregon settlement of Lawrence County where the Bowers operated a gristmill and wool-carding machinery. They kept a storage facility for flour, wheat, corn, wool, and assorted dry goods. Local informants there said the Union army had marched through Lawrence County a week ago Thursday and were somewhere nearby.

The next day, July 4, 1861, the Missourians took the first steps to organize their army. Governor Jackson ordered all the men with weapons to report to the brigadier generals in charge of their districts. This was a confusing directive in some ways because in the trek southward many men found themselves in divisions outside their districts, and they did not know whether to report to a new division or stay where they were. Around 1,800 men reported to Brigadier General Rains, while more than 2,200 divided into the commands of brigadier generals Mosby Monroe Parsons, John Clark, Sr., and William Y. Slack: altogether about 4,000 men. Another 2,000 or so had no weapons. The entire Army of Missouri numbered almost 6,000 men, a marked improvement over the 800 that defended Boonville but far short of the 50,000 anticipated when Governor Jackson issued a proclamation calling for volunteers to resist invasion by the federal government back on June 12.[4]

The State Guard stayed at Camp Lamar less than one day after the junction of the two columns. The Guard commanders made a decision to leave Roup's Point and move further south a few miles past Lamar and wait for General Sterling Price to come up from Arkansas. The troops could do little training. Because of the rain, the artillery caissons and wagons sank into the mud up to their axles as horses and men strained to extract them. Water soaked the gunpowder and provisions that sat unprotected in the wagons. Governor Jackson wrote out his order of march for the State Guard divisions and instructed his generals to be ready to move at 3 P.M.[5]

They broke camp at Camp Lamar on the afternoon of July 4 and began the march southward. Officers herded their raw recruits into columns and kept a close eye that they stayed there. Governor Jackson strictly enjoined officers to keep the men in line and allow no one to leave without permission. His warning anticipated the undisciplined nature of the State Guard recruits and no doubt stemmed from the governor's impression that his army might melt back into the countryside from which it came at any moment. The army cut a wide swath on both sides of the Lamar road, which was little more than a cart path too narrow to accommodate the ranks of the advancing column. Parsons' division took a wrong turn and had to backtrack. Some of the companies marched on the other side of

Muddy Creek. The column crossed over Petty's Creek and swerved west. Heavy underbrush in a bend of Muddy Creek entangled the horses and men, slowing the march to a crawl. They forded the Muddy and caught up with Guard pickets posted the night before — no sign of the federals, yet. The State Guard Missourians came steadily on, down the Lamar road toward Carthage. At about nine o'clock on the evening of July 4, Jackson's army stopped for the night. After about an eight-mile march, they settled uneasily into camp on John Murray's farm six miles south of Lamar. Independence Day brought the news that Franz Sigel was south of Carthage on his way to give them battle. On the eve of the first full-scale battle of the Civil War, two opposing armies of contrasting military character advanced toward each other on the rolling prairies of southwest Missouri.[6]

At this point there needs to be some clarification of the organization and movements of the combatants on the eve of the battle, especially regarding the young inexperienced Missouri State Guard. To do this, it is necessary to consult witnesses to the battle and those who have studied it to resolve disagreements in the historical record. First, the junction of the Missouri State Guard rebel army is important to the understanding of the battle that soon followed because the combined rebel force came together only two days before the battle and entered the fight without equipment or training as a joint force. Exactly where Governor Claiborne Jackson and General James Rains joined forces and what transpired in the hours immediately before the battle are key parts of the battle's history heretofore not well understood.

The original plan in the aftermath of the skirmish at Boonville, Missouri, called for the two independent rebel columns to meet at Montevallo in Vernon County, Missouri, with General Rains coming down with his men from Lexington and Governor Jackson from Boonville. However, heavy storms and swollen streams delayed General Rains. Governor Jackson, after waiting for a while at Montevallo, advanced his column toward Lamar. Stories differ as to the time and place of the rendezvous of the two columns and their movements as they approached Carthage. A popular description of the battle written immediately afterward from the rebel camp on Spring River by Colonel John Taylor Hughes — which appeared in several state and national newspapers — claimed the two columns met on Independence Day. Hughes, traveling with General Rains, wrote, "On the 4th of July our army effected a junction with Jackson and Gen. Parsons' Division on Rupe's Creek." Private Henry Cheavens, on the other hand, also riding with the Lexington column of General Rains, wrote in his journal, "Arrived in the evening (July 3rd) at Camp Lamar, in a pretty bottom. Gov. Jackson, Gens. Price, Parsons, and Clark already there." Cheavens was apparently not aware that General Price was not at Camp Lamar but far to the south near the Arkansas border. Historian Robert S. Bevier, meanwhile, remembered in 1879 that "on the night of the 3rd of July, the column from Lexington formed a junction with Jackson's forces in Cedar County." Jefferson Davis accepted the July 3 date and repeated Bevier's Cedar County location in his memoir. This apparently came originally from Robert R. Howison's "History of the War" who wrote in 1863, "Two days afterwards [after crossing the rain-swollen Marmaton River] the whole force under Raines [sic], Slack and Weightman, effected a junction with Gov. Jackson, at Roup's Point, in Cedar county, where he had arrived a short time before, with the brigades of Parsons and Clarke [sic]." R. I. Holcombe, meanwhile, referred to Rupe's Point being not in Cedar County but in Jasper County, a location repeated by Edwin C. Bearss. Thomas L. Snead who was with Governor Jackson appears to have rendered the most accurate account of the junction of the State Guard columns. In 1886 he wrote, "Governor Jackson reached Montevallo, in Vernon County, and then moved to

Camp Lamar, on the right bank of Spring River, some three miles north of the village of Lamar. There he was joined by Rains and Slack on the 3d of July." The consensus is for a rendezvous of the Lexington and Boonville State Guard columns on July 3, 1861 (not July 4 as Colonel Hughes remembered), at a place near Roup's Point called Camp Lamar in Barton County. The various reports that place Roup's Point in Cedar County or Jasper County, instead of Barton County, reflect the confusion created by the close proximity of the three counties and the dispersion of the large State Guard force. It was a large force of some 6,000 men with almost half as many horses and a large number of wagons strung out for miles across the prairie. This may have contributed to the differing reports that surfaced about the junction of Rains and Jackson in the hours leading up to the battle. Nevertheless, Roup's Point was in Barton County. One old Dade County resident, relating a story about three unfortunate citizens murdered in Barton County, said, "They [the murder victims] reached what is called 'Ruphs' Point on Muddy Creek just over in Barton County." The writer then went on to say, "Ruphs Point is a point of timber where it juts out into the prairies of Barton County." Later on, a longtime resident of Lamar, reminiscing about her childhood at Lamar in the 1920s, wrote, "Little did we dream that place had once been known as Roup's Point for an early day settler, Gil Roup, or that it served as a Confederate training camp during the Civil War and was known as Camp Lamar." Roup's Point still exists at a bend in Muddy Creek where the timber juts out into the prairie — about three miles north of Lamar, as Snead said — near the present Old North Dam in Barton County. Snead, however, placed the point on Spring River instead of Muddy Creek; the latter is actually a tributary of the North Fork of Spring River.[7]

A second point of interest is the timing of the organization of the State Guard and the path of its subsequent movements immediately prior to the battle. The language of Governor Jackson's organization order on July 4 at Camp Lamar was clear. It said, "The commander-in-chief issues the following general orders for the government of the forces now in the field: The several brigadier generals now in the field will proceed forthwith to the organization of the forces from their respective districts." Jackson's order provided, too, that parts of companies of the Second District should report to General Clark; the Fifth District to General Slack; and the First, Eighth, and Ninth Districts to General Parsons. The commanders of the named districts were not on the field, except for General Rains and the Eighth Division. It is not clear why Governor Jackson assigned those troops to General Parsons unless he meant to infer that General Rains had relinquished his division command to take overall command of the State Guard. However, Jackson's order did not explicitly state that. Contrary to Jackson's order, Edward A. Pollard said the State Guard organization took place on the evening of July 3, immediately after the junction of the two State Guard columns at Camp Lamar on Roup's Point. Joseph A. Mudd, a veteran of the Missouri conflict, likewise remembered a July 3 organization. However, both Pollard and Mudd appear to be wrong because Governor Jackson did not order the organization until July 4, only hours before the battle. Pollard's 1863 account is worth parsing because it served as one of the earliest authorities on the battle, notwithstanding its misinformation about rebel troop movements. Pollard said the army had organized by twelve o'clock on July 4, and one hour later took up the line of march for the southwest. He further stated that Jackson marched his command a distance of 23 miles by 9:00 on the evening of July 4, at which hour he stopped for the night. Pollard evidently confused the Guard movements from Montevallo and the time it stopped at Murray Corners. He had the July 3 rendezvous of the two columns occurring in Cedar County, near Montevallo, which was actually in Vernon

County. The distance from Montevallo to Murray Corners is approximately the 23 miles Pollard claimed the Guard marched before stopping on July 4. Governor Jackson's order, however, proves that the Missouri army relocated to Murray Corners on the eve of the battle shortly after organizing on July 4 at Camp Lamar. The importance of the location is the distance the State Guard troops had to march before encountering Sigel's Union army. The actual distance was significantly less than the 23 miles Pollard and others envisioned. The rebel Missouri State Guard left Camp Lamar on July 4 not long after it organized and moved with some difficulty over the muddy terrain to a place about eight miles south at Murray Corners. Cheavens said the army commenced its march from Camp Lamar to Murray Corners about noon, which coincides with Pollard's recollection of an early afternoon departure. They may again be incorrect about the departure time, however, because Governor Jackson ordered the march to begin at 3 P.M., July 4. Cheavens was in the rear guard, meaning he could not have left at noon before the other units unless some had already started their march before the order was in hand. The State Guard went into camp at Murray Corners on the evening before the battle. Surgeon General Taylor placed the new camp eight miles south of Lamar but probably meant eight miles south of Camp Lamar and not the town of Lamar. The documented distance of about six miles that the Guard traveled the next day from this second camp to the battlefield confirms Murray Corners as the second encampment. John P. and Hester Murray's farm was about halfway between Lamar and the present-day town of Jasper, in Jasper County. The rebel camp was about where the village of Boston, or Beloit, Missouri, is today. VanGilder placed it in the muddy bottoms of the North Fork of Spring River, near the point where it receives Petty's Creek, West Fork Creek, and Rose Branch. This was approximately the location of Murray Corners, now Boston, Missouri. North, meanwhile, situated the encampment past Lamar on the north side of Coon Creek, twelve miles north of Carthage, which also roughly coincided with the Murray Corners location. It was here that the rebel soldiers went into camp with their newly organized divisions in the early evening of July 4.[8]

Finally, no one knows for sure the exact number of Missourians who came together at Murray Corners on Independence Day, or the full extent of their preparation, or lack thereof, to do battle. There were many estimates of troop strength. Pollard maintained that about 1,200 infantry fought in the rebel line; the remainder were cavalry, he said. Shoemaker concluded an armed force of 4,000 State Guard and 2,000 unarmed. Rombauer tabulated the total force under arms as

Claiborne Fox Jackson, ca. 1861. Pro-South and in favor of secession, Missouri Governor Claiborne Jackson abandoned the state capital at Jefferson City under pressure from Union troops. He personally took command of the rebel Missouri army. (WICR 11499 in the collection of Wilson's Creek National Battlefield. Image courtesy National Park Service.)

4,200; another 2,000 had no weapons. Bevier gave a lesser number of 3,600 total men, 500 unarmed. Snead put the force at about 6,000, of whom 4,000 had weapons, about 1,800 unarmed. Schrantz gave a complete breakdown of State Guard units by regiment and battalion but confessed an "unknown number of unarmed men." Violette determined the numbers were less for both State Guard and Union forces, setting rebel strength at slightly more than 4,000 and Union numbers at 1,000. Modern research by Denny and Bradbury concluded that the State Guard had 4,375 men with weapons, out of 6,000; 1,358 were mounted cavalry. Denny and Bradbury did not disclose how they arrived at such precise figures. Meanwhile, they adopted the generally accepted troop level of 1,100 men on the Union side.[9]

A fair conclusion from all this is that Governor Jackson moved his column from Montevallo, in Vernon County, and stopped at a place called Roup's Point on Muddy Creek, in Barton County. General Rains caught up with him there on July 3, 1861. They called the Barton County site Camp Lamar. Here they organized for the first time as a fighting force. The next day, July 4, the combined force moved south to Murray Corners south of Lamar (Beloit or Boston on later maps) and a few miles north of Carthage.[10]

On the evening of July 4, 1861, at Murray Corners, Governor Jackson received erroneous intelligence that a force of 3,000 federal troops under the command of Colonel Sigel was immediately to his front at the town of Carthage. Governor Jackson also had word that General Lyon was behind him in pursuit from a northeasterly direction. Another piece of intelligence told him Major Sturgis had a bead on him from the northwest. The two federal forces intended to unite in his rear with a combined force big enough to crush the Missouri uprising. At this point, Jackson personally took command of the Missouri troops. It was the only time during the Civil War when a sitting governor commanded an army in the field, although it would be hard to describe this collection of poorly equipped and pitifully outfitted Missourians, dressed mostly in civilian clothing, as an army. It would be equally difficult to envision Governor Jackson as a military leader, a political leader perhaps, but a soldier no. Nevertheless, Jackson made an impressive appearance. In his middle fifties, tall and angular with a determined gaze, the normally clean-shaven Jackson now sported a full fringe of whiskers from ear to ear that framed a firm, straight mouth and clean-shaven upper lip. One State Guard soldier from Carroll County expressed the general feeling about the governor's political demeanor, saying, "He is a good talker but has hard looks. I was disappointed in his appearance. He is a foxy old 'coon.'" The State Guard army followed the commands of an odd assortment of politicians. James Rains, Mosby Parsons, Robert Peyton, and Ben Brown were all sitting state senators; John Clark, Sr., had left his post as a member of the United States House of Representatives; and there were several state representatives. Except for brief stints in the Mexican War, the State Guard officers were as inexperienced as the men in ranks.[11]

Meanwhile, on the Thursday morning of July 4, 1861, Independence Day, Colonel Franz Sigel's army left Neosho and moved out in column. He turned northward and headed for Carthage, 23 miles due north in Jasper County, away from General McCulloch and Sterling Price to the south and on an approach to confront Governor Jackson's Missouri State Guard. Three miles north of Neosho the State road forked: the road on the right led to Carthage; the left-hand branch went to Grand Falls, 16 miles northwest. Sigel sent a message to Captain Cramer to abandon his reconnaissance mission at the Kansas border and hurry to rejoin him at Diamond Grove by the quickest available route, and to inform Captain Indest to come as soon as possible too.[12]

The federals arrived at Diamond Grove, passing there around noon. It was a hot Missouri summer day, and the diamond-shaped stand of timber offered shade and a brief respite from the heat. They left Diamond Grove and continued on north with approximately another ten miles to go to Carthage. No sign of rebel troops yet. Three miles on, the Union column came into the vicinity of Fidelity. Fidelity was a post office seven miles south of Carthage. When William Clow laid out the village in 1856, it promised to be a town of some importance. It never grew much beyond its original plat, and people living in the vicinity dismissively called it Skeeterville, a fanciful name from its early days. Visitors to Fidelity marveled at the enormous church there, built by the Christian denomination to accommodate 600 people. It could seat Sigel's entire Third Regiment and half of his whole command. Both Union and rebel forces made use of the church during the course of the war, making it a wonder that it escaped destruction.

Sigel's march from Neosho to Carthage sent a bevy of informants scurrying ahead of him across the countryside to warn residents that the Yankees were coming. Lazarus Spence had taken a load of corn to Neosho a few days earlier and brought back word that the federals were in the area. Spence lived east of Fidelity on Jones Creek. He often did blacksmith work for the Moss families who had several farms in the Jones Creek neighborhood. When Dr. D. F. Moss heard that Sigel's army was coming, he hitched his buggy and set out for Carthage. He went straight to former sheriff Norris Hood's house and delivered the news that the Union army was on its way. Hood welcomed the report because he was a good Union man. Moss expressed concern about his livestock, and Hood assured him no harm would come to his property because everyone knew that Dr. Moss also supported the Union. The alert soon spread through Carthage, and everyone waited apprehensively for the Lincoln army to show.[13]

A good distance to the north of the two colliding forces, General Nathaniel Lyon with his force of volunteers and U.S. Regulars continued the slow march from Boonville. They proceeded toward southwest Missouri at a leisurely pace, unaware of the building conflict coming to a head between Governor Jackson's Missourians and Colonel Sigel's Union force at Carthage. Lyon's army stopped to camp late on the afternoon of July 4 outside the village of Smithton in Pettis County, immediately east of the newly incorporated town of Sedville. There was a new railhead here at the terminus of the line out of St. Louis, and the last opportunity to resupply before the trek into southwest Missouri. Here Lyon met two companies of Captain Able Cook's force who had come to Smithton from Benton County to transfer arms to his Home Guard at Cole Camp, 16 miles south. The heavy Union losses from the recent rebel raid at Cole Camp underscored the urgency of the need for action. Lyon worked into the evening, receiving reports from his scouts and formulating his plan for entering southwest Missouri. He laid out a role for Cook's German regiment. Their job would be to clean out pockets of rebel secessionists left in the wake of Governor Jackson's retreat while Lyon's force pursued the governor into southwest Missouri.[14]

Lyon's army broke camp at Smithton early on the morning of July 5, after waking up at 3:30 A.M., the general's usual time to begin the day. They marched southwest toward Leesville and the planned rendezvous with Major Sturgis at Clinton. It started to rain again. The federals marched all day through a continuous line of showers. Thick clouds rolled over the prairie full of lightning and thunder. The men trudged on through the mud. To relieve the burden of wet gear, some of the men dumped their tents and never slept in a tent again for the duration of the campaign. Mules sunk into the mud in some places up to their bellies and wagons to their axles. For all the misery of the conditions, the weather did little to dampen the spirits of the Union army. The soldiers belted out a chorus of "The Happy Land of Canaan" on the hour. Animals foraged contentedly on the pastures and crops as the column progressed. They made Green Ridge before noon and stopped for the night near Belmont in Henry County within less than a day's march of Major Sturgis and his men waiting at Clinton.

Lyon's plan appeared to be coming together. Lyon now descended from the north with 2,500 men; Sturgis waited with 2,200 troops at Clinton; Sigel's 1,500 or so volunteers were near Springfield; and Sweeny had approached from Rolla with another 1,000 men. Neither Lyon nor Sturgis had any idea what was transpiring many miles to the south in Jasper County.[15]

9

Carthage, Blossom on the Prairie

Carthage, Missouri, stood on Spring River where the Ozark highland meets the western prairie, on territory ceded to the United States Government by the Osage Indians in 1825. The soil was rich, and several well-kept farms dotted the landscape. Their comfortable dwellings sat tucked behind lines of hedge fences surrounded by green orchards. The land around Carthage was well settled; out in the country, however, travelers might go for miles without seeing a house or meeting another person. A typical farm setting along Spring River placed the dwelling house and barns on an elevation overlooking a section of rich bottom-land. A road ran along the foot of the hill, a spring flowed from the base of the hill, and clear waters coursed freely across the land finding the easy path before emptying into Spring River. An orchard covered the whole face of the ridge. The land for miles around abounded in waist-high lush grasses. Carolina parakeets and carrier pigeons descended in large flocks on the open prairie. Livestock grazed peacefully. The river teemed with many species of fish, and the timberland along its banks harbored bounteous wild game. Such idyllic scenes made Carthage one of the envied towns of southwest Missouri.[1]

On July 4, 1861, as opposing armies proceeded on a collision course, the pastoral setting of Carthage gave no hint of what was about to happen. The innocence of nature had produced an almost perfect setting for a battle. Situated between the two armies was some of the finest farming land in the country. The land was mostly open prairie with only about one-quarter of the area in timber. There were few places, however, even on the broadest prairies that a belt of timber did not encumber the view to break up the monotony of endless prairie land. One would describe the surface of the land as undulating, a continuous pattern of rolling low ridges and shallow dells punctuated here and there with long stretches of woods, especially along the streams. In places along Spring River and other watercourses, hills rose to the stature of bluffs and the valleys deepened. The timber along the streams was of a heavier nature than that found out on the prairie. The wood-canopied streams of clear running water gave a different character to the rugged bottomlands.[2]

Wild game ran freely everywhere. Deer roamed in herds throughout the day. Turkeys flourished in the timber and were in such abundance around town that citizens shot them from their windows. Flocks of prairie chickens migrated into barnyards and perched on garden fences. Roaming wolves kept many a child up at night with their lonesome howls. The plentiful wildlife in field and stream grew to such abundance that the neighborhood

Group of Osage Indians, ca. 1868. Bands of Osage Indians up from Indian Nation to trade at Linn's store were a common sight on the streets of Carthage. The land around Carthage and across large parts of Missouri once belonged to the Indians before they ceded it to the U.S. government. Many of the Osage joined the Confederate army when the Civil War started. (National Anthropological Archives, Smithsonian Institution BAE GN 4159 C.)

deer took to invading the town to eat up whatever grain and hay might be lying around loose. One resident thought he heard them at work at his oats in his wagon one night. He stealthily crept out with his shotgun and blazed away at what proved to be his neighbor's cow. There was, of course, a lawsuit about that.[3]

Carthage had a population of about 350 at the beginning of the rebellion, perhaps 400 if the census included the surrounding community. The town enjoyed prominence as an agricultural and trade center situated on the prairie at a major crossroads in southwest Missouri. It came to be known as the queen city of the southwest, a town of great business activity and energy, and remarkable for its social qualities and fine hospitality. Nestled against the Ozark foothills, it burgeoned with investors and entrepreneurs eager to gain riches in the "New City" county seat of Jasper County.[4]

On any given day, the town bustled with commerce with an eclectic blend of customers. Buckskin-clad hunters and booted plainsmen jostled with farmers dressed in the familiar homespun butternut and women in dark-colored, full-length dresses with black or gray stockings. Lest that remark leave the impression that Carthage women were of the genteel Eastern class, they were not. The dress of women in rural Missouri stood apart from their counterparts in St. Louis, and certainly from the luxurious fashions of the antebellum South. Fancy carriages were rare. More often than not, the women rode saddleback, clad in a homespun dress and their head covered by a poke sunbonnet. Every woman in Missouri owned a horse and knew how to ride it — the common habit of using tobacco did not limit itself to men or adults.[5]

The occasional business leader in a Boston-tailored suit stood out in the crowd, striking an odd contrast to the handful of blanketed Indians who congregated in front of J. M. Linn's store. A few Osage still visited the area, coming up from the Osage village at Flat Rock Creek near Osage Mission, Kansas, and could be seen on the streets of Carthage in 1861 bringing their furs and skins to trade for tobacco and red calico.[6]

The town had a tranquil quality to it, with children gleefully playing and adults going quietly back and forth. The houses, built of native lumber and a few log structures, sat back from wide dirt streets, with front yards filled with roses and honeysuckles. In the back yards were the woodpiles and the occasional servants' quarters for those wealthy enough to own slaves. A spring or a well, dug deep enough to reach cool water, furnished multiple house-holds. Kids watched wide-eyed when a luscious watermelon sent down to mysterious depths emerged covered with a silvery frost. It is funny how the minor things in life stand out in one's memory like indelible silhouettes, while the greater events seem less important.

A wide piazza surrounded the courthouse, where the leisurely occupants of benches and split-bottomed chairs might elevate their legs on an empty keg or nearby railing. A fence enclosed the grounds of the public square, crossed via a stile. The hotel dinner bell summoned the guests at noon. Businesses ringed the square, each establishment sporting a long rack in front where the horses stood in patient rows, switching off the flies with their long tails.[7]

Carthage had just about anything a civilized population could want. It was a milling center from before the time of its founding in 1842, when one of the early settlers put up a mill on Spring River. It had several mills now, along with three good trade-goods stores, carpenter and blacksmith shops, a bakery and several specialty shops, a fine hotel, a relatively new brick courthouse, and a saloon or two.[8]

The courthouse, five years in the building, was the pride of the community. Patterned

after the one at Neosho, it sat at the center of town, situated on a generous lawn that formed the public square. The two-story structure dominated the skyline. Slave labor built it in 1858 from local stone blocks to replace the old log structure that had served since the town's founding. Large fireplaces anchored each corner of the structure. A fancy cupola topped off the roofline. Two sets of double doors on the east and west oddly opened directly into the courtroom,

Old Jasper County Courthouse, 1854–1863. Built by slave labor, the courthouse was completed in 1854. Slaves were sold at the courthouse door. It became a hospital for both federal and rebel forces at the Battle of Carthage. (Livingston, *History of Jasper County*, courtesy Springfield-Greene County Library.)

which occupied the north end of the building on the first floor. Upstairs was the jail. The main entry on the south opened on the county offices. Down the hall at the southwest corner were the law offices of Johnston and Kerr, both prominent attorneys from wealthy slaveholding families. Since at least May 8, 1861, a rebel flag had flown from the pole on the courthouse lawn. Circuit Court Presiding Judge John R. Chenault said he was a Conditional Union man — meaning anyone so favoring the nation could keep slaves — but everyone knew that deep down he was a secessionist. He kept slaves, too.[9]

No more than a dozen or so male inhabitants of the town openly favored the Union. Norris Hood did, of course, as did Joe and John Turner, blacksmith Obe Stinston, William Sisler, John Crow, the three Tucker brothers and their father, and the shoemaker Shonsone, to round out the Union support. A few more than these supported the central government but kept quiet about it. Young men of Union inclinations unobtrusively drifted away to Kansas or the east to volunteer for service under the United States flag no longer officially seen in Carthage.[10]

A leisurely stroll around the square told the first-time visitor what a fine city this was, with more than a small town's share of colorful characters. The Carthage Hotel sat on the north side facing the courthouse, fronting the street about in the middle. John Shirley had sold his farm back in 1856, built this story-and-a-half country inn, and moved his family to town. Shirley owned several slaves whom he kept in a lean-to on the west side of the building. East of the hotel, extending all the way to the corner, was a board fence enclosing the Shirley stable yards. The stables were about a hundred feet to the rear. Travelers regarded the Shirley Hotel as one of the better destinations in southwest Missouri. Shirley, then in his mid–60s, backed the Southern cause. He had the presence of a true Southern gentleman

curiously displaced in the rugged frontier of the West. His personal library of biographies, histories, philosophical writings, and novels suggested a background more akin to lawyers and intellectuals than a hotel keeper. The townspeople of Carthage respected and liked the Shirley family. Their 13-year-old daughter, Myra Belle, grew up to be a Confederate spy — the legendary outlaw queen Belle Starr. She grew up overly protected and spoiled by her father's success; nevertheless, it surprised many who knew her as a child when she turned to her lawless ways. A Carthage schoolmate remembered her as petite, bright, and intelligent, "but of a fierce nature and would fight anyone, boy or girl that she quarreled with. Except for this trait, she seemed like a nice little girl." One of the Shirley sons, John A. M. Shirley, who they called Bud, joined the Confederate side and died from a

Belle Starr (Myra Belle Shirley), ca. 1866. The daughter of a wealthy pro–South Carthage innkeeper, she experienced the Battle of Carthage firsthand. Classically educated at the Carthage Female Academy, she later gained notoriety as the famous Bandit Queen Belle Starr. (Edna Mae Couch Collection, Research Division of the Oklahoma Historical Society 20738.L.3.3.)

Union bullet in Sarcoxie when militia surrounded the house he was in and shot him as he tried to escape over a fence. Some thought Belle's outlaw ways stemmed from the killing of Bud. When she showed up to help retrieve his body, she wore two large pistols strapped around her waist.[11]

Next to the Shirley Hotel going west of the Carthage square stood W. Kelly Franklin's harness shop adjacent to his house. The Lucy Killgore home sat on the extreme northwest corner enclosed by a neat picket fence. The Killgore family made no secret of their support of the South, especially the daughters, Rachel and Judith, who spoke openly against the Union. Looking away from the square, up North Main Street and a bit to the east, visible through the trees was the old homestead of Henry Percy who built the first house in the area. He built it there near a spring in 1833 when hardly anyone lived in Jasper County, and when the farm animals of choice were iron-shod oxen.[12]

Strolling around to the west side of the square, J. M. Linn's store stood on the northwest corner, facing on Main Street. Linn opened his building, a plain two-story frame structure, to the Masons who held their meetings on the second floor. Linn bargained with local traders and Indians and dealt in trade goods that he hauled to the railhead at Tipton, bringing back goods for sale to the citizens of Carthage. Although his store faced on the public square, it gave off the feeling of a frontier outpost; immediately in the rear westward was nothing but brush and timber, laced with well-worn footpaths.[13]

Linn's store was almost as busy as the new wood frame building next door, which happened to be the local groggery. It had opened just the year before and was run by a young fellow named John Cannon. Cannon liked to style himself as a "hotel keeper" for appearances sake. The long tree-shaded house to the south of his establishment was Sheriff Norris Hood's place. Hood was one of the few outspoken Union men in Carthage.

Next to the Hood residence on Main Street was Bulgin's carpentry shop; and next to it was the printing office of the newly founded *Star of the West* newspaper — lately called the *Southwest News* — started by Christopher Columbus Dawson, who was known around town as Lum. Young Dawson established the first newspaper in Carthage when he was 23, in the back of his father's drugstore. He openly advertised for volunteers for the Confederacy and endorsed all the presidential candidates in the 1860 election, except Lincoln. He brashly posted the motto, "Independent in all things, neutral in nothing." Not everyone in Jasper County appreciated Dawson's politics. Afraid for his life if Carthage fell into Union hands, he turned the paper over to one of his printers, 18-year-old Charles B. Hayward, for salary that he owed Hayward and left town. Young Hayward and his printer brother William held a more moderate stance than Dawson did on the secession question. The Hayward brothers, who lived with their parents on the northwest corner of the square next to John Cannon, kept the newspaper going until a shortage of paper forced it to close. Some said the former owner, Dawson, took some of his printing paraphernalia, went to McDonald County, and later printed state script for Governor Jackson.[14]

On the southwest corner of the Carthage Square sat a log house masquerading as the "grocery" of Lee H. Chrisman, one of the better saloons in town and an impartial destination of partisans on both sides. Turning the corner to the south side of the square, there was Casey's bakery. The Mitchell and Stinson wagon shop stood next to Casey's place. Other than some new construction under way and Elijah Pennington's saloon, the rest of the south side was mostly vacant except for J. L. Craven's store on the southeast corner, where one might purchase anything from fancy corsets and laces to mule collars. Jesse Lamb Cravens was part of a large slave-owning clan. He was the brother-in-law of Brigadier General Rains, and was now traveling with Rains and the Missouri State Guard somewhere to the north. He was a graduate of West Point but not a model cadet; a court-martial found him guilty of disobedience of orders, neglect of duty, and conduct subversive of good order and military discipline. Nevertheless, he and two of the Cravens brothers later served as officers in the Confederate army.[15]

Judge John R. Chenault's store and blacksmith shop anchored the corner of Main and East streets. James and John B. Dale's general store stood across from Chenault's facing west. Along the east side of the square, several buildings housed various offices and businesses. Oliver and Johnston's store stood in about the middle on the east side. Ben E. Johnson had his house and law office on that side, and Dr. James B. Foster located his practice there. Dr. B. T. Love kept a wayside house on the east side and gave his place the provocative name of the Union House. John B. Tibbetts had a modest shoemaking business on the northeast corner. Tucked inconspicuously among the shops, a frame building housed the drug store of Dr. A. M. Dawson, which doubled as the post office and was home to the *Star of the West* during its early beginnings, before the paper moved its printing office across the square to the southwest corner.

Various other shopkeepers and attorneys found offices and places of business in the courthouse or in buildings set back from the main thoroughfares. Carthage boasted an unusual number of doctors; some of whom were at the very beginning of their careers. Dr. A. M. Patterson, a young frontier doctor who entered medicine at a very young age, was still in his mid–20s.

Several schools around Jasper County attested to the people's strong interest in education. From its earliest days, Carthage attracted its share of well-educated citizens. People used to say that John Brooks was the only Jasper County farmer who could and did read the New Testament in the original Greek.

The Carthage Female Academy came into existence in 1858. It sat on Seminary Street (later Chestnut Street) on a north slope in the southern part of town. In a new substantial two-story brick building, the academy had the distinction of being the school of several well-known Missourians, including the infamous Belle Starr who studied the classics and became a better than average pianist. Though called the Female Academy, both boys and girls attended. The young men held their debating society upstairs. A candle on a stick stuck in the soft mortar supplied the light.[16]

Carthage was a town of many stories. In the year of 1849, when California was the destination of gold seekers, William Tingle and David Campbell made a mineral find in Jasper County, not gold but highly valuable nonetheless. Working with pick and shovel in different locations, the two men independently found small chunks of mineral stone that turned out to be lead. The discovery of lead in southwest Missouri opened a new war industry in 1861, supplying this necessary commodity. The mining of it reached princely proportions after the war, making this part of Missouri one of the major lead-producing centers of the world. It existed in such large deposits throughout the region that one solid, unbroken mass taken out sometime after the Civil War weighed seven tons.[17]

10

Slavery in Jasper County

Carthage extended out a couple of blocks from the courthouse square in each direction. Scattered houses dotted the landscape outside these limits, mostly to the southwest and on the eastern slope. A small cemetery stood nestled in the brush on the outskirts of town to the southwest. Black oak timber and thick brush lay to the north and west. A person could stand on the cupola of the courthouse and count 61 occupied houses.[1]

A half-dozen slave cabins spotted here and there housed mostly domestic laborers; the large majority of slaves stayed outside the city on the farms where they worked. One Carthage family owned more than 25 slaves but kept them away from town. The oilpaper window-lights easily distinguished the slave cabins from the houses of the white folks. One log cabin, a little larger than the others, housed Judge Chenault's slaves. Slavery had a large foothold in Jasper County. The 1860 census counted 335 slaves. These were not plantation slaves, as in the South, but workers belonging to less arduous owners. Nevertheless, a good male farm hand fetched between $1,000 and $1,500. Women sold for considerably less. As was the custom throughout Missouri, slaves were sold publicly at the Jasper County courthouse in Carthage on the first day of January each year. They were sold at the south door. The slaves were made to climb atop a pile of corded wood so that prospective bidders could look them over.[2]

The people of Jasper County were occasional church-going folk, each to whatever denomination most closely aligned with a family's spiritual and social inclinations. They put off building a church so services were held intermittently in the courthouse. The Methodists sat divided in their congregation, the men on one side, women on the other. Then there were the Campbellites and hard-shell Baptists. Ministers of the different creeds preached enough variety from their pulpits to bewilder the minds of ordinary mortals and shape the behavior of repentant souls. Many black people shared membership in one or another of these denominations and attended services with the white people; they could regularly be found seated in the back on any given Sunday. Being a Christian slave had its merits. A slave named Henry professed conversion one time, and the congregation took him into the fold by immersion. When Henry's sister Emma heard of it, her congratulatory comment was, "One thing, Henry got a good washing." Slaves never were out after ten o'clock, nor at anytime during the night without a pass from a white owner. "Henry has permission to pass and repass until ten o'clock" was the usual form.[3]

The history of the young town of Carthage contains a tragic episode from slavery. From the beginning there were several slave owners in and around the town and a good number of slaves. In late July 1853, a few years before the slavery question boiled over and brought the Union army to Carthage's gates, the citizens took two slaves to the outskirts of the town and burned them alive. The two stood accused of the crimes of murder, rape, and arson. A trail of evidence convinced the excited community of their guilt. They allegedly conspired to kill the master of one of the slaves for his money and in the act assaulted his wife, killed her and a small child, and then set the house afire. The money, a blood-spattered axe, and other proof of the crime turned up in the possession of the hapless black men. After stringing one suspect up on a rope and threatening him with hanging on the spot, he confessed to the crime and gave enough details to satisfy the outraged citizens that they had the culpable parties. A committee of citizens examined the facts of the case and by popular indignation sentenced the two to death. However, differences of opinion soon arose as to the appropriate mode of execution. Some thought that hanging was too good for them. Everyone finally agreed that a vote of the people should decide the matter. The whole town met on the town square. Those in favor of hanging marched to one corner of the square; those in favor of burning marched to a different corner. The vote was two to one for burning. A large number of those present did not vote at all. Three days later, the largest crowd ever seen in Jasper County up to that time gathered to witness the spectacle of execution. It was a hot, sultry afternoon. Storm clouds loomed on the horizon off to the southwest. At three o'clock, guards marched the two condemned slaves to the execution site, a natural amphitheater formed by the hills on the south edge of town. Hundreds of spectators from all over the county and places as far away as 50 miles followed and took their places on the side hills. Local slave owners took special pains to have all the slaves in the county in attendance and saw to it that they had seats closest to the stake. The guards brought the two condemned men into the arena and chained them between two large posts. A band of helpers came forward and piled a cord or more of wood waist high around them, generously supplied with shavings. One man stood the ordeal bravely, singing songs. The other pleaded piteously for his life and screamed for them to let him go. Two black men came forward and lit the fire. As soon as the flames struck their bodies, they struggled briefly until the fire suffocated them and they sank down. In an hour, the flames burned down, but little remained of the dead slaves. That evening a heavy thunderstorm came up and washed away much of what was left of that awful day. Many of the citizens of Jasper County got thoroughly drenched before they reached their homes.[4]

By 1861 public sentiment over slavery and secession divided almost evenly around Carthage. Judging from various discussions, those sympathetic to the South appeared to hold a majority. For the most part, however, the question remained a topic of open and civil discourse right up until hostilities began. Even those who had an opinion for one side or the other sometimes rethought the issue and changed sides. Judge John B. Higdon, for example, warmly endorsed the Union at a public meeting of the County Court's spring term in 1861, and then afterwards took sides with the Confederates. It turned out to be the last time the court served as a political platform for either side. The Jasper County Court did not meet again after the spring term until the end of the war, from May 10, 1861, until October 10, 1865. In another case, voters elected the modest and genial Judge John R. Chenault to the state convention as a Conditional Union man, only to later hear he voted with the secessionists.[5]

Meetings occurred all over Jasper County. Union supporters met at LaForce's Grove.

Other meetings were at Hackney's schoolhouse, Fidelity, Preston, and other places around the county to organize opinion for or against the Union. An unexpectedly stormy meeting at Preston adjourned in confusion and rancor, perhaps signaling a level of animosity soon to erupt in outright violence.

Jasper County mirrored the sentiments all across Missouri. An intense excitement bordering on zealous frenzy impelled the citizenry toward war. Lifelong neighbors and friends practically overnight became adversaries. Any idea of compromise faded under the fervent determination of the one side to save the Union and the other to expel federal invaders from the sovereignty of state soil. Nothing short of actual combat could settle it. Far away in Washington, in Congress and before the public, voices of reason fell silent while impassioned oratory added fuel to the flames.

Kansas border violence, unabated for years, often spilled over into Jasper County and threatened Carthage. Only a few months earlier, someone gunned down James Walker as he stood one morning, just before daylight, on the front steps of his home three and a half miles northwest of Carthage on Spring River. The longtime Jasper County resident in his early 60s had lived in the county since 1832 and raised a large family. Local citizens blamed the killing on border raiders from Kansas but no one knew for sure. Even antislavery men in the county thought the murder of Walker was a shame.[6]

Lawlessness grew with the rise of separatist fever in Jasper County. Travel sometimes took on the tenor of a high-risk adventure, particularly when accompanying certain cargos of value. One day Robert J. Christie, visiting from up north, overtook a team of six oxen, hauling a load of whiskey to the lead mines at Granby. The driver had a kind of happy-go-lucky attitude, the type that politics washes over without much consequence. Christie asked him, "Aren't you afraid with everything that's going on around here that your whiskey will be captured and your oxen killed for beef?" To which the youthful teamster replied, "They ain't mine." He drove on toward the mines in a willing temptation of fate. Someone said later that his cargo ended up in McDonald County at a State Guard camp. In those days, whiskey mixed with a little New Orleans molasses was the drink of men of mettle.[7]

One of the most daring acts of violence in Jasper County was the robbery and murder of George W. Broom at his home northwest of Carthage, near Georgia City, not far from the Kansas line. This happened in August 1861, a few weeks after the Battle of Carthage, but it illustrates the depth of partisan hatred that had spread over Jasper County. Broom, who lived alone, was a bachelor from the state of Georgia who had amassed considerable wealth in his 36 years, owning several hundred acres of good land. Only a few years before, he had bought John Shirley's 800 acres when Shirley decided to move into Carthage and build a hotel. A band of men descended on the Broom place, killed Broom in broad daylight, pillaged his property, and burned the house. No one knew a cause for the raid and killing except robbery, but many suspected that slavery had something to do with it. Broom owned slaves and often advertised land for sale, offering to take slaves in trade. He was embroiled in a lawsuit at the time that had become something of a public embarrassment over a slave he had purchased a year earlier in January 1860. Stephen Hain had willed a 16-year-old slave girl named Charity — a fine-looking black woman of bright yellow hair — to his daughter to own forever. The administrators of Mr. Hain's estate sold Charity to Broom for $1,385, and the whole thing wound up in a lawsuit challenging the validity of the sale. The case remained unsettled well after Broom's death and was still in court in 1876, although the Thirteenth Amendment had abolished slavery in Missouri more than a decade before. Many such lawsuits went on for years after the war as one-time slave owners tried to recover whatever they could of the wealth they had lost because of the end of slavery. Some Jasper County slave owners blamed Broom's murder on antislavery sympathizers from Kansas who, they said, acted in complicity with some of Broom's neighbors who happened to support the Union. A group of secessionists rode out to John Ireland's farm on Spring River not far from the Broom place. They dragged Ireland from his house, gave him a vigilante trial for Broom's murder, and hanged him. The 29-year-old Irishman left a young wife and two small children. Lawmen arrested a couple of his killers, but by that time the war was coming on, the courts in Jasper County had pretty much dissolved, and nothing came of it, except as an incident that drove a wedge further into the widening chasm between the partisans of North and South. There was some question as to whether it was John Ireland the mob hanged or one of Abraham Ireland's other two sons. In the end, it mattered little because all three sons were dead by the end of the war.[8]

Even with Union troops advancing on the town from the south and an opposing army of Missourians descending on it from the north, Carthage could not know that the prosperous beginning the town enjoyed for the first two decades of its existence was about to end. Within a year of the war's beginning, military incursions into the city would destroy the entire town and disperse its population. The town changed hands a number of times in the first three years of the war. Parties from both sides completely ravaged it. A partial list of Jasper County residents who died during the war shows 88 murdered or killed in local skirmishes. Every man felt he carried his life in his hands. Events made it impossible to compile a complete list; practically none of the names of men who fell in battle outside Jasper County were preserved. The entire population deserted the town as scouting parities reduced it to ruins, leaving it little more than a ghost town. The courthouse burned in the fall of 1863. Until this day, no one knows for sure who torched it. The exodus of residents applied to all of Jasper County and much of southwest Missouri. The 1860 U.S. Census counted 6,883 people in Jasper County. By the close of the war in 1865, there were only 30 men found in the entire county. Only five dwellings escaped total destruction in Carthage. Owls nested in isolated chimneys standing gloomily over the desolate scene where houses once stood. Overgrown with weeds, the abandoned public square became the habitat for wolves and deer, except when bands of war marauders wandered into town and stopped to feed their horses, then mount and hurry on.[9]

Just as the fleeing citizens did not foresee ruin, they could not have known at the time that within a decade after the war ended, the city would rebuild and prosperity would redouble beyond its original affluence. Out of the ruins of the Civil War arose the opulence and opportunity of the Victorian era when Carthage boasted more millionaires per capita than any other city in the United States. Wealthy mine owners rode the streetcar to the lead and zinc mines west of town. Deposits of gray marble north of the city added additional wealth and a note of historical distinction by furnishing the stone to build the new state capitol building at Jefferson City. Limestone marble bluffs lined the north bank of Spring River. At the height of stone-quarry production, five quarries shipped out more than 40 rail cars per week. However, all of that was in the future, a future far from certain in the summer of 1861 when slavery became almost completely incidental in the conflict to decide Missouri's future in the Union.[10]

11

On the Brink of Battle

Brigadier General Mosby Parsons, encamped with the State Guard at Murray Corners and not knowing that Union troops were coming up the Carthage road ahead en masse, sent a detachment of 95 men under his quartermaster, Lieutenant Colonel Thomas Monroe, into Carthage to take possession of the mills there. By the afternoon of July 4, Colonel Monroe had collected enough provisions to fill several wagons when rumors began to spread that federal troops were approaching rapidly from the south. He quickly topped off a few wagons and sent them north at top speed. He and the foraging party remained behind and stationed themselves on a hill north of town to watch for the arrival of the national forces. Monroe sent a messenger to General Parsons to tell him that the federals were coming. Observing from across Spring River, he sent word back that Union troops were in strong force in that vicinity and only a substantial show of force could fulfill his mission at the mills.[1]

Garbled reports kept coming into Carthage about the approach of Sigel. Rumors had Union troops coming from several directions at once. Excited couriers rode around the county Paul Revere style exhorting citizens to get ready. On the morning of July 4, young George Gibson, who lived south of Carthage, rode up to the home of Alta Fullerton and hollered, "The Dutch are coming. All the secesh men in Carthage are leaving to join old Claib." Gibson's aim in going to the Fullerton home was to impress the Fullerton daughters as much as it was to spread the word about the Yankees. Gibson sped off toward Carthage, his buggy stirring up little clouds of dust in spots where the sun had begun to dry out the rain-soaked road. He shouted a parting assurance for the benefit of the Fullerton girls: "There ain't no Yankee nag in the county can catch this gray mare." Shortly after Gibson left, another rider came by saying the federals were indeed close behind.[2]

The Fullerton sisters and some neighbor girls climbed to the top of a hill overlooking the road to watch the quick-stepping Germans pass. They stared in amazement at the speed with which the infantry marched. Everyone said Sigel's foot soldiers moved as fast as cavalry. There was a reason that the newspapers called Sigel the Flying Dutchman. A handful of Union supporters walked alongside the federal troops as they approached Carthage. Vain attempts to strike up a conversation with the soldiers told them that the army was not in Jasper County on a diplomatic mission.[3]

Sigel's brigade covered the 22 miles from Neosho in 12 hours before halting southeast of Carthage. Several stops along the way had allowed Captain Cramer's company at Cedar Creek to catch up to the main body, but there was no sign yet of Captain Indest. The Union column reached Carthage about five o'clock on the afternoon of July 4, and went into camp behind Spring River. They bivouacked east of the city, near the big spring located there, and the troops settled in for the night. General Sterling Price and his regiment of Missouri volunteers had passed through here on their way to Pool's Prairie just ten days earlier.[4]

The appearance of Union troops in Carthage solidified partisan differences that had been festering for a long time. Several young men showed up at the federal camp and pledged to the Union cause. They came in from all parts of the county and elsewhere, eager to embrace the romance of war. As soon as George V. Knight, Nelson and Salina Knight's boy who lived east of Carthage, heard Sigel and his troops were at Carthage, he saddled a horse and hurried to join them. The 21-year-old farmer's son left his family to do his part to help put down the rebellion. His Kentucky-born father would later wear the Union uniform, too. Jasper B. Waggoner rode in from Barton County to indulge similar patriotic zeal. Since he had a horse, Sigel signed him up as a scout. Charles B. Hayward, the youthful publisher of the Carthage *Southwest News*, showed up at the federal camp, much to the surprise of many, perhaps hedging his bets in favor of the Union cause, or perhaps just to get a story.[5]

The flow of new recruits was not limited to the Union camp. Jasper County had its own version of home guards operating along the Kansas border. The "Border Guards" at Medoc, in the northwestern part of the county, and the "Border Rangers" patrolled the Missouri-Kansas line helping to quell the violence that spilled over from the Kansas unrest. Both unionists and secessionists rode together in these companies until the Civil War started. Then the companies dissolved and the men joined either Confederate or Union units. While Union partisans drifted into Sigel's camp, pro–South volunteers sped north to join Governor Jackson. One of them, 17-year-old George Buchanan Walker, impatiently sought out the rebel column, partly out of sympathy for the secessionists but mostly for the opportunity to avenge the murder of his father. Walker hurried north. The Missouri Guard would make the Union sympathizers pay.[6]

Local Union supporters in Carthage soon rode out to inform Sigel that a band of rebel foragers had been there that day and had left town when the federal troops showed up and that they might still be somewhere near the mills. Sigel learned, too, that General Price had come through town with a body of State Guard men several days earlier and that Governor Jackson's State Guard troops were on the Lamar road headed south in the direction of Carthage. Jackson had an army reportedly at least 4,000 strong. Hannibal W. Shanks said there might be as many as 20,000 State Guard troops to the north. Mr. Shanks was a local cattle buyer and longtime resident who knew the countryside well. He came from Iowa but was Kentucky-born, and some said leaned toward the South. John M. Richardson, former secretary of state during the Sterling Price era who was traveling with Sigel primarily to confirm the loyalty of visitors, advised him that Shanks might not be the most reliable informant.[7]

That evening about 6:00 P.M., Samuel Benton LaForce, a large landowner in Jasper County, and devoted unionist, met with Sigel and volunteered to serve as his guide across the prairie the next day. The 45-year-old LaForce and his family lived on a farm about three miles northeast of Carthage. Both his parents had been Southerners, but he was a solid Union man. He, too, cautioned against listening to locals with overblown claims of rebel strength. Having been a resident of Jasper County for the past 18 years, a one-time county sheriff, circuit and county clerk, and state representative, he knew the people and terrain as well as anyone in the county and far better than anyone in Sigel's army. Upon Richardson's recommendation, Sigel accepted his offer as a guide. LaForce's advice would prove to be invaluable on the battlefield.[8]

As the opposing forces gathered in Missouri on Independence Day, President Abraham Lincoln made his legal and constitutional case for the preservation of the Union before a special session of Congress in the nation's capitol. He called for congressional approval of at least 400,000 men and $400 million dollars to put down the rebellion, a clear warning of his resolve to hold the Union together. The United States never formally declared war on the Confederacy, therefore no official beginning date of the war exists. Congress acquiesced to President Lincoln's call for support in putting down the rebellion but stopped short of adopting the legal status of war. Nevertheless, Lincoln's speech was, in effect, the use of his constitutional war powers and a declaration of war under the classic definition of war; that is, a conflict embraced by force of arms between nations or, in this case, parties within a nation.[9]

Several dates may qualify as the beginning of the Civil War. The bombardment of Fort Sumter on April 12, 1861, is one date. Lincoln's proclamation of April 15, 1861, in which he called for 75,000 troops to put down the insurrection, is another. The U.S. Supreme Court set the beginning of the war as April 19, 1861, the date the president proclaimed a blockade of Southern ports. The Confederate States passed an act recognizing the existence of war on May 6, 1861. Notwithstanding all these dates, President Lincoln's proclamation before Congress on July 4, 1861, was a clear statement of war on behalf of the United States, and is popularly accepted as the official start of the war. His speech was, in effect, a declaration of war against the rebelling states; the next battle in time would be the first battle of the official Civil War.[10]

Back in Missouri, half a continent away from Washington, a small army of tired Union soldiers camped beside the Sarcoxie road outside Carthage, poised to act on Lincoln's determination. Celebration of Independence Day seemed of little consequence to these men. A few touched off some gunpowder, but most soaked their feet in the cool spring water of James Spring and got ready for tomorrow. Pickets took up posts around the perimeter of the camp, and soldiers went about Carthage in small groups interrogating local citizens to learn as much as possible about the State Guard forces. Almost everywhere they went in the town, they found the streets deserted and windows shuttered out of fear of the federal Dutch. A squad of men went by the courthouse and pulled down the rebel flag that flew on the southeast corner of the lawn and ran up the Stars and Stripes in its place.

One family that welcomed the Union troops was Norris C. Hood and his large brood. Some of the soldiers walked into town along Mill Street and came on the courthouse square. Fronting the square, on the west side of Main Street, stood the Hood home, a long building made partly of logs and surrounded by several shade trees. There in the twilight, the soldiers saw a handmade American flag mounted on a stick and attached to the white gatepost in front of the residence. They walked over to a warm reception from Hood's two teenage daughters, Martha and Lucy. Both girls were students at the Carthage Female Academy and relished the opportunity to strike up a conversation with the young Union boys. They proudly told how they had stitched together the flag from kitchen curtains and intended to fly it even if the neighbors objected. The soldiers learned that the girls' father was the former sheriff of Jasper County, having finished his term just at the beginning of the year. Sheriff

Hood was a South Carolinian by birth and had come to Jasper County, Missouri, by way of Tennessee where several of his children had been born, including Martha and Lucy. It was unusual for a man of such background to be a Union man. He bought a good farm about three miles west of Sarcoxie on Center Creek and settled down. He became a wealthy landowner and had only recently cashed in part of his fortune to build the house at Carthage. As the war came on, events would drive Hood and his family, and many other Union families like his, out of Jasper County. He lost a son in the war, shot at Stockton while serving as a Union scout, a dear sacrifice to the national cause. His neighbor, John Shirley, lost a son in service dedicated to the Southern Confederacy. The two boys grew up as friends, just as the Hood daughters and Myra Shirley and the Killgore girls had shared happy moments together at the Female Academy. The war severed those relationships with hurtful and tragic consequences to all families. Instead of the larger conflict between Northern and Southern states, Missouri pitted neighbor against neighbor. Former friends suddenly became bitter enemies. In every Missouri town, men on both sides quietly went away, singly and in small squads to find a place in the army of their choice. They did not openly duel with each other. The fighting element on both sides seemed by common consent to choose to attach themselves first to organizations of war before doing any fighting. A penitent old veteran many years later, reflecting back on the war, ruefully summed up the sentiments of many when he said, in regard to the Union and rebel forces engaged in the late rebellion, "God only knows which was right." The phrase, "God only knows which was right," appeared many times in the aftermath of the Civil War. On that day, however, it came from a father standing soberly before two graves, his head bowed in remembrance of his sons. Each died in combat fighting for a different side.[11]

While Myra Shirley and the Killgore girls made themselves scarce, the Hood sisters, who had earlier in the day hidden from Lieutenant Colonel Monroe and his rebel foragers, enthusiastically greeted the Union soldiers on the public square. In a moment of testosterone-induced bravado, the Union boys removed the homemade American flag from the gatepost and conspicuously attached it to a stile on top of the fence on the west side of the courthouse. Here they proceeded to serenade it in the best of their guttural tones until their oeuvre of "John Brown's Body," "The Star Spangled Banner," and other patriotic tunes was exhausted. The neighbors were not entertained but the Hood sisters loved it.[12]

The United States as a country turned 85 years old on July 4, 1861. Twenty-four states remained in the Union of the nation's 35. Eleven had already relinquished statehood and a 12th threatened in Missouri. On this day, General Lyon's army was making its way south from Boonville, Major Sturgis and his men awaited them in Henry County, and events in southwest Missouri progressed toward a deadly climax. On this July 4, the nation's birthday marked the start of the apocalypse of ruin that would turn the clock back on Carthage to its prairie beginnings and to erase whatever progress Missouri, as a whole, had made up to this point.

12

First Contact

The Fourth of July found the different players in the unfolding drama busy with their particular parts. Captain Sweeny, a.k.a. acting brigadier general Sweeny, at his headquarters in Springfield soon demonstrated that his political talent did not equal his military skill. A grizzled Mexican War veteran, Tom Sweeny stood five feet nine inches tall with black hair and a full row of whiskers. His penetrating dark eyes and slim, ramrod-straight military bearing made people take notice of him. Without his right arm — a casualty of the Mexican War — he handled his sword with his left hand. A button stayed loose to accommodate an empty sleeve always pinned in the opening of his coat.

None of his military swagger substituted for diplomacy, however. Normally very quiet in his demeanor, Sweeny now felt it necessary to announce his presence in Springfield. He issued a lengthy Independence Day proclamation to the citizens of southwest Missouri in which he harangued Governor Jackson for his treasonous conduct. Politicians and generals, both North and South, held great fondness for proclamations for whatever reason. All of them at one time or another saw fit to issue one or more public pronouncements on the condition of affairs as they saw them. The edicts probably did no great harm but certainly did no good either. Adversaries paid no attention to them except to violate them, and sympathetic followers did not need them. Opposing sides went about nailing each other's proclamations to trees and blacksmith-shop doors as a way of inciting recruitment to their side.[1]

Sweeny's proclamation revealed an interesting Union position on the slavery question calculated to appeal to his Missouri audience. He pledged to put down any slave rebellion should one arise in southwest Missouri and earnestly promised to protect all loyal citizens in the enjoyment of their property, slaves included.

Sweeny called for an oath of allegiance to the U.S. government, as did all proclamations issued by fellow Union officers, as if such an oath to the Union prevented any pro–Confederacy advocate from following a commitment to secession. Sweeny ended his proclamation with the usual ineffectual plaudits of loyalty to the government and the wisdom of the Constitution, which, he said, his soldiers intended to protect.

Sweeny took up the task of organizing the local Home Guards. Other problems almost immediately surfaced. Frustration soon set in when he discovered that the demands for arms and supplies greatly surpassed availability, making it impossible to effectively arm and equip the considerable numbers of loyal Union sympathizers who came forward to enlist in the service of the federal government. Moreover, the military stores at Springfield were inadequate to sustain a long campaign in southwest Missouri. The nearest railhead was more than a hundred miles away at Rolla. Although there was Union sympathy in the region, useful military support seemed unlikely.

This all led to Sweeny making another fateful decision. He withdrew plans to send additional federal troops to support Sigel in pursuit of Governor Jackson because he feared an attack on Springfield. Confederate General McCulloch had a few days earlier issued his own proclamation to the people of Arkansas, effectively calling them to arms to protect the state against the Union threat. Several hundred men gathered in response at Fayetteville, Arkansas. McCulloch ordered Colonel Dandridge McRae, a zealous proponent of the Southern cause, to take this force and make a demonstration on Springfield. The effect of the threatened demonstration was to force Sweeny to call back the Union troops set to march to the aid of Sigel and instead to hold them to defend Springfield.[2]

The Confederate armies of generals McCulloch and Pearce crossed from Arkansas into Missouri on July 4. The Arkansas troops included Thomas J. Churchill's First Arkansas Mounted Rifles — a regiment of 3,000 — and General Pearce's 1,200-strong First Arkansas militia brigade consisting of John Rene Gratiot's Arkansas infantry, David W. Carroll's Arkansas cavalry, and William E. Woodruff's artillery battery, not to mention McCulloch's regular Confederates from the Third Louisiana Regiment. James McIntosh, McCulloch's chief of staff, led the Second Arkansas Cavalry Regiment. They reached General Price's camp at Cowskin Prairie later that same day, picked up Price and a contingent of 800 Missourians, and continued the march northward to rescue Governor Jackson and his men. General Price at the time had about 1,700 men. However, McCulloch soon learned that only 800 were armed. The combined rescue army had more than 6,000 men. McCulloch's informants in Missouri kept him briefed on Governor Jackson's journey south. He knew that the governor had made a junction with General Rains and was nearing Carthage. He knew, too, that federal units were closing in on the governor from two directions. He did not know, however, that his spies inflated the danger by overestimating the federal force in the immediate vicinity of Jackson at more than 6,000, and floated the rumor that Sturgis and Lyon were closing fast, when neither were anywhere near Jackson's location.[3]

McCulloch thought he saw a potential disaster in the making. If the Union forces concentrated against Jackson's disorganized and undisciplined men, they would cut them to pieces, and Missouri would certainly fall under the control of the North. Thinking Governor Jackson trapped between Sigel on one side and Lyon and Sturgis on the other, and fearing there was no time to waste, McCulloch left his infantry and the bulk of his slow-moving command behind south of Neosho at a camp 20 miles inside Missouri territory. Taking 3,000 cavalrymen, he and General Price hurried north to the Governor's relief. Riding in column two abreast, the drumming of horses' hooves made a noise that shook the earth and mysteriously shattered the silence of the open prairie. The Confederates were coming.[4]

That night McCulloch and his army, along with Price and his State Guard, camped on Buffalo Creek in the northwest corner of McDonald County, near the place where H. A. Barlin kept a small steam mill, 12 miles southwest of Neosho. Secessionists who had taken flight from Neosho welcomed McCulloch and offered to guide his forces into Newton County. Early on the morning of July 5, McCulloch learned that Sigel had already moved north against Governor Jackson, and had left a detachment of federals to garrison Neosho, this being the company of Captain Joseph Conrad. McCulloch moved to neutralize the

Union guard that Sigel had left there. About 11:00 A.M., he started two columns by different roads to capture Conrad and his troops some four-hour's march to the north. Colonel Churchill took six companies of his regiment by one route up the Gates road, while the always-able Captain McIntosh — McCulloch wished he had more like him — newly appointed to McCulloch's staff, led another five companies from another direction by way of the Pineville road. Eleven Confederate companies to one Union company would be ample to do the deed.[5]

Meanwhile, Independence Day proved serendipitous for Governor Jackson and his rebel Missourians camped far to the north. On its eve, the Lexington arm of the Missouri State Guard had rendezvoused with the retreating troops of Governor Jackson at Roup's Point, on the same day that General McCulloch marched his Confederate troops into Missouri. While Brigadier General Sweeny waxed eloquent about Union hopes before the citizens of Springfield, Governor Jackson's Missouri State Guard, some 6,000 strong, was less than 35 miles to the front of Franz Sigel's federals.

Colonel Sigel and Colonel Salomon readied their Union men with orders to attack Governor Jackson's band, not knowing that the rebel force now outnumbered their own by nearly 5,000 men. Governor Jackson and the Missourians knew Sigel was somewhere in the area. News of his sudden appearance in southwest Missouri, however, surprised the Missourians. Where did he come from? They expected to meet the forces of Price and McCulloch, not Lincoln's army. Lieutenant Governor Thomas Caute Reynolds, traveling with Jackson, guessed they had come from St. Louis through Rolla to Springfield. "General Lyon," he suggested, "may not be far behind."[6]

As Sigel's Union troops bedded down outside Carthage on the night of July 4, suddenly they heard shots coming from the vicinity of Spring River north of the federal camp. The Union pickets had stumbled upon some of the State Guard commissary troops of Lieutenant Colonel Monroe and opened fire on them. Each side hurriedly threw more troops into the skirmish. It soon promised to become a full-fledged little engagement, with neither side willing to back off. Monroe called for reinforcements and sent word to Brigadier General Parsons to come in a hurry. It became clear after a few minutes, however, that the Union troops greatly outnumbered his rebel detachment. Monroe withdrew his men and faded away into the dusk. This brief but intense flare-up left one Union soldier killed and a guardsman slightly wounded, the first real marks of the high-stakes game now at hand.[7]

At about this time, Parsons, marching in advance of the rebel column, had halted his Sixth Division at Murray Corners, at a place he dubbed Camp Slack, to rest his men and refresh them after the day's march. He had no sooner stopped than Lieutenant Colonel Monroe's message reached him saying that Monroe had encountered the federals on Spring River.

Stories of the dust-up at the Carthage mills found their way into the history books but in varying descriptions of what actually happened. The time of the incident remains vague. If a brief skirmish took place at the mills north of Carthage, its timing leaves open the question as to when the rebel forces at Murray Corners first learned of Sigel's presence at Carthage. General Parsons said he first received intelligence of Union troops at Carthage about six o'clock on the evening of July 4. Snead, traveling with General Clark's division, remembered hearing the first intelligence of Sigel's federals shortly after the sun had gone down. General Parsons obtained his information from Lieutenant Colonel Monroe's courier sent from the vicinity of the mills at Carthage. Monroe must have based his alert on advance intelligence because Sigel's Union brigade did not arrive at Carthage until around 5 P.M.

The courier could not have traveled the 18 miles from Carthage to the rebel camp from the time the federals first came on the scene at five o'clock until General Parsons received Monroe's message at 6 P.M. Parsons' quick reaction to Monroe's demand for relief could not have been in reaction to the skirmish at the mills because the courier did not know about the skirmish, unless it occurred earlier in the afternoon. Such are the minor conundrums of military history. Therefore, the exact time of the first contact between State Guard and Union forces remains unsettled. It is possible that the incident on July 4 was confused with a later encounter on the morning of July 5 when Jo Shelby's pickets met Sigel's advance guard. That encounter resulted in similar casualties to those reported at the mills. However, because the preponderance of authority supports the mills incident, it is the generally accepted account of the first contact between State Guard and federal troops.[8]

When General Parsons received word of the Union presence, he immediately prepared to go to the relief of Monroe's detachment at the Carthage mills and meet the federal soldiers based on what he had learned. By ten o'clock that night, he was ready to move on Carthage. His men were under arms, animals hitched up, and supply wagons loaded with the necessary camp equipment to support a forward campaign. He sent word to Governor Jackson that his division was ready to march. Jackson soon sent back orders that Parsons was to stay put and remain in camp for the night.[9]

Meanwhile, the Union men at Carthage slept uneasily that night. Local reports said Governor Jackson and the State Guard had passed southward through Lamar. What they did not know was that less than 20 miles to the north, above Coon Creek, lay the camps of the Missouri army.

It was a sleepless night for the rebel Missourians, too. No sooner had they turned in when some of the horses broke loose and stampeded through the camp. The men woke up to the hullabaloo and piled out of bed in the dead of night to corral the edgy animals. They passed the night without much sleep. These Missourians, like the federals, had not yet been tested in battle, and they were anxious about their new adventure. Neither side had any idea what war really meant.[10]

The presence of federal troops at Carthage soon alerted all the rebel divisions. The rest of the State Guard followed General Parsons' lead and was ready for battle by midnight. Around 1 A.M. on July 5, Brigadier General Rains received an order from Governor Jackson to be ready in three hours to take up the front of the State Guard line of march with his Eighth Division southward toward Carthage. Why Jackson changed his mind after halting General Parsons and then ordering an engagement is unknown. Perhaps he harbored misgivings about Parsons after the general's tardy showing at Boonville. Maybe for tactical reasons he wished to avoid nighttime maneuvers, or maybe he simply preferred Rains to Parsons.

Jackson and Parsons did not like each other. Their personal animosities dated to the election the year before. Parsons, a zealous, outspoken advocate of slavery and states' rights, publicly expressed his outrage when Jackson abandoned his support of Breckenridge for the presidency and came out for Douglas. "Our party and its principles demands that we should discard him [Jackson] without hesitation," wrote Parsons. He campaigned hard against Jackson in the 1860 election in a losing effort. Jackson handily won the election but bad feelings between the two lingered.[11]

The change of battle order placing the division of General Rains in the lead is telling because on the previous day Parsons' division had led the march from Camp Lamar by order of Governor Jackson. On that day, the State Guard divisions had marched out of Camp Lamar in order of their ranking generals, Parsons and Clark in the lead with Rains and

Slack following. This order was reversed, however, when the Missourians formed in line of march the morning of July 5 with General Rains at the front of the column and Parsons at the rear.

The first hints of a dysfunctional command structure began to surface not long after the two State Guard columns came together at Lamar. General Rains had command of the largest body of men from Lexington by virtue of his appointment by General Sterling Price when Price departed for southwest Missouri. However, General Parsons, traveling with Governor Jackson's column at the time, was the senior brigadier general on the field. General Parsons' stature as the ranking division commander surfaced a few days after the Battle of Carthage when General Price made a point to acknowledge Parsons as the ranking brigadier general. Writing at Cowskin Prairie to announce an upcoming absence from command, Price assigned interim command to Brigadier General Parsons, "the senior brigade-general in service of the State of Missouri." The order of march from Camp Lamar on July 4 suggested Governor Jackson's recognition of General Parsons' rank, but he then acquiesced to General Rains' superiority as head of the larger Lexington column. Jackson solved the command controversy by exercising his role as commander in chief and taking command of the army himself.[12]

The governor's decision to place General Rains at the head of the rebel column may or may not have been a sign of his dislike for General Parsons. Other practical considerations likely guided his assignment of the impetuous Parsons. General Rains made his home at Sarcoxie and was well acquainted with the geography of the area. He knew many of the people in and around Carthage and seemed better suited than Parsons to lead the column into battle. In any event, after directing General Rains and the forward divisions of the State Guard to prepare to move out, Jackson sent orders for General Parsons' division to take up the rear of the rebel column. The strategy was apparently to organize the divisions of Rains and Parsons at either end of the column with the divisions of generals Slack and Clark in the middle. When deployed in line of battle, Rains and Parsons would anchor the rebel flanks with their large cavalry units.

As soon as the Missourians in rank heard the news, they knew there was going to be a fight.

13

The Advance

At 4:00 A.M., orders came down from Governor Jackson to march immediately. The Missourians moved at daybreak, July 5. With Captain J. O. Shelby's Rangers in the advance guard, the men of Brigadier General Rains' division led the main Missouri column out of camp, many of them before they had time to fix breakfast. Some of the men complained about going into battle on an empty stomach. Governor Jackson thought hunger would make them fight harder. Companies of men formed quickly and struggled into line to take up the march.[1]

The Army of Missouri advanced in columns. Brigadier General William Yarnell Slack's Fourth Division followed Rains. Brigadier General John B. Clark, Sr., commander of the Third Division, was behind Slack. The Callaway Guards, after only a day's rest following their long and trying march to join Governor Jackson's force, sprang into place at the head of General Clark's division. Being the best-drilled and only uniformed company on the field, they made a conspicuous display leading the division into battle. Brigadier General Mosby Monroe Parsons' Sixth Division was next in line, ordered to take up the rear of the column, a position intended to place him on the extreme left of the line of battle when it became necessary to deploy. Governor Jackson and his staff brought up the rear. General David Rice Atchison, former United States senator, and most of the state officers rode with Jackson. By 6:00 A.M., the last rebel elements joined the line of march.[2]

All knew Sigel was on the move, and the Missourians would meet him. With new life in their step, the rebel army marched out in quick and regular order. The untried and undisciplined Missourians, poorly armed if armed at all, were cheerful and in good spirits on the eve of their first battle, despite the perilous circumstances of their position. Very early on the morning of July 5, with a large federal force in their rear and another blocking them in front, the Missourians broke camp and marched out to meet Sigel. A muffled rumble jarred residents awake as a thousand horses of the Army of Missouri passed in the early morning light. These were men and boys not used to military service. What passed for cavalry, with their rope bridles and rope stirrups, struck one of the State Guard officers as looking like "Don Quixote and Sancho Panza, on Rozinante and Dapple." The raw State Guard soldiers did not care to march on foot. Many of them rode horses and mules, so many that General Ben McCulloch later said half factiously that the State Guard had enough horses to outfit

an army of 50,000, a pecuniary observation because a good horse fetched
more than $150 in Confederate cur-
rency. One veteran later remarked, "All,
to the poorest, had horses." The number of mounts, however, was greatly
disproportionate to equipment and
training for mounted soldiers. They
were cavalry in name only.[3]

The rebel column passed to the
west of the trading village of Coon
Creek, forded the creek, and marched
into Jasper County. The Missourians
angled southwest and headed in the
direction of Carthage. The road soon
opened onto the rolling prairie, passing
over the highest elevation of Jasper
County. A panoramic view of seemingly endless grasslands spread before
them in the early dawn.[4]

A few miles to the front, the federals broke camp at Carthage about five
in the morning. The sun was just showing above the horizon. It looked like a
beautiful day in the making. The
national troops moved up the State
road, which bypassed the town on the
east, and then turned west along the
town's north edge. Most of the town's
residents remained cloistered behind
locked doors, fearful that the Dutch
would see them. Only a small crowd
came out to watch the troops go. The
Hood girls stood beside the road
prominently waving their homemade
Union flag.

Joseph O. Shelby, ca. 1864. Captain Shelby's Rangers
made first contact with Sigel's advance guard a few
miles north of Carthage. His cavalry company checked
the forward progress of the Union troops. (WICR
31493 in the collection of Wilson's Creek National
Battlefield. Image courtesy National Park Service.)

The federals angled west down a steep grade past a house on the hill. An ice-cold
spring flowed from the foot of the hill below the house, emptying into a large inviting pool
of clear water. A stone springhouse sat on the west side of the pool, and cool shade trees
bordered the whole scene like a view in an Arcadian landscape. The Germans thought it
an ideal summer gathering place for young couples on a Sunday afternoon or a nice place
to dine on the precooked meal that each soldier carried in his rucksack. About a mile further
on, the column came to Spring River, normally a placid stream but up from recent rains.
Trying to hold muskets, ammunition, and rations above their heads to keep them dry, the
soldiers descended the steep embankment, waded across the swollen ford, and marched out
onto the prairie.[5]

About a half mile past the Spring River crossing, the road inclined sharply up a small hill that fanned out for a distance on both sides north of the river. Looking back, Sigel had a commanding view of the river as he watched the wagons cross over and begin the slow climb up the grade. To the north lay the open prairie. Samuel LaForce, the Jasper County farmer riding with Sigel at the head of the column, pointed out the lay of the land as they peered out across the open space. LaForce would remain on the field the entire day.[6]

The Union column followed the Lamar road. A mile out of Carthage, past the Spring River crossing — then known as the Walton Ford — the newly surveyed State road from Carthage to Fremont (Stockton) angled off to the northeast toward the LaForce farm. The federals stayed on the main road and continued northwest. After another mile or so, they came to a crossroads. The road to Fort Scott, Kansas, went to the northwest; the Lamar road led due north.[7]

Rebel scouts swarmed over the great plateau north of Carthage and watched Sigel's movements from close range. Sigel recalled, "They were almost within our sight." Union scouts likewise rode ahead looking for the main rebel force.[8]

Continuing some distance north, the Union troops encountered the first rebel squads of mounted riflemen. When some five miles northwest of Carthage, Sigel's advance pickets, operating ahead of the main army, met a particularly defiant detail of Captain Jo Shelby's riflemen, and a brief firefight broke out near Vincent Gray's house. Old man Gray's farm was located in Marion Township on Buck Branch where he lived as a widower with his adult children. The family was in the middle of morning chores when lead started flying, and everyone ducked for cover.

The encounter at Vincent Gray's is another of those perplexing little incidents of history that keeps the record unsettled. It is unclear what time the first contact occurred between Union and State Guard forces on the morning of July 5. About as many chroniclers of the battle mention the encounter at Vincent Gray's house as do not mention it. The timeline of subsequent events suggests possible confusion with a different encounter. The news circulated quickly among the rebel column that Shelby's State Guard pickets had tangled with the Lincoln pickets. They said a Guard trooper suffered a wound in the hand and one of the Lincoln pickets died in the skirmish. (The Missouri boys liked to call the Union soldiers the Lincoln army in derision of President Abraham Lincoln.) A different story of the encounter circulated in Sigel's camp. The Union pickets had attacked Shelby, driven him off, and taken three prisoners. Back in Carthage, the rumor circulated that each side had lost one man killed.[9]

Though in doubt as to the exact time and place, Shelby's advance guard of Missourians was the first to meet the approaching troops of Colonel Sigel, and had the honor of receiving the first fire from the outlying federals. Better trained and disciplined than the rest of the State Guard cavalry, Shelby's men were constantly in the saddle, tirelessly reconnoitering the Union movements. Shelby's Rangers, 43 in number, had shadowed Sigel's advance since he left Carthage, observing his march and pestering the Union outposts. Young George Walker guided Shelby's men through the unfamiliar terrain. The teenage Jasper County native stood out among the grizzled, bearded rangers, his youthful whiskers not yet cultivated. Shelby's men pressed the federal column. Each time, the federal skirmishers drove them away back toward the main rebel force.[10]

The Union troops pushed forward. "With these troops I advanced slowly towards the enemy," Sigel wrote later, "our skirmishers driving before them numerous squads of mounted riflemen, who were observing our march."[11]

The baggage train followed the federal column at a distance. Its three dozen wagons strung out across the prairie for more than a quarter of a mile. Sigel crossed Buck Branch and moved out onto the high prairie. When he was about halfway between Buck Branch and Dry Fork Creek, he could plainly see the rebel army massing its forces to the north. The land was flat and open. Peering through his glass, Sigel saw them forming at a substantial distance.[12]

The federal army advanced northward, and the Army of Missouri marched southward toward them. From the State Guard position, the Union army first appeared three miles away directly in the path of the rebel column. General Rains passed the word to his commanders that the federal troops were in their path and blocking the road ahead. He ordered the regiments in his division to ascertain the number of companies properly armed and supplied with ammunition. Not a single regiment was at full strength. In Colonel R. L. Y. Peyton's Third Regiment Cavalry, for example, only Companies A and B, and part of Company H out of nine companies had the necessary ammunition. The remaining six and a half companies were armed but had no ammunition and no prospects of obtaining any. Nevertheless, General Rains ordered Colonel Peyton, as senior colonel, to take command of the cavalry and advance in the direction of the federals. In addition to his own two and a half companies of troops, Peyton's amalgamated command included the mounted battalions of Colonel James McCown and Lieutenant Colonel Richard A. Boughan, along with the companies of captains Thomas E. Owens and J. S. Stone of Henry County, altogether some 600 mounted men. The balance of Peyton's cavalry, unable to fight because of lack of ammu-

nition, stayed back under command of Lieutenant Colonel James D. White and did not immediately join the others in the line of battle. The infantry regiments and artillery batteries followed Peyton's cavalry in regular battle order.[13]

It was a bright morning as the rebel army made its way across the high prairie plain. They had covered about five miles when word came around 7 A.M. that Union troops were in force to the front about seven miles north of Carthage. General Rains rode ahead to reconnoiter their movements and get a firsthand look at the ground. He raised his glass and watched the Union column advancing on a stretch of open prairie headed north toward Dry Fork Creek, a tree-lined stream that formed a dividing line between the two armies. On the declivity of a hill, he could see a long line of soldiers with glistening bayonets and bright guns. At the outer edges of the prairie, timber on both sides framed the Union column as it neared the objective of its nine-mile march.[14]

James Spencer Rains. Brigadier General Rains commanded the Missouri State Guard Eighth Division at the Battle of Carthage. He lived at Sarcoxie, Missouri, only a few miles from Carthage. This rare photograph is the only known picture of him. (Courtesy Richard K. Rains, Jr.)

Governor Jackson saw the Union troops approaching in the distance. Unable to sit comfortably on a horse, he drove up to General Rains in his carriage and pointed in the direction of the federals. "Don't be excited, Governor; don't be excited, sir," Rains said in a patronizing way. "I'll disperse them in a few minutes."[15]

Rains knew that a battle was imminent and sent orders to Shelby, now leading the advance of the rebel column, to halt and detain the whole State Guard command back out of sight. It was General Rains' plan to lure the Union troops into an indefensible position. If he could induce Sigel to cross Dry Fork Creek, the federals would be obliged to defend the low bottomland while he, Rains, and the Missourians deployed in force on the heights above it. By keeping the main Missouri force out of sight, he hoped to entice Sigel to cross the creek. The rebel column halted. Shelby placed a guard at its front to stop anyone from prematurely advancing while the order of battle formed. The quartermasters corralled the supply wagons at a proper distance back of the main column. The State Guard baggage train bore little resemblance to a military supply train. There was little or nothing in the way of camp and garrison equipment. Tents were unheard of. Large numbers of state government officers and civilians traveled with the Jackson column as part of the rush to escape central Missouri. To offset the lack of guns and materials of war, the supply train had, in Lucien Carr's words, "a surplus of baggage, some of which, as, for example, the feather beds and frying pans, were scarcely suited to a column in light marching order." General Parsons' small division alone trailed more than 40 wagons dressed out in harness made at the state penitentiary. The spectacle of the rebel train caused one observer to remark, "The old State Guard was not a very gorgeous looking array — but if not an array with banners it certainly was one with wagons, and if by any means the teamsters could have been put in the ranks we would have had three full regiments of them."[16]

The cavalry, or part of it, moved to the front of the column and advanced first. Commands rippled through the ranks to prepare for battle.

Men in the Clay County company marching toward the rear of the column were skeptical. James A. Broadhurst with Brigadier General Slack's division mumbled, "Just another of Rains' scares." He had hardly uttered the words when they met one of Shelby's Rangers sporting a bloody bandage wrapped around his hand. "Get ready, boys," he said. "This is the real thing."

After marching another mile and a half to two miles, the State Guard troops came to the top of a low prairie hill. The Missourians had marched about seven miles when they came over the brow of the hill north of Dry Fork Creek. The rebels halted and shortly the artillery came up.[17]

14

State Guard Order of Battle

Colonel John Taylor Hughes put the number of federal troops at 2,500, and the rebels, he thought, at about the same number, although poorly armed compared to the Union boys. Few on either side knew that the Missouri Guard was nearly 6,000 strong. Brigadier General Rains tallied the men under arms in his division at 1,812, including 1,204 infantry and artillery, and a sizeable mounted contingent of 608 cavalry. The divisions of brigadier generals Slack, Clark, and a part of Parsons' division added another 1,700 men to the center of the rebel column. Brigadier General Parsons' 500 mounted brought up the rear. Another 2,000 unarmed Missourians broke off from the order of battle and remained back with Governor Jackson.[1]

These were hardly the figures of a well-organized army. No one knows how many Missouri State Guard troops actually took up arms at the Battle of Carthage. Several students of the battle tried to fix the number. Livingston gave the number of men in the First Brigade as 1,204, plus artillery, and in the Second Brigade, 1,812, adding up to 3,016. Another 2,000 unarmed men rounded out Livingston's tally. He apparently confused the two brigades, however, causing him to omit about 1,000 Guard troops. Schrantz, meanwhile, arrived at a total number of 4,027, plus 2,000 unarmed, a total figure substantially larger than Livingston's estimate. Schrantz prepared a careful breakdown of his total by individual units and reiterated his findings a decade later with only slight modification. VanGilder endorsed Schrantz's figures. The settled estimate is approximately 4,000 infantry, cavalry, and artillery, with another loosely counted 2,000 without arms.[2]

The Missourians could only guess at the strength of the advancing federals. Captain Shelby, now riding well in advance of the rebel line, generously overestimated Sigel's approaching force at 3,000 of all arms. General Rains judged the Union army to be about 2,000 strong, a thousand less than Shelby's guess but still well above the number of federals actually on the ground. Shelby wondered how the federals had managed to evade General Price on the Neosho road. They must have gained the front by marching on a line parallel to General Price, he thought. He did not know that Price had already moved his force to the south and was with General McCulloch somewhere around Neosho and in no position to assist against Sigel, although he and General McCulloch were trying hard at that moment to reach them in time.[3]

The Missouri Guard prepared to draw up its line of battle, having spotted Sigel's army advancing toward them. The first units of the young State Guard swung into position around 8 A.M.; the column filed to the left of the road and began to form in line, blocking the path of the federals. The two forces were about a mile apart when the State Guard began to form its battle line. Divisions went into place in the order of their line of march: Brigadier General Rains' division in the lead, Shelby's Rangers forming the advance guard. In the absence of Sterling Price, and with Governor Jackson well to the rear, Rains was effectively the field commander of all State Guard forces on the field. He ordered his lead cavalry to move west and deploy on the far right of the rebel line. Colonel Peyton, at the front of the Rains cavalry regiment, guided what was left of his mounted command into place. Most of his men stayed back for lack of ammunition. Those who could fight, the 115 or so with weapons, left the road and moved 400 or 500 yards down a sloping plain to wait for further instructions. At that point, Colonel James M. McCown's First Battalion of 250 independent cavalry filed to the right of Peyton and took a position some 300 yards ahead of him on the extreme right wing of the rebel line. As they waited, Colonel Peyton received an order from Rains to send his regiment of two and a half companies to join Shelby in some unstipulated special service, perhaps to aid in checking the advance of the federals. Mildly irritated at the order, Peyton sent only one company under Captain William H. Doak. General Rains did not yet have a strong reputation as a military leader. His officers saw him as a politician. Nevertheless, on this day all went into battle under Rains, whose reputation as an ineffective commander Peyton thought he already knew.[4]

Chaos of command plagued the actions of the rebel divisions from the start and became the hallmark of the Battle of Carthage for the Missouri State Guard. Hints of open dissatisfaction with the command structure, in that no division commanders addressed a report to General Rains, the supposed field commander, however, are generally unfounded. Attempts by military scholars to discredit General Rains in this respect are overemphasized and do not relate the entire story. To understand some of the confusion allegedly reflected in the after-action reports, it is necessary to look ahead to July 11 and General Prices' reorganization of the State Guard following the Battle of Carthage. Price designated five divisions, commanded respectively: First Division, Brigadier General Parsons; Second, Brigadier General Rains; Third, Brigadier General Clark; Fourth, Brigadier General Slack; and Fifth, Brigadier General A. E. Steen; the Steen division being made up of State Guard troops previously assembled by Price at Cowskin Prairie. Of the four divisions engaged at the Battle of Carthage, only Clark and Slack retained their original command titles under Price's new organization. The battlefield reports of the Battle of Carthage, most of them written after the Cowskin reorganization, reflect in part the status of the different commands after reorganization. For example, General Parsons addressed his Carthage report to Governor Jackson and signed it Sixth Division M.S.G., First Division Army Corps. In his mind, it was a necessary distinction because by that time he had been designated commander of the First Division by General Price. In similar fashion, General Rains addressed his report to the adjutant general according to protocol for an overall field commander, and one who perhaps could not bring himself to address either General Price or Governor Jackson. Rains signed his report from the Second Division instead of the Eighth to reflect his new status assigned by General Price; Colonel Peyton did the same. Other subordinates, however, remained somewhat confused, addressing their reports to General Rains of the Eighth Division instead of the Second. Meanwhile, General Clark sent his report to Governor Jackson, commander in chief; and Slack addressed his to General Price, commander in chief. It is easy to see how historians would conclude that the division commanders of the State Guard did not have a clear idea of who was in charge of the Army of Missouri entering the Battle of Carthage.[5]

The State Guard line of battle continued to form. Coming on line next to the cavalry of colonels McCown and Peyton was Lieutenant Colonel Richard A. Boughan's Vernon County Battalion of the Seventh Missouri Cavalry. Already 200 strong, attached to his battalion was another 100 men from St. Joseph under the command of Lieutenant Colonel Charles P. Hyde. All together, more than 650 cavalry anchored the right wing of the Missouri line, a mounted force more than half the size of Sigel's entire federal army. They extended westward down the open ridge almost to the timber.[6]

As the State cavalry maneuvered to form the right wing of the rebel line, the First Infantry Brigade of the Eighth Division came on line, Colonel Richard Hanson Weightman commanding. Weightman was himself a cavalryman and one-time artilleryman, but in his new capacity as a brigade commander, he organized his brigade of foot soldiers with the skill and efficiency of a veteran infantryman. His troops were the first to move into order of battle while the cavalry units on his right trotted off to take their places on the right flank.[7]

None of the State Guard commanders lacked colorful personal histories. Weightman was a strong secessionist with Southern roots, and a refugee of the Kansas-Missouri border wars. His Missouri First Regiment Cavalry, organized only recently in April 1861, was at Rock Creek on June 13, when some of the regiment's own men accidentally shot and killed regimental commander Colonel Edmund Holloway, the first blood seen by many of the young rebel recruits. Weightman had quickly assumed Holloway's duties as full regimental commander before then moving up in rank to become brigade commander

Weightman issued orders instinctively as he readied his brigade for battle. His command of the First Brigade was new, having assumed it only two weeks ago. Drawing on his experience as an artillery captain in the Mexican conflict, the first company of his brigade to come on line was the artillery battery of Captain Hiram Miller Bledsoe.

Like Weightman, Bledsoe had participated in the Kansas troubles, seeking to make the territory a slave state. He was a veteran of the Mexican War, too. When not at war, he engaged in farming in Lafayette County, Missouri, and plied his avocation as a minister. Although there was some question as to the exact date of Bledsoe's birth, most took him to be about 35 at the time of the Battle of Carthage.[8]

Bledsoe's three-gun, 46-man battery of a 12-pounder and two six-pounder cannons unlimbered in the middle of Colonel Weightman's line with an infantry regiment on either side of it. The Independent Infantry Regiment of Colonel John R. Graves with 271 men was on Bledsoe's right; Lieutenant Colonel Walter S. O'Kane drew up his Warsaw Battalion of 350 on the left. Everyone knew O'Kane as the Benton County warrior who at the head of his Warsaw Grays led the daring raid at Cole Camp to clear Governor Jackson's retreat from Boonville.[9]

Almost half of Colonel Weightman's brigade was missing. Colonel Edgar V. Hurst's Third Regiment of 521 men was about three miles back, having stopped with Colonel Weightman's permission to make breakfast before the alarm came that the federal army was on the move. Weightman quickly sent for Hurst to come up at speed and take a position on the right of Colonel Graves. Without Hurst, a force of 1,400 infantry and cavalry eased into place to finish forming the rebel right wing.[10]

The rebels continued to assemble in large numbers across the ridge, all the time watching Sigel move his small army forward across the prairie toward them. With Brigadier General Rains' cavalry and Colonel Weightman's brigade of infantry in place, the other State Guard divisions began to form the left wing of the line in succession as they came on ground. The line of battle reached eastward as the end of the rebel column moved up, faced left, and marched forward off the road into the line. Brigadier General William Y. Slack brought his Fourth Division into position at the center of the rebel line next to Weightman's brigade, joining on the right with the infantry of Colonel O'Kane. Slack's division comprised about 1,200 men, including Colonel John T. Hughes' regiment of infantry along with the infantry battalion of Lieutenant Colonel John C. C. Thornton. About 700 foot soldiers altogether served under Hughes and Thornton.[11]

William Yarnell Slack, ca. 1860. Brigadier General Slack commanded the Fourth Division at the Battle of Carthage and later led the division at the Battle of Pea Ridge, Arkansas, where he fell mortally wounded. This image, taken from an original glass negative, is the lone surviving photograph of him. (Library of Congress LC-B812-3026.)

The Missourians formed their line of battle as best they could. Orderly Sergeant Salem H. Ford of Hughes' regiment soon discovered there was not an officer in his outfit that knew how to form a line of battle. The 25-year-old Ford had closed his store in Plattsburg and said goodbye to his wife, Sallie, and infant daughter, Cora Bell, to follow the Clinton County State Guard into battle. His family was on his mind for some reason as he took his place on the rebel line. Sergeant Ford awkwardly spread his men across the line in double-rank close order and took up a position with the officers at the front.[12]

Colonel Benjamin A. Rives' regiment of 500 cavalry next eased into a place of support behind the infantry. Rives commanded the First Cavalry Regiment of General Slack's Fourth Division. A good many in his regiment were Carroll County boys looking for their first fight. Some of them thought it had been too long in coming. Shortly after Fort Sumter, citizens of Sugar Tree Bottoms got together at Moss Creek Church and enrolled a home-guard unit, the first company raised in Carroll County and one of the first in the state in opposition to federal authority. Colonel Rives' men nervously waited as the federals grew closer. Looking on was Private Henry Martyn Cheavens. Cheavens, from Boone County, ended up assigned to Rives' cavalry because he owned a horse. Like most of his Missouri compatriots, the Boone County teacher had no military experience.[13]

The Missouri army had a clear view of the approaching federal troops. Looking across the open prairie, the rebels could easily see them passing over the next ridge. General Slack saw them from his position at the center of the rebel line and overestimated their size at 2,300 men. His fellow commanders had done the same. Slack's error was less telling, however, because he was not a military man. William Yarnel Slack was a citizen soldier. He owned neither riches nor military pedigree. His Quaker heritage taught him to reject offensive war but justified armed defense as a Christian act. Slack represented the American dream, rising from poor and humble beginnings to become an accomplished public official and a brigadier general in the Missouri State Guard, and eventually the Confederacy. He came to Missouri as a toddler when his parents carried him from Kentucky to northeast Boone County, Missouri. He never forgot his Southern roots. He entered the law profession in Chillicothe, Missouri; married; and began to raise a family. When still in his twenties, he entered politics, won election to the Missouri General Assembly, and served at the Missouri Constitutional Convention of 1845. Slack knew Sterling Price from their common service in the war with Mexico. Despite his Quaker sentiment, he had emerged as a strong supporter of the invasion of Mexico. He returned home from the Mexican War and resumed his law practice, perhaps grateful to have his military years behind him. He aligned himself with the Southern wing of the Democratic Party. The attack on Camp Jackson, in St. Louis, turned him and many others who had first opposed secession against the federal presence in the state. Now in his 45th year, the patriotic conflicts of duty plagued him. He once publicly said of the Mexican conflict, "Our country has declared war and I am for my country, gentlemen, first, last, and for all time." These words haunted him in 1861 as he took up arms against the Union. He painfully decided in the end that his loyalty must go to his Southern homeland. Governor Jackson appointed Slack brigadier general, and he raised a command from the Fifth District of Missouri but now led the Fourth Division of the State Guard. Slack's new commission as Fourth Division commander took effect on the eve of the battle he was presently organizing his men to fight. Despite his reputation as a strict disciplinarian, Slack's men held a special affection for him. Perhaps these ragged Missourians, with no uniforms and hardly anything with which to wage war except hope and determination, identified with his humble background. All who knew General Slack knew him as a man of much more than ordinary ability, cool and clearheaded, and a model of soldierly bearing.[14]

The organization of the Missouri State Guard roughly followed the pattern of the federal model. Local organizers recruited companies and placed them in regiments. A regiment usually comprised ten companies, each company with a designated number of privates, augmented by units of cavalry and artillery. The regiments formed into brigades; brigades formed into divisions; and the divisions constituted an army. However, divisions in the State Guard were not divisions in the military sense. Divisions in the case of the Missouri State Guard meant political subdivisions and not military troop strength. Missouri was divided into eight military districts. Governor Jackson appointed a brigadier general to each district responsible for raising a "division" of armed troops. Legislation, passed before General Lyon ran the state government out of Jefferson City, provided for nine military districts but the state effectively had only eight. The St. Louis district never formally organized because Union troops were in total control of it. In the other eight districts, units seldom reached full strength in practice. A company usually contained fewer than the prescribed number of men, regiments seldom made full strength, and brigades rarely mustered the requisite number of regiments. Depending on recruitment success in their respective districts, State Guard units were much less likely to be at full strength than the Union regiments. Large discrepancies in size characterized the respective state divisions. For instance, the Eighth Division, made up mostly of men from the western border counties, enlisted well over 2,000 volunteers, while the Third Division, located north of the Missouri River in the north-central region of the state, fielded only about 400 men. State Guard companies elected their respective officers, as did Union volunteers. Regimental commanders usually were the organizers of the regiments. Governor Jackson appointed the field commanders of the Guard. Jackson served as commander in chief by the authority of the state legislature. He had taken personal command of the rebel army two days earlier, but as fighting loomed ahead, he stayed well back of the front line and left each division commander on his own, roughly accountable to General Rains, the presumed ranking field general.

Governor Jackson wrote two specific orders on July 4, one stipulating the order of march and the other the time of march. He apparently issued no order turning command over to General Rains. The assumption of field command by Rains on July 5 — if he did assume command — probably came from his assignment by General Price as commander of the Lexington column and Jackson's concurrence by making him the lead division in the State Guard column. The absence of a functioning command structure further caused the State Guard performance at the Battle of Carthage to be fragmented, uncoordinated, and generally ineffective. Jackson's earlier decision to take overall command of the State Guard was one way to smooth over ripples of dissension among the commanders. It may also help to explain General Parsons' aggressive role on the battlefield.[15]

15

Itching for a Fight

The Third and Sixth Missouri divisions came up next, beginning with Clark's Third. Brigadier General Clark, upon learning that the federals were in force ahead, dismounted his men who were mounted and led them forward on foot. Those who had arms to join in the battle followed him. Everyone who had a gun formed into line of battle. The remainder stayed back with Governor Jackson. Clark's small Third Division comprised 365 men. Riding at the head of his division, he was personally guiding his troops to close with Colonel Weightman's Brigade on his right when he observed the Sixth Division rapidly overtaking his position. It was at this point that the rebels made a last minute change of order in the battle line. As Brigadier General Clark's Third Division neared the line of battle formed by Rains, Weightman, and Slack, Clark suddenly saw Brigadier General Parsons advancing rapidly from the rear with his artillery and infantry trying to align next to the commands of Slack and Weightman. As Clark maneuvered the Third Division forward along the ridge, the Sixth Division passed him.

The divisions of Parsons and Weightman were the only ones with artillery batteries. Parsons saw that his artillery would be of no use unless he could position it on the high ground in the proximity of Weightman. Parsons' division had lagged slightly behind the rest of the State Guard column because Governor Jackson had sent him to the back of the line. When he received word that the federals were forming in line of battle on the plain below, in front of the Missouri army, he enthusiastically brought his men forward in rapid motion. Within a few minutes, he arrived to find the advanced units of Rains, Weightman, and Slack already in place. The terrain masked the Union troops from Parsons' view as he came up, and he did not yet know their numbers or position. He swung his division around General Clark's and quick-timed to the front. Clark politely marched his men to the side to let Parsons pass, and Parsons' Sixth took a place near the center of the rebel line.[1]

Mosby Monroe Parsons was a daring military man, fearlessly impetuous, and a fast appointment as one of Governor Jackson's brigadier generals. A Southerner by birth, he moved from Virginia to Cole County, Missouri, as a teenager, eventually making his home in Jefferson City. A lawyer by vocation, he volunteered for the Mexican War where he gained a reputation for gallantry. Returning to Missouri after the war, he married but tragically lost his wife of three years in 1853, leaving him with an infant son. He entered politics and served as United States district attorney for western Missouri. Voters sent him to the state legislature in 1856. Nominated for lieutenant governor in 1860, he still held his seat as a state senator when Governor Jackson called for his military service in 1861, despite their serious political differences. His political opponents liked to characterize him as someone who carried water on both shoulders, the vernacular way of saying he told people what they wanted to hear. A strong States' Rights Democrat, he strongly opposed Claiborne Jackson for governor, but his sympathy lay with the Confederates. When the secession crisis erupted in Missouri, Parsons readily answered the governor's call to lead the Missouri Sixth Division.[2]

Parsons quickly brought up his artillery battery of three brass six-pounders and swung into position on the battle line. It was then for the first time that he saw Sigel's army forming for attack several hundred yards to the front. From where he was, it looked like they were between 2,500 and 3,000 in number. The rebels still did not yet know that the federals had fewer than half that number on the field. General Parsons advanced his artillery to the front of the rebel line ahead of the guns of Bledsoe's Battery, closing the ground between his troops and those of the gathering federals. Captain Henry Guibor maneuvered his three-gun light-artillery battery into position, two guns toward the center of the rebel line, a third well down the line on the left. Guibor's Battery entered the battle with barely ten days of training. The first trial of the guns had been only two days earlier at Camp Lamar, when Guibor fired a salute to the rendezvous of the two State Guard columns. Each man in the battery knew how to do only one job. Only Guibor himself had gunnery experience from his Mexican War days. On his right, a short distance away, was Bledsoe's battery; on his left stood Colonel Joseph M. Kelly and his legendary One-Hundred. Kelly's Irish regiment was the best fighting unit in the whole State Guard that day. His men carried the Springfield Minié-type rifled musket, more accurate and easier to use than the old .69-caliber smoothbores.[3]

Mosby Monroe Parsons, ca. 1860. State senator from Cole County, Missouri, Brigadier General Parsons set aside political animosities with Missouri Governor Claiborne Jackson to command the Missouri State Guard Sixth Division at Carthage. (WICR 32048 in the collection of Wilson's Creek National Battlefield. Image courtesy National Park Service.)

General Clark's Third Division, having given way to Parsons ostensibly to give a better line of fire to Guibor's Battery, came rapidly on line at this point next to Parsons' Sixth. Seeing Parsons' movement, he gave ground and veered his column to the left, thus placing his command east of Parsons on the battle line. General Clark's three regiments — little more than companies in size — were under the commands of Colonel John Q. "Jack" Burbridge; Lieutenant Colonel Edwin Price, son of General Sterling Price; and Major John B. Clark, Jr., son of the division commander. Clark's men now anchored the left flank of the Missouri Guard line. John Bullock Clark, Sr., at 59 years of age was the oldest of the State Guard generals, seven years senior to Sterling Price. He was another one-time bitter enemy of Governor Jackson; at one point Jackson challenged him to a duel, which fortunately never materialized. Old animosities disappeared as circumstances now found them together on common political ground. Clark had the look of a citizen soldier, finely dressed in a black broadcloth frock coat and black slouch hat that covered an enormous head. A most picturesque character, his imposing stature of six feet two inches helped him stand out in a crowd, a crowd that seemed always to gather wherever he went. A good storyteller, he apparently convinced his biographer that as a boy he lived a year with the Indians as a hostage to guar-

John Bullock Clark, Sr., 1859. At the time of the Battle of Carthage, Brigadier General Clark served as U.S. Representative from Missouri. He commanded the State Guard Third Division at the center of the rebel line. His participation in the Battle of Carthage ended his distinguished political career in the United States Congress. (Library of Congress LC-DIG-ppmsca-26806.)

antee a treaty between them and white settlers. Unshackled by the constraints of a formal education, he taught himself law and was something of a folk legend for his courtroom demeanor, known to shed tears as a defense lawyer to appeal to the emotions of the jury. Another time, he hired a man to ride all over the county and get petitions signed asking the judge to free his client. The evidence against the man was strong, and few people signed. Then he asked all who refused to sign one of the petitions to sign a remonstrance against the man. By the time the court met, every man in the county except one had already declared the defendant innocent or guilty by his signature on one petition or another. The court could not find a jury to try the case. Clark entered politics in 1850 and was a sitting member of the United States House of Representatives when he took the field against the federal government. In better times, his name had circulated as a possible presidential candidate. Congress expelled him on July 13, 1861, for taking up arms against the Union, citing actions principally at the Battle of Carthage, for which he now readied his troops. Clark's wily legal and political reputation came with considerable experience as a military man, having served as an officer of the Missouri Mounted Volunteers during the Black Hawk War; he had been a major general, too, in the old state militia.[4]

When General Clark's Third Division came on line next to General Parsons' brigade, Parsons immediately sent his cavalry under Colonel Benjamin Johnson Brown to take a

Map accompanying report of the Battle at Dry Fork Creek, Mo. on the 5th of July 1861.

Map No 524 for Plate 33. Map 6

position to the far left of General Clark on the extreme left wing of the rebel line. Ben Brown was a state officer, serving as president of the Missouri State Senate until roughly tumbled out of office by General Lyon's blitz up the Missouri River.[5]

The Missouri battle line was now complete: artillery in the center, cavalry on both ends, and infantry companies strategically aligned throughout. This is the settled opinion as to the general order of battle; a more exact alignment is debatable. Just as it is nearly impossible to know the real number of men in the line, it is equally challenging to know precisely what the order of battle was and who was based where by looking at the after-action reports of the State Guard commanders. Weightman said Parsons' guns were on his immediate left. Parsons confirmed that, stating that he advanced his artillery battery to the front and to the left of Colonel Weightman's battery. Parsons also noted that General Clark's division came into line on his left. General Slack, on the other hand, claimed to have been in the center of the line with General Clark on his left, and does not mention Parsons. Clark said the division immediately on his right was Parsons' and not General Slack's.

The unceremonious jockeying of the State Guard in forming its battle line led to arguments about which division actually ended up where. Despite the confusion, most observers placed General Slack's division and not Parsons' to the immediate left of Colonel Weightman. Others, however, claimed that General Parsons' division and not Slack's fought next to Weightman, citing battlefield commanders' reports. A careful parsing of the reports, however, may resolve the debate. The reports specifically mentioned the actions of the artillery. Parsons brought his artillery battery on line near Weightman's battery because of the advantage of the terrain, apparently separate from the movement of his infantry. General Rains noted that Parsons "unlimbered on the left of my division"; Parsons wrote that he came on line, "advancing my batteries to the front and to the left of Colonel Weightman's"; and Weightman said that Parsons "had unlimbered in gallant style immediately on the left off my brigade." General Clark acknowledged that Parsons sought a position next to Weightman, but reported that his, Clark's, division fought next to General Parsons' regiments and not General Slack's, who Clark pointed out was elsewhere on the battlefield with Colonel Weightman's troops and out of his sight. Meanwhile, Thomas Snead, who was with General Clark's division during the entire fight, listed the order of battle as Weightman, Slack, Parsons, and Clark, with the cavalry of Rains and Parsons on either flank. However, Snead's account came 25 years after the battle, and his credibility on the matter suffered from the fact that he apparently misstated the alignment of forces at the Battle of Wilson's Creek, which came soon after the engagement at Carthage. Nevertheless, subsequent action at the Battle of Carthage as the battle developed tends to support Snead's version of the battle line. There is also speculation that Parsons did not know at the time that most of Colonel Weightman's brigade had not yet come up. The 500 men of Hurst's regiment were still some distance back when the other divisions came on line. Parsons may have thought he was next to Weightman's large body of men when it was Slack's division of infantry instead.[6]

A clearer picture of the State Guard battle line may come ironically from the Union side. Franz Sigel looking across the prairie from his Union position said, "Two regiments, forming the wings, consisted of cavalry, the center of infantry, cavalry, and two pieces of

Opposite: Map of the Battle of Carthage, or Dry Fork Creek, Missouri, 1861. Brigadier General Thomas W. Sweeny included this map with his report on the Battle of Carthage. This previously unpublished original copy is the oldest known map of the Carthage area. An edited version appeared in the *Official Records* of the war 30 years after the battle. (Courtesy National Archives Cartographic Division.)

artillery. The other pieces were posted on the right, and one on the left wing. The whole force within our sight may have numbered 3,500 men, besides a strong reserve in the rear." The pell-mell deployment of Parsons' artillery also explains why Sigel's adjutant, Lieutenant Max Tosk, saw only five rebel guns instead of six. Parsons pulled one gun out of the battery and sent it to the left flank where Tosk did not see it. Colonel Sigel's keen eye, however, did, and he immediately spotted the placement of the rebel artillery. Sigel went on to describe the fragmented deployment of the rebel force. He said the first line formed in three regiments — actually, divisions in State Guard parlance — which suggests that the diminished sizes of the divisions caused him to count three regiments instead of four as the rebel troops came on line. Sigel's description implies not only that General Parsons divided his artillery battery and posted guns at different places along the rebel line, it indicates that Colonel Rives did not initially join the left wing with his cavalry, as some thought, but remained back of General Slack's Fourth Division until after the battle started.[7]

The rebel line extended east from a point due north of Thomas Nelson's house, beyond the place where J. C. Pitts later built his house, and west over the hill out of sight — a line a mile in length. The Nelson house was located ten miles due north of Carthage. The Pitts property fronted that of Moses J. Gresham. Gresham's house stood about in the middle of the forming rebel line; Brigadier General Slack's infantry centered on the Gresham place. Here again, though, is the opportunity for a second opinion. Discrepancies in the descriptions of the initial location of the State Guard line add to the foggy recollection of the beginning of the battle, alongside the unknown number of men on the line and the order in which they aligned. Where exactly did the State Guard form its line, on the Moses J. Gresham farm or along a line joining the Nelson and Pitts properties? The Nelson property was immediately south of the Moses Gresham place and slightly east, situated in Township 29N Range 31 Section 4. According to one description, the rebel line started at about the west edge of the northeast quarter of Section 4, near the north edge of the Township 29N line. The modern townships of Marion and Preston now meet at this line. The line of battle extended west into Section 5, all in what was then the North Fork Township of Jasper County, North Fork being one of the three original townships of the county. This location of the northern boundary of the battlefield is generally the same as that illustrated by Thomas Sweeny's map of the battlefield. These descriptions of the battle suggest that the State Guard formed on the Gresham property and then moved forward to make its initial stand south of the property lines between Gresham and his neighbors.[8]

Moses Gresham had predicted there would be a battle and expected it to be somewhere along the Lamar-Carthage road since both sides marched along it from opposite directions. He had no way of knowing it would start on his farm. When he heard the first shots of Shelby's skirmish with the federal pickets, which took place across a little knoll south of his house, he loaded his wife, Millie, and their two-year-old on a wagon with a few personal belongings and left. He drove southwest a short distance to the next farm over and picked up his older half-brother George; George's wife, Elizabeth; and their two toddlers. Heading away from the fight, they took shelter with relatives who lived on the west side of the county, well out of the line of fire. The entire clan eventually left the county to take refuge at Fort Scott, Kansas.[9]

The Lamar-Carthage road veered west of the Gresham house for a half mile then curved back east. The road was little more than a trail cutting across the prairie and jutting through the Gresham farm. A low ridge ran perpendicular to the road, continuing out some distance on either side of it. The rebel line first formed along the crest of this ridge in the fields of the Gresham farm. The land on both the west and east sides of the road belonged to the Gresham families. Fields of waist-high corn spread across the prairie protected by wood fences blocking parts of the rebel line. Another small farmhouse stood a little to the east unprotected in the line of fire.[10]

Governor Jackson rode in his carriage going back and forth at a safe distance behind the line. Four thousand Missourians lined up for battle. Another 2,000 had no weapons. These unarmed volunteers took a position to the rear, well behind the battle line to create the appearance of a reserve corps. Governor Jackson established his command post with them. In the bottom of the plain below, the Lincoln army posted on the main road and began forming its own order of battle. Salem Ford watched from the rebel side. He said later, "I thought that I had never seen so many men in one body, they being well drilled and armed. I could not help admiring their beautiful movements in their formation of line of battle. Our side it was quite the reverse."[11]

The Missourians flew three different flags over their ranks. Two secession flags flanked the state flag of Missouri displayed prominently in the middle of the line. General Sterling Price had laid out the design of the state flag in June 1861, ordering each regiment to carry a four-by-five-foot blue marine banner with the Missouri coat of arms in gold gilt on each side and mounted grandly on a nine-foot pike; but hardly any of the regiments had such a flag. A few of the mounted companies carried smaller white guidons with the letters M.S.G. in gilt on either side. For the most part, however, battle flags were in short supply. The organization fell short, too, of Price's order that each company should have a drum and fife and each mounted company carry two buglers. The difference between Price's grand vision of the Missouri State Guard and its reality was palpable.[12]

The federal troops carried the national flag.

16

Sigel's Nationals

Since early morning, Colonel Franz Sigel had marched his Union men north from his camp southeast of Carthage into the path of Governor Jackson and the Missouri State Guard. Jo Shelby's harassing State Guard pickets confirmed what Sigel already knew; the main body of Missourians was nearby.

Sigel pushed on to Dry Fork Creek and eased down the gentle prairie slope to its banks. He approached the bend in the creek and crossed over the ford. There was no bridge. People crossed streams at natural low-water crossings or hauled rocks and dumped them into the creek to build a ford. The men waded into the creek and struggled against the current of the thigh-deep water to the other side. They marched up the slope on the north bank and began their approach to the rebel position. Three miles beyond the creek, the rebels were forming their order of battle across the road.

Sigel sent his advance guard ahead of the main force. He left posted behind the creek one company of the Third Regiment and one piece of artillery to intercept movements of cavalry that might try to cut off his main force from its supply train. He had parked the supply wagons on the backside of the creek about three miles in the rear under the protection of a company of pioneers. The supply train was critical to the success of Sigel's army in the field; it maintained the lifeline of the Union troops. The critical job of the pioneers was to keep the army moving. When not engaged in assigned duties, they were fighting like the rest of the troops or, in this case, standing guard over the federal wagons. As the officer in charge, Captain John Foerster had the responsibility for all equipages of the wagons of the Union train. Loss of the train meant the loss of Sigel's army.[1]

Sigel's forward guard soon made contact with the Missourians and was exchanging shots. Shelby's Missouri Rangers continued to harass the Union advancing front. As soon as the federal advance guard had crossed the creek, and gone about three-quarters of a mile, Shelby's company came forward as a line of skirmishers to check them. Sigel hastened two companies of the Union Third Regiment and two pieces of artillery forward to assist the advance guard. About 8:30, a few spherical-case shots from the federal guns sent Shelby in an orderly withdrawal back to the safety of the rebel line. Shelby's men demonstrated parade-like precision before the lines of both armies and retired to a position behind the line of battle. The federal gunmen said later that the artillery shots fired at Shelby were blanks.[2]

Upon reaching the elevation beyond Dry Fork Creek, a little southeast of where C. W. King later built his house, Sigel could see in the distance the moving mass of Missourians spread out across the prairie. The panorama of men and horses presented a formidable foe for Sigel's little army. The Union brigade was not at full effective strength. One company of the Third Regiment was at Neosho under Captain Conrad. Captain Indest — earlier dispatched to Grand Falls to guard the Military and Kansas Line Road — had kept his company there, and had not returned by the time hostilities began. Sigel left a third company behind Dry Fork Creek as a rear guard with one piece of artillery. Colonel Salomon, meanwhile, having deposited garrisons of men from Rolla to Sarcoxie, reached Carthage with only seven of his normal ten companies.[3]

The sorting of the Union battle line presented the same vagaries as the State Guard. At full strength, Sigel's Third Regiment had twelve companies: two rifle companies and the ten companies that normally constituted a regiment. These rifle companies had designations of A and B, the same as the regular line companies A and B, which explains how Sigel could forego the reassignment of three companies and still come on line with nine. It does not explain, however, the loss of the mutinied company at Lebanon that Sigel replaced with Greene County Home Guard soldiers. Depending on how Sigel counted his companies, the Union line possibly comprised no more than 800 infantry soldiers facing a mob of 4,000 State Guard recruits. Nevertheless, the generally accepted troop strength of the Union force was 1,100 based on Sigel's battlefield report of 950 men and the assumption of another 150 in Backhoff's artillery. In his official report, Sigel said that he had a total effective strength of 550 infantry in the Third Regiment and Colonel Salomon 400 in the Fifth. It is unclear if he included in his count the men of the two batteries of artillery that made up the remainder of his field command, or if his numbers included any support troops or local volunteers. Lieutenant Tosk, Sigel's adjutant, said Sigel had 600 men and Salomon 500. However, Sergeant Otto Lademann, also in the Third Regiment, remembered a number of 2,000 muskets and eight guns. The *Fort Scott Democrat* reported on July 7, 1861, that the Union force numbered 1,500 in all. Sigel's figures understandably became the historically accepted troop strength going into the battle. The number has been repeated without much question every since the battle. Snead said Sigel's force included about 1,100 men, and eight pieces of artillery; the *St. Louis Republican*, July 11, 1861, published a number of 1,100; Schrantz set the number of Union troops based on Sigel's battlefield report and said the Union column consisted of 1,100 men. Shoemaker accepted Schrantz's numbers and so did VanGilder, who also made a point to include Backhoff's artillery that he said was down to 150 men; VanGilder

Charles Eberhardt Salomon ca. 1863. Major Salomon accompanied Colonel Franz Sigel to southwest Missouri and commanded the Fifth Regiment of U.S. Missouri Volunteers at the Battle of Carthage. (Courtesy of Kent Salomon.)

mentioned a number of additional men left with the supply train. And so on. Therefore, on the Friday morning of July 5, the settled number for the Union Second Brigade was 950 infantry in ranks, including officers. Colonel Salomon's Fifth Regiment of Missouri Volunteers numbered about 400 men in seven companies; Sigel's Third Regiment had an effective strength of approximately 550 men in nine companies. Two batteries of artillery with four guns each and about 150 men to serve them rounded out the force. There was no cavalry. An unknown number of unnamed local home-guard volunteers supplemented the federal army.[4]

The German soldiers that came on line at the Battle of Carthage represented what was left of the St. Louis Missouri Volunteers of the Second Brigade. A month prior to the battle, the Missouri adjutant general listed troop strength in the units later dispatched to southwest Missouri: Sigel's Third Regiment, 1,103 men; Salomon's Fifth Regiment, 926; and Backhoff's Artillery, 253; 2,282 total. With the assignment of various parts of his command to other duties, and with expired enlistments, Sigel prepared to engage the Missouri rebels at Carthage with about half the number of soldiers enrolled in June 1861.[5]

The federal drummers started the cadence of the long roll, signaling the Union troops to prepare as quickly as possible for action. The ominous sound of the muffled drums started very slowly, then gained velocity to a rapid roll before tapering off again, and then repeating. Soldiers shifted cartridge boxes to the front, brought weapons to the ready position, and pressed forward. Sigel's men carried the old .69-caliber rifle muskets with an effective range of 100 yards and capable of discharging an ounce of lead with each load, assuming cartridges were available. The cartridge boxes the men carried were nothing more than flat containers shaped like cigar boxes. The boxes were without any kind of retainers to hold the shells in place. After a week of marching and jostling the boxes around, a soldier was lucky if he did not have a box full of loose powder and bullets dangling from empty paper cases.[6]

A good musketeer could get off about two shots a minute, three if he practiced. The soldier had to stop and hold the musket upright, pour in a cartridge of powder, shove in a ball and ram it home with a ramrod, half cock the hammer, place a percussion cap on the nipple, run to catch up with his line, raise the weapon to his shoulder, cock it, aim, and pull the trigger. A soldier needed a good set of front teeth. He bit off the end of the cartridge with his teeth, poured in the powder, and rammed the ball home. If a man's teeth gave out so did his usefulness as a soldier. After a few volleys of biting off cartridges, a musketeer had a wad of gunpowder-flavored paper that he gnawed like chewing gum. A man guarded his cartridges as best he could. Any lost cartridge or one fired without orders cost the soldier ten cents a cartridge. In the heat of a fight, a weapon sometimes misfired. Men often reloaded a musket amid the noise of battle without even knowing it had misfired. Someone reportedly found one weapon at Chickamauga with 17 loads.

Sigel's poorly equipped federals did not know at the time that the rebels were even worse prepared than they were. Fully one-third of the rebels were without any arms, facing Sigel with nothing more than pitchforks and the courage of their convictions. If these rebels were to confront anybody, it would have to be mostly hand-to-hand combat. Those who had arms largely carried their own shotguns and gaming rifles brought from home or borrowed from neighbors. A few of the old hunters on the rebel side loaded their heavy hunting rifles in deliberate fashion. They took their time to place a piece of cotton or buckskin over the muzzle; press down the ball a little, pull an old knife from a pocket, cut off the patching, return the knife and ram the ball gently down; put on a cap, then gaze under the smoke and look for a shot.[7]

A mile and a half further on after crossing Dry Fork Creek and routing Shelby's skirmishers, the Union force found the main Missouri line drawn up in battle formation about 1,500 yards to the front. Second Lieutenant Tosk, situated near the head of the Union column, in his excitement estimated their number at 5,000, chiefly cavalry. He miscounted five guns — four six-pounders and a 12-pounder. Contrary to Tosk's observation, the State Guard had six pieces on the field. The rebels had deployed in multiple regiments, well positioned, and arranged in line on a ridge of ground rising gently on an elevated swell of land oriented east–west. What Sigel thought he saw before him was not a ragtag band of rebels, as he perhaps expected, but a well-led militia of volunteers properly deployed at military intervals and positioned in proper line of battle. Two regiments of cavalry formed the wings of the rebel line. At the center was the rebel infantry, backed by cavalry and supported by two batteries of artillery. Sigel thought the rebels had posted other guns on the right, and maybe one artillery piece on the left wing. He estimated the force within his sight at 3,500 with an unknown number held in reserve. Off to the east, he saw another large group of cavalry coming rapidly onto the rebel line of battle. Sigel glanced at his watch; it said 9:30 A.M.[8]

Colonel Sigel formed his initial battle line three-quarters of a mile south of the rebel line. Major Henry Bischoff's Second Battalion, Third Missouri Infantry, was on the left wing. Next to Bischoff's infantry on the right were four pieces of Major Franz Backhoff's battalion of Missouri artillery. The diminutive Major Backhoff was a close friend of Sigel and intensely disliked by his men. A little over four feet tall, he was, like Sigel, exceedingly ambitious and openly vain. Cruel and heartless, he liked to parade like a king riding up and down in front of his troops on a big horse, berating them, screaming obscenities, and bellowing like a maniac. He became so angry once that he actually frothed at the mouth. One time he arrested all of his officers. The Americans made fun of him, but the Germans tolerated him as one of their own. As the battle line formed, he rode up to give a cursory check of the deployment of his battalion, and then went to the rear where he pretty much stayed the whole day. He would be the Union's most ineffective officer on the field that day.

The first four pieces of Backhoff's artillery came on line under the command of Captain Theodore Wilkins, who patiently positioned his battery of three-month volunteers. Most of Backhoff's artillerymen, including the 40-year-old Wilkins, dated their enlistments from late April and would soon end their period of service, like the majority of the soldiers in Sigel's force that day. Wilkins' men trampled the waist-high prairie grass and cutting across the soft field wheeled the four guns into position.

Private John H. Bell, in General Clark's State Guard Third Division, watched Colonel Sigel's brigade, with bayonets glistening in the sun, form their line of battle down in the low part of the prairie. One of the Union batteries directly in front of him took a position at the lowest part of the dell. One of the rebels asked, "Why do they take a position down in that hollow?"

Private Bell answered, "Because they think they can take better aim if they shoot up, and we must be careful or we will overshoot when shooting downhill."[9]

The Fifth Infantry Regiment of Missouri Volunteers, in two separate battalions under Lieutenant Colonel Salomon and Lieutenant Colonel Christian Dietrich Wolff, were at the center of the Union line. Wolff's battalion centered about on the Moses Gresham place. Another three pieces of Backhoff's artillery under Captain Christian Essig took a position on Wolff's right. Essig, 35, commander of Battery A was, like his counterpart Wilkins in Battery B, an April enlistee. On the extreme right wing of the Union line was Lieutenant

Colonel Franz Hassendeubel's First Battalion of the Third Missouri Regiment. Colonel Sigel, meanwhile, remained a convenient distance to the rear mounted on a coal-black horse looking as much like a schoolmaster as a commanding general.[10]

The battle lines edged closer. Men on opposite sides of the battlefield knew each other. Some from Carthage and elsewhere around Jasper County grew up together but chose to fight for two different causes. Soldiers peered across no man's land straining to identify anyone they might know. A few veterans of the Mexican War knew that they faced former comrades. Colonel Weightman on the Missouri side and Lieutenant Colonel Hassendeubel on the Union side had served as fellow officers in the same unit under Sterling Price. On this day, however, Weightman and Hassendeubel were at opposite ends of the battle lines; they would not directly face each other. Hassendeubel's infantry aligned due south of Brigadier General Parsons' infantry — Parsons being yet another Mexican War veteran.

Every Union and State Guard officer on the field knew Franz Hassendeubel, if not personally, by reputation. Already a distinguished military officer, he was a lieutenant in Fisher's Light Artillery Battery during the Mexican War. Sterling Price had officially commended him for his acts of bravery. When the conflict between Missouri and the federal government appeared unavoidable, Price remembered Hassendeubel's exemplary war experience and invited him to a meeting at the Planter's House hotel in St. Louis to ask him to join the Missouri State Guard. Unknown to Price, however, Hassendeubel was already secretly drilling the Home Guard at the Turner Society, and plainly expressed to Price his devotion to the Union cause. Hassendeubel did not know that his old commander was not on the field that day as the two armies faced off for battle.[11]

Sigel extended his line as much as prudently possible, but the State Guard cavalry still overlapped his flanks. Nevertheless, he advanced his line another 400 yards until they were within a half mile of the rebel line. The Union line halted a few hundred feet forward of a small stream called Double Trouble Creek at the foot of the rise looking up toward the rebel army. Less than a thousand yards separated the two lines. Double Trouble Creek was little more than a trickle in dry weather. Two converging sources east of the road fed the stream, which conspired in wet weather to flash flood the crossing, giving the branch its double-trouble name. Sigel first deployed his troops just north of this muddy little stream. He posted his artillery along a low rise of ground approximately where the Pugh brothers later built their house. He moved most of his infantry ahead of the artillery about a hundred yards and ordered them to lie down in the grass out of sight of the rebel artillerymen. Recent rains made the ground soft and cool, a nice relief from the morning sun, for it was a bright sunny day.[12]

The Missouri Guard battle line simultaneously moved from the top of its ridge down the incline to a position slightly forward of the ridge line to flatter ground. The cavalry on each wing pressed southward, threatening to enclose Sigel's army. The time was approaching ten o'clock, and the morning sun began to assert its presence. The July sun beat down as if to add its own measure of misery to whatever was to come next.

The Missourians had at least two tactical advantages despite the poor condition of their force: the high ground and more than a third of them were mounted. They could afford to mass their troops in line. The federals, on the other hand, had no cavalry and consequently had to bring their units up formed in column of companies to guard against cavalry attacks on the flanks. This impaired the mobility of the Union army. However, Colonel Sigel had another weapon. The good guns of his artillery outmatched the six old cannons of the Missourians — the only heavy guns in the entire Missouri force.

Here on the prairie of southwest Missouri, two Missouri armies, one for the Union, one for the State, maneuvered their regiments to face each other in the first major land battle of the Civil War. Later engagements of the war quickly eclipsed the Battle of Carthage as more symbolic of the war's impending calamity; but in the beginning, almost everyone recognized that the first serious engagement between the two sides happened not in the East but in the West, on the isolated prairies of southwest Missouri.[13]

It was a pathetic beginning to an awful war. Two armies of Missourians faced each other on the field of battle, one badly equipped and unsupported, the other with field equipment and armament much worse. The gray-clad federals looked only marginally more like an army. There was at least a consistency in most of the uniforms: gray jeans trousers, gray jackets — a few with yellow piping — and black shoes. Each soldier wore a wide-brimmed hat. The rebels had no uniforms. Mostly unorganized and untrained recruits, they were clad in the dress of the Missouri farmer in those days, the homespun butternut jeans and plain homespun work shirts that they had on their backs when they joined the Missouri State Guard on its march south. Those that had weapons carried mainly the old Kentucky rifles and shotguns brought from homesteads or collected from secessionist sympathizers along the way. A lot of them wore a large knife tucked in their belt. The only fully uniformed company in the whole State Guard was the Callaway Guards of Burbridge's Infantry Regiment, of General Clark's division, and they were dressed in gray.[14]

The two battle lines stood facing each other. The sporadic small-arms fire coming from either side suddenly stopped. Silence came over the scene. Only the sounds of creaking leather drifted in from the rebel flanks as horses pranced and riders nervously shifted in their saddles. Now and then, a restrained oath disclosed the impatience of a restless soldier. Neither side knew what to expect. Some of the St. Louis Germans were veterans of military service in Europe. A few on each side had seen limited service in the Mexican War, but in that war, all Missourians were on the same side. Here north of Carthage, Missourians faced Missourians, eager for a contest but in the back of their minds wondering what it would be like actually to shoot at each other.[15]

William P. Barlow, a young rebel lieutenant in Captain Guibor's Battery, recalled what those first moments of the battle were like. "I remember feeling the beauty of the scene as our mules maliciously wheeled the pieces into battery, and we looked down from our slight ridge and saw the bright guns of the federal battery and their finely uniformed infantry deploying on the green prairie about 800 yards distant. Both sides formed in silence and stood looking at each other." It was as if no one wanted to fire the first shot. The tall grass rippled across the landscape; now and then, a lone tree swayed back and forth in the gentle morning breeze.[16]

17

Shotguns and Cannons

Governor Jackson since February had worked to secure arms for the state's defense. His efforts had been severely set back at Camp Jackson with the capture of the state militia. General Lyon and his Union volunteers had relieved the militia of a dozen fieldpieces and a large number of small arms shipped from Jeff Davis' Confederate stores at Baton Rouge as part of the futile attempt to take control of the St. Louis Arsenal. Jackson's men had managed to transport a few arms to Jefferson City along with a supply of gunpowder, but Union troops confiscated everything else, including the siege guns borrowed from President Davis.

Missouri Quartermaster General James Harding scavenged what he could in the way of military hardware to supply the new State Guard. He retrieved seven old Mexican guns brought to Missouri after the Mexican War and hidden away in a dark vault under the portico of the capitol building at Jefferson City. He managed to recover one or two wagonloads of materials of war from the capitol basement and a few hundred old flintlock muskets, literally antiques believed to have last seen service during the War of 1812. Harding had some of the muskets converted into percussion and set up a cartridge factory at the penitentiary. He sent the seven old Mexican cannons to St. Louis to have them recast into four six-pounders. He had carriages, limbers, and caissons built after the style of the ones at the St. Louis Arsenal, one of which he borrowed from the arsenal as a pattern. These four guns unfortunately remained behind in St. Louis during the hasty flight of the State Guard from Jefferson City. They were still at a St. Louis foundry when Governor Jackson and the state officers abandoned the capital ahead of General Lyon's advancing Union army. The setback at Jefferson City came on top of the rebel losses at Camp Jackson. By the time Jackson reached Boonville, he had hardly any heavy arms at all and very little else in the way of weapons to arm his fledgling Missouri State Guard. He counted two old six-pounders without caissons, a little more than a thousand rifles and muskets, and about 100 sabers and swords, a third of which were useless. The swords and sabers were, in Quartermaster Harding's words, about as useful as so many bars of soap. Along the journey south from Boonville, the weapons taken in the rebel raid at Cole Camp added a few more muskets to Governor Jackson's column. General Parsons' division brought three bronze six-pounders taken from the Liberty depot, and a supply of pistols, muskets, and sundry other items. General Rains'

Lexington contingent fielded three artillery pieces along with a motley collection of small arms. The limited weaponry of the divisions of generals Clark and Slack rounded out the official armaments of the Patriot Army of Missouri. Volunteers supplied the rest from home in the form of shotguns, fowling pieces, and their personal hunting rifles. The armaments within the rebel divisions lacked uniformity to say the least.[1]

The six heavy fieldpieces in Rains' and Parsons' divisions were the core of the State Guard armament. Without them, the rebel army would have been practically defenseless and no match against the Union's superior firepower. Three of the six guns came from the rebel sacking of the U.S. Arms Depot at Liberty in April 1861, when Governor Jackson tipped his hand on his intent to oppose a federal military presence in Missouri. The three brass six-pounders ended up in General Parsons' division. Twelve other six-pounder iron guns and a small three-pounder taken from Liberty at the same time never made it into the meager arsenal of the State Guard troops. Neither apparently did a good supply of ammunition. One of the recurring complaints of the Guard batteries was the lack of ammunition for the guns; yet, the depot at Liberty gave up close to 900 rounds of all kinds, including canister, a shot the rebels claimed not to have had. The raid at Liberty also produced about 500 vintage rifles and muskets in working order, an equal number of swords, and 923 pistols, which for an army of 6,000 facing off at 800 yards were useless. Some of the infantry soldiers wondered if they would ever get to use their weapons. The opposing armies faced off at such a distance beyond the effective range of the small arms of either side that one corporal on the Union side later complained, "Our infantry was not able to accomplish anything."[2]

The six rebel fieldpieces divided into two light artillery batteries, one commanded by Captain Hiram Bledsoe and the other by Captain Henry Guibor. The Guibor Battery came together on the retreat from Boonville when the three bronze pieces from Liberty wound up in Guibor's hands.

Henry Guibor brought experience to the gunnery arm of the rebel force. A St. Louis printer by trade and a citizen soldier, he had been a gunnery officer with the state militia and active in the Kansas troubles at an early date. Taken prisoner at Camp Jackson when Union soldiers seized it, he looked for a chance to get even for the St. Louis massacre. Federal organizers knew his military skill. Upon his parole from Camp Jackson, they offered him a commission as a colonel in the Union army. He declined, whereupon officials promptly issued a warrant for his arrest. Of Northern birth, he nevertheless strongly defended Missouri's claim to states' rights. Guibor and another Camp Jackson parolee, William P. Barlow, who had likewise declined a federal commission, struck out by different routes to find Governor Jackson's State Guard. Guibor told his family he was going to the country on a short trip. Avoiding federal authorities, he met up again with Barlow about 20 miles outside St. Louis, and the two of them headed southwest looking for Jackson. Distrusted by both sides, secessionist partisans arrested them twice as spies before they caught up with the governor at Warsaw. Jackson immediately released them and put them in charge of General Parsons' battery of three brass six-pounders. When Guibor took over the battery, it hardly resembled a serious military entity. The equipment amounted to four caissons, a battery wagon, and three gun carriages, each drawn by a four-mule team in plough or wagon harness and driven by a long lean Missourian with a single check line. It took considerable horsepower to move one of these brass guns; each alone weighed 882 pounds. Other meager equipment included a traveling forge and a small assortment of tools that came with the guns from Liberty. There was about a half supply of ammunition and nothing to work the guns but one sponge-

Free-State Kansas Battery, 1856. *(Left to right)* Owen Brown, George B. Gill, Tauy Jones, Augustus Wattles, August Bondi, James Redpath. Heavily armed companies of Kansas militants terrorized the Kansas-Missouri border. Free-Staters stole a Mexican War era cannon like this one from militant Missourians. A companion 12-pounder known as Old Sacramento went into the formation of Bledsoe's Battery at the Battle of Carthage. (Kansas State Historical Society.)

staff. There were only three guns in the Guibor Battery and not four as some thought. The battery did not have four guns until after the Battle of Wilson's Creek; there were four six-pounder caissons but only three guns, the three bronze Model 1841 pieces taken from the Liberty depot. Neither Guibor nor Barlow saw their families again until the end of the war. Guibor's short trip to the country lasted four years. From 1861 until the close of the war, he went wherever his guns took him, from Carthage to Wilson's Creek to Vicksburg.[3]

Operating alongside Guibor's Battery, further west down the rebel line, stood Hiram Bledsoe's three-gun battery consisting of an eclectic mix of a 12-pounder and two six-pounders, one of iron the other bronze, altogether only marginally better off than Guibor's Battery.

The lone 12-pounder in Bledsoe's Battery was the fabled Old Sacramento, a retooled piece captured in Mexico. It was a trophy of the Mexican War, captured by the First Regiment Missouri Mounted Volunteers of Doniphan's command at the battle of Sacramento Creek. The U.S. government gave the gun — and several others taken at the same time —

to Doniphan's Missourians who brought the guns home after the war and stored them at different places around the state. Some went to the capitol at Jefferson City where Quartermaster Harding found them; some to the U.S. depot at Liberty, in Clay County; two more to Platte County; and one to Lafayette County. The Lafayette County gun was the fabled Old Sacramento. It stood on a bluff overlooking Lexington and laid at Lexington for a long time, used only on Fourth of July occasions when boys of the city would ram it half full of powder and brickbats to fire the national salute. When rebellion threatened to break out in Missouri, Captain Bledsoe, who made his home in Lafayette County, formed the first Missouri battery of the Civil War in the spring of 1861. He had first organized a company of mounted rifles at Jefferson City, but the mounted company unfortunately suffered the handicap of having no horses, and Bledsoe joined the State Guard exodus to Lexington. Bledsoe, who rode with Doniphan and was instrumental in the capture of the Mexican guns at Sacramento Creek, appropriated the Lexington gun for his battery. It was originally a long, nine-pound gun. Bledsoe had it shortened and bored out at Morrison's foundry in Lexington to a 12-pounder. Quartermaster Harding furnished Bledsoe a carriage for the gun at Jefferson City. Bledsoe had come to Harding looking for a carriage on which to mount the gun. The only carriage Harding had at the time to show him was a primitive-looking thing with ironwork forged and fitted at the penitentiary for a six-pounder gun previously ordered up for duty during the Kansas border quarrel. The commander of the Kansas mission thought it too light for the rough roads of border service and rejected it. Bledsoe looked at it, thought it would answer his purpose, and took it home with him. He mounted Old Sacramento on that discarded carriage with its funny equipment and shoe-box-looking limber chest that held 30 rounds.[4]

Union sympathizers told a different story about Old Sacramento. They said it never was part of Bledsoe's Battery; that proslavery Missourians took Old Sacramento from the Liberty depot and used it in the Kansas border conflict. Kansas Free-Staters claimed to have, in turn, liberated the gun from the Missourians during the border war and buried it near Lawrence. They dug it up and used it to celebrate the admission of Kansas to the Union in January 1861. The tale of the capture of the gun was both colorful and dubious. The *Osawattomie Herald* printed reminiscences of it in July 1861 that told how "Old Sac" ended up on the Union side. Proslavery men kept the gun near the border for a long time under the guard of six Missourians, bringing it out as needed to terrorize Kansas citizens. In the summer of 1856, under the stealth of night, so the story goes, a man from Shawnee and three Kansas women, two of them teenagers, stole the gun away and whisked it off to the Kansas Territory to use it, in the words of the *Herald*, to annihilate the traitors in Missouri. After the Free-Staters captured it from the proslavery side, they claimed it was never again in rebel hands. A variation of this story said that among the ten guns Doniphan's Missourians originally captured at Sacramento Creek were two Old Sacramento cannons, both nine-pounders; one went to Jefferson City and then to Lexington, and the other went to Platte City. The Lexington gun admittedly went into service in the Civil War with Bledsoe. It was the Platte City Old Sacramento that Missourians carried into Kansas to support proslavery efforts in the early border troubles. Some say the name of the Kansas gun was not Old Sacramento but Old Kickapoo. In any event, it remained in Kansas until 1896 when it exploded near Lawrence when fired over the spot where someone drowned to raise the body. Remnants of it are in a museum at the University of Kansas.[5]

Bledsoe's Old Sacramento of Civil War fame had a peculiar bark that identified it above other cannon on the field. In the conversion from a nine- to a 12-pounder, the machine shop at Lexington turned the chase off smooth, thus reducing the thickness of the metal to give the piece an unusual sound when fired. The gun soon became familiar to rebs and feds alike. The gun's odd ring when fired became a signature of Bledsoe's Battery at Carthage and many battles of the Civil War thereafter. Allegedly cast by the Mexicans from church bells with a high silver content, the gun's distinctive sound inspired all who heard it in action. Men referred to it affectionately in the feminine. "That's Old Sac; She's at it again!" was a familiar refrain. Worn out and badly grooved from use, Old Sacramento ended up at Memphis, Tennessee. Some said that unbeknownst to Bledsoe the gun went to the Confederate navy yard at Mobile, Alabama, and there a foundry eventually recast it into other guns. Others say it was lost in the Mississippi River, while some claim that after Memphis, no one could find it.[6]

The legend of Old Sacramento in the Civil War is one of the war's memorable stories, one of the colorful sidebars of the war. The gun began its epic Civil War journey on July 5, 1861, north of Carthage, Missouri, on the prairie of Jasper County. Notwithstanding some differences of opinion about its origin, and how it came into the war, there is ample evidence that Old Sacramento formed the core of Bledsoe's Battery.

Bledsoe, like Guibor an experienced artilleryman, had misgivings about taking command of the tattered battery. Joseph A. Wilson remembered being with Bledsoe in the first days of the battery. "From Jefferson City our 'army' came to Lexington, where we found three pieces of artillery, a bronze nine-pounder captured by Missourians in Mexico [Old Sacramento], an iron six pounder cast at Lexington, and a brass six-pounder taken from the depot at Liberty, Missouri." The brass six-pounder actually came from Platte County and not Liberty, as Wilson thought, having made its way to Lexington by way of Independence. The iron six-pounder smoothbore gun was new, cast at Morrison's foundry in Lexington. Two other iron guns that Bledsoe helped to seize in the raid on the Liberty depot and took back to Lexington turned out to be unserviceable. Nevertheless, Bledsoe was with some difficulty persuaded to take temporary charge of Old Sacramento and the two operable guns; thus, they formed one of the first and most famous and effective batteries of the Civil War. There is no popular support, however, for the claim that Bledsoe brought Old Sacramento on line at the Battle of Carthage drawn by a yoke of steers. Nor that

William P. Barlow, ca. 1890. Lieutenant Barlow turned down a Union commission, choosing instead to fight with the rebel light artillery battery of Henry Guibor. He fired the first rebel shot at the Battle of Carthage. (Scholten, Missouri History Museum, St. Louis.)

Bledsoe's Battery could fire six effective shots a minute for each gun. A legend can only go so far.[7]

While the rebels struggled to field six working cannon, on the federal side the Union guns gave Sigel's force a key advantage in firepower. Captain Christian Essig's battery fielded four 12-pounder howitzers, and Captain Theodore Wilkin's battery had two 12-pounder howitzers and one six-pounder field gun, a fourth piece having stayed in reserve behind Dry Fork Creek. The rebel guns had only solid shot: no exploding shells, no shrapnel, and no grapeshot. The Union guns fired all four.

Solid round shot came in different sizes of solid spherical iron balls. A bronze six-pounder cannon, for example — the regulation light artillery piece of its day — fired a three-inch caliber ball launched by upward of a pound and a quarter of gunpowder. A practiced artillery crew could fire a six-pounder three times a minute, up to a range of a mile depending on the size of the gun and type of projectile. The swath of death and destruction widened with the size of cannon, and Sigel had at his disposal the full complement of firepower. Deadly variations of solid shot came in the form of shell, or hollow iron balls, filled with gunpowder and fitted with a fuse timed to explode at a calculated range. The same ball filled with musket balls and a bursting charge of powder took the name spherical case shot. Such ammunition, correctly fused, burst anywhere from 50 to 130 yards short of its target, usually at a height of 15 to 20 feet in the air. The musket balls and shell fragments continued on to the target at the same velocity as the original projectile and with devastating consequences. Grapeshot, meanwhile, was the term for large cast-iron balls bolted together as steel disks into a cylindrical group that when fired separated in flight with the same deadly consequences as case shot but with even greater destructive force. A variation of grapeshot was canister, smaller cast-iron balls mounted in thin sheet-iron containers that burst when fired from a gun. These had a particularly deadly effect at short range. Sigel had ample canister.[8]

The federal guns wheeled into position. The Missouri artillery batteries staked their cannon on the side of the hill. Brigadier General Slack and Colonel Weightman aligned their infantry — those with arms — on either side to support the guns. Captain Bledsoe's three-gun battery took aim at the Union front 800 yards away. Colonel O'Kane edged his men forward on Bledsoe's left toward the federal center. Captain Guibor's men finished building gunnery fires from which to light their cannon.

General Rains, a red sash tied around his waist to signify his rank, maneuvered his cavalry toward the federal left flank. Rains set up his operational command post there with his cavalry. It was a bad decision, one that seriously compromised his effectiveness as overall battlefield commander because the Missouri Guard line extended west from where he was for more than a mile. It would be impossible for him to direct the artillery or the battle from his chosen position. On the other hand, perhaps Rains did not consider himself the overall field commander, leaving that assignment to the self-appointed command of Governor Jackson stationed at the rear and likewise in no position to direct the battle. Jackson stayed back with the baggage wagons and all the unarmed men, some 2,000 of them, who formed a faux reserve that amounted to little more than a line of spectators.[9]

The battle scene was set.

The Union army occupied the low ground two miles north of the timber that shielded the bank of Dry Fork Creek. The Missouri State Guard commanded a ridge of prairie directly in front. A distance of from 700 to 800 yards separated the two lines. The ground sloped gently southward, broken here and there by shallow gullies and undulations. Between

the two armies were two large cornfields, one that extended along the west end of the battlefield almost over to the timberline on the creek, which angled northwest toward the rebel
line. A similar field ran along the east end of the battlefield. Cornfields dotted the prairie
because corn was Jasper County's most important agricultural product. These open grain
fields presented a tactical advantage for the State Guard cavalry to advance against the Union
flanks. The Gresham house stood like an abandoned sentinel, left alone to guard the desolate
prairie.

The federals had marched ten miles, eager to demonstrate their superior military training. The Missourians, too, arrived on the battlefield in high spirits. After a sleepless night
and a similar march of about eight miles, a cool drink of water would have been welcome
but there was none. The federals were between the thirsty rebels and the creek.

Captain Henry Guibor's battery stood on the left-center of the rebel line, deployed on
a portion of high ground not far from Bledsoe's Battery on the right. General Parsons rode
up to Guibor's Battery. As soon as the guns were in place, Guibor galloped over to him and
asked permission to open the fight. Lieutenant Barlow carefully aimed the right-hand piece,
Guibor nodded his head, and the first shot fired in earnest went screaming through the air.[10]

18

The Cannonade

The cannonading commenced sharply at ten o'clock "vigorously on both sides at the same time," as one State Guard Missourian recalled. General Slack looked at his watch, which indicated eleven o'clock, apparently an hour fast. Both General Slack and General Clark thought the cannonade began at 11:00 A.M. Surgeon General Taylor said it began promptly at ten minutes to ten.[1]

No sooner had the rebel guns opened than Sigel's artillery returned fire with a heavy barrage of round shot, shell, spherical case shot, and grape. The Union artillery fired almost simultaneously, perhaps at the smoke of the Guibor gun. General Rains had just galloped up and dismounted near the rebel guns when the shelling commenced. Captain William McCown remarked to him, "We are going to catch it." To which Rains replied, his field glass to his eye surveying Sigel's position, "Oh! No, we are not in range." Barely had the words passed his lips when solid shot tore through a section of the rebel line, killing one man and wounding three others. Another case shot exploded in the ranks, creating great confusion among the green rebel recruits. Captain McCown observed, "General Rains, in a very unmilitary style, mounted his horse, and without a word of command, rode out of range very hastily." A few of General Rains' detractors liked to tell how his horse bolted and raced to the rear with the general holding on for dear life. The anecdote did not say how General Rains was able to mount the frightened animal before horse and rider sped away. Rains managed to quickly get the wayward animal under control and return to his position on the line of battle.[2]

It was not clear exactly who fired artillery first. Witnesses to the battle came away about evenly divided. Some said Sigel did, and Bledsoe replied. Others said that Guibor's Battery in Parsons' command opened the battle and the federal guns returned fire before Bledsoe joined in. General Clark was of the impression that Guibor's guns opened the battle and fired first. "Sigel's guns quickly answered the rebel cannon," he said. Bledsoe then joined the duel. On the Union side, Lieutenant Max Tosk said the Union guns opened the battle. Another observer claimed that the federals opened but with a blank shot, answered by a solid shot from the Missourians. John Buegel, on the other hand, wrote afterward in his diary that the rebels fired first and the federals replied, firing six cannon all at once with the effect that "the earth trembled."[3]

Buegel's mention of six cannon brings up yet another controversy surrounding the Battle of Carthage, this one about how many guns Sigel lined up against the six pieces on the State Guard side. It is another of those conundrums that shadows the details of the battle. A few chroniclers of the battle repeated Buegel's reference to six cannon on the Union line and maintained the federals fired first. General Clark, on the other hand, thought the Union opened with eight guns posted 1,000 yards to the front and held to his claim that the State Guard guns opened the battle first. Notwithstanding General Clark's eyewitness position, Sigel did not have eight guns on line as Clark imagined and possibly had only six. Of the eight cannon originally in his brigade, he left one piece with his rear guard behind Dry Fork Creek and had previously sent two pieces from Neosho with captains Cramer and Indest to scout the western border. One of these guns may have remained with Captain Indest who arrived from his border mission too late to participate in the opening shots of the battle. Indest's description of the border excursion includes mention of the accompanying artillery. "We started on the 4th of July, with Company I, and two pieces of artillery as detachment, to Cedar Creek, from whence the company went on a scouting excursion to Grand Falls and five miles below on the Texas Road; next day [July 5] returned to Grand Falls and went to Carthage." By the time Indest arrived at Carthage, the battle was under way. When the cannonading commenced, Captain Indest was still a distance away from Carthage.[4]

Hiram Bledsoe. The light artillery battery of Captain Hi Bledsoe rained a deadly cannonade on the Union line. His aggressive tactics on the battlefield inspired the rebel Missouri State Guard troops to push Sigel's federals into rapid retreat. Bledsoe went on to become one of the Confederacy's most effective gunners of the Civil War. (Bob Younger Photo Collection, State Historical Society of Missouri.)

Sigel did not say the two guns were specifically with Indest. He implied that the two detached guns were with Captain Cramer, who did return from the border mission to the main Union force in time to enter the fight. Did Sigel have six guns or seven? He made a point to say that he directed Major Bischoff to direct all seven Union guns at the rebel line, and specifically emphasized the number seven. His battlefield report, generally accepted as a fair description of events, nevertheless has overtones of fantasy. Major Bischoff, for instance, was nowhere in sight when the guns opened fire. The statement also softened the effect of Sigel's earlier decision to send a heavily armed Indest and Cramer on a goose chase to the western border while he marched his decimated army into the jaws of a rebel force more than four times the size of his own. There are no official Union reports of the Battle of Carthage besides Sigel's to dispute his version, except that of Lieutenant Tosk who, when not acting as Sigel's adjutant, was an artillery officer, and he sidestepped the point. In his report to the press, Tosk discounted the rebel artillery to five pieces instead of six and said that on the Union side there were "several pieces of artillery." He had said in a dispatch before that there were eight field guns, probably referring to the original artillery strength of the brigade when it left Springfield and not the number of pieces that lined up at the Battle of Carthage.[5]

In the end, it mattered little whether there were six or seven pieces; the Union guns took a deadly toll. The first federal shot took off the left arm of Private William D. Hicks and the right arm of Private Thomas Doyle in the front and rear ranks of Colonel Kelly's infantry, standing sturdily just to the left of Guibor's Battery on the rebel line. Both Hicks and Doyle were privates in Company A of the First Regiment, in Parsons' Sixth Division.[6]

The Missourians immediately answered the Union cannons.

The calm silence of the Ozark prairie, bathed in the morning sunshine of a clear July day, was suddenly broken by the deafening roar of artillery. Lieutenant Barlow, working the Guibor guns on the left, said, "For the next half hour I remember little. It was an almost continuous roar of whizzing shot and bursting shell." Each side intended to inflict as much damage as possible.[7]

Bledsoe's Battery immediately opened a steady fire from the rebel right, determined to pour maximum misery on the Union boys. Captain Bledsoe worked the right-hand battery himself. Bledsoe's physical appearance belied his intense personality and tough demeanor. His cadaverous, lean-looking expression was almost humorous because he had a proclivity for wearing hats several sizes too large so they rested just above his eyebrows and perched on his large ears. A gangly six feet six inches tall, he moved awkwardly but could sit a horse with the best of men. A generous full moustache seemed to borrow from his short-cropped hair and sparse goatee. A religious man, he would sit in silence before a battle, knees drawn up, head resting on his folded arms. Appearances aside, Bledsoe instilled intense loyalty in his men. His unblinking and determined gaze left no doubt that he would give the federals no pity. He directed his barrage at the densest parts of the Union force. Those federals still standing in the vicinity broke ranks and found refuge out of sight in the depressions of the prairie until the shelling let up. As soon as they reappeared, Bledsoe resumed shelling them.[8]

Infantrymen on both sides lay flat on their faces at the first shots, cowering in the tall prairie grass and praying a shell did not come their way. No sooner had the men in General Clark's division formed and dressed their line when cannon balls came streaking through the air. Orders came for the men to lie down in the grass. For the next 30 minutes, they watched the Union guns unleash their firepower on the rebel line. They watched with a mixture of apprehension and surreal wonder. Cannon balls came rolling and bouncing through the grass from the low-ground position where Sigel planted his guns, seeking the hilltop where the State Guard boys held the high ground.

Cannon balls struck where men lay on both sides, kicked up ground, and spread shrapnel of death and mayhem. Solid shot embedded deep in the soft soil. One apocryphal tale told how a rebel ball landed beside one federal infantryman, passed beneath him, and came out the other side before rolling on down the slope without touching the lucky soldier. In a similar incident on the other side, Salem Ford saw a Union ball coming at him on a direct line, bouncing along the ground. His first inclination was to catch it but better judgment told him to let it go. It bounced toward Bo Roberts lying flat in the grass immediately behind Ford. The shot passed between Roberts' body and left arm and continued up the slope of the hill behind the prostrate soldiers.[9]

A cacophony of guns, shouting voices, and a mix of the sounds of frightened horses and mules filled the air. Mules drew all of Guibor's field guns and part of Bledsoe's. A few of the gunnery horses reared and screamed, spun about and charged full speed to the rear with their handlers struggling to get them under control and return to the fight. Some panicked and pranced through the ranks stepping on many of the hapless prone soldiers. Guibor's Battery worked its three brass sixes and continued shelling the Union right. Guibor's gunners had broken up an old rail fence and made a fire near each gun. To fire the guns, they poured powder over the vent holes of the cannon and touched it off with pieces of the burning fence. A small supply of quick match made of cotton rope soaked in turpentine proved less sure than a powder horn and a burning splinter. They faced a well-equipped battery opposite them in Essig's company, but with steady aim and unruffled improvisation, they took the fight to the Union troops.[10]

With all the fuss of these first barrages aimed mostly at each other's artillery batteries, there were surprisingly few casualties. The thinness of the rebel line presented no depth to

the federal guns and their ability to inflict mass damage was limited. Major Thomas H. Murray of O'Kane's battalion had his horse shot from under him by grapeshot; the second discharge from the federal guns went over the rebel line and felled two horses in Colonel Rives' cavalry; and two of Kelly's men received severe wounds, but considering the concentration of Union fire, the damage was light. Only two men in Guibor's Battery received slight wounds. One of them, however, was Lieutenant Barlow. The field hospital quickly repaired him and sent him back to duty.[11]

While the rebel line bore the brunt of the shelling, the cavalry maneuvered to draw the fire of the federal guns. In one audacious incident, the rebel cavalry taunted the federals. Captain Emmett MacDonald led his men onto the field although not a single rider owned a weapon. MacDonald, already a man of reputation, had been the lone man who refused

Emmett MacDonald, ca. 1861. At the Battle of Carthage, Captain MacDonald maneuvered his cavalry parade-style, taunting the federal army in an exhibition of horsemanship done in full view of the Union troops. (WICR 30826 in the collection of Wilson's Creek National Battlefield. Image courtesy of the National Park Service.)

General Lyon's offer of parole after the federal capture of Camp Jackson at St. Louis. When the first shots of the Battle of Carthage rang out, Captain MacDonald further demonstrated his insolence toward the Union. Joseph Mudd, a soldier on the rebel line, described what happened. He said, "At the battle of Carthage, in the temporary confusion due to the separation of the unarmed cavalrymen to be sent to the rear preparatory to the cavalry attack upon the enemy's flank, Captain MacDonald took his company out on the high prairie in full view of every man in each contending army and in the midst of the flying shell and canister made it perform all the best maneuvers of the tactics. It was a beautiful sight and very inspiring to us who there got our first view of real war."[12]

The most intense moments of the artillery exchange came at the opening barrage. As Brigadier General Clark led his troops into line of battle, a cannon ball struck his horse in the neck, knocking him to the ground. A continuous shower of grape and shell poured into Clark's troops and caused momentary confusion in the line. The men were already under severe duress from the shelling, and when they saw the general go down, they broke in confusion. General Clark got to his feet, caught another horse, and rallied his men. The disruption soon quieted as men and officers received the fire with the poise and coolness of veterans. Those who were there said Clark's division suffered the most in the fight.[13]

General Clark had reason to be especially concerned for the welfare of at least two of the line officers in his division. Lieutenant Colonel Edwin Waller "Stump" Price, eldest son of General Sterling Price, commanded Clark's Third Infantry Regiment. The 26-year-old Price had barely escaped capture at Camp Jackson at the time General Lyon imprisoned the entire camp, starting the chain of events culminating in the face-off now above Dry Fork Creek. The younger Price inherited the distinctive character of his father. Ordinarily of good cheer and full of sunshine, his warm handshake and polite nature made him welcome in any Chariton County home. On the battlefield, however, his good nature dissolved into an aggressive, if somewhat less than competent, fighter, someone trying vigorously to defend the Cause and make his father proud. The other officer on the battlefield of great immediate concern to General Clark was his own son, Major John B. Clark, Jr., commander of the First

John Bullock Clark, Jr., 1864. Colonel Clark commanded a regiment of the Missouri State Guard at the Battle of Carthage in the Third Division led by his father, Brigadier General John Bullock Clark, Sr. (WICR 31453 in the collection of Wilson's Creek National Battlefield. Image courtesy National Park Service.)

Infantry Regiment. At age 30, he was a few years older than Stump Price but had been in the position of regiment commander for only two days.

The Missouri State Guard troops proved to be steady and calm in the face of battle, a remarkable testimony considering that most of them had never seen battle, let alone found themselves thrust into the front line of one. Despite the relative intensity of both the rebel and federal barrages, losses up to this time continued to be small.[14]

The Union guns adjusted and unleashed another devastating barrage. Sigel ordered the concentration of all of his cannon directly against the center of the rebel line. Bledsoe's men took the brunt of Sigel's fire. They suffered severely. A round wounded Bledsoe and some of his best men fell. Bledsoe's wound was more serious than those around him thought it was at the time. His brother, Robert D. Bledsoe, writing years later, said, "At the battle of Carthage he [Captain Bledsoe] received a severe wound; really a dangerous wound, but he remained with the army, and came back [home]." The rebel ranks broke but quickly rallied. The Missourians held their position despite the destructive discharges against them. One gun in particular was the target of the federal cannon, the lone 12-pounder in Bledsoe's Battery, the fabled Old Sacramento. The Wallace brothers, Curtis O. and Charley C., along with four of their companions, worked the gun under withering fire. Incoming fire wounded both Wallaces. Mules reared up, stood on end, and tried to break free. One team, still hitched to its limber, stampeded toward the Union line, getting well into no man's land between the rebel and federal lines before a daring mounted officer overtook them and brought them back, an act of courage that drew the admiration of both sides.[15]

The heat was extreme. The gunners became exhausted in the hot sun. The hard work and excitement of battle caused some to collapse. Many infantrymen, too, fell beneath the blazing sun as they worked to support Captain Bledsoe's relentless barrage against the Union line. Bledsoe, a veteran of the Mexican War, had battlefield experience. Now, his courage and that of his steady gunners inspired the raw volunteer militia who were for the first time in their lives facing the galling fire of canister-loaded artillery. Smoke belched from the guns. The acrid smell of burned gunpowder hung in the air and stung the nostrils. Across the battlefield, puffs of smoke burst out in silence, followed by the sound a few seconds later, delayed by the distance between the battle lines. The awful interval between sight and sound could be an eternity for the soldiers because each one knew if he heard the sound, he was OK. A column of smoke, white at first, then rapidly changing to blue, belched forth from each gun 25 to 30 feet from the muzzle before anyone within its range heard the sound rumble over the prairie. Missiles of death and destruction discharged with a loud roar. Solid shot gave off a peculiar sound like a combination of a muffled railroad whistle and the flaring of a torch in high wind, an eerie, venomous kind of sound.[16]

The Missourians had little in the way of ammunition with which to charge their guns. In lieu of grapeshot, they filled their canisters with scrap shot — bits of iron, trace-chains, rocks, and anything else a country blacksmith shop could supply to fire at the federal troops. Looking out onto the plain below, a swath appeared to cut through the columns of the Union troops with every shot of the Missouri batteries.[17]

Union officers repeatedly rallied their stricken men. Once again, there were surprisingly few casualties, with one notable exception. Private Peter Glock, a Union Third Regiment mounted orderly, died instantly, cut down by a rebel ball. The 43-year-old Glock had proudly joined the Third Regiment at St. Louis less than two months earlier, furnishing his own horse to the Union cause. Both he and his horse lay killed on the field. A companion of Private Glock later claimed that Glock died in the encounter with the advance State Guard scouts three miles north of Carthage before the battle began. Glock and his companion allegedly shot five rebels in the encounter. The pioneers supposedly found and buried Glock's body not far from his horse. Sigel's six mounted orderlies constituted the only cavalry on the Union side, and now they were down to five.[18]

The federal guns answered with more roars, like distant thunder in quick succession. The federals had the superior firepower and used it mercilessly on the rebels. The Union guns soon reduced the secession flags to tatters. From the Union side, the rebel line stood silhouetted against the prairie ridge. Every time a shell exploded from one of Sigel's guns, a large gap appeared. In their youthful exuberance, the Union soldiers cheered to see so many Missourians fall in the onslaught of their firepower. They, with their ignorance of war, however, were soon educated. The fallen rebels never stayed down. They always got up again, and the gap in the line was filled. It soon became clear that the Union artillery was not having the expected effect.[19]

The roar of artillery resounded across the normally serene prairie. People living 20 miles or more away heard it. Men from Fort Scott swore they heard the firing of cannon all the way to the Kansas border, 35 miles from the battlefield. Many could not identify the deep roll of the guns. Several thought it was thunder, although they thought it odd that such a bright sunny day could produce a thunderstorm. The sound carried all the way to Sarcoxie. Margaret Jane Rains, wife of the rebel brigadier general, and her daughter stood on the porch of the upper portico of their home and listened. Mrs. Rains had not previously felt the anxiety of war but felt it now, worried for the safety of her husband and her brother, Jesse Cravens. Henry Zellers, a unionist living in Madison Township, recognized the sound of Old Sacramento from the days when he rode with Doniphan in the Mexican War. He thought it regrettable that the gun should now serve such an ignoble cause.[20]

Campbell A. Smith lived on Spring River northwest of Carthage near the James Walker place. His wife, Sarah Ann, was standing in the yard looking to the north for signs of a storm when her father rode up. "What's that noise?" she asked him. A former Jasper County sheriff, he answered calmly, "Why, honey, that's Rains fighting the Dutch." North of Spring River, the daughters of Hannibal W. Shanks climbed on the roof of a farm shed to watch the cloud of battle smoke rise from the battlefield.[21]

The muffled sounds of the battle wafted into Barton County, to Lamar, where the day before sons and husbands had left loved ones for the excitement of war, the din of which now echoed over Muddy Creek and across Muddy Bottoms. Over near Cave Springs, east of Carthage, the noise caused considerable excitement on the Brice Henry farm. John W. Henry stopped in the middle of his farm work, looked at his father, and said, "This is it." He put down his tools, strapped on his revolver, and picked up a rifle. He saddled his best horse and galloped off to enlist in the Union army. Elsewhere around the county, the sounds of battle fueled similar passions on both sides. Thomas B. Glass operated a woolen mill along Spring River. When the firing commenced, Amanda Glass was bedridden and eight months pregnant. It sounded to her as if the battle could be on Spring River, and she worried about her husband's mill. Fearing for its safety, the Glasses earlier had gone out of their way to declare their neutrality on the secession issue. However, a month later the couple suspended their neutrality long enough to name the new baby Sterling Price Glass. Moses and Susan Carver heard the rumble of the guns 20 miles away at their farm near Diamond Grove. They guessed the commotion was somehow connected to the Union soldiers who had passed through Diamond Grove the day before, and they wondered what it might mean for their future as slave owners. The Carvers held a unique place in history. Not long after the Battle of Carthage, bushwhackers kidnapped a female Carver slave and her baby. Authorities recovered the baby, and Moses and Susan raised him to be George Washington Carver, the distinguished educator and scientist.[22]

The noise of battle became more distinct closer up the road toward Carthage, the road on which Sigel's army had marched only yesterday. Widow Alta Fullerton and her daughters heard it and guessed the soldiers who tramped past her place had found their battle. James M. Hickey heard the sounds rumbling in the distance from his farm near Fidelity. He, too, thought it was a storm coming on and hurried up with his plowing. A friend came by and said it sounded to him like cannon. Hickey mounted his horse and rode by his house to tell his wife, Lucinda, that something was going on in Carthage, and he thought he would ride up to see. He wheeled his horse around and started north.[23]

Business went on as usual in Carthage. Most of the stores remained open. Merchants stood outside their doors and looked anxiously in the direction of the battle. A few people milled about in the streets exchanging speculation about the state of events to the north. Norris Hood thought there were too many Missourians for the federal boys to make a fight of it. "They'll be eaten up alive," he said, as the bellowing artillery rumbled afar. No sooner had the first sounds of the battle drifted over Carthage than Captain Joseph Indest and his rifle company came into town hurrying from their earlier assignment at Grand Falls. The company broke into a run when they heard the cannon.[24]

After about 20 minutes of the cannon duel, Brigadier General Parsons became concerned about the exposure of the rebel infantry who had taken direct hits from the federal guns. He decided to use his cavalry to harass the Union right flank and draw fire away from the middle of the State Guard line. He ordered Colonel Ben Brown's regiment of cavalry to feign an attack on Sigel's right flank. At the same time, Brigadier General Slack sent Colonel Rives and his regiment of mounted riflemen, which had remained behind Slack's infantry, wide around the Union right wing toward Buck Branch to take possession of the crossing there, cut Sigel off from a possible retreat, and threaten the federal rear. Rives' cavalry rode over from the center of the line to the far left where his horse soldiers could swing around the right flank of Sigel's army. Simultaneously, sensing that the Union line might be wavering, General Clark conferred with Colonel Kelly who was on his immediate right and indicated his intent to advance his troops toward Sigel's line. At that moment, General Parsons came up from his batteries and gave a similar order. General Parsons left orders for Kelly that as soon as the cavalry began its movement around Sigel's flank, Kelly was to advance the infantry toward the center of the Union line.[25]

The federal guns continued to concentrate on the rebel core. Colonel Weightman's First Brigade on the right center of the rebel line was immediately in front of the Union line of attack. It received the wrath of Sigel's fire. The initial phase of the battle took place in the open prairie, without shelter for the infantry or artillery. The Union guns delivered a severe fire on Weightman's exposed troops, but the green rebel volunteers stood steady, displaying the calmness usually reserved for disciplined veterans.[26]

Meanwhile, Brigadier General Rains, operating on the far Missouri right flank, saw the same opportunity to turn the left side of Sigel's line that General Parsons had seen on the federal right. Sigel lacked the number of troops to extend his battle line enough to protect both of his flanks. General Rains also saw the plight of Weightman's uncovered brigade. He ordered his cavalry around the Union left flank to divert the Union guns away from Weightman's infantry.

In the absence of General Sterling Price, the State Guard was without a field commander. When the battle intensified, each division commander began to operate independent of the other. Some thought Governor Jackson had temporarily handed over field command to General Rains, but Rains leveled his attention on his own division.

Jackson, meanwhile, was not on the field.

19

Rebel Cavalry on Both Flanks

The Union guns leveled a relentless fire at the rebel line. As they did so, the mounted regiments of the Missouri State Guard began a wide circle from both flanks to turn the federal left and right. Colonel Rives' cavalry was on the extreme left of the rebel line, some 700 or 800 yards from the guns of the Union artillery, determined to fulfill his mission to circle the right flank of Sigel's infantry and threaten the rear of the federal force. Colonel Brown and his regiment maneuvered alongside Rives. General Parsons now saw a possibility that his cavalrymen could surround the Union army before it reached Dry Fork Creek. He ordered Colonel Brown to circle wide around the Union right flank and hasten to Dry Fork to occupy the timber at the crossing. There he would join with Colonel Rives from General Slack's division and block any chance of a Union retreat.[1]

The cavalry movements had the desired effect of drawing attention away from the rebel line and diverting the shelling from the front as intended. Sigel shifted the positions of his infantry and artillery to respond to the movement of the mounted regiments. Two of his guns swung away from the rebel infantry and trained exclusively on Rives' cavalry.[2]

The rebel cavalry quickly drew fire. The first discharge of shot did little damage. The second was lethal. Two horses fell, killed immediately by grapeshot. The men tumbled to the ground, shot out of their saddles. Shells fell thick on the cavalry ranks. The officers and men remained surprisingly cool, considering again that for most of them this was the first military engagement of their young lives. After covering several yards under fire, Rives' men stopped. A strong plank fence was directly in their path. Several men dismounted and set about tearing it down, all the while in the sights of the federal guns. A masked Union gun out of sight of Rives' men suddenly opened fire on them with a barrage of grapeshot and shell. Four men fell. Captain John Norton Stone, Private James Herrin, and Private William R. Burton died instantly or fell mortally wounded. Ordinance First Sergeant Joel Stamper tumbled from his horse wounded. Henry Cheavens was with Rives when the rebels attempted to cross the field. He saw Captain Stone fall. As soon as he got to the cover of a cluster of trees, he volunteered with some others to go to his captain's assistance. The would-be rescuers ran into the open, back across the field. Another round of federal artillery tore through the air above their heads. They reached Captain Stone to find him lying in the field in a pool of blood. A six-pound ball had struck him in both of his legs, knocking him from the saddle and killing his horse. The shell tore a piece of flesh from the back of his left leg just above the knee but missed the bone. He had bound a strap above the wound to stem the bleeding; his horse lay 50 feet away dead. Unable to carry Stone back to the rebel lines, Cheavens and his comrades carried the injured captain to the Widow Smith's house, which was nearby. A nicely laid out breakfast was still on the table in the Smith house but no one was home. They made a bed of quilts on the floor and tried to make the captain comfortable. He took a drink of water. One of the men tightened the strap around his leg. After a while, a doctor arrived, but the wound proved to be more serious than first thought. Captain Stone died later that day at about three o'clock. He was 32. The Ohio-born farmer from Utica, Missouri, had taken up the secessionist cause on behalf of his Virginia ancestry, whose legacy remained embodied in the slave ownership of his family in Livingston County. His uncle, Judge John Stone, cut a wide swath in north Missouri politics. Bent on protecting his Baptist ways from outsiders, the judge served against the Mormons to force them out of the state. It was against this background that Captain Stone gave his life, the first officer of the secessionist army to die in Missouri.[3]

At the exact moment that Colonel Rives' cavalry came under fire on the left, on the extreme right side of the Missouri line, General Rains' rebel cavalry was also drawing heavy fire from Sigel's artillery, which belched forth a steady barrage of various kinds of munitions. The federal guns shortly checked Rains in his advance as he vainly maneuvered his cavalry looking for a route to Sigel's left flank. Each time the rebel wings tried to bring the cavalry into position on the Union flanks, Sigel turned some of his guns in that direction, wreaking mayhem, and causing the horses to stampede.[4]

Rains' cavalry on the rebel right comprised the Third Regiment Cavalry of Colonel R. L. Y. Peyton; the First Battalion Second Cavalry under the command of Colonel James M. McCown; and Lieutenant Colonel Richard A. Boughan's Vernon County Battalion. From Colonel Peyton's position, he could see the federal batteries on the left, positioned to the southeast, north of Dry Fork Creek. They were about three-quarters of a mile away with a large cornfield separating the rebel cavalry and Sigel's guns. A little more than a half mile directly south was the timber line of Dry Fork Creek, with a sturdy fence in front surrounding the grain field. They would have to pass through this open field to get to the creek. Colonel

James B. McCown, ca. 1862. Colonel McCown commanded the First Battalion Second Independent Cavalry of the rebel Eighth Division that followed General Rains in a failed attempt to pass the left flank of the Union line and circle behind Sigel's forces. (WICR 31479 in the collection of Wilson's Creek National Battlefield. Image courtesy National Park Service.)

Peyton continued to rest his command at the edge of the field, awaiting further orders from General Rains. Peyton's "regiment" was down now to only 60 men because he had earlier sent one of his companies to join Shelby. It was at this moment that General Rains appeared on the field and personally took command of the cavalry column and turned it left toward the Union position.[5]

Colonel McCown's 250-man battalion was next to Colonel Peyton on the extreme right wing of the rebel line as far west as the line extended. The 44-year-old McCown, a prominent Johnson County politician from Warrensburg, and his lawyer son, William H., had been early enlistees in the State Guard. The younger McCown commanded a company in his father's battalion. The elder McCown had first enlisted in his son's company but now commanded the battalion. They were on the battlefield together, eager to meet the Lincoln army. A few minutes into the cannonade, General Rains ordered McCown's battalion to advance in the direction of the Union artillery and to get ready to charge the federal guns. McCown made his way into the grain field on the west end of the battlefield between the opposing lines. He had advanced just beyond a cabin near the middle of the field when Rains joined him at the head of the column. Rains stayed at or near that position for the remainder of the battle. He passed the word: "On a given signal, you are to charge upon the enemy's battery. The signal will come from the commanding officer of cavalry on the east wing." That officer was Colonel Brown, who was now positioned more than a mile to the east. With that, Rains rode off. Colonel McCown waited for the signal. He neither saw nor heard any signal to charge, either from the east wing or from General Rains.[6]

As McCown and Peyton guided their units into the grain field, Lieutenant Colonel Boughan brought up the 200 men of his Vernon County cavalry. Only about a third had proper arms. The rest carried common rifles and shotguns. Another 100 men from Colonel Charles P. Hyde's command of St. Joseph volunteers joined Boughan's battalion. Most of Hyde's Buchanan County boys had never seen Jasper County before. The lads from nearby Vernon County, however, knew it well. These were home-grown, southwest Missouri boys with local names and generational ties to the area. They fully believed it was their duty to defend their homeland from the invaders. Boughan's battalion took a position on the left of Colonel Peyton's command. Acting with Colonel Peyton's troops, Lieutenant Colonel Boughan's men prepared with the other Missourians to charge the Union battery. Boughan's command moved forward in two squadrons. A hundred men went with Colonel Hyde, the rest with Boughan. The Vernon County recruits and their St. Joseph compatriots were anxious to fight. Hardly had they begun their advance toward the federal guns, though, when they, too, encountered a strong fence running north–south parallel to their path and impeding their ability to make a direct assault on Sigel's artillery. They found themselves in the same large field of wheat and corn as McCown and Peyton, stalled by part of the same heavy fence. Unable to breach the fence quickly and attack in line of battle, Boughan and Hyde fell in behind Colonel Peyton's small band as they progressed across the field, tearing down pieces of the fence as they went. With the fence partly down, the remainder of the cavalry entered the field and came up on the rear of McCown's men. At this point, General Rains abandoned the assault on the federal artillery and instead ordered the whole cavalry through the field to gain the safety of the timber along the creek. A sudden commotion at the head of Peyton's column and an overall lack of progress in eliminating the fence prompted Boughan to veer his command to the right of Peyton with the intention of bypassing the fence and coming around it to the rear of the federal line and charge from that direction.

McCown, meanwhile, had led his men through the field with the intention of carrying out his own flanking movement around the federal left.[7]

As McCown's men came out of the cornfield, the Union guns fired on them. The open position exposed them to a barrage from the Union cannons. Private George W. O'Haver had his arm shot off and died two days later; Private Elijah M. Wood lost his left leg. Shots killed six horses and wounded several more.[8]

The federal guns now trained on Lieutenant Colonel Boughan's troops. The terrain had generally masked the movements of Boughan's men up to this time. As they came over the brow of a low hill, the open ground suddenly exposed them to a raking fire from Sigel's guns. Canister and round shot peppered the field. The Union guns rained down on the rebels as they tried to cross the open field. The fire was heavy and severe. Lieutenant Francis M. Kimble's leg was broken and his horse killed under him by a cannon ball. A shell struck the saber and scabbard of Lieutenant Albert Badger, breaking it in two but luckily causing no other damage. The horses of Captain Jesse F. Stone and Private John R. Huckaby were simultaneously killed beneath them, and Private Gilbert Wilson lost his horse moments later. For nearly a quarter of a mile, the men rushed through the federal barrage. The shelling continued until they reached the sanctuary of the woods.[9]

After passing through the field in the midst of fire, General Rains again took charge and guided his men into the body of timber. The young volunteers continued to stay remarkably calm for inexperienced soldiers under fire. Gaining the timber, the rebel cavalry halted at its edge under cover of the trees. As the battle raged to the southeast of them, they waited in the forest north of Dry Fork Creek. The creek at this point angled northwest away from Sigel's guns, and General Rains found himself still to the front of the federals after his cavalry reached the wood line.

As the Missouri cavalry moved east and west away from the ends of the rebel line, it caused great intervals to open between them and the center of the line. Sigel saw an opportunity to try to break through the rebel line. He concentrated all his artillery on the right-center of the State Guard line, aiming it at Bledsoe's Battery, and for a short time gained an advantage. The rebel Old Sacramento 12-pounder appeared to be dismounted, and Guibor's Battery fired at longer intervals, a sign they were running out of ammunition. Two pieces from Essig's Battery were moved from the Union right to the left wing to add firepower against the rebel right. Bledsoe's entire battery now appeared silenced. A line of riflemen formed as skirmishers between the federal guns to make an assault.[10]

It was a critical moment in the battle.

Sigel made it known to his commanders that it was his intention to gain the heights by advancing with his left and taking a position on the right flank of the rebel center. At that precise moment in the battle, Captain Theodore Wilkins, commander of Backhoff's left artillery battery, called out, "I am out of ammunition. I cannot advance." It was a decisive instant of judgment for Sigel. No time could be lost. The rebel cavalry was advancing against both ends of his battle line. The wings of the federal line were already engaging with them as the horse soldiers worked their way around the Union flanks. Without the full force of his artillery, an assault on the front was likely to fail and turn into a rout.[11]

The Union assault stalled. Realizing his plight, Sigel called off the risky attack and decided to withdraw back toward Dry Fork Creek.

The brisk artillery exchange between the two sides had lasted approximately 30 minutes, a half hour of a hot and bloody duel, before Sigel began to fall back. For some it seemed shorter, no more than 20 minutes. Archie Thomas in the rebel Carroll County company said the cannonade lasted 20 to 30 minutes, which coincided with the recollection of General Clark. Others swore it lasted longer. Missouri Colonel J. T. Hughes said it seemed like the cannonading went on for an hour. General Slack claimed to have clocked it at precisely 55 minutes. All during the dueling between batteries, each side prayed that the other side would run. Neither side did. Whether it was the encircling rebel cavalry, the Missourians' superior numbers, or the loss of half his artillery, the empty Union guns offered an excuse for Sigel to extract his army from an untenable and perhaps impetuous action on his part. Sigel now feared that he was in danger of losing not only the battle but also his supply train and perhaps his entire army. He ordered a complete withdrawal and sent word for the supply wagons to advance toward him as rapidly as possible to be under the protection of the army.[12]

The Missourians, too, were at a breaking point. No longer able to withstand the federal cannon barrage and not knowing that some of the Union guns were out of ammunition, the rebel infantry simultaneously prepared to charge. When the Union guns faltered, General Parsons, sensing a turn in the battle, ordered an immediate advance of his division. General Clark did the same. Colonel O'Kane's battalion in Weightman's brigade joined them in a quick movement in the direction of the federal line. Soon the whole rebel line was rapidly closing with the federals.[13]

The Lincoln troops fell back and the State Guard soldiers took up the pursuit. The Missourians threatened to overwhelm the federal line by the utter size of their force. The

Union's superior arms and training were not enough to offset the four-to-one troop advantage held by the rebels. The Missourians pressed forward about 50 yards. Suddenly, the Union line made a quick retrograde movement in double-quick time back over the ridge where they had initially posted. Sigel, anticipating a threat from both sides by the rebel cavalry, slowed his pace and deliberately and slowly fell back some 200 yards to the rear of his initial position, and recommenced the engagement.[14]

Colonel Weightman advanced his whole brigade in battle order toward the wavering Union line. He closed rapidly, and for a few minutes the two sides engaged at close quarters. The aggressive advance of Weightman recalled a time in

Richard Hanson Weightman, 1848. Colonel Weightman led the First Brigade of the Eighth Division Missouri State Guard infantry and artillery at the Battle of Carthage. This engraving made at the time of the Mexican War is the only known image of him. (Library of Congress LC-USZ62-58521.)

the Mexican War when he and Bledsoe had dodged their artillery about the battlefield, taking their guns to within 50 yards of the Mexican redoubt at Sacramento Creek. Those acquainted with R. H. Weightman well knew him as an intelligent and adventurous individual, if not a little hotheaded and unsettled. He grew up the son of a prominent Washington, D.C., family, and a product of his Virginia private education. He studied law but never practiced; went to West Point but never graduated. He moved to St. Louis in 1846 and from there entered the war with Mexico as a captain in the Missouri Volunteer Light Artillery. The Southwest attracted him after the war, and in 1851, he moved to New Mexico Territory to edit the *Santa Fe Herald*. He served as Indian agent and carried the credentials of an antebellum delegate to the United States Congress in 1851 as the Territory's first representative. His unsuccessful petition to Congress for New Mexico statehood showed early on his passion for states' rights. The rights of all people come from a just government, Weightman concluded. He killed a man in Santa Fe, supposedly in an argument over the proposed route of the transcontinental railroad. He next went to Kansas from New Mexico, and then eventually to settle in Independence, Missouri, in 1861. His restless spirit made him one of the first to take up arms in the sectional dispute that now found him in close pursuit of the retreating Union troops.[15]

Bledsoe's guns reopened fire at the federals at each closing interval. His was the only rebel artillery still operating. The three six-pounders of Guibor's Battery on the Missouri left fell silent, out of ammunition. The federals still had most of their artillery while the Missourians effectively now had only three pieces in use. Some in the ranks of the infantry complained that had the artillery been more efficient, they could have taken the complete federal command.[16]

The rebel infantry continued to advance south toward the Union line. At the same time, General Parsons' cavalry aggressively pressured the right flank of the federal troops, trying to cut off Sigel's retreat before he could reach Dry Fork Creek about a mile behind the Union position. The resupplied Union guns stalled the rebel advance again. A steady fire from the Union infantry and well-aimed artillery shelling managed to slow the progress of the Missouri mounted soldiers, but Sigel, detecting the progress of the Rains cavalry movement toward his left flank, thought it prudent to withdraw from the field. He saw immediately the intent of the advancing cavalry to encircle him. After only a few minutes of cannonading from his second position and under cover of fire from his artillery, he began an orderly retreat by his right flank, much to his mortification, slowly pulling the right of his line back to match the advance of the rebel cavalry.[17]

When the federals fell back from their initial position on the ridge, dropping back 200 yards, they passed into a ravine. The terrain briefly concealed the federals from view. Thinking that Sigel had fallen back to gain a position on the Missourian's left to make an attack on their flank and counterattack the rebel cavalry, the commands of O'Kane, Dills, and Kelly suddenly stopped their frontal assault and changed their direction from south to east. They closed with General Clark's division on the left, and marched in separate columns east for about a half mile, intending to keep the Union troops to their front and thwart Sigel's anticipated tactic. When they came over the hill, however, they discovered the federals not to their front as expected but in full retreat toward Dry Fork Creek. Sigel had not moved east as expected but had continued his retreat to Dry Fork, while the rebels had almost marched themselves out of the battle.[18]

The superior firepower of the Union cannon gave Sigel's men time to fall back without much obstruction as they began a calculated withdrawal in the direction of their supply train now located about three miles from the scene behind Dry Fork Creek. The federal troops executed a textbook example of a deliberate retrograde movement, retreating by the right flank ahead of Brown and Rives' rebel cavalry, which pressed them on the east. As the federals withdrew, the rebels slowly followed. Each time the Union line gave way, the rebel line pressed forward.

Two incidents from this part of the battle suggest that the fighting during Sigel's retreat to Dry Fork Creek was more intense than an orderly withdrawal might imply. As Colonel Brown's cavalry pressed forward toward the creek to follow the retreating Union soldiers, the Union infantry began to collect in the wood line north of the creek completely out of sight of the advancing Missourians. The trees were in full leaf along the creek bank. Thick undergrowth hid the federal position. Brown sent a squad of 40 or 50 mounted riflemen ahead to check the easternmost position of the Union flank. As soon as they approached the federal line, Sigel's rear guard fixed bayonets and moved out to meet them. A squad of infantry fired a volley at close musket range into the advancing rebels, causing them to withdraw in disorder and provoking hearty cheers from the Germans in the Union ranks. The sight of flashing steel in the hands of the Union Dutch emerging from the woods startled the rebel cavalry who turned and withdrew toward the protection of their own line. One Missourian remembered the moment the Union line broke and said, "A small portion of [State Guard] cavalry succeeded in reaching their rear," before the Union troops repelled them. Other witnesses confirmed this brief clash between the federal infantry and rebel cavalry, although they said it occurred during the cannonade. However, they included the initial artillery duel and the standoff at Dry Fork Creek as parts of the same vigorous cannonading, which some said lasted two hours. The State Guard cavalry attack on the Union rear failed when Sigel turned his battery upon them, dropping three-second shells among the untrained horses of the cavalrymen.[19]

Meanwhile, a mystery remains unsolved about the engagement before Dry Fork Creek in the Union's clamor to cross 15 companies of foot soldiers and two batteries of artillery over the rain-swollen stream. The only suitable place to cross was at the narrow ford. The *New York Times* and *Sacramento Daily Union* reported, "At the crossing of Dry Fork, our [Union] lines were very near being broken, when, by the timely arrival of 200 Union men from Shoal Creek, they crossed with but a loss of five killed and two mortally wounded." This brief reference suggests that local Union patriots participated in the battle alongside the mostly German volunteers from St. Louis. Confirmation appears to come from the State Guard side. Surgeon General George W. Taylor, writing shortly after the battle, identified, in addition to Sigel's well-armed and well-equipped infantry and artillery, two companies of cavalry. The Union Second Brigade had no cavalry. The identity of the mystery horse soldiers remains unknown. There was a Union Home Guard company organized in June 1861 in Caldwell County, north of the Missouri River, called the Shoal Creek Rangers; however, it is unlikely that this band was anywhere near southwest Missouri at the time of the Battle of Carthage. The passing reference to the heroism of the Shoal Creek men at Dry Fork may have been a self-serving imaginary addition by the Kansas City correspondent who furnished the information to the newspapers, perhaps attempting to add the Caldwell County boys to the folklore of the battle. The mystery unit, on the other hand, may have been part of the Lawrence County Home Guard. While there is not a Shoal Creek associated with this regiment, it was a sizable force of almost 1,000 men at the time of the battle, some of whom accompanied Sigel to Carthage. Captain William D. Gatton's Company F joined Sigel at Mount Vernon as a guard company, and Lawrence County resident Private Owen

Smith Nichols claimed he served as Sigel's color bearer and paymaster. It is possible that companies of the Lawrence County regiment not mentioned in Sigel's after-battle report participated in the fighting and then returned to Lawrence County. Another possibility for the Dry Fork 200 may attach these mystery men to Shoal Creek in Newton County, although no evidence exists of a military unit organizing with that name in this heavily pro–South county. Shoal Creek flows westward through Newton County immediately south of Jasper County where the battle took place. The creek gave its name to a small village located at the time up in the northwest corner of the county. When the editor of the *Neosho Herald*, Archibald M. Sevier, fled Neosho — being one of only a few outspoken Union men in town — about 150 less-vocal unionist men from Newton County accompanied him to Mount Vernon. The murder of Tom Rea of Shoal Creek by unknown marauders prompted Sevier and his compatriots to abandon the deeply secessionist Newton County soon after Sigel and his troops occupied Neosho. The sojourn from Newton County to Mount Vernon is its own mystery. It is unclear whether they departed from the county before or after the battle. In any event, if they were the Shoal Creek boys at Dry Fork Creek, Sigel made no

mention of them in his report, and like Gatton's Lawrence County company, they managed to keep their participation in the Battle of Carthage a secret.[20]

Before Sigel began his withdrawal, some of the men who were pinned down on the State Guard line by the federal guns saw General Rains and his mounted men begin their movement south. They anticipated he would scurry around the Union flank, reach the ford at Dry Fork Creek, and there dismount his cavalry and hold the federals in check until the State Guard infantry caught up. It made a logical scenario. They did not anticipate Sigel's calculated withdrawal. Almost as soon as Rains had started his advance toward the Union left flank, the Union forces were out of the hollow and on

Joseph Conrad, ca. 1864. Colonel Franz Sigel left Captain Conrad and his company as a protective garrison at Neosho, Missouri, while the remainder of the Second Brigade continued on to Carthage. Confederate troops captured Conrad and his men without resistance. (Massachusetts Commandery Military Order of the Loyal Legion and the U.S. Army Military History Institute.)

their way back toward Dry Fork Creek. The State Guard commanders ordered the rebel infantry to charge, but Sigel's guns had the range. He stopped two of his guns on a small knoll long enough to throw a few shells at General Rains' men. It stopped the cavalry advance and erased any possibility that Rains would reach the ford ahead of the retreating rebels. The untrained men and untrained horses of the State Guard cavalry scattered amid the barrage of bursting shells. The few rounds dropped on Rains' men probably saved Sigel from capture.[21]

The Missourians failed to stop Sigel's retrograde movement. He managed to withdraw back across Dry Fork Creek to the position of his rear guard behind the creek. He crossed over the creek and hastily formed a line of battle on a knoll of ground behind a cluster of trees on the south side of the creek, now about a mile and a half south of his first position. He posted a section of artillery on a steep eminence on the south bank on the east side of the road and deployed five companies of infantry along the bank of the stream to cover his retreat. These five units south of the creek guarded the withdrawal of the rest of the Union force. The larger force soon retired to the other side of Dry Fork Creek and passed up the road and through the timber that skirted its banks, leaving the five-company detachment as a rear guard on the south side of the creek.[22]

The Missourians did not have a coordinated response to the Union retreat. Each State Guard division commander acted more or less independently. Neither General Rains nor Governor Jackson gave a command to advance the State Guard line. Rains, the ostensible field commander, was out of position at the far right flank of the rebel line and not able to direct the action on the battlefield. The governor, meanwhile, stayed at the rear well back of the fighting. Consequently, no one was in overall command. The two sides of the rebel line formed on either side of a half-mile gap. The respective commanders had no idea how their counterparts were progressing. The rolling terrain complicated movements on the field. General Clark, for example, could not observe from his position the maneuvers of Slack and Rains. The rebel situation on the right flank was entirely different from the action on the left.

On the west end of the rebel battle line, General Rains' cavalry steered clear

James McQueen McIntosh. Brigadier General McIntosh resigned his commission as a U.S. Army officer at the outset of the Civil War and joined the Confederacy. As colonel of the Second Arkansas Mounted Rifles, he led a raid on the federal garrison at Neosho, Missouri, that resulted in the capture of a company of Franz Sigel's Third Brigade, the first hostile action of a Confederate force inside Missouri. (Courtesy J. N. Heiskell Individual Photograph Collection/UALR Center for Arkansas History and Culture.)

of the left flank of Sigel's line until the artillery barrage let up when the Union army began its retreat. The Rains cavalry had passed through the cornfield that stood between them and the federal left and gained the woods along the creek. The young Missouri volunteers of the State Guard stood ready now to obey any order to place them in the fight, but the call to fight never came. They passed instead over to the trees where they halted under cover of the woods, reformed, and waited.[23]

The first major engagement of the two armies had swung quickly in the secessionist's favor. Many in the fledgling Missouri State Guard saw as the objective of their action the independence of the State of Missouri, and if they must, they would fight to defeat the Union army to preserve what they regarded as nothing less than their liberty. It had become necessary to seek help from the Confederate States. That was the great object of this battle and their march southward to join forces with General McCulloch and his army of the South. When the battle began, with Sigel's powerful force of well-armed federal troops blocking their way in front and a column of veteran Union soldiers under General Lyon and Major Sturgis threatening their rear, prospects for success had by no means been certain. Now, the cause so dear to all took on a new hope. They had the federals on the run.[24]

20

Standoff at Dry Fork Creek

All morning the dull sound of the guns had drifted far over the countryside. Twenty-five miles to the south, Captain Joseph Conrad heard it at the Newton County courthouse, in Neosho, and wondered what it meant. He sent a patrol of 20 men to investigate. Around 1:00 P.M., he got a message back from John M. Richardson, the former secretary of state turned brigade quartermaster, saying Union troops had met the Missouri army in force and that he, Captain Conrad, might want to consider retreating to Sarcoxie.[1]

At about the same time Captain Conrad received Richardson's message, the first of General McCulloch's Confederate cavalry descended on Neosho from the south and west. Major McIntosh's column arrived near the town first, covering the distance from the McCulloch camp at Barlin's Mill in three hours instead of the anticipated four. Fearing that the federals would detect his presence and attempt to escape before Colonel Thomas Churchill's men could come up, he determined to make the attack alone. He sent Captain Carroll's company of Arkansas state troops on a detour around the town to come in on the north road and block a possible escape in that direction. He dismounted the other four companies of Churchill's Arkansas Mounted Riflemen under his command about a quarter of a mile from town and marched forward at double-quick time, halting about 200 yards from the courthouse where the Union company had its headquarters. He sent a volunteer aide-de-camp by the name of Dr. Armstrong to Captain Conrad to demand surrender of the Union garrison and gave Conrad ten minutes to decide his answer. As Conrad weighed his options, literally within minutes of receiving Richardson's message about the dire situation north of Carthage, the rest of Colonel Churchill's column of Arkansas Mounted descended on Neosho from several directions. Six more companies of sharply dressed cavalrymen, well armed and mounted on dapper steeds, quickly surrounded and easily overwhelmed the small Union force. The Confederates captured Conrad and his men without firing a shot. They confiscated anywhere from 100 to 150 weapons and seven wagonloads of supplies, which they distributed among themselves. The abundant supply of commissary stores provided welcome additions to their haversacks, empty after marching most of the night and all the day before.[2]

The capture of Captain Conrad and his company of Union volunteers marked the first action involving Confederate troops on Missouri soil and the first Confederate captures anywhere outside the fall of Fort Sumter. Churchill placed the federal troops under guard at the courthouse until General McCulloch could decide what to do with them. The number of soldiers captured at Neosho is unknown to this day. Major McIntosh said he took into custody 80 federals; other independent reports put the number at anywhere from 94 to 137.[3]

A popular story of the Neosho incident at the time provided a somewhat different account of the capture. It held to the capture of 80 men of Sigel's command quartered in the brick courthouse. An astonished witness said, "Arkansas troops suddenly appeared on the hills." The story went on to say, however, that after the capture of Conrad's company, a messenger arrived from the federal commissary at Granby and asked for Colonel Sigel. The captors pointed him instead to Colonel Churchill who took the courier's letter and immediately dispatched a detail to Granby to arrest Sigel's train. Sigel, of course, was nowhere near Granby at the time. Perhaps some of his supply wagons had parked there at the lead mines for obvious reasons. This embellishment of the capture of the federals at Neosho became an example of the lively stories that flowed from events in the early days of the war.[4]

The Confederates secured the town and waited for General McCulloch and General Price to come up with the remainder of the Confederate command. At about the time that the federal command in Neosho was surrendering to McCulloch's Confederates, the Union army north of Carthage was retreating from Governor Jackson's State Guard. Under pressure from the Missouri cavalry on both flanks, the federal troops had retired across Dry Fork Creek.[5]

After crossing back over the creek, the Union army halted and prepared to fight a delaying action a short distance back of the creek crossing. Sigel saw an opportunity here to delay his retreat and make a stand. He decided to fight a defensive action and redeployed his command. He divided his force in two parts. One part he positioned to conduct a rear-guard action at Dry Fork Creek to check the advance of the rebel line. The second part proceeded rapidly south to protect the supply wagons from the encircling rebel cavalry, some of which by now had already crossed the creek further east and was making its way across the prairie to get behind his army. Sigel pulled parts of Lieutenant Colonel Hassendeubel's First Battalion of the Third Regiment and Lieutenant Colonel Wolff's battalion of the Fifth Regiment from the right flank of his line and ordered them to the rescue of the supply wagons. With the four-gun battery of Captain Wilkins trailing them, they went high-tailing to the rear to defend the supply train against an anticipated attack by the rebel cavalry. The train still remained parked on the prairie about a half mile to the rear, under the command of First Lieutenant Sebastian Engert, and lightly guarded by Captain Foerster's company of pioneers.[6]

With the larger of the two components of Sigel's army withdrawing in the direction of the supply train, the smaller element of troops stayed back and began a movement to take control of the woods on the south side of the creek. From this position behind the creek and in command of the high ground, the relatively small force of federals could inflict serious casualties on the rebels and perhaps hold the ground indefinitely. Sigel drew up the federal troops on a ridge of ground just beyond the creek and reformed his line behind a thick skirt of timber. Captain Essig's four-gun battery took a position above the south bank of the creek on the east side of the road. From here, behind the ford, his guns covered the only ready crossing point along the creek. Sigel set up a rear guard consisting of five companies. Lieutenant Charles Stephani with a company of infantry from the Fifth Regiment took a place west of the road on Essig's left, and two companies of the Third Regiment under Captain Adolph Dengler and Lieutenant Hugo Golmer took up positions to the east on Essig's right, extending along the creek as far as possible. Two more companies of the Fifth commanded by Captain Charles E. Stark and Lieutenant Bernhard Meissner backed up the two wings as reserves, one company behind each flank. The Union troops had a strong position. Essig's artillery set atop a steep hill that rose up from the creek bottom masked in heavy timber. They occupied the ground a few yards east of the crossing and directly in the path of the rebel advance. The federal infantry spread along the south side of the creek about a quarter of a mile, ready at the timber's edge almost as if in ambush. The advantages of the terrain suddenly reversed. The Union guns now held the high ground while the rebels would have to fight from the bottomland.[7]

Meanwhile, the rebel Missourians wanted more than ever to complete the defeat of Sigel's army and drive the Union troops from the state. Sigel had fallen back with what the rebel generals observed to be considerable loss and surely could not withstand a concentrated attack. However, the generals were wrong. Union losses up to that point had been relatively light.[8]

The Missourians did not immediately follow up their initial gains. It was about 11:30 when the rebel army finally started its advance toward Dry Fork Creek. After advancing about a mile and a quarter and taking a considerable amount of time to reorganize, the State Guard drew up its line again for an assault on Sigel's new rear-guard position. Colonel Weightman took the lead and ordered Captain Bledsoe's Battery to engage the federals. Bledsoe planted the State guns in the creek bottom at a distance of 400 yards, and another artillery duel began. Weightman next ordered his infantry forward to attack the Union troops guarding the creek. The divisions of Slack, Clark, and Parsons joined in the attack following Weightman's lead. Soon, the entire rebel line took up the assault.[9]

Even troops idle during the first cannonade joined the fight. Taking notice of Sigel's withdrawal, Colonel Hurst brought his reserve regiment up from the rear of Weightman's brigade at double-quick time. Hurst's regiment, which had lagged behind when the battle opened, now came up and took a position in Weightman's line on the right of Colonel Grave's regiment, adding another 500 fresh troops to the rebel attack. At the same time, the men of Colonel Peyton's regiment, held back that morning with Lieutenant Colonel White for lack of arms and ammunition but chafing to get into the action, refused to remain sidelined. Sixty-three of the men scraped together enough arms and ammunition to follow White into the fight on the left side of the rebel line.[10]

A line of timber and brush ran for several miles along either side of Dry Fork Creek, giving way to open prairie beyond its edges. A segment of this skirt of woods lay between the rebels and Sigel's men. The creek ran along the center of the timberline about 30 yards back from its edge. Weightman ordered his whole brigade forward in line of battle, down the slope toward the creek. Proceeding along the road, as he came near the timber lining the bank of the creek, Weightman could see Sigel's artillery down the road through an opening in the woods. They had posted in the timber on the brow of a hill on the opposite bank of the creek about 400 yards in front of him. He could see them only through the gap in the timber. From any other vantage point, the timber masked them from view. Weightman moved Bledsoe's Battery up closer under cover of Parsons' advancing infantry and planted it in the road on the north side of the creek immediately in front of Sigel's line.[11]

Only a narrow prairie waterway separated the two armies. Between the federals and the rebels was Dry Fork Creek, a clear stream about 30 feet in width. At its normal height, Dry Fork was an especially beautiful stream of clear and pure water. The creek was up from recent rains, running at near flood stage. Thick timber and undergrowth lined both sides and extended out from the banks of the creek for a distance of about 30 yards in either direction. The steep, wooded banks and the depth of the water made it difficult to cross even at the ford. Sigel stationed his guns to command the ford completely.[12]

Sigel commenced his delaying action. The opposing batteries faced off again. The Union artillery opened a brisk cannonade on the rebel front ranks at a distance now of about 300 to 400 yards.

The Missouri artillery readied to return fire. Captain Bledsoe's artillery was on the road pointed straight through the gap in the trees. Lieutenant Colonel Thomas H. Rosser, a druggist from Westport, in Jackson County, in civilian life, took personal charge of one of Bledsoe's cannons and readied to open fire. Rosser, a veteran of the Kansas statehood dispute, came innocently from Virginia seeking to settle anew in the promised land of Kansas. Pol-

Joseph M. Kelly, 1862. A native of Ireland, Colonel Kelly commanded the First Missouri Infantry Regiment of the Sixth Division. His men took the brunt of the Union cannonade at Carthage and were the first to reach Dry Fork Creek to engage Sigel's federals. He received a wound in the hand at the Battle of Wilson's Creek and later led the famous Irish Brigade of the C.S.A. (Courtesy Maureen McGrath.)

itics drew him into the border hostilities, eventually costing the life of one of his sons who died in a confrontation with John Brown. Rosser afterward joined Sterling Price in the fight for Missouri, in command of the First Infantry Regiment, the regiment of the infamous Rock Creek blunder that accidentally killed Colonel Holloway but lately redeemed in its steady performance on the battlefield. After steadily unlimbering the gun, Rosser opened a carefully aimed fire directed down the road at the Union troops. One participant who watched Rosser meticulously aim the gun said, "He had all the calmness of a professor of entomology examining a rare addition to his collection." This took place amid a storm of cannon fire from the Union guns. Grapeshot tore up the ground around them and disabled men and horses. A shell struck a powder keg near Captain Bledsoe, exploding it and injuring him. A blast of case shot hit Private Thomas C. Young, of Lexington, and Charley Young, two brothers in Bledsoe's Battery. Another shell knocked Private Eldridge Booton to the ground.[13]

The federal cannon rained down hard on the Bledsoe Battery. Amid the hail of artillery, the rebel guns answered. At the height of the duel, Captain Bledsoe and Lieutenant Curtis

O. Wallace of the artillery and Captain F. M. McKinney of the infantry personally operated guns in place of the fallen and disabled gun crews. The previously wounded Lieutenant Wallace remained with his gun although twice wounded in the leg. Eight privates fell wounded in the federal barrage. The Union shelling killed four horses and hit another three animals. It was during this exchange of fire that Lieutenant Charles W. Higgins, one of Bledsoe's officers, fell, seriously but not fatally wounded. Shot down at the gun he was serving and badly wounded, he struggled to his feet and continued loading his piece, then collapsed exhausted beneath its muzzle. The sun bore down intensely. It was a stifling hot day. Most of the men had been on their feet since before 4 A.M., many without food and water. More than one fell exhausted and unable to continue.[14]

General Parsons immediately saw the potential danger of Sigel's move to control the field of fire and quickly ordered a rapid movement of his infantry to get possession of the timber on the rebel side of the creek. A large field extended south from the rebel line to the north edge of the timber, opposite the right wing of Sigel's position. Without any hesitation, the rebels ran into the open field, Colonel Kelly's regiment in the lead. Major Dill's battalion was close on his right with the Warsaw regiment of Colonel O'Kane to the right of Dill. Colonel Clark brought his infantry up on the extreme left. Sigel's batteries had a clear view of the field from their high position across the creek and now used every effort to break the rebel advance. For a time, Captain Essig's guns held off the advance of the rebels across the field. Essig fired rapid volleys of grape, shell, and round shot into the charging State Guard troops. It looked for a while as if they would be unable to reach the creek, but the rebel soldiers did not waver. The Missourians crossed the open field exposed to raking federal fire before coming to the corner of the woods near the Union front. They reached the south side of the field, rapidly regained their lines, vaulted the fence, and quickly deployed into the timber. They had not lost a man.[15]

Colonel Kelly's command was the first to close the pursuit. His regiment, uniquely made up of St. Louis Irish volunteers, stood out as he rapidly led them forward in pursuit of Sigel's men. His infantry had posted on the left of Henry Guibor's guns during the first cannonade and in good position to pursue the right flank of Sigel's retreating line. Kelly dispatched his men as skirmishers into the timber along Dry Fork Creek. By this time, Sigel's infantry had moved up into the timber on the south side of the creek. The Missourians advanced through the timber on the north, firing from the cover of the trees. From the woods came the sounds of Kelly's Irishmen firing away and practicing their first rebel yell as they confronted Sigel's line across the creek.[16]

The other State Guard infantry flanked around Kelly and picked their way through the brush along the creek. Lieutenant Colonel O'Kane, having rapidly crossed his infantry battalion over the field, occupied the skirt of timber next to Bledsoe's artillery. Bledsoe eased his battery into closer proximity of the Union line and opened a deadly barrage to complement the assault and steady advance of the rebel infantry. Then, in a bold move, O'Kane led his infantry battalion of 350 men, aided by units of General Clark's division, forward confronting the federals at close range. From here, his men engaged the federals through the woods and across the ford. A portion of Brown's cavalry came up, dismounted, and with the infantry exchanged a withering fire of small arms at close range with Sigel's troops, separated only by the width of the creek. With the sure aim of shotguns and rifles, they matched the federals shot for shot. Some of the Missourians tried to ford the creek and gain the other side before Essig trained his guns on the crossing and turned them back onto the open prairie.[17]

Farther up the rebel line, General Clark had rushed his four companies across the prairie to the edge of the marsh on the rebel side of the creek. There was a lull in the fighting at this location and Clark had paused to rest his men. He was sitting on his horse while several of his men perched upon the rail fence of a small wheat field to catch their breath in the sweltering sun. They wanted to get all the air they could after racing across more than a mile in pursuit of the retreating federals. They had barely caught their breath when a courier hurried up to General Clark and delivered a message from Governor Jackson. Jackson apparently had observed the action on the field and now exercised his prerogative as commander in chief of the State Guard to issue an order to General Clark. Clark rose in his stirrups, drew his sword, and said, "Boys, Governor Jackson says the Dutch are in this swamp, and he wants us to drive them out." Jackson's direct order to one of his field commanders revealed that he retained nominal command of the battle.[18]

Without forming his men into line, Clark led his division helter-skelter into the willows and wild vines. His voice rising above the noise of the attack, "Come on boys," he shouted, "and drive them out." Notwithstanding the lack of organization, the separated units of the Third Division reached the bank near the creek at about the same time. As soon as they came within range of the federal riflemen, the Germans opened fire on them, killing and wounding several men. The rebels inched forward and returned fire through the willows causing a sizable reduction in Union numbers. The two opposing forces traded shots with relentless determination to drive the other back from the creek.[19]

Up to this point, the battle had been at long range. The previous intense artillery duel that started the fight gave the raw Missouri recruits a first taste of the big guns of war until Sigel fell back to his position across Dry Fork Creek. Now they experienced, many for the first time, the deadly effect of small-arms fire. A brisk standoff ensued in some of the most severe action of the day with shotguns and game rifles against the better arms of the federals.

Amid the shouting and rapid-fire exchanges, men found their own personal moments of battle. One of General Clark's Callaway County boys rushed through the willows to the bank at the edge of the creek. Across the stream, he saw a federal in the willows on the other side at the same time the federal saw him. Each man in a hurry to shoot first missed, and then commenced the race to reload. The Callaway lad filled his charger with powder. As he poured the powder into the muzzle of his rifle, he cast a glance at the federal across the creek in time to see him biting off the end of his cartridge and ramming it into his musket. Realizing the Union soldier would load first, the rebel nervously called to one of his comrades, "Shoot that fellow before he loads."

"I can't see him, I can't see him," came the reply.

"Then give me your musket. I'll shoot him."

Kneeling to get a clear view through the willows, the Callaway soldier took deliberate aim and fired. The recoil of the musket sent him sprawling full length on the ground. Lifting himself up, he handed the piece back to its owner. "Sir," he said, "I believe you have loaded that musket every morning since you left Fulton. If the other end was any worse than mine, that federal won't bother us again."[20]

The action to the east of the creek crossing became particularly severe. Union and rebel troops were no more than 100 feet apart as they fired repeated volleys across the narrow creek. The withering rifle and musket discharges were deadly at that range. The rebels were particularly vulnerable as they pressed forward trying to cross the timber, under the close vigilance of the Union sharpshooters, to get within range of their homegrown weapons. The action east of the road was the scene of the heaviest fighting of the battle, a point severely contested with great loss, especially to the rebel side. General Clark's Third Division lost ten killed and wounded, and Parsons' Sixth Division, while comparatively light in casualties, suffered its greatest losses of the entire battle at the Dry Fork Creek charge. The officers of the State Guard led their men gallantly from the front throughout the attack. Captains Stephen F. Hale and George H. Vaughn rushed forward into the conflict at the creek. Captains Francis O. Gray and James McElwrath, and Lieutenant Peter Taylor all distinguished themselves in this brief but deadly skirmish. Lieutenant Colonel Edwin Price had his horse killed beneath him. Colonel O'Kane had his horse shot from under him. His unit lost two killed and 20 wounded, including Captain Leonidas Warren who reached the edge of the creek only to take a grapeshot through the lower leg.[21]

The loss on both sides from this sharp engagement was considerable. One story said, "Blood ran in little rivulets down the sloping banks into the waters of Dry Fork, coloring the stream for some distance." So severe was the fighting, the Missourians thereafter referred to the whole battle as the Battle of Dry Fork Creek. They were not the only ones to call it that. The map accompanying the battlefield report of Union commander Thomas W. Sweeny also referred to the battle as the Battle of Dry Fork Creek. Union documentarian Frederick Dyer in one instance called the battle the Battle of Carthage and in another instance the Battle of Dry Fork Creek; he recorded Sigel's Third Regiment engaged at Carthage but listed Salomon's Fifth Regiment in action at Dry Fork, as if they were somehow at different battles. Meanwhile, Surgeon General George W. Taylor inexplicably called it the Battle of Spring River.[22]

The heated exchange in the woods at Dry Fork Creek continued for about 30 minutes before it let up. General Clark said the two sides exchanged sharp volleys of small-arms fire for a half hour, and claimed Sigel also suffered his heaviest loss of killed and wounded in the Dry Fork standoff. Clark's observation that one piece of federal artillery had to be left on the field, however, was never substantiated.[23]

The rebels had the advantage of numbers to press the attack but were unable to cross the creek because it was running deeper than usual from the recent rains. Sigel's artillery, meanwhile, prevented them from using the ford. The rebels could not cross at that point without serious losses. It looked like the two sides stood locked in a stalemate. Thick smoke blanketed the ground, hanging low above the prairie and twisting through the heavy woods that lined the creek. The two forces faced each other eye-to-eye, each waiting for the other to blink.

The distraction of Essig's guns to the east gave Weightman an opportunity to advance his troops on the west. He directed the infantry on either wing of his brigade into the timber to the right side of the creek crossing, to pass through the woods and confront Sigel's line at close quarters as other elements of the rebel line were doing on the left. Weightman's infantry pressed forward through the woods west of the road matching what the men from General Clark's and General Parsons' divisions were already doing further east. The regiments of colonels Graves and Hurst of Weightman's brigade surged into the timber passing to the right of the rebel artillery and advanced through the woods toward the creek. Fighting across Dry Fork on the west side of the road was less deadly than on the east side. Only one federal company defended that side. They pushed the federals back and reached the edge of the stream but found the water too swift and the banks to steep to effect a crossing. They found it impassable at that point and proceeded downstream to find a suitable place to ford the fast-flowing water. At about the same time, Colonel Hughes' command, of General Slack's division, followed Hurst and Graves into the timber, aiming to bring more small-arms fire to bear on the federals. When Hughes attempted to occupy the woods skirting the Union position, deep water again prevented his troops from crossing at the most opportune location.[24]

The Union held its line for some time on Dry Fork Creek. From start to finish, Sigel maintained his position behind the creek for nearly two hours and inflicted some of the heaviest losses of the battle on the Missourians. Triumphant shouts rose from the U.S. Volunteers as the flag of the rebels fell twice. Yet the rebel line continued a relentless advance toward the Union position.

Meanwhile, the main columns of the rebel cavalry maneuvered to surround the federal army. Because of the skill of Sigel's retrograde movement, the cavalry had been unable before to gain a position behind the federal line, but the Union troops by now had backtracked across the creek. The artillery and infantry of both sides faced each other across the creek, all but ignoring the rebel cavalry. With the threat of shelling finally removed, the rebel horsemen advanced.

As the skirmish across Dry Fork Creek raged on, Colonel Rives led his cavalry across the creek well out of range of the federal guns and crossed the open prairie, swinging wide to the left of the Union wing. He circled his men around Sigel's line to a position about a mile and a half to the rear of the Union army and formed his regiment at the small creek called Buck Branch, blocking Sigel's passage back to Carthage. Colonel Brown's First Regiment Cavalry soon joined him there. While the fight continued at Dry Fork, the rebel cavalry waited, prepared to intercept a Union retreat. The Union troops and their entire supply train seemed trapped between two bodies of the State Guard. The cavalry had outflanked Sigel and stood between him and safe passage back to Carthage.[25]

21

Charge at Buck Branch

The Union line extended almost three-quarters of a mile up and down Dry Fork Creek, pushing the five federal companies along the creek beyond the breaking point. The Missourians began to gain the upper hand. Several of them tossed piles of dead timber into the creek and began to cross over in large numbers. Some of the first sporadic hand-to-hand combat took place at this point. Sigel saw the danger and stubbornly ordered his men to fall back. The Union troops pulled out of the woods away from the creek and toward their main line, all the time under added pressure from Bledsoe's Battery. The State Guard infantry vigorously pressed them on the front, pushing them steadily in the direction of the State Guard cavalry waiting in the Union rear at Buck Branch.[1]

The federals found themselves cut off from retreat to Carthage, caught between elements of the rebel army. It was a desperate situation. Sigel had no mounted cavalry to counter the rebel blockade. To engage the army behind him and to free his supply train, he would have to weaken his line to the front where the bulk of the Missouri State Guard was now pressing against his forward elements. To dislodge the rebel cavalry in his rear, about 500 infantry foot soldiers would have to go against an equal number of mounted riflemen. Sigel immediately saw the peril of his situation and ordered another retrograde movement. The real danger of the cavalry behind his lines was not great. He knew he could easily disperse them with his artillery. However, the possible loss of his baggage train was another matter. That and the effect on morale of having the Missourians behind his lines prompted his decision to abandon the battlefield.[2]

Sigel fully realized by now the untenable position he had taken in his headlong pursuit of the Missouri army. Overpowered by the State Guard numbers to the front and now at his flanks, and the rebel cavalry threatening the rear, the federals finally gave way and under cover of artillery suddenly began another withdrawal. At about half past noon, Sigel abandoned his position on Dry Fork Creek and turned attention to the protection of his supply train. He quickly disengaged the remainder of his force, caught up with the main body, and together they rejoined their wagons and began a speedy withdrawal south. State Guard Surgeon General Taylor clocked the time of the battle from the cannonade to the retreat from Dry Fork Creek at about two and one-half hours, beginning at ten minutes to ten o'clock until 12:30 P.M. He said the Union retreat from Dry Fork Creek was a hasty one, not as orderly as the first. "A rider mounted each horse attached to a gun carriage or baggage wagon. Whip in hand, the riders put the horses into a gallop and raced across the prairie." Numerous stories circulated about the fight at Dry Fork Creek, mostly untrue. Unionist claims that Sigel's troops picked up a wagonload of weapons after the fight and took them to Springfield never happened. Sigel was in steady retreat and never stopped to pick up anything. Secessionist tales that Sigel abandoned his wounded on the battlefield and lost several of his supply wagons were equally untrue. A State Guard rumor surfaced that Sigel had abandoned his companies at Dry Fork Creek and was not present at the time of the fight. An eyewitness on the Guard side wrote a book about the fight for Missouri many years later and claimed that Sigel left the detachment at Dry Fork and retreated with the main body of his troops toward Buck Branch. Sigel felt a need to correct the author and wrote to him in 1886 to say that he, Sigel, had personally remained in command of Essig's Battery and the force at Dry Fork Creek up to the end of the fight. Only then did he join the troops that had taken a position with the train between Dry Fork Creek and Buck Branch.[3]

After retreating about a mile from Dry Fork Creek, Union scouts brought word that the State Guard cavalry had indeed succeeded finally in circling around the federal line and now occupied the ford at Buck Branch in force, blocking the Union retreat south and preventing Sigel from escaping. The Union army appeared trapped between the two Missouri forces: the State Guard cavalry threatened ahead, while the rebel infantry advanced on the Union rear.

When the retreating army came to within a little more than a half mile of Buck Branch, Sigel deployed his forces around the supply train to protect the wagons from all sides. He drew the wagons into a tight box of eight rows with four wagons to a row. The formation was the classic European-style infantry troop formation popular in 19th-century European wars but rarely used on American Civil War battlefields. He positioned artillery alongside the train to shield it from possible attack by the rebel cavalry, placing Essig's cannon on either side, two guns on the left, and two on the right. Colonel Salomon and Lieutenant Colonel Wolff brought up their battalions in column to support the artillery. Wilkins' Battery of Backhoff's artillery formed a rear guard supported by two companies of infantry under the command of Lieutenant Theodore Schrickel. Their mission was to fight a delaying action against the main rebel force coming up from Dry Fork Creek, should the rebels try to keep pressure on the retiring U.S. volunteers.[4]

When Sigel abandoned his position at Dry Fork Creek and started back in the direction of Carthage, it allowed the entire army of the State Guard to cross over unimpeded to the south side of the creek and take up the chase in pursuit of the federals. The attention of generals Clark and Parsons had been completely on the left side of the Missouri line, and they had no idea what had transpired with the elements of the Guard on the right. Around 1:30, General Parsons rode back up the hill on the north side of the creek to a high point of ground to get a view of the battlefield. It was from here that he discovered that the entire Union force was in general retreat. He ordered his already fatigued division to pursue them.[5]

Out ahead, Sigel marched his column en masse toward the rebels at Buck Branch. Three companies of Lieutenant Colonel Hassendeubel's battalion swung around the baggage train and formed a column to the front. The remainder of the Union army trailed behind. It was an unorthodox order of march in which the supply train preceded the army. The retreating federals approached the rebel blockade to within a half mile. The only place to cross the Union supply wagons was at the Buck Branch ford. The marshy ground on either side of the crossing was impossible to traverse, meaning the wagons would have to cross the ford single file, slowing the Union retreat with the State Guard army in pursuit.[6]

Colonel Rives' First Cavalry and Colonel Brown's First Missouri Mounted stood directly in the path of the Union column. They had dismounted and deployed along the south bank of Buck Branch behind the stream in front of the approaching federals. There is some question as to whether the rebel troops formed in front of Buck Branch or behind it. Sigel claimed they were behind the branch. However, he may have used a different orientation because he also claimed that the blocking rebel force came from the extreme right of the rebel line when in fact they had come from the extreme left.[7]

Colonel Rives watched the Union column approach. He realized his dismounted cavalry was no match for Sigel's artillery and sent word north by courier for reinforcements.

The rebel infantry had taken its time crossing Dry Fork Creek and could not offer any immediate support for Rives and his cavalry. Momentarily satisfied that the federal troops were dislodged again, the Missourians had been in no hurry to catch them and content to let Sigel fall back in an orderly retrograde movement to Buck Branch about two miles distant, not knowing that the cavalry had gained a position behind him. Weightman's brigade had only now rejoined the rebel line. Hurst and Graves, forced to find a ford further downstream, had crossed over Dry Fork Creek at a place well beyond the Union flank. By the time they came back upon the federal position, Sigel had already abandoned the fight and for the third time was retreating across the prairie. General Rains' cavalry appeared to be completely out of the picture somewhere to the west.[8]

It was past two o'clock in the afternoon, and the men in Colonel Weightman's brigade, with the exception of Graves' command, had been on their feet since 4 A.M., Colonel Hurst's regiment operating without any breakfast. Ignoring General Parsons' orders to pursue the federals, Weightman decided to give his men a rest and camp on the ground of the brigade's victory, the ground that Sigel had recently occupied. No sooner had encampment procedures begun, when word came that Colonel Rives of General Slack's command had led his cavalry into an engagement with the retiring Union troops at Buck Branch and needed help. Colonel Hughes' regiment, also of Slack's command, which had likewise returned from crossing Dry Fork Creek downstream, immediately took up the pursuit. Weightman called out his weary brigade once again and took up the chase, too.[9]

The Missourians might easily have captured the entire federal army, but they continued to suffer badly from disorganization, and lacked experience and practice in averting some of the more difficult terrain that impaired troop maneuvers. The rolling terrain, crisscrossed with streams that were in places impassable, proved to be unsuitable to horse soldiers. General Rains' cavalry, for instance, posted on the far right flank of the rebel line, never got into the chase at all. This proved particularly problematic because Rains, potentially the overall field commander, could not direct the Missourians in battle from his extreme flank position, and consequently field command was practically nonexistent. From the end of the initial artillery cannonade on, General Rains kept his cavalry out of the fight for reasons perhaps both real and imagined. He had a reputation for wanting to shield his men from danger. His losses up to this time were consequently relatively small. As the Union guns began to let up from the initial duel, the Rains cavalry had made its way through the cornfield on the right with a view to flanking Sigel's left flank just as the large body of cavalry from the other divisions had threatened Sigel's right from the rebel left. They had waited by the cornfield for the order to attack, but no order had been forthcoming. They now decided to advance toward Dry Fork Creek to try to come up behind the federal line. While

Franz Hassendeubel, ca. 1861. Lieutenant Colonel Hassendeubel served as Colonel Franz Sigel's second in command at the Battle of Carthage. The St. Louis city engineer turned down a commission in the Missouri State Guard from General Sterling Price, opting instead to fight with Union forces. (Roger D. Hunt Collection, U.S. Army Military History Institute.)

they picked their way through the timber, Sigel began his series of retreats. Finding it too late to get between the federal troops and Dry Fork Creek, Rains' men went downstream to locate suitable crossings over the creek. This proved to be a very time-consuming maneuver. They followed the old road that led past the Widow Shoemaker's, and, having eventually crossed over Dry Fork Creek to the south side, they consequently came out of the timber on to the prairie a good distance west of the battlefield. Here they halted again to organize and await further instructions from General Rains. The rebel cavalry had been there waiting only a short while when Captain Doak of Colonel Peyton's command rejoined the regiment, his mission to assist Captain Shelby apparently completed. Nothing else happened. Sigel, meanwhile, had retreated across the prairie toward Buck Branch.[10]

The Rains column, after waiting for some time, cautiously moved forward, keeping an eye on Sigel's troops retreating in the distance and giving the other missing components of the brigade time to catch up. Colonel Boughan took his command down Dry Fork Creek and crossed over at the first crossing he could find. South of the creek, he came out on the prairie considerably west of the rest of the cavalry brigade. He caught up with them, but by this time, Sigel was gone. Because of a series of tactical miscues, the rebel cavalry of the Eighth Division was never a serious threat to the Union line. After the dust-up in crossing the cornfield, they saw little action. Boughan's Vernon County Battalion, for instance, was never close enough again during the battle to give or receive a shot from the federals. A rumor circulated that after crossing the creek some of Rains' cavalry came on a thick patch of blackberries and stopped to pick their lunch. The berries were plentiful in early July in that region with large patches everywhere around the prairie. The general absence of Rains and his men from the battle gained the unfortunate designation of his command thereafter as the Blackberry Cavalry. It turned out to be a mean-spirited prank that probably traced back to the bickering at Murray Corners about who should be the ranking commander, Rains or Parsons. Captain William McCown who served as captain of Company H, Second Regiment Cavalry, in Rains' division, said it came from the men in General Parsons' division. McCown who was part of the Blackberry Cavalry considered it a base slander on the cavalry.[11]

Sigel's wagon train approached the rebel cavalry blockade at Buck Branch. The State Guard had dismounted and deployed in line of battle. Newspapers later printed a fanciful account of the clash that followed, even though there were no reporters present. They said Major Backhoff sent two artillery pieces on the left of the wagons in an oblique movement to the left, making a similar movement to the right with the guns on the right of the train. Sigel's battalions followed the maneuvers left and right as if to pass the extreme flanks of the rebel blockade and go around it. The rebels closed up their flanks and tightened their battle line. When the Union artillery was within range of the rebel cavalry, the Backhoff batteries executed a transverse oblique and opened a crossfire on the waiting Missourians. The phantom reporters gave a similar report of how the artillery batteries on each side of the wagon train had leapfrogged across the prairie, one firing at the trailing rebels, and then retreating while the other fired, to take a new position from which to cover the federal withdrawal. What actually happened during the retreat and at Buck Branch was much less colorful. There was no running battle across the prairie. The rear-guard guns occasionally fired a round in the direction of the pursuing rebels, but Weightman's brigade was still at least a mile behind Sigel when the commotion at Buck Branch broke out. The Eastern press kept trying to manufacture a romantic war out of a shameful internal conflict between the citizens of a fractured state.[12]

The frontal assault on the rebel cavalry at Buck Branch was much more straightforward. Lieutenant Edward Scheutzenbach's two guns from Captain Essig's battery, which had been crucial to the defense at Dry Fork Creek, opened the assault head-on. Although Essig received no special mention in Sigel's after-action report, he came away nevertheless as the hero of the battle. The performance of his battery throughout the action, especially at Dry Fork Creek where he held off the advance of the State Guard, and now at Buck Branch, made it possible for the Union army to withdraw to positions of safety and ultimately to escape capture by the rebel Missourians.[13]

At the same time Essig's guns prepared to open fire on the rebel blockade at Buck Branch, Lieutenant Colonel Hassendeubel's three companies of the First Battalion Third Regiment spun into action and deployed in line between the Union supply wagons and the dismounted rebel cavalry. His advance guard was the first to encounter the rebel cavalry at Buck Branch. After leaving Dry Fork Creek, his men had marched in columns of companies back across the prairie from whence they had come earlier in the day, and stopped now about 1,000 yards from where the rebel cavalry had drawn up. Lieutenant Sebastian Engert, one of Hassendeubel's staff officers, saw the Missourians first through the tall prairie grass — some of it as high as a man's head — and pointed them out to his commander. The heads of the dismounted riders were just visible above the banks of the stream. As the Union artillery opened up on the rebels, Hassendeubel maneuvered his three infantry companies to advance in line, ordinarily a tactical blunder when deploying foot soldiers against cavalry. He ordered his battalion to attack. Otto Lademann, first sergeant of Hassendeubel's Company E, told how this critical moment in the battle unfolded. Colonel Sigel came galloping up on his horse and expressed incredulity at the audacity of Hassendeubel's deployment of his unit. "What are you doing there, Colonel Hassendeubel?" asked Sigel.

Hassendeubel replied, "I am deploying my battalion." As if to say, what do you think I am doing?

"For God's sake, stay in column," warned Sigel. "Don't advance in line. They are cavalry and they will cut you to pieces."

Hassendeubel knew what he was doing. He had served under General Sterling Price in the U.S. Volunteers in the Mexican War and had led similar bayonet charges of his unit to help quell the Taos uprising. He was a veteran army officer. Here on the high prairie of southwest Missouri, the safety of the Union army in the opening battle of the Civil War in the West now fell squarely on his shoulders. "Ah! Nonsense, Colonel Sigel, those fellows haven't got any sabers," he said.

With that, he commanded, "Forward! Double quick! March!"[14]

The storied lieutenant colonel — Sigel's second-in-command — was something of a military legend. The 44-year-old Hassendeubel was German-American, one of the thousands of German descent who passionately supported the Union, and who the Missourians derisively dubbed the Union Dutch. Of average height and athletic build, Hassendeubel's healthy and fit appearance gave him a ready if not imposing military presence. Prominent cheekbones framed a slightly oversized nose cushioned by a full, wide moustache and whiskers. He wore his dark hair short and combed back to reveal a high forehead and mildly receding hairline. His thin wire spectacles gave a hint of his considerable intellectual merits. He possessed a good sense of humor and often provoked laughter through some gesture or timely witticism. To everyone who knew him, he appeared unassuming in manner and speech, never speaking of himself or his considerable accomplishments. Born on the Rhine River and educated in the classics, mathematics, and civil engineering, Hassendeubel immigrated to America when he was 27 and settled in St. Louis. He became city engineer of St. Louis and was instrumental in designing and overseeing the building of a series of forts around the perimeter of the city. When tensions began to grow between the rebel Minute Men and the Home Guard, he turned his duties as city engineer over to his brother and volunteered for Sigel's Third Regiment of Missouri Volunteers. Hassendeubel was an expert rider and an able military tactician, quick to seize an opportunity to act when it presented itself. Because of his unassailable character and notable reputation in the Mexican War, he had the respect of his men who trusted and followed him enthusiastically.[15]

His infantry charged forward at double-quick time. The German volunteers responded with a loud cheer and rushed headlong through the tall prairie grass straight for the rebels in what seasoned military men later described as a novel spectacle and one contrary to the settled rules of warfare at the time. The rebel cavalry was about 900 yards away when the Hassendeubel assault began. The federals had closed to within 400 yards when a few men stopped to catch their breath. Out of nervousness or sheer panic, someone fired his musket. Thinking the engagement was on at this point, the whole battalion fired off a volley, although at such a range as to do very little damage to the opposing rebels. This was the first small-arms volley seen by either side. Although accidentally discharged, it produced the effect of what a real battle could sound like with more than 200 muskets all pointed in the same direction and fired simultaneously. Neither side had ever heard anything like it. Within seconds the whole prairie in front where the rebel cavalry had been was alive with fugitive, mounted men scurrying away in the direction they had come as fast as their horses could carry them and circling back to rejoin their line. Colonel Rives went west to link up with Rains, Colonel Brown fled east. A single volley routed the rebel cavalry completely, amid thunderous cheers from the little Union army. A determined charge of Union infantry had dispersed the waiting Missourians. The only casualty in the whole confrontation was one unfortunate rebel captain captured when his horse was shot from under him by one of Sigel's artillery discharges.[16]

Arriving at Buck Branch, Sigel briefly took up yet another defense to provide cover for the supply train while its 32 wagons crossed over the Buck Branch ford. He was now about a mile and a half back of his position at Dry Fork Creek.

The Union wagons crossed the creek without incident. By the time the pursuing rebel infantry got to Buck Branch, the Union troops had already gone. The federals crossed the prairie headed in the direction of Carthage. Sigel again pulled his batteries back to protect the rear of his column. Next, he would have to cover his retreat while getting his army across the ford at Spring River. Sigel ordered another retrograde movement, this time retreating about five miles across the prairie to the heights north of Spring River, scattering a few rebel cavalry in the process. The Union wagons raced across the level prairie at a rapid rate, the horses in a gallop until they reached the hills of Spring River about a mile from Carthage. He crossed the open prairie unmolested by the State Guard who followed at a respectful distance.[17]

Meanwhile back at Dry Fork Creek, General Clark's division had found it impossible to cross the creek because of the depth of the water and the steep embankment. After the outnumbered Union sharpshooters began to fall back and the Union artillery was finally no longer a threat, some of Clark's division went down the creek to the rock ford and crossed over where Sigel's men had crossed. Other parts of his division went upstream looking for another place to cross. By the time they took a half-mile detour up the creek and found a crossing, Sigel's troops had engaged the rebels at Buck Branch and broken through. They could hear Sigel's cannon discharges but were still a mile away and too far to join the skirmish. Out of the fight for the time being, they hurried forward to try to catch the federals before they reached Carthage. General Clark's division was never again together after the Dry Fork standoff. They all went haphazardly across the prairie in pursuit of Sigel's army. "There was no more forming of lines," Private Bell remembered, "but every man for himself."[18]

Meanwhile, the divisions of Slack and Parsons had crossed the creek and were somewhere out on the prairie. To the west, the Eighth Division under General Rains and his officers — Peyton, McCown, and Boughan — had crossed Dry Fork Creek downstream and left the timber line a couple of miles west of the initial battle scene. Rains was planning to cross the prairie to the timber on Spring River, expecting to gain a position in the rear of the retreating Union column. After covering a few miles on Colonel Sigel's trail, General Rains halted his column while he rode over to confer with the commanders on the left side of the rebel line. He left instructions for no one to move until he returned. Colonel Peyton, apparently tired of Rains' stop-and-go tactics, marched his column forward anyway without Rains, with the intent of catching Sigel before he could get to Carthage. Rains later concurred in Peyton's movement. Nevertheless, when Rains returned from his intended meeting with the other line commanders, his command was gone. He caught up with it shortly at Buck Branch. They were once more too late; Sigel was long gone. Taking charge again, Rains marched the cavalry rapidly forward past Buck Branch and across the prairie toward Spring River. Rains later tried to cover the slow performance of his cavalry saying, "Sigel retreated so rapidly that my plans to surround him were defeated."[19]

It was past three o'clock, and Sigel had been in retreat at least since half past noon. The success of his withdrawal was not because of any daring speed on his part but instead resulted from a deliberate and skillful use of his artillery in a series of carefully executed rear-guard actions that allowed his troops to retreat methodically toward Carthage. That and the higgledy-piggledy actions of the State Guard commanders greatly enhanced the appearance of Sigel's battlefield performance.

22

Spring River Crossing

The federal troops and their supply train crossed Buck Branch and retreated without serious interruption toward Carthage. The rebel cavalry had regrouped by now and entered the pursuit of the retreating Union army. Sporadic light skirmishes occurred across the prairie; the federals withdrawing, and the rebels pursuing at a distance. Sigel withdrew his men as fast as the Missourians would let him, stopping periodically to send a shot or two in their direction. The afternoon sun blazed down on the unsheltered combatants. Men on both sides were exhausted. The state troops stopped to rest a few minutes, and then took up the chase again.

After marching some two and three-quarter miles beyond Buck Branch, Sigel halted his men about two miles north of Spring River and used the openness of the prairie to reorganize his army. There was a house at this location, and Sigel feigned a line of battle around it to stall the advancing rebels while he prepared for a full retreat through the dells of Spring River in the direction of Carthage.[1]

The Union troops and baggage train reached the heights north of Carthage relatively unimpeded. Sigel next took up a protective position on the high ground northwest of Carthage before Spring River. He drew up his artillery while the remaining infantry and wagons passed on to the river crossing. He posted a defensive line on top of a steep hill to protect the crossing of the river and cover the army's entry into Carthage. The hilltop defense became known in local folklore as the Ornduff Hill stand; however, the property did not come into the Ornduff family until 1882, long after the time of the battle. Local citizens know the site today as Quarry Hill, but in 1861 it was simply the big hill on the Lamar road. The hill was about a half mile north of the Spring River ford where the Union army had crossed that morning. This gravel-lined ford, called Walton Ford, made it easier for the federal wagons to cross than Walker Ford located further downstream. (The name of Walker Ford later changed to Loveless Ford.) The federal train comprised 32 wagons loaded with the ammunition and materials of war needed on the Union expedition; it would take time for them to cross the river. Sigel had managed to keep the wagons out of rebel hands so far.

The federal hilltop defense had a commanding view of the pursuing rebels spread out across the prairie. The elevated ground ran directly across the road, extending out on both sides into a high plateau. To the north was the open prairie; to the south flowed Spring River, running west and threading its way though bands of timber that reached out a short distance from the stream's edge. The path of the road went down the hill and ran southeast before angling east about a mile into Carthage. The river took a wide bend to the north at this place, putting the ford crossings well within range of Sigel's hilltop position. He deployed all eight of his artillery guns on this hill, aimed to cover Walker Ford and the rear of his column as it approached the Spring River ford. Walker Ford crossed about a mile downriver west of where Sigel planted his guns. He thought the State Guard cavalry probably would attempt a flanking crossing there and somewhere upstream to close around him before he could reach Carthage. Sure enough, within an hour part of the rebel cavalry swung over toward Walker Ford. Another body of cavalry eased up further in the distance to the east, but most of the rebel cavalry concentrated heavily to the west.

Having failed to beat Colonel Sigel to the timber line on the north side of Spring River and get behind him, General Rains and his cavalry now had to cross the river to stop the Union retreat. However, by the time they arrived, Sigel's guns had the crossings targeted. The Union artillery opened fire. Sigel's cannon leveled a barrage on them and drove them back. The rebel cavalry tried again to gain the crossing. A second barrage hit Colonel McCown's battalion as his men

The Cockrell Brothers, ca. 1864. Native-born Missourians, the Cockrell brothers of Johnson County led units of the Missouri State Guard Eighth Division. Lieutenant Jeremiah Vardaman Cockrell *(right)* was with Colonel James McCown's cavalry; Captain Francis Marion Cockrell *(left)* fought with Colonel Edgar V. Hurst's regiment, in Weightman's brigade. (F. M. Cockrell: Monroe Cockrell Photo Collection, State Historical Society of Missouri; J. V. Cockrell: WICR 31999 in the collection of Wilson's Creek National Battlefield. Image courtesy National Park Service.)

approached Walker Ford. A shot from one of the cannons burst in their midst, hitting Private John Byler in the left leg, toppling him from his wounded horse and spilling him down the river bank. A couple of men rushed forward, plucked young Byler from the water, and carried him in a blanket up the hill to the Walker house. Thirteen shell fragments struck him but he survived to return to his family in Knob Knoster. As the Walkers cared for Byler, Mrs. Walker anxiously awaited news of her own son in the battle. Only the year before, her husband had died on the steps of this very house, shot down by unknown assailants. It had been such a peaceful house before, one they had built together beside the river just three years ago. It seemed her life knew nothing but violence lately.[2]

The artillery barrage that struck Private Byler had unsettling personal consequences for Colonel McCown. Byler soldiered in the company commanded by Colonel McCown's son, Captain William H. McCown. The shell that struck Byler could as easily have brought down his son. It all added to the worries of the elder McCown. The previous February authorities had linked the young McCown to an election-day separatist killing in Warrensburg. Both McCowns barely escaped a mob that threatened to hang them. Unless the secessionists succeeded in this conflict, they could never return to Johnson County. William H. McCown went on to attain the rank of colonel in the Confederate army and never did go back to Johnson County; after the war, he became a resident of Carthage. His father did return home but died in 1867.[3]

The Union guns continued to shell the ford, denying the State Guard all access to the crossing. The heavy artillery stalled the rebel advance and repeatedly drove the cavalry back from Walker Ford. Sigel had positioned his guns perfectly. Here on the bluffs northwest of Carthage, the German colonel once again demonstrated his tactical genius in fighting a holding action while his army withdrew across the river.

It was at this point that General Rains' cavalry broke off contact again. Colonel McCown followed Spring River downstream, traveling some distance away from the engagement in order to find a suitable safe crossing. Rains and the remainder of his force also looked for a crossing to take downriver. They planned to circle around to the south and come upon Carthage from the rear.

The crossing of the Union supply wagons took a while. Rebel sharpshooters kept pace with the retreating federals, stationing themselves in small numbers along the wayside. The sharp crack of small-arms fire told of further losses to the uncovered Union soldiers as they worked their way over the rolling terrain and patchy woods the final mile into Carthage. The guerrilla-style attacks took a toll but the federal muskets kept the rebels at bay, and the main body of the State Guard was unable to harass the Union column because of Sigel's deployment of his artillery. With his wagon train safely across the river, Sigel disengaged from his rear-guard position on the hill and continued his withdrawal. He formed a new line on the south side of the river. At a point just west of the Spring River ford, he stationed part of his artillery and a detachment of infantry on the south bank to cover the remaining retreating troops. This deployment of force followed the same tactical pattern Sigel used all day, that of using a stepwise retrograde maneuver, placing defensive positions behind his main army to cover its progressive withdrawal. He simultaneously sent Lieutenant Colonel Wolff with two companies of infantry and a section of artillery under Lieutenant Schaefer to pass Carthage and occupy the high ground east of town above James Spring on the State road, near where the Union army had camped the night before. He ordered Captain Cramer to take two additional guns and the two infantry companies of captains Zeis and Indest — the latter having finally rendezvoused with the retreating federals — forward and post them to guard the western city limits, thus forming a corridor through which the Union army could withdraw. Once all the wagons were across Spring River, Sigel sent them on into Carthage. The federal supply train stretched out from Spring River halfway to Carthage. After the wagons cleared, Sigel abandoned his south-shore river defense, and accompanied the rest of his troops into town.[4]

James Hickey had ridden up from his farm at Fidelity out of curiosity and came on the Carthage square about the time the federals got there. He saw a deserted public square except for about 25 women gathered at the northeast corner engaged in animated conversation. There were no men anywhere. No sooner had he reached the center of town than he saw federal soldiers coming out of the timber to the northwest and moving toward the courthouse. Hickey swore he saw hand-to-hand fighting at the edge of town as local secessionist sympathizers apparently put up a feeble defense of the town. He stayed long enough to see some of the wounded federal soldiers from the day's fighting brought into the courthouse. Hickey, pro–South himself, quickly concluded that this was no place for him, and he rode toward home as fast as his horse would gallop.[5]

Sigel arrived at the courthouse in the town square around dusk, between 6:00 and 7:00 P.M. The fight had now been going on for ten hours. The courthouse was a two-story brick affair with four chimneys and too many windows on all sides; more of an architectural curiosity, Sigel thought at the time, than an imposing county seat of government. A curious cage-like design sat high atop the pitched mansard roof. Sigel bypassed the courthouse and stopped in front of the Norris Hood home, intending to set up a temporary headquarters there while turning the courthouse into a hospital for Union casualties. The Hood sisters walked across the street to help attend to the wounded. A few other women joined them to serve as nurses.[6]

Once inside the city limits of Carthage, Sigel took steps to calm the residents. They had heard the fighting north of town all day long. Now the Union army occupied the center of town, and the rebel Missourians were apparently close behind them. The citizens feared for their safety. Sigel and Quartermaster Richardson spoke calmly with Hood who worried that Sigel's troops risked capture. "There is no danger," Sigel assured him. Fourteen-year-old Thomas C. Hood stood by his father's side and heard Sigel repeat in a relaxed tone, "There is no danger."[7]

It was late afternoon, and Sigel felt safe within the city and tried to convince the residents that the danger had passed. The Union rear guard took possession of the town. Sigel ordered the remainder of his troops to get some much-needed rest. Footsore and dog tired, they had marched more than 18 miles, been in action since nine o'clock in the morning, suffered from intense heat, and almost all with nothing to eat or drink. This, after a 22-mile forced march the day before from Neosho, made for a very exhausted army. Some of the Union soldiers rested, perhaps thinking that the rebels had abandoned their pursuit. Some took time to draw water and drink refreshingly from the wells. James Whitehead and Stephen Crum, who had walked in from their farms on Center Creek to see what was happening, watched the troops crowd into the square and carried water from the town well to the worn-out men. One of them offered a drink to Sigel who gratefully accepted it. A few of the locals gathered around to hear an account of what had happened, only to be told by the federals that they had whipped the State Guard and killed anywhere from 200 to 500 of them.[8]

Sigel expected the rebels to break off the engagement. Nevertheless, he placed precautionary defenses around Carthage to discourage possible attacks. Lieutenant Colonel Wolff's detachment and the two guns of Lieutenant Schaefer bore upon the east approach to the square, while the companies of Indest and Zeis guarded the west side of town. The rear guard, which at this point amounted to only a few companies, posted around the courthouse square. The remainder of the troops in the main force fell back into the hollow near James Spring that they had left that morning. After a day of running battle, they welcomed the return to this idyllic place. A large spring flowed from underneath a high bluff of limestone rock, creating a stream of clear, pure water that coursed northward through several acres of well-shaded prairie ground before emptying into Spring River. For all its inviting beauty, however, Sigel chose not to try to defend it. The Union infantry crossed the spring branch and marched over the hill, halting in the road south of a house. Sigel intended to give the men some much-needed rest, and by posting his infantry behind the spring, he was in a position to meet any flanking movement that the rebels might send from the river crossings north of town. He placed the remaining pieces of his artillery on the high ground southwest of the spring. The precise placement of Sigel's guns is unclear. Some said that he placed two guns west of the square and the remaining six southeast of Carthage. Others related that he sent two guns to guard the west side of town and two guns to occupy the eastern heights on the Sarcoxie road southeast of Carthage. This presumes that he kept four pieces with him, which he later used on the heights behind Carthage to protect the Union retreat. There were two separate defenses at Carthage yet to come, one on the heights about a mile from town, and a second at the entrance of the Sarcoxie road at the woods two and one-half miles southeast of Carthage.[9]

Remnants of the Missouri State Guard spread across the prairie, all the way to Dry Fork Creek. Many soldiers gave up the pursuit along the way and stood idly along the route, exhausted and wanting no more of the fight. Private Henry Cheavens, who had stayed with the mortally wounded Captain Stone, came upon many soldiers sitting on the prairie, in their minds convinced that caution was the better part of bravery. Private Cheavens had remained with Captain Stone until he died, and then washed the body and laid him out before leaving around three o'clock to catch up with his unit. He found many members of his own company scattered along the road. He rallied a few of them to try to find the rest of their outfit and rejoin Colonel Rives, who by then had fled Buck Branch and circled wide to the west in an attempt to get behind Sigel's troops before they could cross Spring River into Carthage. The prairie between Dry Fork Creek and Buck Branch widened out to about three miles. All over, pockets of the State Guard milled around in various states of action, some attempting to reorganize, others advancing individually or in small bands. At several places along the road, the wounded came under the protection of whole squads of soldiers who exhibited no signs of wanting to renew the battle. Private Cheavens informed them that the ambulances were not far behind and would soon be there.[10]

Meanwhile, most of Brigadier General Clark's command broke off the chase entirely and did not engage the federals anymore after the standoff at Dry Fork Creek. A handful continued on but without Clark. General Clark had entered the battle with only the bare nucleus of a command, able to field fragments of but four or five companies. Easily the smallest of the four State Guard divisions, his troops were from the Third District of north Missouri, which lay above the Missouri River. The only recruits he had with him were those able to cross into lower Missouri before General Lyon's occupation of Boonville and his subsequent control of the river. Up until the time of the battle, there was the impression that John Bullock Clark, Sr., had entered into the secessionist movement reluctantly, that he would have rather stayed quietly at home to enjoy the pleasures of old age. Many looked upon him as just another political officer and placed a rather low estimate on his military abilities. All that changed when he led his small division across the field into the concentrated fire of the federal guns at Dry Fork Creek. Clark's assault on the Union forces greatly changed everyone's perception of this United States Congressman. The men at once saw in him a fearless commander. This old man of high national prominence suddenly became the pride of the men who followed him. When the assault was over, stories quickly circulated recounting the evidence of his daring. A Minié ball had cut a groove through his hat; bullet holes marked his clothing in several places; and his horse had fallen, shot dead from beneath him. No one could remember afterward another officer making such a narrow escape. The battle ended for General Clark at Dry Fork Creek. He would leave to others the chase of Sigel and the Union army back across the prairie.[11]

Brigadier General Parsons, still more than two miles from Spring River, advanced his infantry and two pieces of artillery with the objective of renewing the battle with the federals. However, Sigel did not intend to meet the Missourians on the open prairie. By the time Parsons' troops came up, Sigel had completed the withdrawal of his men across Spring River and taken up a position inside Carthage. The attempts by the cavalry to intercept Sigel at the Spring River crossing had fallen short again because of the heavy fire from the Union guns.

The rebel cavalry passed temporarily out of the picture while the commanders searched up and down the river for suitable places to cross out of range of the Union guns. Colonel Brown had taken his cavalry on a wide circle to the east, out of sight of the Union army, after the dust-up at Buck Branch and was approaching Spring River from that direction. Joshua Kendrick and several men were in a field about two miles northeast of Carthage harvesting grain when they heard the commotion down on Spring River. The farmer's son, Thomas J. Kendrick, taking a summer break from teaching school, rode toward the river to see what was going on. He later said, "I saw about a million men riding toward me." These were the Missourians converging on Carthage. He could see large numbers of riders across the prairie; some had gathered around the Kendrick house, situated about a mile north of Spring River. Built by the slaves of Senate Rankin, a wealthy Jasper County farmer, the Kendrick house stood out on the prairie as a symbol of Rankin's success. William Kendrick, of Newton County, had just bought the house from Rankin in 1860, and the Kendrick family had barely moved in when hostilities erupted across the state. The Kendricks abandoned it and went back to Neosho until the war ended. Both rebel and Union forces eventually occupied it; however, on this day, the Missourians turned it into a rebel hospital.[12]

By late afternoon, many in the State Guard army had given up the chase. The more relentless ones, however, intent on catching Sigel and his federal invaders, descended on Spring River seemingly from all directions. Their numbers spread for miles along the river looking for places to cross over it and get at the Union army.

All soon knew the fight was not over.

23

Melee in Carthage

The action of the Missouri State Guard continued to be a tale of disorganization. The Missouri army behaved more like a mob of several large gangs than a coordinated force of disciplined military troops. One fellow said, "The different commanders apparently did whatever seemed best to them at the time." The one thing each band had in common, though, was a desire to catch the Union army in Carthage and either destroy it or prevent its escape. With the threat of the federal artillery now gone at the Spring River crossing, more and more of the State Guard pressed forward toward the river. The Missourians moved their commands forward cautiously, not to repeat the experience at Dry Fork Creek. The relentless rebel army slowly advanced its center. Once again, however, the State Guard troops were too slow to pursue the retreating federals. It was after six o'clock when the first elements began to ford the river. Sigel was already in Carthage by that time. Nevertheless, the rebel infantry and artillery were not far behind as they crossed the river and made their way toward town.[1]

The first units of the rebel infantry to cross Spring River were those of Colonel Weightman. He had earlier rushed his regiment forward in an attempt to reinforce Colonel Rives at the Buck Branch blockade but arrived too late to help Rives before Hassendeubel's charge scattered the rebel cavalry. Weightman's weary brigade had promptly responded to Rives' call for help, but by the time they arrived, Sigel had broken through Rives' cavalry and was gone again. With the infantry of Brigadier General Slack close behind, Weightman elected to take his brigade forward into Carthage. His infantry and artillery went across the main ford where Sigel's army earlier had crossed. The rebel infantry picked its way through the timber on the south shore of the river and began to emerge into the open prairie northwest of Carthage. As the Missourians were traversing the woods and struggling to reform their ranks on the south bank, the federal guns opened up on them again. These were the guns concealed by Sigel on the west side of town to stall the advance of the rebels while the remainder of his army retreated. The federal guns poured grape and canister into the exposed ranks of the Missouri men and drove them back into the woods. Weightman hurried his artillery into position south of the river to answer the federal guns. Bledsoe's Battery wheeled into place below the ford on a level piece of ground west of the road, about where Sigel's guns had been earlier. The rebel cannon unlimbered and opened a barrage directly on

150

Carthage, intending to cover the crossing of the State Guard infantry but taking a heavy toll on the town itself. Private H. B. Kramer, a Union gunner out of Captain Wilkin's battery, arriving on the square soon after Sigel did, ran into Dale's store on the east side to buy a plug of tobacco. He no sooner passed through the door than one of Bledsoe's cannon balls hit the building. Kramer left without his tobacco and dashed out to catch up with his section. Another shot hit the courthouse, tearing up the roof and shattering the windows. A shell arched over the town to the southeast corner and struck the bell tower of the Female Academy, sending the sound resonating across the grounds. Someone found the bell years later beneath the rubble when clearing the ruins of the old academy building. The bell passed down through generations as one of the surviving relics of the day that Carthage first felt the fury of the Civil War. No one was in the academy at the time. The students had gone home and now huddled with their families in cellars beneath their houses.[2]

Surprisingly only a few buildings caught the impact of Bledsoe's guns as he rained shells down on the federal rear guard. Most of the citizens remained in town, hunkering down and taking shelter wherever they could. Remarkably, no one died and there were apparently no serious injuries, although there were narrow escapes. The house of David S. and Mary Holman was hit twice. The first shot came through the roof and struck a pillow on the bed. The pillow flew off the bed and went spinning around on the floor. The Holmans and the Bulgin family, who lived in the house with them, fled to the cellar only to hear a second ball rip through the wall and come to a stop on the floor directly above their heads. The shots fortunately were not of the exploding type. One pro–South witness said the Holman house was the only one hit and not by Bledsoe but by federal guns firing from the vicinity of the spring southeast of town. Mr. Holman, who had been a South Methodist preacher in Oregon, Lafayette, and Crawford counties before opening a business in Jasper County, greeted their deliverance with mixed feelings. He had helped lay out the nearby town of Avilla, Missouri, in 1858, but now had second thoughts about settling there. He moved his nursery business to Springfield and never returned to the area. There were many such stories of residents who fled and never returned to tell what they had seen.[3]

The rebel Missouri cavalry maneuvered wide to the right and left around Carthage, this time with a plan to take control of the Sarcoxie road and block Sigel's further withdrawal to Mount Vernon and on to Springfield. The left wing of the rebel cavalry took its time crossing the river at a ford almost directly north of town. The right wing, meanwhile, looked for a crossing downriver.

While the cavalry struggled to get across the stream at Walker Ford, the Missouri infantry crossed over on Sigel's route at Walton Ford. Under the protection of Bledsoe's artillery, Colonel Weightman's brigade finished crossing the river, followed closely by the regiments of General Slack. Once on the south side of Spring River, Weightman directed his Second and Third Regiments under colonels John R. Graves and Edgar V. Hurst off the road to the right and into the timber, to circle southwest and come up on the flank of the federal outpost west of town. Colonel O'Kane's Warsaw Battalion followed them in reserve. As Weightman's troops took a wide turn to the west, Colonel John T. Hughes of Brigadier General Slack's division made a frontal assault on Sigel's west guard, spearheading the attack on the Union line northwest of Carthage. Hughes mounted an intense attack on the federals. Colonel Hughes once had been among the most outspoken proponents of keeping Missouri in the Union. He now marshaled all the force at his command to destroy the Union troops. Colonel John Taylor Hughes was a Kentuckian by birth, moving to Missouri when he was very young. A cousin of Sterling Price, he served with Price in the Mexican War. A schoolteacher by profession, he was a polished writer and gained national fame for his book about his personal experiences in the Mexican campaign. After the Mexican War, he worked as a newspaper editor and school superintendent, and served as a state representative while maintaining his private life as a planter and slave owner. He expressed strong views on all questions then before the public. Known for his energy and great force of rhetoric, political opponents respected him for his courteous and considerate accommodation of opposing views. He was in his mid–40s when sectional strife broke out. Of average build, ruddy complexion, and dark brown hair, his gray-blue eyes and strongly cut features gave him the countenance of a seasoned leader. Like his kin, Price — who was more like a brother to him than a cousin — Hughes was a strong Conditional Union man until the Camp Jackson affair. He strongly resisted efforts to take Missouri out of the Union, opposed the state convention to consider the question, and then when it convened argued forcefully for the election of delegates who opposed secession. The federal actions at Camp Jackson, however, caused him to abandon his support of the government and join Missouri's rebellion against federal occupation of the state. He joined the Missouri State Guard as colonel of the First Regiment, Fourth Division, from northwest Missouri where he was a political leader.[4]

Approaching the Union defense west of Carthage, Colonel Hughes ordered his battalion

commanders, Lieutenant Colonel James A. Prichard and Major John C. Thornton, to bring their men in close proximity to Sigel's line along a low, wooded ridge west of town running north and south. Forty or 50 of the federals had taken a position in a cornfield at the edge of town. They opened fire from their concealed position as the rebels advanced on them. Colonel Pritchard, coming out of the brush at the head of his command, reacted with sanguine battlefield humor at the ambush. Turning to his men emerging from the brush behind him, he said, "Come on boys here they are."[5]

His men opened a deadly fire. By one local account, the rebels killed 15 of the federals in the cornfield and sent the rest scurrying back to town. It made a good war tale even if it had an apocryphal ring to it. The federal artillery opened fire on the advancing Missourians but did little to stall the rebel

John Taylor Hughes. Colonel Hughes' First Missouri Infantry, in General Slack's Fourth Division Missouri State Guard, saw some of the most severe fighting at the Battle of Carthage. His men were among the last to give up the chase of the retreating Union troops. (WICR 30121 in the collection of Wilson's Creek National Battlefield. Image courtesy National Park Service.)

assault. The Union flanking artillery battery fired freely into the rebel ranks but proved to be relatively ineffective in defending against their attack. Placed primarily to discourage an advance of the rebel cavalry, the guns were useless against the guerrilla-like tactics of the dismounted rebels coming through the woods.[6]

A few blocks away, the two Union cannon placed southeast of the square joined the barrage, lobbing shells over the top of the Female Academy into the city cemetery five blocks southwest of the square where the rebels were trying to pick their way through the timber. The federal guns apparently had the range. To the surprise of many, only one house took a hit by a Union cannon ball and that on the east side of town when a stray shot ricocheted into it.[7]

From out of nowhere east of town, a rebel gun answered the federal barrage. Henry Guibor's battery had somehow crossed Spring River and swung around to a position northeast of Carthage.

Meanwhile, the two federal infantry companies of Sigel's west guard under the command of Captains Zeis and Indest tried to defend against Colonel Hughes' attack, opening fire from behind buildings and fences within two or three blocks of the courthouse. They managed for a time to hold Hughes' infantry at bay, preventing his forces from reaching the streets of Carthage. A few minutes into the fight, Colonel Graves and Colonel Hurst of Weightman's brigade came on the scene. They had led their units through the skirt of timber until they came into town from the south on the rear of Sigel's army, coming up on the southwest perimeter to the right of Hughes. They edged forward, as one rebel remembered, "hoping to get close enough to use our shotguns and squirrel rifles." Some of Hurst's men armed with long guns broke ranks and raced ahead to get a shot. Somebody said later if they had not done that, they might have captured the entire Union battery. "When we got through the woods into the town of Carthage," one soldier said, "we were stopped in the street and all at once the enemy fired." In the waning daylight, Hurst and Graves were uncertain about the identity of the troops in front of them and did not fire at once. As soon as it became clear, however, that these were Union troops and not their rebel comrades, they joined Hughes and opened a withering fire on the lagging federals that broke and ran toward the square.[8]

Other units of the State Guard started to deploy in multiple directions around Carthage as they crossed the river and circled around the town. General Parsons had finally crossed over Spring River and heard the cannonading start. He ordered his commanders to pass their troops around Colonel Hughes' left and come in from the north side of town: first Major George K. Dill's infantry, followed closely by Colonel Kelly's men, and Captain Alexander's cavalry. Elsewhere, General Rains and his cavalry were somewhere at a point south of Carthage, dismounted and moving in the direction of the action. They could hear the distant guns of Bledsoe and Guibor opening up on the federal defense.

Sigel quickly decided to abandon Carthage and fall back toward Sarcoxie. It was a short rest for the federal soldiers. While the Union rear guard readied to abandon the town square, the Missourians entered the town and came on them. Colonel Hughes and the battalions of General Slack's command were the first to reach the square. The federal soldiers made a courageous but brief stand as their fragmented forces fired at the advancing rebels. They took shelter in and behind houses, walls, woodpiles, and fences, and put up an obstinate resistance. Bullets riddled many of the houses in Carthage. The fighting in the streets was at close range. There were unknown casualties. Some said several men died in the streets, but a different account of the fighting inside Carthage quickly surfaced. One informant said that he overheard a messenger from the secession camp say that they had killed but one man after entering Carthage. The State commanders acknowledged that the federals made a strong stand here. After some 40 minutes of this ambuscade, the Missourians chased the last of the Union troops out of the town square. Some of the men, who came into the fray late, estimated that the clash in town lasted no more than 15 to 20 minutes, the time it took to oust Sigel's men. There were longer estimates of the length of the fight but those included the time it took to engage the federal troops and drive them beyond the city limits.[9]

The federals abandoned the town in haste. Under intense pressure, they swiftly fled east out of the public square, and rapidly withdrew from town in great confusion. Isolated skirmishes took place all around the town as the routed federal rear guard tried to reach the cover of the main Union force at James Spring. In street fighting in and around town, the rebel losses were small. Private Thomas W. McKane, a 16-year-old farm boy in Hughes' regiment, received a Minié ball wound in the leg, which proved fatal a few days later; a ball grazed William Marrow's head and knocked him down; and a shot slightly wounded Archie Thomas in the arm. Conflicting accounts of Union losses said they ran higher, although never officially acknowledged. The Union wounded at the courthouse had no chance to avoid capture by the occupying rebels. The Missourians took them prisoner, along with several other Union stragglers and their weapons. Those too wounded in the skirmishes to flee or who found themselves cut off from the main federal force likewise became prisoners of the State Guard. As the federals retreated, they outran part of their prized baggage train, and this, too, fell into the hands of the Missourians.[10]

The women of Carthage were especially happy about the success of the State Guard troops, and rejoiced at having the federals driven out of town. The hyperbole of the moment

found its way into local folklore. One woman, so the story goes, ran through the streets when the bullets were flying, shouting, "Hurrah for Jeff Davis, liberty and independence forever. Down with the Dutch."[11]

The State Guard came across the square, pausing only long enough to accept offers of food and water from sympathetic women before hurrying on after the Union troops as they chased them east out of town. The smoke had not cleared before the rebel flag again flew over the courthouse lawn. Someone tore down the American flag the federals had put up the night before and put the secessionist flag back up.

Men carried both rebel and federal wounded into the temporary hospital at the courthouse and placed them down side by side without consideration of politics.

Amos H. Caffee, 1865. Dr. Caffee was a 26-year-old physician from Center Creek who happened to be in Carthage on the day of the battle. He worked alongside State Guard surgeons at the courthouse to treat the wounded rebels, and then volunteered as a surgeon for the Union. (Roessler, Missouri History Museum, St. Louis.)

Courthouse doors taken from their hinges became litters and operating tables. The sheriff's office at the southwest downstairs corner of the building became an operating room. Animosities disappeared as men and women worked to attend to the wounded inside the courthouse. Local doctors worked alongside military surgeons. Dr. David F. Moss, who had driven in that morning from Fidelity and stayed in town, went to the courthouse to help. Moss, a sometime preacher with an avocation of farming on the side, offered a complex blend of compassion, spirituality, and medicine. Another Union man, Dr. Amos H. Caffee, pitched in as well. Caffee had a practice in Sherwood in Center Creek Township in the western part of the county near the Kansas line. In Carthage on business, Dr. Caffee, Ohio-born and educated, put aside political differences and joined Dr. Moss to tend to the wounded regardless of which army they came from. The courthouse could not hold the large number of wounded, more than 100 the townspeople estimated. Some went to local homes; some wound up in the Shirley Hotel. The five wounded federals lay in a corner of one of the rooms to themselves.[12]

The courthouse remained open. A steady stream of visitors passed through, some looking for friends among the wounded, others simply passing through out of curiosity. The federal prisoners attracted a great deal of interest from the mostly Southern sympathizers, who commonly boasted that one Southerner could whip five Yankees. Sigel and his Germans drew special contempt from the secessionists who derisively called them the lop-eared Dutch. The Germans to them were nothing but hirelings going to fight wherever their wages took them.

A group of spectators came up to the five wounded federal men lying in the courthouse, and one of them said, "Now then, how do you Yanks like getting shot? You would not have hired out to come down and fight us fellows if you had known this was coming to you, would you?"

Not expecting a reply, the delegation was about to leave when one of the wounded prisoners turned toward them, half raised himself on one elbow, and said in perfect English, "Mister, we are fighting to save this Union. We believe it ought to be preserved and we volunteered to fight to preserve it."[13]

The young federal soldier spoke without a hint of a German accent. It became immediately clear to the visitors that the Dutchmen were fighting for something after all and that not all of Sigel's men were German. Nevertheless, the five federal wounded caused a spectacle when surgeons removed them from the courthouse outside to the lawn to make way for rebel wounded. Local pro–South citizens gathered to stare curiously at them and hurl insults at the silent German mercenaries.[14]

24

Chase Up the Sarcoxie Road

A coordinated State Guard attack on the town of Carthage would almost certainly have spelled capture for the Union army. As it was, only a relatively small part of the rebel force opened the action without forming any kind of order of battle. By the time the rest of the Guard came up to join in, Sigel was on the run again. Some of the state infantry and a large part of the state cavalry still had not crossed the river. Those that had crossed did so in disjointed units separated from their home companies and battalions. General Parsons arrived at Spring River with remnants of his infantry division to learn that Captain Guibor had already crossed with two pieces of artillery and was at the front a mile away waiting for the infantry to come up. The point at which Parsons chose to cross the river was relatively deep, and the infantry, exhausted from the exertion of the battle, found it difficult to cross. General Parsons turned back and used his personal carriage to help ford some of them over the river. This took considerable time. As soon as his men regrouped on the other side of the river, he turned toward Carthage. After a while, he heard cannonading coming from town about a mile to his front. His delay in crossing Spring River meant that another part of the rebel army and not his was taking the initiative. Parsons hastened forward as quickly as possible but well off the timing of the other advancing parts of the State Guard.[1]

Having failed to impede Sigel's withdrawal at Buck Branch, Colonel Rives and his mounted soldiers, now riding with General Rains, received orders from Rains to try to intercept the federal retreat. The rebel cavalry had trouble once again. Many of the riders had difficulty getting their mounts across Spring River. By the time Rives got his cavalry across the river, the Union troops had already left town with Colonel Hughes and his men in hot pursuit. General Parsons, hurrying up his infantry, arrived in Carthage to find Rives' band of rebel cavalry coming on the scene. Parsons immediately ordered them to the front. Rives caught up with Hughes, dismounted his men, and joined the chase on foot.[2]

Colonel McCown and his cavalry crossed Spring River about two miles downstream and started back toward town. After crossing over to the south side of the river, they traveled the road leading to Carthage until they were within about a mile and a half of town. They heard artillery fire in the distance coming from up ahead. The cavalry quickened its pace, riding in the direction of the fighting. They veered off to the right of the road, continued to a point about a mile outside town, and stopped at a stand of timber opposite the city's south side. They dismounted in the road, formed a line to enter the town, and marched into Carthage. There was no resistance. Once more, they were too late to engage in any action. The rebel infantry had already chased the federals east out of town. Sigel had departed. Shortly thereafter, Rains and other elements of his cavalry arrived at the outskirts of town. He, along with Colonel Peyton, like McCown, had dismounted the whole command to come to the aid of the infantry, but Rains, too, had arrived inside the city after the fight was over. Forced by Sigel's artillery to cross Spring River downstream, Rains had crossed his men at Tucker's Ford, a good two miles away. Coming up from the south, he dismounted his men and came in from the rear, arriving just in time to see the federals leaving. Except for a brief and deadly moment in that open grain field above Dry Fork Creek, the Eighth Division cavalry fought the entire battle under wooded cover, always arriving too late to engage the Union troops. The cavalry was never decisive in the battle, except by its movements at the outset of the fighting above Dry Fork Creek that caused Sigel to begin his withdrawal. While the infantry moved into Carthage to meet Sigel's troops and eventually oust them in street-to-street fighting, the cavalry circled the town.[3]

Being late to enter the fight had one advantage — aside from staying healthy — and that was the collection of spoils. The confusion of getting the cavalry across Spring River caused Captain J. H. McNeil of Colonel Rives' command to lose contact with the rest of the State Guard troops. Coming into Carthage after the Union troops had left, he took possession of part of the Union supply train and baggage left by the fleeing federals. Sigel had deserted it because he had no horses left to pull it. The Missourians confiscated a second wagonload of goods when federal looters abandoned a cache of items lifted from the citizens of Carthage. Private Salem Ford happily discovered the loot contained an ample supply of blackberry cordial. The rebels passed the stuff around and all declared it fine.[4]

The Missourians occupied Carthage in large numbers, by now coming in from three directions, and adding duress to Sigel's beleaguered retreating army. The federals retired from the city east along Seminary Street — the old mill road before the Female Academy gave it a new name. The rebels were in close pursuit harassing the Union soldiers from all sides. Rough native-stone fences along parts of the road offered minimal protection for the federal troops. As Sigel's precious wagon train came through Carthage, it suddenly came under attack. When the train had yet to clear the town, rebel cavalry came in from a flanking position and charged straight into the wagons. The federal infantry responded and drove them off, taking a position afterward on either side of the train to escort it out of town. In the hullabaloo in and around Carthage, eyewitnesses disagreed on the timing of the rebel assault on the Union supply train. One group said it happened as the leading wagons were coming into town; others said it occurred as the train was leaving. Both agreed, however, that the Union infantry turned back the cavalry attack with heavy musketry. The State road passed around the town square on the east side of town. It intersected with Seminary Street southeast of the city limits and continued southeast to the Sarcoxie road. It is unclear whether some or all the wagons detoured around Carthage on the State road or proceeded through the town ahead of elements of the infantry that fled the town square and abandoned the town up Seminary Street.[5]

Seeing his position was untenable, Sigel ordered a further retreat towards Sarcoxie. Heavy woods covered the Sarcoxie road. Sigel made it his objective to reach the road, reasoning that the State cavalry could not follow him there into the timber. As the Missourians closed in on the city, the federals took up the tactic of withdrawing and firing. It was an orderly retrograde movement once again using rotating elements of artillery and infantry to cover the withdrawal of the rest of the army. Under pressure from the rebel Missourians, Sigel continued his retreat, gaining the admiration of the opposing generals for his skill and eminent ability on the field.[6]

Under hot pursuit by Colonel Hughes' command and constant rebel fire, Sigel managed to position his guns on a rise of ground a mile from the center of Carthage east of town at about the place where the Union soldiers had camped the night before. Here, beyond the outskirts of town, Sigel formed a new line of defense to protect the retreat of his rear guard. He deployed his artillery along a low wooded ridge running north and south across Seminary Street, guarded by a company of infantry to check the rebel pursuit. Sigel personally took charge of the defense on the State road. He ordered Captain John E. Strodtmann's Company E of Colonel Hassesdeubel's First Battalion to hold the rebels until further orders. Strodtmann and Sergeant Otto Lademann formed the company across the road; the artillery positioned strategically along the line. The right flank of the line ended near James Spring. The two guns of Lieutenant Schaefer, sent initially by Sigel to guard the east side of town, occupied a place on the heights nearby. With his guns in place on the high ground, Sigel now had a position to cover the retreating infantry. He paced back and forth behind the guns as his retreating rear guard came up on the run.[7]

It may be useful at this point to suspend the action of Sigel's withdrawal for a moment to settle different reports of what happened next. Upon vacating Carthage, Sigel drew up his Union guns two more times in defensive alignments aimed at covering his retreating infantry and supply wagons. There is disagreement on the exact placement and descriptions of these defenses. Sigel said only that he took a first position "on the heights behind Carthage, and then at the entrance of the road to Sarcoxie into the woods two and one-half miles southeast of Carthage." The first defense was near Carthage. He had previously ordered two pieces of artillery to pass Carthage and to occupy the eastern heights on the State, or Sarcoxie, road. This marked the approximate location of the first defense, as generally confirmed by the State Guard commanders. General Slack located Sigel's defense "on the heights one mile east of town." Colonel Hughes concurred in the distance but placed the Sigel defense "on a hill one mile south of town" and said it was the Union's last position, suggesting that he did not consider the second Union defense that came further along the road as meaningful enough to mention in his after-action report. General Parsons, meanwhile, appeared also to describe the first defense on the eastern heights when

Otto Lademann, 1863. An early enlistee in Sigel's Third Regiment Missouri Volunteers, Lademann participated in the raid on Camp Jackson, in St. Louis, and then accompanied Sigel to southwest Missouri. Sergeant Lademann, later Captain Lademann, was with Sigel at the final line of defense southeast of Carthage. (Holke and Benecke, Missouri History Museum, St. Louis.)

he said he "passed east of town and found his artillery engaged at a mile distant." Describing the first defense as being east or south of Carthage refers to the same location, which was actually southeast of the courthouse square. Sergeant Otto Lademann who was with Sigel's Third Regiment picked up the story at this point and related how it was his Company E that Sigel left in support of the artillery to cover the retreating federal infantry. Lademann gave his recollection of the alignment of the guns. He told first of fire being returned "in a languid manner by two of our guns," doubtless referring to the two guns Sigel initially posted on the eastern heights. He then went on to say, "Here Colonel Sigel personally ordered my company — Company E of Captain John E. Strodtman — to remain and hold the enemy in check until further orders." Lademann continued, "Captain Strodtman formed the company in column of platoons, across the Sarcoxie [State] road. The sun went down; all troops to the right and left of us marched off, our company being left solitary and alone on the prairie, about 300 yards from the timber fringing Spring River, the place where we had camped the night before." Spring River in this case referred to the stream issuing from James Spring and not Spring River north of Carthage. Marvin VanGilder later used these descriptions to help identify the site of the first defense as about where the present River Street and Chestnut Street intersect — at that time called the State road and Seminary Street, or the mill road — on a north–south ridge near the present River Street. VanGilder said, "The right of his [Sigel's] line then was approximately at what is today the entrance of Carter Park [then called James Spring]." Study of the topography in this area suggests that the defense line probably formed just east of the present River Street. It extended across Chestnut Street, or Seminary Street, at the place where Seminary and the State road turned into the Sarcoxie, or Springfield, road. George Knight, a young man at the time of the battle — who said he rode with Sigel the entire day — remembered, "The battery was formed in line of battle on that ridge, three guns south of the road, two at the road and one just north of the road." Knight's memory, however, produced a different story of what happened next. General Sigel was off his horse walking back and forth in front [and not behind] the battery and looking toward Carthage. There was no firing at this point, according to Knight. He said, "General Sigel told me later that he would have given them the contents of the full battery from that point had they followed him out of Carthage." Thomas Hood, another local boy who witnessed the fight, had a different recollection of Sigel's State road stand. He wrote years after the battle, "At the ridge, another stand was made by Sigel and considerable firing was done. This was, I think at about the intersection of what is now Chestnut and River streets, but possibly a little south of that point." Accounts of the same events often varied widely at the Battle of Carthage. Notwithstanding a few dissenting opinions, the Union stand at the State road was a bloody affair. Sigel's guns did fire into the pursuing State Guard men with deadly effect.[8]

Private Owen Smith Nichols, the Lawrence County Home Guard private who Sigel had allegedly pressed into service as a color bearer, was in the escaping rear guard trying to make his way out of Carthage to the safety of the Union defense. He later told how he carried the brigade banner as fast as he could up Seminary Street, running backward and facing the pursuing rebels. No man wanted to be shot in the back running from the field of battle. A charge of grapeshot from one of his own Union artillery guns suddenly exploded at close range and Nichols dropped to the ground. His comrades, thinking him killed, paused long enough in their retreat to retrieve the flag and move his body to the side of the road where they left him. The pursuing State Guard passed close by without taking notice of the fallen soldier. Hours later, he came to unhurt, alone at the edge of the road, the battle finished. The bursting shell had knocked him unconscious but left him otherwise unscathed. The only wound turned out to be a dent in his belt buckle from a shell fragment. He got to his feet, caught a horse, and hightailed out of Carthage. He caught up with Gatton's Lawrence County Home Guard company two days later on the other side of Marionville. The Lawrence County boys went back home to do what they first organized to do: that is, protect the citizens of Lawrence County. Nichols later enlisted as a sergeant in the Union Eighth Missouri Cavalry and eventually returned to Jasper County after the war to marry Eliza Coats, the girl he left behind in the rush to join Sigel. Owen and Eliza settled on a farm near Bower's Mill and raised a large family. Many a time he told the story of how in the stampede to get out of Carthage he was left for dead on the side of the road.[9]

The battlefield around Carthage was a patchwork of skirmishes. The rebel infantry surrounded the town, joined by various companies of the cavalry to the right and left. General Parsons, unaware at the time of Sigel's new defensive position, passed to the east of town about a half mile out and to his surprise discovered part of his own artillery unlimbering to engage the federals. Sigel's James Spring defense lay some 400 yards further on in a patch of timber to the left. Parsons had serendipitously arrived on the Union right flank. Captain Guibor's battery wheeled into place at close range while Bledsoe of Weightman's brigade, a distance away, brought up his artillery to bear on the front of the Union position.

Sigel's guns opened fire on the pursuing Missourians, shooting into the advancing State Guard lines at point-blank range. The Union guns put up a wall of cannon and musketry. The muskets of the federals quieted when the artillery of Bledsoe and Guibor responded to the Union fire. The artillery faced off again and a spirited exchange ensued. Some of the deadliest fighting of the day occurred here. The federal guns halted the advance of the rebel troops, preventing them from pressing the attack. Sigel's James Spring defense held the Missourians in check while his main body of troops broke off and continued to withdraw up the State road, leaving Company E and the battery of guns alone, implanted across the mill road directly in the path of the State Guard. At the same time, the Union wagons moved steadily ahead toward the Sarcoxie road, passing the mill east of town.[10]

The Union stand on the edge of Carthage was the strongest of the day from the rebel point of view. The artillery exchange was one of the bloodiest skirmishes of the battle. The Union guns repeatedly fired rounds to cover the retreating federal troops scurrying toward the security of the woods on the Sarcoxie road. It was here that Captain Fountain S. McKenzie fell. A Union shell burst on Colonel Brown's regiment killing McKenzie, the Company B commander. Many knew McKenzie as a hero of the Mexican War and one of the first to stand up for Missouri's independence, helping to organize the Clark Township Southern Mounted Guards of Cole County. General Parsons grieved his death especially, remembering their long association and friendship. McKenzie had fought with Parsons through Doniphan's campaign in the Mexican War, serving as his orderly sergeant. Together, they had fought in defense of the country to uphold the very flag that now floated above the heads of the federal invaders. McKenzie was 41 years old, and many back in Cole County mourned his loss. Not far from where McKenzie fell, another shell wounded Private William Kimball.[11]

The sun was dipping toward the horizon when Strodtmann's federals noticed that the edge of the timber about 300 yards away was beginning to fill up with men. Colonel Hughes' command had pressed forward under cover of a band of woods, coming out in close proximity to the rear of Sigel's position. Colonel Kelly arrived about this time, too, with his infantry, and advanced immediately on the Union right flank to roust the federals from their spot in the woods. In the light of dusk, one of the State Guard officers rode up to the

Union line and inquired of First Lieutenant E. H. Poten what regiment it was. When the two men discovered they were on opposite sides, Poten fired his pistol at the hapless rebel but missed.

The Missourians immediately opened a volley on the flank of the Union defenders. A sharp firefight ensued. Captain Strodtmann fell from a wound in the right shoulder. Private Charles Mick, a 27-year-old enlistee who had a position near the captain went to his aid and caught a bullet in the right shoulder himself. Strodtmann's men tried to return fire but their formation faced west and hindered them from effectively responding to the flanking rebels coming from the north. The engagement was brief, lasting for about 20 to 30 minutes before the State troops dislodged the Union soldiers again and forced them from their last stronghold. Three or four hundred Missourians burst from the woods and charged the federal guns, cheering and firing as they advanced. The Union boys picked up their wounded captain, gathered the rest of the wounded as best they could, and hastily abandoned their position. They went scurrying off under particular pressure from Major Dills' infantry and Captain Alexander's mounted service before those two broke off the chase. However, the relentless Colonel Hughes' stayed after the retreating federals and did not break off the pursuit. Once more using the shelter of the woods, Hughes caught up with the fleeing federals and again brought his command close to their rear where he opened a destructive fire at their lines as they retired.[12]

Sigel's rear-guard detachment had run about a mile, pursued in a running skirmish by the unrelenting Missourians, when they encountered a lone rider who turned out to be Lieutenant Colonel Hassendeubel. It surprised him to discover it was his Company E that Sigel had ordered to remain behind in the path of the pursuing rebels. Hassendeubel apparently lost track of them in his own retreat. The company quickly rallied, reformed, and moved out to catch up with the rest of the Union army.[13]

Sigel renewed his tactic of alternating the withdrawal of his artillery and infantry, pulling his guns, back then his infantry, in stages as the army leapfrogged on a trot up the road. In this way, he succeeded in protecting the rapid withdrawal of his shattered and disorganized column.

Nightfall began to set in. The men of Colonel Hughes' infantry, who had led the pursuit of Sigel's army up to this point across the prairie and through Carthage, fell back. Exhausted, Colonel Hughes' men finally gave up the hunt. The infantry returned to Carthage and went into bivouac spent from exhaustion. A handful of men from some of the other infantry units continued to hound the federals, inflicting additional losses on the Union troops. However, for the most part, as darkness settled, the pursuit of Sigel's men on foot ended.[14]

Up to this point in the conflict, the rebel artillery and infantry did most of the fighting. The cavalry was raw and poorly equipped, and except for the threat they initially presented to Sigel's flanks, were not a major factor in the battle. They had difficulty negotiating the terrain and not all were of the caliber of Shelby's Rangers when it came to maneuvering in the field. As the battle wound down, at about the time that the infantry broke off the chase, some of the cavalry units found passage through the heavy timber along Spring River and came up on the backside of the retreating federals. As Hughes' spent infantry retired from the field, a detachment of Colonel Rives' cavalry under the command of Captain McNeil replaced the foot soldiers and took up the pursuit of Sigel's shattered army. McNeil, who had separated from the rest of Colonel Rives' cavalry, continued to harass the flank and rear of the retreating federals until well after sunset. His cavalry came up behind Sigel and dealt

162   THE BATTLE OF CARTHAGE

a persistent aggravation to the retreating federals for another hour, inflicting several more casualties.

There would be one more light engagement before the battle ended. Once again, mixed opinions about this last engagement invite scrutiny. Some said it resulted in large numbers of casualties for both sides. Others claimed there were hardly any losses at all. According to one story, "The last attack was made three miles southeast of the town, near the timber, about dusk, which lasted some twenty minutes, which resulted in a heavy loss to the rebels, and scarcely any to the other side." Most people, however, look upon this final skirmish as minor and do not give it the same emphasis as the first Union defense at James Spring with regard to casualties. Probably this final defense by the Union troops is the same perfunctory defensive line mentioned by Sigel that occurred "at the entrance of the road to Sarcoxie into the woods two and one-half miles southeast of Carthage." Sergeant Lademann described it not so much as a line of defense but a salutary act of defiance before the Union troops disappeared up the Sarcoxie road. The rebel cavalry continued to annoy the withdrawing federals at a distance until darkness blanketed the prairie. They followed for a mile or two until around nine o'clock before turning back. Night put a stop to the conflict. The State cavalry fell back and abandoned the chase. Nightfall and fatigue put an end to the battle. Sigel was now in general retreat up the Sarcoxie road.[15]

Colonel Sigel continued to withdraw, breaking off contact with the rebels, and bringing up the remainder of his rear-guard units. The Union army next retired to the entrance of the Sarcoxie road at a point where the State road became properly the Sarcoxie road, about where the road leaves the prairie and begins the Ozark woodlands. Taking a position near the timber, Sigel made one final defiant gesture. It was about 9:00 P.M. when he formed the Union brigade for the last time across the road in the dark, forming a line of battle at the edge of the woods. He fired three salutes of artillery and three volleys of musketry in the direction of the State Guard troops, although there were none seen. A few

Henry Martyn Cheavens. Educated at Yale University and Amherst, with a degree from the latter, Private Cheavens gave up his teaching job to join the Missouri State Guard. He rode with Colonel Rives' cavalry at the Battle of Carthage. (Virginia Easley Photo Collection, State Historical Society of Missouri.)

of the men reckoned that only God and Colonel Sigel knew the military reason for this fireworks demonstration. Sigel's clear commands — "Load! Ready! Aim! Fire!" — sang out in the dark, followed immediately by the deafening roar of cannon and muskets as the last sounds of arms echoed across the silent prairie, after which the Union soldiers quickly turned about, silently ducked into the woods, and headed on to Sarcoxie. The Union troops continued from here without further incident, and the battle ended.[16]

Darkness settled in as Sigel made his escape under cover of night. The Missourians had forced the federals to retire some 20 miles from their initial position at Dry Fork Creek. The heavily outmanned Union force had broken camp at 5:00 A.M., marched more than 20 miles, and fought a running battle over a ten-mile stretch of open prairie. By ten o'clock that night, they were back of where they started, exhausted but with many more miles to go before reaching safety.

The Missouri State Guard troops pulled back from their pursuit and went into camp all around Carthage with parts of different units camped on farms far south of town. That night some stayed in the courthouse yard while others camped at James Spring where the Union army had camped the night before and by which it had passed on its retreat back to Sarcoxie. Private Henry Cheavens, who had put in appearances at various stages of the battle beginning with the dying Captain Stone at the Widow Smith's house, caught up with his unit about nightfall, just in time to participate in the final rebel assault on Sigel's James Spring defense. After it was over, he made his way back up Seminary Street, went into a vacant house on the edge of town, and slept on the floor. Covered in blood, dust, and sweat, he never slept more soundly.[17]

Many of the men slept on the ground beneath their horses wherever the battle ended for them. Private C. L. Smith found himself stepped on more than once. Too tired to spend much time thinking about it, he wondered, though, what the outcome of the battle would have been if Rains' cavalry had turned the federal left flank the way General Parsons had turned the right. They could have captured the entire Union army if the Eighth Division boys had not missed the chance by halting to eat a hat full of blackberries.[18]

Young George Walker spent the night at home, on the bank of Spring River. A State Guard friend stayed overnight at the Walker place and the wounded State Guard Private John Byler stayed there, too, under the care of the Walker family. George was an immediate celebrity around Jasper County. Not only had he survived the battle that dealt the Union its first defeat in Missouri, he had ridden with the legendary Shelby's Rangers, all at the age of 17. If the battle had not revenged his father's murder, it was at least a good beginning. George did not stay long at home. He soon enlisted in the Confederate army, along with three of his brothers, and served until wounded. When well enough to ride again, he and a companion named Ed Hall joined the Jasper County guerrilla band of J. J. Petty and rode with Thomas Livingston's Cherokee Spikes, continuing to heap misery on the antislavery interests that he held responsible for the death of his father.[19]

25

A Late Supper

The exhausted Missourians broke off the chase and retired from the field. Evening settled over the prairie. The rebel surgeons tended to the wounded, and that night the rebel army camped at Carthage on the same ground that the Union troops had occupied the night before.

With the Union army in full retreat, driven beyond the mills east of Carthage, Brigadier General Parsons halted his division and reminded his officers that occupying the mills had been his original intention before the ensuing battle. He turned his attention to what his mission had been and directed his commissary, Lieutenant Colonel Sidney Roberts, to take a detachment of men to the mills and take possession of whatever quantity of flour he could find. The remainder of Parsons' Sixth Division retired into camp about a quarter of a mile east of Carthage. Parsons' division gave a good account of itself on the field that day. The ability and daring of Colonel Kelly's men and that of Major Dills proved to be decisive turning points in the battle. The precision of the artillery of Captain Guibor and Lieutenant Barlow won a position on the field. Guibor and Barlow several times worked the guns themselves. It is a remarkable fact that during the whole engagement Captain McKenzie was the only one in Parsons' division to lose his life. The number of wounded was seven. In an act of chivalry uncharacteristic of commanders after a battle, General Parsons gave no estimates of Union casualties. He had fought admirably in a hotly contested battle. It was over and time to move on.[1]

The battle was over, but there was little boasting on either side. The Army of Missouri rightfully claimed victory, but most participants were simply glad it had ended. Lieutenant Barlow later wrote, "I well remember that we all thought this … a great battle and a great victory, and when our last shot was sent rolling over the prairie, about a half mile beyond Carthage, after dark, and the pursuit ceased, we were very glad the awful battle was ended, and went into camp thoroughly tired out." General Parsons cited Lieutenant Barlow and Captain Guibor for their personal valor and complimented them on the effectiveness of their gunnery. They and their battery of artillery received much credit for helping to turn the tide of fighting. Neither man could know at the time what lay ahead in the war, that the experience of real fighting in real battles would quickly reduce the Battle of Carthage in the history of the war to a contemptible little skirmish.[2]

165

Colonel Weightman's exhausted brigade camped in and around Carthage. Like most of the rebel army, many had not eaten for more than 24 hours. The battle had extended over a distance of ten miles and had continued for twelve hours. He counted two in his brigade killed in the action, with 38 wounded. There were those who said his brigade contributed more to the success of the day than any other troops. Throughout the long battle, Weightman drew the admiration of his men for his cool and collected demeanor. When it was over, he, too, did not try to compute the losses on the other side.[3]

General Clark's fragmented division went into camp in various places. Colonel Burbridge bivouacked near town and waited for the exhausted stragglers of his command to drift in. Of his four companies that entered the fight in the morning, only about 20 men kept up with him and were with him at the last charge to the east of town that sent Sigel scurrying toward Springfield. Only three were still standing from the colorful Callaway Guard — the only State Guard company in matching uniforms. The others had fallen prostrated beside the road in the sweltering heat. Big, strong, muscular young men could not keep the pace that Sigel set for them. Colonel Burbridge issued a supply of cooking utensils and a part of the flour and bacon captured from the federals, some of the spoils of battle that came to what remained of his decimated regiment for being in the right place at the right time.[4]

Brigadier General Rains arrived at Carthage with his cavalry just in time to see the rout of Sigel's army. Most of his men dismounted and went into camp shortly thereafter. A few joined the chase of Sigel's Union troops up the State road. Other than Colonel Weightman's brigade, assigned that day to the Eighth Division, Rains' men saw little action. There were those who said his performance as overall State Guard commander fell short of expectations. Few bothered to consider that no order ever surfaced naming him overall commander. He drew criticism, too, for not engaging the Union guns. However, in not doing so, he proved perhaps to be the more sensible commander on the battlefield. He took great care to protect his men. After the initial cannonading north of Dry Fork Creek and the loss of several men while attempting to circle around Sigel's left flank, Rains saw immediately the vulnerability of his inexperienced cavalry. From that point on, he became overly cautious about throwing his men into the fight. His critics said many times that he did not intercept Sigel because he did not want to attempt it with his undisciplined troops. He intentionally took wide detours, they said, to arrive late. The truth perhaps lies in his actions both at Dry Fork Creek and at Spring River where in both instances he rode miles downstream to find suitable crossings well out of range of Sigel's guns. General Rains knew the country well and had a great many men with him from the immediate locality. They knew the waterways, too, and could easily have utilized a good ford without going so far to the west. In doing so, however, he spared his men the consequences of attacking an already defeated and retreating Union force that had repeatedly proven itself capable of driving off any kind of rebel threat. Nevertheless, his initial command at the head of the State Guard column at the outset of the battle and the perception of the press afterward that he was in charge made him the scapegoat for the Guard's muddled performance at the battle. His political detractors consequently rumored him unfit for command, undisciplined in leadership, and too poorly organized to be a field commander. Moreover, the Eighth Division cavalry suffered the unfortunate indignity of becoming henceforth the Blackberry Cavalry, another unfounded criticism. The nickname of a command was a reflection of its reputation. Almost every unit down to the company level had a colorful and sometimes extra descriptive moniker. The alleged undisciplined sojourn of Rains' cavalrymen into the neighboring fields to gather blackberries became an unfortunate derisive footnote to General Rains' war record that accompanied him throughout the war.[5]

Colonel Hughes' regiment of General Slack's Fourth Division was the last to give up the fight, breaking off the pursuit of Sigel well after other rebel commands had retired. His regiment along with the battalion of Major Thornton from Clay and Platte Counties had the front position in every attack made. Hughes' and Thornton's men occupied the post of greatest danger all day, and their losses were more severe than in any other unit. At least 15 men died and more than 40 were wounded, several of them critically. As his troops went into bivouac on Spring River, Hughes lamented that he had lost some of his best officers and men: three company captains killed and his sergeant major mortally wounded and left at Carthage in the care of a local doctor. In the several close engagements, some died instantly while others later died from mortal wounds. At the end of the day, General Slack's command, of which Hughes and Thornton were a part, held eight prisoners and two baggage wagons filled with tents and other field supplies. For more than eight hours, Colonel Hughes and Major Thornton had pressed the attack. Their soldiers called it the "Running Battle of Carthage."[6]

Soon after the Missourians had settled into camp in and around Carthage, a squad of rebels showed up in front of the Norris Hood home. The Missourians arrested Hood and took him at bayonet point through the streets to the State Guard command headquarters set up in a blackjack oak grove southeast of the square. A handful of profane rebel officers intensely questioned Hood about his Union sympathies, generously lacing their interrogatives with obscenities to underscore the seriousness of his situation.

"Mr. Hood," they said, "the time has come when every man must take his stand on the issues now agitating this country."

"I have taken mine sir, as you are well aware, long ago," replied Hood.

"Those who are not for us are against us," warned one of the officers.

"I am against you, sir, with my whole mind and strength."

The rebel commanders apparently found the former sheriff's answers to be acceptable. When he had the audacity to ask permission for the Hood family to feed and care for the wounded federal prisoners, they granted it.[7]

Every woman in Carthage that night prepared food for the hungry Missourians. Some did it happily, some not. Those rebel soldiers not able to get a meal did the best they could. While Norris Hood was undergoing questioning by the rebel commanders, some of the State Guard officers went to the Hood home about 10:00 P.M. and asked the Hood women to cook a meal for them. The local grapevine said Governor Jackson along with some of his aides were among them. This went on at the Hood place until 2:00 A.M. when the visitors finally allowed them to retire. No sooner had they turned in than some unknown anti–Union goon threw a rock through a window. The rebel officers rewarded the hospitality of their hosts by having a guard placed around the Norris home for the night. The Missourians released Norris Hood the next day and allowed him and his family to leave Carthage, which they did.[8]

Thousands of good Union families, like Norris Hood's, went to Fort Scott, Kansas, to escape the war-ravaged counties of southwest Missouri. Government-sponsored trains, sometimes stretching across the prairie 250 wagons long — six mules to a wagon — carried refugees and their belongings across the border to safety. Another to leave was Dr. D. F. Moss, the longest-practicing physician in Jasper County, who abandoned his property and fled. Anyone else who had joined Sigel or openly supported the Union struck out for safer territory by whatever means available to them. George Knight who had rode with Sigel during the entire battle wasted no time in finding refuge in Kansas. Young Charles B. Hayward, the recently installed editor of the *Southwest News*, walked the 60 miles to Fort Scott. He decided to take no chances that his previous appearance in the Union camp might draw repercussions. He found numerous former Jasper County citizens at Fort Scott cautiously settled in, like Dr. Moss and Norris Hood, for the duration of the war. Many of them never returned to the county, choosing to go elsewhere when the war ended, and taking with them recollections of that fateful summer of 1861. Both Moss and Hood did return, the latter to rebuild in Carthage and Moss to his medical practice at his home southeast of town, one of the few houses to survive the destruction of Jasper County.[9]

The engagement on July 5 from start to finish lasted more than 14 hours, from the first exchange of shots between the Union and rebel pickets, through the cannonade and standoff at Dry Fork Creek, and into the running retreat and pursuit of Sigel's federals beyond Carthage. For 11 of the 14 hours, the two armies fought continuously. The introduction to war came quickly for the new State Guard recruits. Less than a week had passed for many of them from the time these young Missourians left their homes and jobs as farmers, stockmen, merchants, and a host of other domestic occupations, to this moment of military victory over a trained force of United States troops commanded by an officer regarded at the time as among the most able of Union commanders. In the span of a few hours, they organized and prepared during a sleepless night, marched eight miles, and entered battle without food or water. Poorly armed and having no military experience, most of them fought from ten o'clock in the morning until well into the evening, driving the federal army before them across ten miles of prairie, killing and wounding many as they went, and advancing steadily, sometimes in the face of withering fire.

On the other side, the Union boys, although pressed hard by superior numbers, never panicked. Their withdrawal was orderly. On more than one occasion, they drew the admiration and respect of the rebel officers.

Men on both sides, most of them new to battle, behaved like veterans. A rumor circulated among Union sympathizers after the battle that some of the State soldiers had retreated in the heat of battle. Eyewitness accounts, however, said that not one soldier gave a single foot. State Guard soldiers were from all parts of the state. After the battle, they wrote letters home. "The boys from Carroll County all acted boldly and nobly so far as I could learn. Not one flinched in the whole time," wrote Archie Thomas. Letters went out to all parts of the state and beyond, telling the news of the battle. During the entire Civil War, the United States mail ran as if nothing whatever was going wrong anywhere. In almost every city, the mails arrived and departed regularly.[10]

The excited Missourians were prone to exaggerate the number of participants on both sides in the heat of the opening guns and the jubilation of victory. Private H. L. Boon, writing home, overestimated Sigel's opposing force at more than 3,000 fighting men, against those of his comrades who he erroneously thought numbered about 1,800, although many more were on the ground, he said, not armed. After some of the Union soldiers became prisoners of the Missourians, the rebel captors listened in disbelief when told that Sigel had but one and a half regiments, none of which was at full strength. It would be a long time before anyone on either side had anything that approached an accurate accounting of the strength of the two armies.[11]

Rumors circulated in the Union ranks that the rebels had lost not less than 350 to 400 killed and wounded. At the same time, a story in the rebel camp estimated losses to the

Union side at 150 to 200 killed and 300 to 400 wounded. Colonel Hughes swore that Union losses were at least 130 killed and some 300 wounded. The spoils of battle, Hughes reckoned, included 20 prisoners, a piece of artillery, several baggage wagons, and a good many horses; none of this squared with the Union version of battle losses, however. It is common practice in any given conflict for both sides to magnify its own achievements and minimize the achievements of its adversary. It was so at Carthage and at every battle thereafter for the duration of the Civil War. One Confederate officer once reported that he killed more Union soldiers than the opposing federal commander reported he had in action.[12]

There were stories, too, of those who fell. Private Albert F. Withers, of Liberty, Missouri, fell at the final Union defense, shot down at the close of the action. About age 22, the son of a large Clay County plantation owner, Albert had been among the first to join Captain Thomas McCarty's company to redress what he saw as senseless violence by unionist sympathizers. Both Northern and Southern patriots blamed slaves for the cause of sectarian violence. Gunmen murdered a Withers slave just for fun, a repugnant act to young Withers. Those who knew Withers greatly admired him for his humane character and friendly disposition. A special sadness gripped his comrades when they learned he was dying. They watched over him with tender care in remorseful silence. He survived only about three hours and died. Softly and tearfully, they buried him at Carthage in a place dark and dreary and far away from home.[13]

That night the Missouri State Guard had a new confidence. They had driven the federal intruders back and secured a vital outlet southward. They had met the invaders and defeated them. Once mortified by their defeat and retreat at Boonville, the victory at Carthage redeemed them. Writing from camp to his father in Howard County a couple of days after the battle, Private Boon boasted, "The fight at Boonville was child's play compared to the work of Friday. We fought from ten o'clock until after dark, driving the enemy from every position they took. The cannonading on both sides was terrible."[14]

Pro-South Missourians, anxious for any good news, reveled in their first triumph. The Army of Missouri had demonstrated that the people of the state could rely upon it in an emergency. The inexperienced soldiers took the field with great apprehension and left with the first taste of victory of the young war. It was an inspirational victory for the Missourians and a wake-up call to the federal commanders in the West. The German volunteers and regulars out of St. Louis expected to encounter little more than a few rebellious Southern sympathizers, easily put down by a modest policing action. They seriously underestimated the depth of feeling against the federal government and the degree of contempt invited by anyone who thought they could substitute tyranny for liberty.[15]

The rebel Missourians declared victory because they held the field. The daylong battle drove the Union army back, forcing it to fight a desperate rear-guard action to escape death or capture. Many in the rebel infantry said that a vigorous concerted effort would have resulted in the capture of the entire Union army, had it not been for the cavalry circling the battlefield. Thus, the battle revealed that the Missouri State Guard was not yet ready for war. With superior numbers and the advantage of mounted riflemen, the rebels failed to destroy or significantly damage the Union force. However, the path was now open to General Price and General McCulloch. The battle succeeded in giving the new army time to train and equip under the protective umbrella of the Confederacy. Tonight the State Guard boys would rest at Carthage, and tomorrow they would continue on their way southward.[16]

26

Uncertain Victory

An alarm went up in the Confederate camp at Buffalo Creek on the night of July 5, 1861. Word reached Confederate Brigadier General Ben McCulloch that there was heavy cannonading to the north during the day signaling that Governor Jackson and his Missourians were fighting their way toward him.[1]

McCulloch's advance detachment of cavalry waited for him at Neosho, greatly enjoying the success of having captured a company of Sigel's Union army. The men at Neosho felt edgy as darkness came on, halfway expecting the federals to descend on them at any moment. It looked like a fight was on. They did not yet know what had transpired at Carthage. Around midnight, the sentinels fired a few rounds and everyone jumped to their feet, grabbed their guns, and fell into ranks, only to learn that it was a false alarm. In a heightened state of vigilance, the sentinels had opened fire on a horse.

Upon hearing news of the battle at Carthage, General McCulloch immediately mounted his Confederate command and caught up with his detachment at Neosho before morning. He paused long enough to secure the town and rest his troops in the same way Sigel had two days earlier in the same place. After a short rest at Neosho, McCulloch started his entire command north on July 6 to form a junction with the Missouri rebel army at Carthage.[2]

Joining his Confederate army on the march was the command of Major General Pearce of the Arkansas State Militia. Pearce brought a force of nearly 2,000 men, a sufficient number to convey the friendly intentions of the Southern Confederacy toward the State of Missouri. Riding with them, too, was Major General Sterling Price and his growing band of Missouri recruits. General Price placed his men under the command of McCulloch, bringing the total number of reinforcements to more than 6,000 troops in the vanguard of the Confederate force. Another sizable contingent followed in the rear, including additional units from Arkansas and Louisiana. The Confederates started north to make contact with the State Guard of Governor Jackson. Pickets went out to watch for Sigel.[3]

Several miles away Sigel's Union Second Brigade trudged toward Sarcoxie. They passed through dense, heavy timber along a rough stony road. The defeated army marched silently through pitch darkness. The wounded and those unable to walk rode on the wagons. The thin crescent moon had already set and revealed nothing in its waning final phase. The

170

night was still. The Great Comet flamed in the sky, orienting the travelers along the road. The comet bore silent witness to the battle. None who wrote of the Battle of Carthage ever mentioned it. No newspaper accounts, no diaries, no official documents said anything about the Great Comet as if to speak of it might somehow visit its curse upon the writer.

The evening passed clear, calm, and awful.

The beaten federals came out of the woods onto the open prairie and there rested before marching on. The prospects of food and drink were at last in sight for them as the heat of the day abated. Sigel continued his retreat through the night and did not stop again until the following morning when he was some 15 miles from Carthage and well beyond the reach of the Missouri army. The exhausted federals plodded on, no longer an army of untested volunteers.[4]

The first elements of Sigel's retreating army reached Sarcoxie at 3:00 A.M., Saturday, July 6, relieved to find it not occupied by General Ben McCulloch. The streets were empty. No one in this secessionist town turned out to welcome the Union troops. The remainder of the column reached town about daybreak and began a slow course of recuperation from the prior day's combat. They hurriedly set up camp and broke out their cooking utensils to fix some breakfast from the meager provisions they carried. The soldiers had been on their feet without food for 24 hours. They had neither hard bread nor canned meats with them. The whole campaign relied mainly on flour and fresh beef slaughtered from the countryside during halts. When marching and fighting there was no meat at all. Thoughts went back to Neosho and the last time they ate a good meal with fresh bread. The best of cooks among them struggled to convert flour into bread using a crude dough substitute of flour, water, and salt to produce a form of flapjacks baked in a frying pan. Without any baking powder or yeast, the culinary result had all the appeal of shoe leather. Before breakfast was ready, an alarm reached the camp. "They are coming! They are coming!"[5]

The report said that the rebel cavalry was behind them and within striking distance. The exhausted federals immediately poured their meal on the ground, repacked their cooking pans, broke camp, and hastily reassembled their ranks. They marched at the double-quick through Sarcoxie and started toward Mount Vernon. As it turned out, all the excitement proved to be a false alarm. Sigel had pressed into service a few local home guards to serve as scouts. These men dressed like the rebel State Guard in homespun butternut attire, and they carried Kentucky rifles and shotguns like the Missourians. These loyal Union men, eager to protect Sigel's force, mistook each other for rebels and rushed back to Sigel's camp to report that the Missourians were advancing from two directions. Such a scenario repeated itself many times in the early stages of the war in southwest Missouri when reconnoitering squads frequently sighted patrols of their own side and reported them as the opposing force. It soon became apparent to Sigel that no rebel troops pursued them, and he took up a more leisurely pace. Details of State Guard cavalry were out feeling around the country looking for him, but by now, he was miles away and well out of range of the rebel pursuers.[6]

Mount Vernon, Missouri, the county seat of Lawrence County, was 25 miles northeast of Sarcoxie on the Springfield road. Slightly more pro–Union than either Carthage or Sarcoxie, the defeated federals expected to find reinforcements there from the Union garrison at Springfield. As dawn broke and the day wore on, the searing heat of a very hot July sun blazed down on the weary men. Still carrying their wounded, they made frequent halts to rest. Stragglers spread along the road for miles unable to keep up with the main body. The head of the Union column reached Mount Vernon late Saturday afternoon, July 6. It was 9 P.M. when the last of Sigel's beleaguered troops straggled in, "utterly fagged out," as one soldier put it. They stacked their arms, collapsed to the ground and fell asleep, too exhausted to cook and eat.[7]

The performance of the Union Second Brigade in the events leading up to the Battle of Carthage, the fight itself, and the aftermath of the battle underscored the awful depravities of war. In hindsight, it was almost superhuman. On July 4, the brigade had marched 22 miles from Neosho to Carthage. Up at daybreak the next day, they marched 18 miles in searing heat from Carthage to Dry Fork Creek and back, maneuvering on the battlefield and engaging in cannonades and skirmishes the entire time. They withdrew without stopping another 15 miles to Sarcoxie, and then continued 25 miles to Mount Vernon. They covered better than 80 miles and fought a battle in the process, with barely two meals, over the course of three days.[8]

While the exhausted federal troops settled in on the evening of July 6, the earth passed through the tail of the Great Comet. As the long midsummer day ended, the sky appeared strange. It had a yellow, aurora look, and the sun gave but a feeble light and a peculiar phosphorescent illumination of the landscape. An ethereal veil covered the sun. People in their homes lit lamps at seven o'clock to dispel the sensation of darkness.

The Missouri State Guard did not advance on the defeated federals as expected and chose not to follow up their victory. Rather they elected to continue southward toward the Missouri-Arkansas border where Governor Jackson and his generals planned to join General Price and the Confederate troops of General McCulloch. They would then march on Springfield with their consolidated armies, and then on to other destinations in the state with the ultimate goal of liberating all of Missouri from the Union invaders. The victorious Missourians did not know that McCulloch and Price were already somewhere on the Neosho road approaching Carthage from the south.

On the morning following the battle, Thomas Hood climbed a knoll east of town looking for the old family cow. His daily chores amounted to rounding her up and driving her back to the Hood home. She ran loose and grazed wherever she chose but always ended up on that knoll, apparently to catch whatever breeze there was for keeping off the flies because it was one of the high points of the town. From the top of the knoll, he could see the State Guard army camped in every direction. Campfires dotted the countryside. He saw activity and bustle everywhere; men busied themselves with getting breakfast. Wagons, horses, and men spread out as far south as the eye could see. Horses neighed impatiently under the excitement and chafed at their restraints. Hood thought the number of men could not be less than 18,000, a count greatly inflated but understandable coming from an impressionable lad of 14 who lived in a town where a gathering of 500 people was the biggest crowd anyone had ever seen.

Obe Stinson, a Union man, lived close by and came out into his yard to see what was going on. Thomas climbed down from the top of Stinson's fence and with a solemn face and heavy sigh remarked, "The Union's gone up for sure, Mr. Stinson; the United States government can't never whip out all that bunch of men."[9]

That morning, July 6, the State Guard troops left Carthage to resume their journey southward. The people of Carthage filled wagons with provisions as best they could before the men left town and saw to it that each soldier received cloth, thread, and needles to make new clothing. Those in the courthouse who were too wounded to move stayed. Throughout the night, screams and pitiful moans had drifted over the public square. The impressionable eyes of young Thomas Hood saw a pile of limbs outside the southwest corner of the court-house. The pile grew larger with each retelling of the story, ultimately to a wagonload of amputated arms and legs, pitched by the surgeons through the courthouse window to the lawn below. Someone supposedly buried the ghastly mess before dawn in a trench cut across the courthouse lawn. It took a ditch 30 feet long and three feet wide to contain all the remains, as Hood told it. Such stories added to the tapestry of the war, although the material used to weave the tapestry was often less fabric and more fabrication.[10]

The Missourians had marched out of Carthage about three miles and stopped for dinner when news arrived that General McCulloch and Major General Price were only about three miles ahead of them. After a rapid march of approximately 20 miles, the Confederates had come within sight of Governor Jackson's men. An enthusiastic McCulloch overestimated the State Guard force at 7,000 strong. The two armies approached each other. This would be the joining of the State Guard and the Confederate troops, which the Union army had tried unsuccessfully to prevent.[11]

The rebels planned at first to march out to meet McCulloch. As soon as they were in line of march, however, they were ordered to halt and form up for review. They had been standing for an hour or so when McCulloch and Price appeared. Brigadier General Parsons met the two leaders and escorted them along the review line. No one needed to point out the striking contrast in appearance of the two armies. The State Guard soldiers stood in tattered civilian clothes, carrying personal weapons, and mounted on farm horses. McCulloch's men rode good-looking mounts and dressed in carefully tailored Confederate uniforms. When they saw McCulloch, one Missouri soldier remembered, "We were all young then and full of hope, and looked with delighted eyes on the first Confederate soldiers we had ever seen, the men all dressed in sober gray and their officers resplendent with gilded braid and stars of gold."[12]

The first to pass by were Governor Jackson and Major General Price. General Price removed his hat, a sign of honor and respect for the State Guard soldiers. The State Guard troops greatly admired Sterling Price. They affectionately called him Old Pap. He went out of his way to identify with them, often dressing in a suit of linen clothes "not over clean," as one observer noted. He carried a saber and rode an "old looking gray horse"; just like any old Missouri farmer, they said. General McCulloch with General Parsons at his side followed Price and Jackson. McCulloch removed his hat, too. It was an awkward gesture. McCulloch made no secret of his disrespect for the ill-clad and poorly organized Missourians, acquitted now as veteran soldiers. Behind them came all the other generals of the State Guard, a regular parade of newly made heroes. Major General Price introduced the head of every command to General McCulloch. After passing down the front of the line, the entourage returned along the rear to complete the review. Amid deafening cheers and waving of flags, the parade broke into a great rejoicing at the victory over the Union Dutch. The victorious Missourians were elated to hear that McCulloch had taken 100 German prisoners and their arms as he passed through Neosho. The capture of a few muskets by the Confederates, however, did not resolve the general lack of weapons in the State Guard. In a postscript to one of his letters, Private Boon wrote to his father, "I do not think McCulloch has any arms with him, but he says we will get them soon, and plenty of them."[13]

The Missourians were eager to relate news of the battle to the Confederates. They had met 2,000 federal troops, they said, ten miles north of Carthage and fought them the whole day, forcing the Union army back on its own path, and soundly defeating it. Talking to General McCulloch, the Missourians confided that they did not know the number of their own casualties but reckoned they had lost about 12 killed and 60 wounded. They thought the Union loss was at least equal to that.[14]

Except for the capture of the Union garrison at Neosho, McCulloch and the Confederate troops did not factor into the battle at all. Had McCulloch moved his command forward sooner, he could have at least blocked Sigel's retreat. Sending all or part of the Confederate cavalry up the Sarcoxie road from Neosho would have placed them in the Union path and prevented their escape. Some years after the war, John Snyder, who served in McCulloch's command, spoke openly of the general's incapacity as a field commander. He was brilliant as a leader of mounted scouts but as a general commanding an army, according to Snyder, he was lost, "entirely out of place; did not know what to do, or how to do it." Nevertheless, McCulloch's lack of action at Carthage did not prevent him from taking partial credit for the rebel victory. That such a disorganized army of poorly armed, green recruits from Missouri could rout a Union army of superior arms, McCulloch thought, could only mean that Sigel and the federals did not want to face his Confederates. They must have heard that he was in the area approaching the federal position and took the opportunity to make a rapid retreat toward Springfield. This was not only a rationalization for his tardiness, it was also his way of justifying to his superiors his presence in southwest Missouri. McCulloch felt uneasy about bringing his Confederate army into Missouri without authority. Jefferson Davis was not enthusiastic about Missouri and from the beginning tendered only lukewarm support from the Confederacy. Davis took a cautious attitude toward Missouri politics. He considered Governor Jackson's pledge to General Lyon at the Planter's House meeting in June 1861 to be an attempt at double-dealing to the point of being dishonorable and suspicious. In that meeting, Jackson and Price offered to use state troops to drive Confederates out of Missouri if necessary to preserve the state's doctrine of armed neutrality. Lyon rejected the offer but it compromised Missouri's place in the Confederacy from the beginning. Nevertheless, late in June 1861, the Confederate War Department authorized McCulloch to cross the Missouri border if necessary to protect Arkansas and the Indian Territory, but only "when necessity and propriety unite," they said. Only the pleas of General Sterling Price and the plight of Governor Jackson's troops trying desperately to reach the shelter of Confederate protection finally convinced McCulloch to intervene in the heretofore neutral territory.[15]

After the parade review, the State troops went back into camp and General McCulloch returned to his command. From where the Missourians were camped, they could see McCulloch at the head of his Confederate column of mounted horsemen filing up the road to unknown parts. As they watched him go out of sight, they hoped that he was looking for Sigel. The State Guard formed ranks and continued down the Neosho road toward Fidelity. That evening Governor Jackson dined at the home of Alta Fullerton. He and his entourage sat down to dinner served by the Fullerton slaves.[16]

The next day, General McCulloch, holding his troops at Neosho, considered his next move. First, he wondered what to do with Captain Joseph Conrad's company of federal soldiers held as his prisoners. He placed them in the courthouse where they remained while he decided what to do. Town leaders called for the execution of Conrad and his men by firing squad in the streets of Neosho. The story traveled all the way to New York. One East Coast newspaper reported that McCulloch captured 200 and executed all of them; another report said most survived, when in fact there were no casualties at all in the Union company, which was considerably smaller than the 200 men the press reported. State officials wanted to shoot them but McCulloch would not agree. He and the Confederate officers treated the Union officers and men in a friendly and respectful way. The citizens of Neosho were not so charitable. The St. Louis Germans were the targets of insulting and brutal treatment from residents and the enlisted State Guard Missourians. Around 5:30 on the afternoon of July 8, General McCulloch released them on their oath that they would not bear arms against the Confederate States for the duration of the war. Private Henry Cheavens witnessed the application of the oath and asked one of the freed German prisoners why they fought, to which he replied, "Nothing to do in St. Louis." Local sympathizers continued to threaten the federal soldiers when they left town that evening. McCulloch sent an escort of 30 men to accompany them the first four or five miles out of town on their journey to Springfield. Captain Conrad and his men wasted no time getting out of Newton County. They marched day and night with only short intervals of rest. Rebel troops had taken their canteens and haversacks. They marched without any rations, walking 85 miles through unfriendly territory and arriving in Springfield in less than two-and-a-half days with little water and hardly any food at all.[17]

Still uncertain about his authority to be in Missouri at this point in the war, General McCulloch decided to fall back to his position in Arkansas, near Maysville, and there to await further orders for future operations and to rest his men. The Confederates had been on the move for several days and nights, subsisting most of the time on a diet of beef and salt and what meager provisions they could secure from the countryside. None complained. Their only regret was a missed opportunity to prove the superiority of the Confederate army over the Union troops. That would have to wait for another time.[18]

The rebel Missouri forces took up the line of march on July 8, for McDonald County in the far southwest corner of the state. McDonald County was about as far southwest as a traveler could go and still be in Missouri. Its location offered protection to General Price and his ragtag Missouri State Guard. The Cherokee Nation bordered on the west, and to the south was the Confederate state of Arkansas. Here Price could organize and train his army for his mission to deliver Missouri to the Southern cause. The State Guard victory at Carthage bought valuable time to organize and train the growing Missouri army, and opened the southern route for supplies and reinforcements from the Confederacy. It kept alive hope for Missouri's independence and an opportunity to recapture the state. Perhaps most importantly, victory avenged the previous defeat at Boonville where the inexperienced State Guard had been roughly tumbled out of the central part of the state by the sharp actions of General Nathaniel Lyon only days earlier. The morale of the state troops improved measurably. They marched out of the Battle of Carthage with the swagger of experienced warriors, confident that they could meet anything the federal government could throw at them. The victory at Carthage meant one other thing. With Sigel and his troops chased out of the area, the rebels could reclaim stashes of hidden gunpowder and work the Granby lead mines for badly needed ammunition.[19]

The success at the Battle of Carthage marked an accomplishment of some magnitude in the earliest days of the war. An untrained and poorly armed rebel army of homegrown volunteers had routed an army of United States troops. The result of the battle was important to the cause of political and private liberties for every Missourian. The steady courage of the raw recruits that made up the rebel army made it clear that Lincoln's plan to put down the rebellion by force of arms would not be easy. The Battle of Carthage transformed the Army of Missouri in one day from untested boys into an army of seasoned veterans. Union pundits admitted that the State troops behaved much better than expected, and they acknowledged relief that the Missourians did not have better arms.[20]

After a fatiguing march, the Missourians halted on the other side of Elk River on Cowskin Prairie, the five-mile square patch of grassland where General Price had set up his camp. Here, under the nearby protection of McCulloch's Confederates in Arkansas, the Missourians could train and prepare for the next battle with Union forces; a battle Price felt was sure to come. Some of the men washed their filthy clothes and sat naked on a rock in the sun until they dried. Others took the bolts of cloth proffered by the citizens of Carthage and made new clothes. That evening, happy to return to solid Confederate territory and forgetting the 15-mile march just completed, the footsore rebel soldiers had one of the greatest hoedowns you ever saw, dancing into the night without stopping.[21]

The mission of the Missouri State Guard was to reestablish the state government of Missouri and in the process to restore the liberties of the people. To do so, nothing less than the eviction or destruction of Lincoln's invading army would be required. General John B. Clark, Sr.—U.S. representative, and brigadier general of the Missouri State Guard— ended his summary of the Battle of Carthage with foretelling vision. He wrote, "The citizen soldiery of Missouri have given to the world an earnest of their determination to defend their rights and redress their wrongs, and which inspires hope of success in the stormy future upon which we are now entering." Even though they now found themselves pushed hard against the border of the state, buoyed by victory at Carthage, they vowed to return under the motto: "We come to deliver you." General Price set about trying to convince General McCulloch to join them in a campaign to retake the state.[22]

General McCulloch's Confederates arrived back at Camp Jackson, outside Maysville, Arkansas, on the evening of July 9, after a six-day campaign into Missouri and back. McCul- loch sat down to pen a brief report to the Confederate secretary of war at Richmond. He warned the secretary that General Lyon would likely move on to Springfield and concentrate his forces for an attack on General Price's State Guard, now camped five miles inside the Missouri border. He saw an urgent necessity to make an attack on Springfield before the Union could gain strength. Unless orders came from the C.S.A., he said, he planned to join generals Pearce and Price to make an advance as soon as Price could sufficiently organize his forces. He intended to march despite a lack of arms and ammunition and a crippling lack of support from his superiors. The contest for Missouri remained unsettled and there was not time to wait.[23]

27

Hell on Retreat

Late on the night of July 6, word reached Sigel's encampment at Mount Vernon of General McCulloch's capture of Captain Conrad and his company of men garrisoned at Neosho. The news added to the bitter defeat of the Union plan to stop Governor Jackson's southward march to join McCulloch's Confederate army.

Everyone in Sigel's Union camp anticipated an attack from the Confederate and State forces who local informants reported were now advancing in great numbers on Mount Vernon. They were, in fact, marching in the opposite direction. Around 3 A.M. on Sunday, July 7, another alarm rousted the federal brigade up and into action. Union scouts reported the rebels advancing from the west and south. The federal troops took up a position on the outskirts of town and stood under arms for seven hours until about 10 A.M. when Colonel Sigel determined the intelligence to be another false alarm and ordered the men back into town to enjoy a cup of coffee and a breakfast of sole-leather flapjacks.[1]

Finding time to relax for the first time in the campaign, some of the men took the occasion to remedy one of the great inconveniences of summertime military duty, doing their laundry. The only clothes the men of Sigel's brigade had were those on their backs. Marching in the July sun made it necessary now and again to wash a few things. To do this, one located a convenient creek, stripped off every stitch of clothing and laundered it as best he could, staying in the water until his clothes were again dry enough to wear.[2]

Back in Springfield, acting brigadier general Tom Sweeny was in the process of setting up his headquarters in Springfield when he learned of Sigel's plight at Carthage. The message said Sigel's command faced superior numbers and stood in danger of capture by the secessionist State Guard troops. Sweeny hastily collected about 400 men of the Fourth Regiment Reserve Corps under Colonel B. Gratz Brown to go to the aid of the Union side. Brown's companies had barely settled in, only having reached Springfield from St. Louis on the day of the battle. Sweeny nevertheless ordered them to go to Sigel's rescue at once. They did not start for Carthage for another three hours. The battle by then had turned against Sigel, and he had withdrawn his troops. It would have been impossible for reinforcements to reach the besieged Union force in time anyway since the battle was already over when Sweeny learned about it, and the distance from Springfield to Carthage was at least a two-day march.

Far to the north, on the morning of July 7, General Nathaniel Lyon left Leesburg and pushed southward, not knowing that Sigel had been defeated at Carthage and that the State troops were now in practical control of southwest Missouri. Major Sturgis' Kansas volunteers broke camp at Clinton, intending to cross the Grand River and wait for Lyon on the other side. The rains had sent the Grand out of its banks. Sturgis took a detour downriver looking for a suitable place to cross his army. The mud was terrible. That evening, about nine miles outside Clinton, Sturgis came upon a large body of troops assumed to be State Guard. It turned out to be the army of General Lyon. There at the ferry on Grand River, on the road from Clinton to Osceola, the two Union armies came together. They fired an eleven-gun salute to mark the occasion. Lyon linked up with Major Sturgis ready to move southwest in pursuit of Governor Jackson, expecting all the time that Sigel would successfully interrupt Jackson's flight south. He had no idea that his bold plan to destroy the state government and its army was in shambles. The southwest arm of his pincer movement instead waited in defeat at Mount Vernon, anticipating an attack from the rebel State Guard at any time.[3]

Colonel Sigel stayed at Mount Vernon for a while, allowing his men to recuperate and watching for any sign of rebel activity. He half expected that the rebel Missourians would take up their pursuit once they had rested and replenished their provisions. While he waited, he began planning for the defense of Springfield. He would need reinforcements. Around four o'clock on the afternoon of July 7, he sent his adjutant, Lieutenant Max Tosk, ahead on a mission to St. Louis to give a full report of the situation in southwest Missouri and plead for reinforcements. Five miles out of Mount Vernon, Tosk met Sweeny's command, and 15 miles further on encountered Colonel Brown, both pressing forward to reinforce Sigel. The 26-year-old Tosk rode the 153 miles to Rolla in 29 hours, and then went by evening train to St. Louis.[4]

Sweeney and Colonel Brown got to Mount Vernon late on July 7. By the time they arrived with their reinforcements, they found the defeated Union army waiting for them. The reinforcements were only 400 in number, but to the recovering federals of Sigel's little band, they looked like 1,000. Sigel's defeated army remained in camp at Mount Vernon for a couple of days. On Monday morning, July 9, accompanied by Sweeny and Brown's detachment of reinforcements, they left Mount Vernon and started back to Springfield, 35 miles northeast. They arrived there without incident the following day around 10 A.M. and bivouacked south of the city on the Forsyth road.[5]

Exaggerated tales of the battle reached Springfield in advance of Sigel and his retreating army. It seemed that every loose-tongued braggart claimed to have witnessed the fight. One such self-identified correspondent reported rebel losses at an even 1,000, while claiming the Union had lost only 47. All over Springfield, different men asserted with equal confidence casualty lists for the rebels from a low of 16 killed and wounded up to an absurd figure of 1,200. Another correspondent, said to be reporting from the field, put the rebel losses at more than 700, compared with a mere 28 on the Union side. Never mind there were no newspaper reporters on the field with either the Missourians or the federals. Partisan swagger began with the first shot and never faltered thereafter. Rumors circulated among Union sympathizers that Governor Jackson was on his way to Mexico where he could safely squander the treasure he had stolen from the state capitol. Contradictory statements about the battle were soon afloat everywhere. While several newspapers reported that Sigel had suffered total rout and destruction, others acclaimed his success as the most glorious victory ever to shed luster on the Star-Spangled Banner. When reports of the battle reached St. Louis, and the newspapers on the East and West coasts picked them up, exaggerated stories painted a picture of Union success and described Sigel as a hero. They said Colonel Sigel and the United States Volunteers of Missouri kept at bay and severely punished a very disproportionate force of rebels. The North tried hard to avoid characterizing the battle as a Union defeat. They hailed Sigel's successful withdrawal in the face of overwhelming odds as a victory. When Sigel died in 1902, the *New York Times* actually stated as one of his military accomplishments that he had won the Battle of Carthage. The press praised him for eluding the grasp of a superior sized force and skillfully leading a successful retrograde movement. A few less partisan newspapers pointed out that in the German revolution Sigel had fought all his battles getting away. The Battle of Carthage reaffirmed his reputation. "Sigel is hell on the retreat," they said. Congressman Frank Blair, Lincoln's front man for Union troops in Missouri, testifying the following year before the Joint Committee of Congress on the Conduct of the War, dealt Sigel's hero status a personal blow when he told the committee, "The so-called battle at Carthage was but a retreat."[6]

One must nevertheless give Colonel Sigel his due. The Union was defeated on the field at Carthage but saved from disaster and disgrace by his skilled battlefield maneuvers. His brilliance in avoiding capture and the complete destruction of the Union presence in southwest Missouri outshone his bad judgment in placing a much smaller force in the path of a determined army of Missourians. His Second Brigade of Union Volunteers proved to be men of great skill and bravery. An overwhelmingly larger army of Missourians menaced them all day, intent on driving them from the field, capturing them, or destroying them. Under Sigel's able command, the lightly equipped federals defended one position after another, and faced sustained attacks by the rebel infantry and cavalry, front and rear, without a single man leaving the ranks. The cost of their bravery was high, although apparently surprisingly modest in comparison to the other side.

One of Sigel's first orders of business upon arriving at Springfield was to check the wounded into a local hospital. For five days in the heat of a July sun, the wounded had suffered in pain, some with life-threatening injuries. Twenty-three checked in with gunshot wounds, nine alone from Sigel's Third Regiment Company A, which saw much of the rear-guard action at Carthage. Most remained in hospital several days; some stayed a matter of weeks, and a few until the end of their enlistments. The war was over for them.[7]

Some Springfield Union women came in a whirl of excitement to assist the wounded. They came laden with ice water, buttermilk, and other delicacies to see what they could do. A young angel of mercy approached the bedside of one of the patients, who was wan and weary from his recent experience. Pity filled her heart. "Can I not do something for you?" she implored. "Would you like me to bathe your face?"

Looking up at her with sad eyes and in deadpan earnest with genuine gratitude for her good intentions, the soldier replied, "I have had it washed seventeen times today, Miss, but you can do it again if you want to!"[8]

Many are the stories of spent youth and maimed lives from the Battle of Carthage. Private William Roth, a 19-year-old, German-born volunteer, had wounds so severe that doctors amputated his right arm. The handsome brown-eyed youth with light hair and fair complexion was but one of many casualties whose brief enlistments in a single battle changed life for them forever.

Another story in particular stands out. Two weeks after the battle, two figures sat in silence on the train leaving Rolla. A mother had journeyed from her home in St. Louis, traveling overland to the hospital at Springfield to find her son and bring him back with her. She found him, sitting and waiting for her, blind and helpless, a Minié ball having struck him in the head. She was of the poorer German class, her faded calico gown worn and patched. Her eyes deep-set from the fatigue of the trip, her cheeks pale and drawn, the two quietly rode in somber idleness, the sightless eyes of the son closed, his hands pathetically folded in his lap, and his life's work done. Yet, there was unspoken joy. Although blind and helpless, he was alive. She had him safe, and the wings of peace folded around him as only a mother's love can do.[9]

The Union troops at Springfield now numbered about 2,600 officers and men, not counting the local Home Guards. These were trying times in Springfield. Those citizens of pro–South persuasion took great offense at a town full of German soldiers. The town in general disliked them. There were more soldiers around Springfield than there were civilians. Many of them behaved badly, becoming so troublesome and rude that one Southern-minded woman complained to General Sweeny. Sweeny suggested that if she would give rooms to two of his staff officers, they would protect her property. And so it turned out that Union officers found good quarters in the home of an unabashed secessionist follower.[10]

General Sweeny believed that behind the defenses at Springfield he could hold out until help arrived. General Lyon and his army were now within two or three days march. No one could confirm his exact whereabouts, only that he was perhaps two or three days out. The combined armies would amount to around 7,000 men under arms, a large force but less than half the number fielded on the rebel side now gathering in McDonald County several miles away — and not circling Springfield as Union alarmists imagined.[11]

It took two tedious days for General Lyon's Union army to cross the Grand River and resume the march southward. Somewhere near the Osage River on July 9, Lyon's men first heard the rumors of the fight at Carthage. The news was dire. Reports said the Missouri rebels had surrounded Sigel, and he could not last more than three days. By the time Lyon got the message, Sigel had already escaped Carthage on his way to Springfield. General Lyon knew nothing of the military situation in Springfield and had only the worst details about the fight at Carthage. He was still north of the Osage River when word reached him of Sigel's defeat. Lyon hurried to the crossing of the Osage, five miles above Osceola, and quickly prepared to ferry his men and supply trains across the river. It took time to cross his army over the Osage. The Union troops spent the day and continued into the night crossing the rain swollen and inhospitable stream.[12]

Still not fully aware of Sigel's retreat, General Lyon sent a letter to Sigel on July 10, 1861, from Huffman's Crossing on the Osage, just above the mouth of Sac River, outlining a strategy to stop Governor Jackson.

"I have heard of your fight with Jackson," he wrote, "and regret I could not have supported you. Get all your forces together so as to sustain yourself and if you cannot join me hang on Jackson's flank or rear if he advances to meet me. I have to cross both this and the Grand River which is 20 miles back and where my trains are still crossing by means of ferrying which is a very slow process. I hope to get off however in two or three days more and before I can get more provisions from you or from Springfield I shall be short as I have now but six days rations. Call on Gen. Sweeny at Springfield to support you."[13]

In the early hours of July 11, the army finished making the crossing and prepared for a forced march to go to Sigel's rescue. The men rested for a couple of hours after crossing the river, and at around 4 A.M. headed toward Carthage to relieve Sigel. They had barely started when they intercepted a courier with a message from General Sweeny at Springfield. Colonel Sigel had been badly defeated. Sweeny painted a bleak picture, "The enemy had concentrated and occupied a line from Springfield to Carthage. They numbered from thirteen to fifteen thousand, with eighteen pieces of artillery." Lyon left Sturgis' Kansas force at the Osage crossing, along with most of his baggage wagons and artillery, and hurried ahead. The last Union man in Sturgis' command did not cross over until 1 A.M. on the 12th. By then, Lyon had marched his men across two counties.[14]

Desperate to reach Springfield, Lyon marched his men 53 miles over barely traversable terrain and on two hours sleep. In hot July weather, the Union soldiers covered the distance in 24 hours, only to learn that Sigel was in no immediate danger. The feat goes down in history as one of the most rigorous forced marches ever. Anyone who was on that march never forgot it.[15]

The frantic race to save Sigel and the federal army at Springfield exposed a festering discontent in the Union ranks for the German element, particularly among some of the Kansas regulars. Some thought it a desperate effort to retrieve the errors of another volunteer in command, a not-too-veiled criticism of Sigel. When it circulated that Sigel had retreated, it caused even more rancor.

"It makes me ashamed of my country," wrote one captain, "when I see the old Stars and Stripes always in retreat, and the courage and devotion of our private soldiers rendered useless by bad leaders."

"One feels as if we were sold to the Dutch in this army," complained another. "Dutch is the prevailing language.... Damn the Dutch element of Missouri. They are useful but cowardly, and never become Americanized."[16]

These were scathing words for an army of which almost four-fifths were German Americans or men of German descent.[17]

Meanwhile, officials in southwest Missouri awaited news of Lyon's whereabouts. A courier by the name of Hindman carrying Lyon's July 10 letter to Sigel and unable to locate Colonel Sigel delivered the letter instead to Brigadier General Sweeny. Sweeny received it about 10:00 A.M. on July 11. This was the first reliable news Sweeny had heard from Lyon. He immediately sent Hindman back to Lyon with a letter detailing the outcome of the battle.[18]

When General Lyon learned that Sigel was safe and in no immediate danger, the column changed its direction away from Carthage more eastward toward Springfield and slowed the march to a more leisurely pace. It was now July 12 and the affair at Carthage was a week old. Lyon's army covered about five miles that day, a dramatic change from previous days, and camped near the small town of Melville (later named Dadeville), a town full of Union men and women to a person. The army continued toward Springfield the next day, marching 20 miles and coming into Greene County on Saturday the 13th. They stopped in the western part of the county and set up camp about ten miles west of Springfield near a place called Pond Spring. The Union army encamped amid picturesque prairie and timber country to reflect on their march of 200 miles. They had left Boonville just ten days before. While they made do temporarily on half rations anticipating new provisions from St. Louis, Major Sturgis' Kansas regiments caught up from the Osage River crossing and joined them in camp. The two armies had met at Grand River, in Henry County, bent on crushing Governor Jackson and his State Guard against the wall of Franz Sigel's German brigade. There would be unification with Sigel's brigade all right but under much different circumstances than originally planned.[19]

General Lyon's plan to trap and destroy Governor Jackson and the Missouri State Guard had failed. He had arrived too late to figure in the Battle of Carthage. Sturgis, too, had fallen short in his drive to prevent the rebel army from escaping. General Lyon attempted to organize his dwindling army in the following days. The four Union leaders — General Lyon, Colonel Sigel, Major Sturgis, and Captain (a.k.a. acting brigadier general) Sweeny — gathered their men at Springfield, trying to hold together a dwindling force as best they could to meet the rebel army growing in strength on the prairies of southwest Missouri. Of the 7,000 federal troops gathered at Springfield, some 3,000 of them were only days from the end of their 90-day enlistments. Badly clothed, poorly fed, and imperfectly supplied, none had been paid and few were willing to reenlist. Lyon looked in vain each day for reinforcements promised by the War Department that never came. General Sherman said later that he watched in dismay at the indifference of Washington toward the Western theater in the first days of the war.[20]

Word spread quickly of the Union defeat at Carthage as pundits tried to fashion a victory out of Sigel's skillful withdrawal to avoid capture by Governor Jackson's overwhelming rebel force. Victory for the Missourians was more real. When the federals left the field, it signaled defeat for Sigel's mission to stop Governor Jackson and his State Guard volunteers. The rout of the federal army ended General Lyon's pincer movement to crush the rebels; and it cleared the way for the Missourians to continue toward a linkup with General Price and the Confederates marching north from Arkansas. The rebel victory at Carthage opened communication between Missouri and the Confederates to the south, giving the young Army of Missouri access to arms and ammunition.

The Great Comet disappeared. Missouri's star clung precariously to its own universe. It teetered in the balance between the creed of equality of all men on one hand, and on the other the freedom to decide the destiny of a nation. The meaning of liberty is not necessarily an easy thing to decide.

All accounts reaching St. Louis now pointed to a forward movement of Union forces against the secessionists gathering in southwest Missouri. Heavy-hearted mothers and wives contemplated an anxious summer. From south of the Missouri border, Private Erasmus Stirman wrote home to report that McCulloch's army in Arkansas was preparing to go to Missouri again in a few weeks. "The next time we go," he said, "we expect to clean out the state."[21]

Postscript

The Battle of Carthage became a footnote in the history of the Civil War. The ordinary soldier passed from memory, mentioned now and then in a family history somewhere, their name scribbled on an index card tucked away in a file at a place most of them never saw. History remembers not the names of the enlisted men who fought the war but the generals who led them. Of the four men who prosecuted the war in southwest Missouri, none lived long to tell about it. The four senior commanders who saw their first major Civil War action in southwest Missouri all soon died either in battle or from consequences directly or indirectly related to the war. General Nathaniel Lyon died in a charge up Bloody Hill at the Battle of Wilson's Creek on August 10, 1861. General Ben McCulloch fell mortally wounded at the Battle of Pea Ridge on March 7, 1862. Governor Claiborne Jackson left Missouri in exile and died from stomach cancer on December 6, 1862, at a farmhouse outside Little Rock, Arkansas. General Sterling Price completed the war as a Confederate general. He fled to Mexico at the conclusion of the war, returning broken and indigent in 1867. He died September 29, 1867, in St. Louis, nine days past his 58th birthday.

Many of the field commanders at the Battle of Carthage suffered similar fates. Colonel Richard Hanson Weightman lost his life at Wilson's Creek, shot down within minutes and less than 100 yards from where Union General Nathaniel Lyon died. Brigadier General William Yarnell Slack fell mortally wounded at the Battle of Pea Ridge, and Brigadier General Mosby Monroe Parsons went into exile with General Price in Mexico where Mexican forces shot and killed him August 17, 1865. Brigadier General John Clark, Sr., ended his military service after the Battle of Carthage and accepted an appointment to the Confederate Congress. He followed the exile expedition to Mexico but returned to Missouri and practiced law until his death on October 29, 1885. Brigadier General James Rains continued a controversial role as a Confederate commander. He spent his last years in Texas where he lived until his death on May 19, 1880. State Guard line officers Benjamin A. Rives, Robert Y. L. Peyton, and John T. Hughes, all of whom figured prominently in the Battle of Carthage, died tragically in the war. Colonel Rives saw action at Wilson's Creek and died from a mortal wound at Pea Ridge. Colonel Peyton served in the Confederate Congress and died in office on September 3, 1863, from complications of disease contracted while defending Vicksburg. Colonel Hughes died from a gunshot to the head at the First Battle of Independence, Missouri, on August 11, 1862.[1]

On the Union side, the field commanders experienced somewhat different results after the Battle of Carthage. Of the four principal leaders — Colonel Franz Sigel, Colonel Charles E. Salomon, and lieutenant colonels Franz Hassendeubel and Christian D. Wolff— only Hassendeubel lost his life in the war. He died as the result of an explosion at the siege of Vicksburg. Colonel Sigel served as a Union commander in the East until he was relieved of command in 1864. He retired to civilian life and died in New York City on August 21, 1902. Colonel Salomon took command of a regiment of Wisconsin volunteers from his home state and served as a Union officer for the duration of the war. He died on January 9, 1881, in Utah. After the Battle of Carthage, Lieutenant Colonel Wolff accompanied a detachment of three-month volunteers back to St. Louis. He served in various capacities with the Enrolled Missouri Militia before returning to civilian life as an elected officer of St. Louis County. He died in St. Louis on May 21, 1899.

The officers of the Union artillery who proved so indispensable in Sigel's retreat at the Battle of Carthage for the most part disappeared from the war record after the Missouri campaign. Captain Christian Essig drowned in the Mississippi River during the Vicksburg Campaign. Nothing is know of Captain Theodore Wilkins, except that he advanced to the rank of major, accepted a discharge in 1863, and later appeared on the Civil War pension rolls.

On the State Guard side, the indefatigable Hiram Bledsoe and Henry Guibor both enjoyed long and distinguished military careers after the Battle of Carthage. Captain Bledsoe took his artillery skills and Old Sacramento cannon to many Civil War battles on both sides of the Mississippi River. He returned to Missouri after the war, later to serve in the Missouri senate. He died on February 6, 1899, at age 73. Captain Guibor, meanwhile, suffered a serious wound at Vicksburg, fought through the Atlanta campaign, and came back to St. Louis where he worked in various capacities for the city. He died in St. Louis on October 17, 1899. Guibor's gunnery mate, Lieutenant William P. Barlow, became editor of the Mobile, Alabama, *Register*, and later chief of police in Mobile. He returned to St. Louis in 1877 and worked as a printer until his death on December 27, 1896.

Union enthusiasts liked to say, "Missouri was seventh in population in 1860 and seventh in the number of men sent to the Union army." On the other side, Southern partisans boasted that no seceding state sent more men to fight for the Confederacy than Missouri. The facts sometimes flew loose in partisan speeches. Missouri, nevertheless, did send more men to the Civil War in proportion to its population than any other state. The division of loyalty to the North and South never abated. The sons of Missouri brought honor to both sides in the Civil War, willing to sacrifice their most precious gift on a field far from home that future generations might see the truth of national sovereignty as they saw it. For example, there were 39 regiments of Missourians at Vicksburg: 17 Confederate and 22 Union.[2]

Writing from Memphis on August 10, 1861— coincidentally the day of the Battle of Wilson's Creek — Governor Claiborne Jackson confided to General Sterling Price that he had secured from Confederate authorities at Richmond an appropriation of a million dollars to support the rebellion in Missouri, with hopes of more to come. Recognition by the Confederate leadership of the importance of Missouri to the war effort, however, came too late to turn back the gains that federal troops had already made to secure the state for the Union. The rump legislature of the deposed Missouri government eventually seceded from the Union and became the 12th star of the Confederate flag. The rump legislature met from October 28 to 31, 1861, at Neosho, Missouri. By that time, though, a state convention had stripped the elected state government of its legitimacy and Missouri stayed politically and militarily bound forever to the Union.[3]

Appendix: A Story of Casualties

No one knows how many men fought on July 5, 1861, at the Battle of Carthage. Early organizational records of the Missouri State Guard are nonexistent. No one knows how many died. No official report was ever made of rebel losses. Estimates vary from a few to numbers many times greater than those suffered by the Union force, guesses based largely on the superiority of the federal artillery. The rebels lost between 40 and 50 killed and 125 to 150 wounded, according to one observer. Another witness conservatively counted the number killed and mortally wounded on the State side at 11 with 35 wounded. Soldiers within the rebel line guessed that the losses within their ranks could not have been less than 60 killed and many more wounded. A rebel prisoner taken at Buck Branch when asked the number killed on his side put the number at 250 to 300. The U.S. government simply put the rebel casualties at 200 killed and wounded.[1]

Careless reporting by the press did little to mask the boastful and pernicious tone of partisan stories of the battle. A few of the State Guard field commanders refrained from making guesses about losses outside their own divisions, but others quickly jumped into the press frenzy seemingly with whatever figure came to mind, and the more sensational the better. The result was a plethora of estimates about the dead and wounded on both sides that greatly confused perceptions of the outcome of the battle. Carelessness and self-aggrandizement marred individual identity and sacrifice. The stories of how the numbers of the fallen entered the history books underscore the depravities of war. A few examples illustrate the point.

Lieutenant Max Tosk, Colonel Sigel's adjutant, first mentioned the number 200 with respect to rebel casualties in the *Missouri Republican*, July 11, 1861. He filed his eyewitness account of the battle with major newspapers, including the *Missouri Republican* of St. Louis, the *New York Times*, and *Sacramento Daily Union*. Historians continued for several years afterward to republish his version of the battle despite statements in it that turned out later to be incorrect. The National Park Service, which oversees national battlefields, still uses Lieutenant Tosk's estimate of 200 State Guard casualties. Meanwhile, in a dispatch that Colonel Sigel sent by Lieutenant Tosk to Colonel Chester Harding at the arsenal in St. Louis immediately after the battle, the Union commander gave a number of 24 federals killed. Later in his official battlefield report, he changed that number to 13 killed, 31

185

Found on the person of Genl Lyons when killed at Springfield 10 Augt 61.

Springfield Mo.. July 11th 1861.
2 o'clock p.m.

Dear Lyon,

Mr. Hindman, the bearer of this, arrived here at 10 o'clock this morning with your note to Col. Siegel, dated Hoffman's Crossing, which I was much pleased to receive, as it was the first reliable news I have recd of your whereabouts. Siegel and Solomon had an en=gagement with Jackson and Rains near Carthage, on the 5th. which lasted from 10 a.m. until dark, the loss on our side being 17 killed and about 30 wounded; their loss is supposed to be very great. Siegle commenced falling back in this direction, abandon=ing a company he left at Neosho, which was captured by McCulloughs troops, who formed a junction with Jackson the next day, swelling their force to quite a respectable size. I recd the news on Saturday about 7 p.m., and fearing Siegle might be surrounded and cut to pieces before he could reach here, I collected together about 400 men, and started with 5 days provisions, to his relief at 10½ o'clock that night, and joined him at Mount Vernon next day at noon, having only stopped about an hour at Little York to give the men a cup of coffee. We remained there until Tuesday morning, when we took up our line of march for this place, having heard that Jackson's army (8000 strong) had fallen back towards Arkan-sas. It is said they intend attacking this place, but I think I can hold it in spite of them. though I'm very short of ammu=nition for artillery. I will try and send you provisions

wounded, and 94 captured. He also amended Tosk's estimate of 200 rebel casualties and put State Guard losses at 350 to 400.

The heavily pro-secessionist *Morning Herald*, in St. Louis — countering reports in the pro–Union *Missouri Republican* — described the road tracked with blood and dotted with dead bodies of escaping federals for 12 miles. Vitriolic stories of Missouri victory quoted anonymous sources claiming that the State Guard cavalry had split the Union forces in two and inflicted as many as 700 federal casualties. "The Missourians shot them down like rats,"

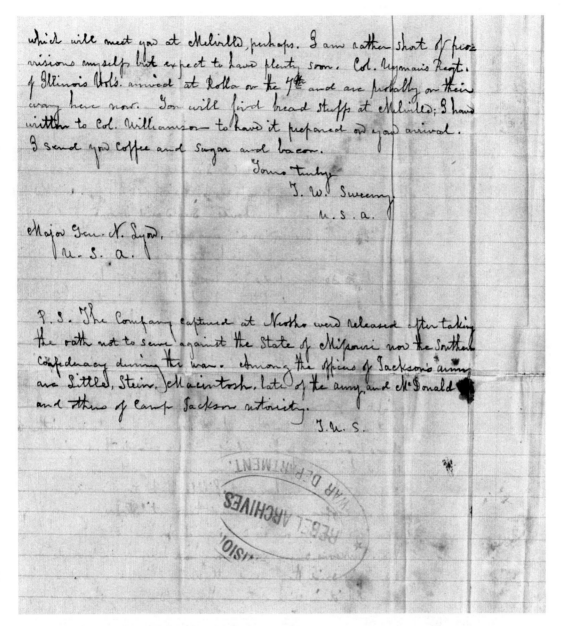

Opposite and above: Brigadier General Thomas Sweeny sent this letter to General Nathaniel Lyon, July 11, 1861, to report the defeat of Union forces at the Battle of Carthage, Missouri. Caretakers found the letter in General Lyon's pocket after his death at the Battle of Wilson's Creek. (National Archives and Records Administration.)

they said. When the Germans resisted, "the Missouri boys rode up and cut their heads off." By one account, 30 federal wagons and several pieces of artillery fell into State Guard hands. Such stories laced with palpable hatred for Lincoln's army clouded the facts of the battle. Press reports on both sides became so irrational that one newspaper gave State troop casualties as four killed in one story and 46 killed in another story in the same edition. The public had no idea of the real outcome of the fight.[2]

The Battle of Carthage, 1861. Northern newspapers printed elaborate stories of the Battle of Carthage that stirred up unionist patriotism against the rebellion. Artists drew imaginary scenes of the battle while reporters wrote fabricated descriptions based on loosely rumored accounts. This full-page engraving appeared in *Harper's Weekly* complete with a bridge across Dry Fork Creek where none existed. (State Historical Society of Missouri.)

Union claims of federal losses are questionable. The only official Union casualty list extant is in the National Archives in Washington, D.C. It is a greatly minimized short list of only four missing soldiers filed by Colonel Franz Sigel for his Third Missouri Infantry Regiment. The report lists no killed or wounded. One of the four men listed as missing in the report later turned up on a State Guard hospital list as wounded and taken prisoner. There are apparently no complete casualty reports for any of the Union regiments or battalions at the Battle of Carthage. Why Sigel's abbreviated report in the archives consists of only four men missing defies explanation. Sigel's battlefield report and estimate of casualties drew criticism almost immediately. A captain in Major Samuel D. Sturgis' Kansas Regulars said, "I don't believe a word of it. I think he ran like a coward."[3]

Rebel reports had their own anomalies. The first written estimate of casualties from the rebel side was that of State Guard Colonel John Hughes written July 6, the day after the battle, and published a few days later in the *Liberty* (Mo.) *Tribune* and *Charleston* (Mo.) *Courier*. Hughes said 130 Union men died with 300 wounded. His estimate of Guard losses amounted to 15 killed and 40 wounded. On July 7, a much different story from an anonymous source surfaced in the *Fort Scott Democrat*, a Union newspaper, in a story picked up immediately by the *New York Times*, which estimated State Guard losses at 300 to 500.[4]

There were equally fantastic stories of the details of the battle. Claims by one eyewitness that the State troops captured seven of Sigel's guns, including two mortars, greatly stretched the truth. He had only eight cannon total and no mortars. Springfield, Missouri, editors hurried sketchy dispatches to the St. Louis press. East and West Coast papers picked them up and filed every kind of inaccurate and dubious information. One fictitious account of the battle included a night attack on Sigel's retreating forces. The story said that in this alleged sequel to the battle secession troops attacked Sigel's retreating army after dark while it encamped southeast of Carthage, and it was "badly cut to pieces," losing 300 to 1,000 as killed or taken prisoner. The secessionists, according to the story, lost 1,000 to 2,000. Another informant put the number of Union troops killed in the night attack at 400, and 600 taken prisoner, besides the capture of three pieces of Sigel's artillery. The Northern public clamored for such tales, and the *New York Times* did not disappoint them. A headline proclaimed, "Great Battle in Missouri; Fifteen Hundred National Troops against Ten Thousand Rebels." The newspapers sensationalized the rebellion beyond common sense and without much regard for the truth. The editors appeared to have no idea where Carthage, Missouri, was. In a single sentence, the *Times* reported Carthage as the county seat of Jackson County, located seven miles south of the battle at Brier Forks Creek, none of which squared with the geographic facts. The *Times* also reported the death of General Rains, a victim of the battle, but quickly retracted the erroneous story of the general's demise. A similar false report had Union Lieutenant Colonel Wolff left dead on the battlefield. In its haste to make war heroes of Sigel and his Union brigade, the Northern press freely invented the content of their stories, once crediting the federals with the capture of 50 rebel prisoners at Buck Branch, along with 85 horses without riders, 65 shotguns, and numerous pistols and Bowie knives left scattered on the ground — none of which was factual. Tabloid newspapers, such as *Leslie's Illustrated* and *Harper's Weekly*, tended to fantasize the battle even more than the mainstream press, often with little adherence to the facts. All this spurred on Northern sentiment to punish the secessionist rebels. The outrageous exaggerations of casualty estimates that fed the press often had no other purpose than to stir up patriotic zeal and Union sentiment against the South.[5]

The local press had its own stories to tell. The Leavenworth, Kansas, *Daily Times* writing a few days after the battle said,

> We conversed yesterday with five families who have just been driven out from Southwestern Missouri, and are on their way to Illinois. They appear to be intelligent, industrious, and honest people. They are from Jasper County, and about six miles from where the Battle of Carthage was fought — They say that the battle was far more desperate than we had heretofore supposed; that fifteen hundred secessionists were killed, that they were from Friday until the next Thursday, in burying the dead. They say that Sigel's artillery was terrible in the work of death; that all along the line of the retreat, the ground was covered for miles with the dead — men and horses; that the day after the battle, the battlefield presented a scene of terrible carnage. They report that the loss of the Federal troops was small, owing to the great skill of their commander, and the superior management of their artillery.[6]

Soldiers in the battle told their versions of casualties. Henry Martyn Cheavens, writing sometime between July 5 and July 9 in his journal, put opposing Union losses at 200 to 250 killed, wounded, and taken prisoner. He claimed that the first shot from Bledsoe's Battery killed eight and wounded 16 federals, numbers that he somehow derived from his location a half mile away. He recorded State Guard casualties as eight killed and 39 wounded. However, Cheavens' claim that he saw 75 Union dead tossed into a pond eroded his credibility as a reliable source on the casualty issue. Elsewhere, Thomas Hood who witnessed the aftermath of the battle estimated that there must have been more than 100 of the wounded alone in the courthouse. He claimed to have watched the surgeons operate and pitch amputated limbs out the open south window of the courthouse. He said the pile of arms and legs amounted to a full wagonload.[7]

Brigadier General Rains, the ostensible rebel field commander, stated that the State Guard lost 44 men killed and wounded. He attached a list of killed and wounded to his report. The list was lost, and he gave no estimates of Union casualties. However, the figure 44 could not be representative of total losses taken by the State Guard because Rains' subordinate officers reported losses totaling at least 70. Weightman reported 40 casualties in his brigade alone; another 14 killed or wounded were in Slack's division; eight in Parsons' command; and Clark lost ten men killed and wounded. None of the field reports of the State Guard commanders satisfied the *Fort Scott Democrat* and *New York Times*, which estimated the loss of Governor Jacksons's side to be very great, citing an informant who said he counted between 70 and 80 wounded on the field and in houses by the wayside.[8]

Vivid descriptions of the battlefield painted a picture of bodies everywhere. General Clark spoke of dead scattered along the Union line of retreat. One chronicler of the battle wrote a particularly stirring account. He said, "The bodies of dead men and horses lay where they fell. Walking wounded sought aid at farm houses along the battle route.... The Rev. David Holman, the town's sole resident pastor, scurried about the field of battle helping to tend the wounded and pausing to pray over the bodies of the dead." It was a suffocating, hot day. Some said that many of the soldiers littering the battlefield had collapsed in the heat but later recovered. If so, the newspapers ignored that possibility. The *Fort Scott Democrat* reported,

> At Dry Fork a large amount of beef was thrown out of the wagons, it is supposed, to make room for the dead.... Another informant, a resident of Carthage, states that he passed over a part of the battlefield yesterday morning [July 6], and says he saw wagons and hacks passing in every direction, gathering up the dead for interment.... The ground in many places was strewn with dead horses, and the stench was sickening.

Such were the stories that fed the national newspapers, and they reprinted them verbatim all the way from California to New York.[9]

A *New York Times* article dated July 15, 1861, citing St. Louis correspondence ten days after the battle, set Union losses at 28 and State Guard losses at more than 700. The *Times* story initially put Union killed at ten and 18 wounded, but two days later ran a correction that said 11 of Sigel's troops died of their wounds, bringing the total killed to 21, and revised the estimate of Guard losses down from 700 to 500. Similar casualty numbers appeared in the *Sacramento Daily Union*. By July 22, however, the *New York Times* acknowledged on the Union side 47 killed and wounded but admitted no real knowledge of Guard losses, citing figures anywhere from nine killed and seven wounded, up to 1,200 casualties with as many as 1,000 killed, all in the same article. The *Times* was not solely to blame for its bad reporting. These were the numbers circulated in Springfield, Missouri, in the aftermath of the battle. A newspaper correspondent traveling with General Lyon from Boonville and lately arrived in Springfield reported the rumors he heard to the Northern press although he had no personal knowledge of the battle. One Missouri State Guard officer grew tired of reading such exaggerated Union accounts and wrote his own version to the Northern papers. Surgeon General George W. Taylor writing on July 20, 1861, gave his rebel account of the battle. He said 12 State Guard soldiers died with 31 wounded and claimed losses of not less than 200 Union soldiers. (The *New York Times* held up Taylor's rebel account and did not publish it until early October 1861.)[10]

The official record of the Battle of Carthage did little to clarify the outcome of the battle. The battlefield reports that appeared in the *War of the Rebellion Official Records* were in some cases edited versions of the original reports. For example, the only surviving original casualty list of any of the State Guard commanders is that of General Slack. He included in his handwritten report the names of 14 casualties from his Fourth Division: two killed, four mortally wounded, and eight wounded. The published report in the *Official Records*, however, inexplicably gives only 12 casualties for Slack's command and omits their names.[11]

Early histories of the Battle of Carthage reflect the ambivalence about casualties. Campbell, in 1866, adopted Sigel's report of 13 killed and 31 wounded for the Union, while concluding there had been "great slaughter" on the rebel side with 300 to 500 casualties. Blankenbecker, writing a decade later, concluded the opposite, that there was "slight loss on both sides." Bevier, in an 1879 account of the battle, gave Union killed at 150 to 200, with 300 to 400 wounded, citing old press accounts. He said Union killed and wounded were scattered over a space of ten miles or more, an observation he probably took from General Clark's battlefield report that made a similar claim. Bevier said State Guard casualties amounted to between 40 and 50 killed, and 125 to 150 wounded. These figures apparently satisfied C.S.A. President Jefferson Davis because he included them word for word in his 1881 memoir. Meanwhile, North, writing in 1883, gave Sigel's numbers of 13 killed and 31 wounded for Union casualties and estimated State Guard losses at not less than 300 killed and twice as many wounded with the caveat, "The rebel loss was not published officially, and never can be accurately ascertained." To be fair, neither can the losses of the federals.[12]

A reputed official statement of Union casualties for the Battle of Carthage is that of Frederick H. Dyer in *A Compendium of the War of the Rebellion* (1908). Dyer placed Union losses at 18 killed, 53 wounded, and five missing. He did not give rebel losses. The origin of Dyer's numbers is unknown. He allegedly derived his figures from official sources showing Union troops engaged in each event and losses sustained, "where such was officially reported." However, he does not cite a specific source, leading to the speculation that he had at his disposal certain official records not otherwise available in the battlefield reports. Exactly when these figures became public is likewise uncertain. Dyer published his *Compendium* in 1908; however, the figures he gave also appeared in the *Atlas to Accompany the Official Records of the Union and Confederate Armies* published 16 years earlier. The *Atlas* gave "Confederate" losses — although there were no Confederates at the Battle of Carthage — as 44 killed and 30 wounded. Both the *Atlas* and Dyer's *Compendium* give rise to skepticism because the Union casualty figures of 18 killed, 53 wounded, and five missing are exactly the same as the Union casualties reported for the Battle of Big Bethel on June 10, 1861, in Virginia, down to the number of missing. The National Park Service pointedly ignores these numbers for the Battle of Carthage in favor of Sigel's report of 13 killed and 31 wounded, and a general estimate of 200 State Guard losses. The National Park Service gives 79 casualties for Big Bethel. Nevertheless, the Dyer figures for the Battle of Carthage are the ones often cited in histories that mention the Battle of Carthage.[13]

The issue of casualties at the Battle of Carthage has not become clearer with time and remains unsettled. In 1923, Ward Schrantz, working primarily from battlefield reports, invoked Sigel's original Union numbers of 13 enlisted killed and 31 wounded, adding five wounded and left on the field and captured, for a total of 49. He calculated the loss to the Missouri State Guard as ten killed and 64 wounded, some mortally, as gleaned from officers' reports. At the same time, however, Schrantz stated, "The official tabulation at Washington gives the Southern losses as 35 killed, 125 wounded, and 45 captured." He does not identify the source of the official tabulation at Washington, nor does he comment on its variance with his own estimate of Guard losses.[14]

By the mid–20th century, there were two prevailing estimates of casualties for the Battle of Carthage: the numbers from Dyer's *Compendium* and the official Washington tabulation cited by Schrantz. Shoemaker published a 1942 variation on Schrantz, giving State Guard losses as 30 killed, 125 wounded, and 45 captured. For Union losses, he used Sigel's figures of 13 killed, 31 wounded, and 94 captured. Later he modified his position on rebel casualties to acknowledge Schrantz's figures of ten killed and 64 wounded, taken from battlefield reports. He included the caution that government officials compiled Confederate losses after the war, implying possible inaccuracies in their tabulations.[15]

In 1961, Virginia Easley published Henry Martyn Cheavens' journal. Instead of using Cheavens' estimate of casualties (200 to 250 Union, 47 State Guard), she applied those of Dyer and the *Atlas of the Official Records*: federals 18 killed, 53 wounded, 5 missing; rebels 44 killed, 30 wounded. VanGilder, meanwhile, in 1961, adopted Schrantz's "official U.S. government records" list of State Guard casualties at 35 killed, 125 wounded, and 45 captured, but took notice of Schrantz's compilation of incomplete State Guard records that showed ten Guard soldiers killed and 64 wounded, some mortally. On the Union side, he accepted Sigel's numbers.[16]

The difference between Sigel's reported casualties and the Dyer *Compendium* figures is the sum of the controversy over Union losses. On the rebel side, there is no consensus. Hinze and Farnham cautiously concluded that Missouri State Guard losses amounted to approximately 12 killed, 64 wounded, and one missing; the dead being the number originally set forth by Surgeon General Taylor shortly after the battle in 1861 and generally confirmed by Schrantz and VanGilder. These numbers and those for Union casualties — 18 killed, 53 wounded, and 5 missing — total almost the same for both sides, although by this count the Union experienced more deaths.

One of the most astonishing statements about casualties at the Battle of Carthage came from Frank P. Blair, a key political figure responsible for events leading up to the battle. On February 7, 1862, in testimony before the joint committee of the U.S. Congress impaneled to investigate the conduct of the war, Blair said, "Sigel killed a great number of them and succeeded in drawing off his force, with a loss of not more than two or three men."[17]

It is likely that the true number of dead and wounded on both sides will forever remain unknown, let alone the names of those who died. Countless names of the fallen never made a casualty list. Many fell in the conflict unknown and forgotten. This was particularly true of the unrecorded recruits of the State Guard. Private Boon, who counted on his side 15 killed and more than 50 wounded, mentioned that a schoolmate named Simpson died in a charge and that two Howard County friends fell wounded, but neither Simpson nor the friends showed up on a casualty list. Sergeant Major William Hyde of Colonel Hughes' regiment later died of his wounds. Buried at Carthage, his name, too, appeared on no casualty list, and so it went. Two privates, remembered only as Privates Garrison and Turner, of Captain Thomas McCarty's Company A, suffered wounds but did not show up on a rebel list. Private James T. Riley, also of Captain McCarty's company, likewise fell wounded but unaccounted for. The men of McCarty's Company A were particularly hard hit because they were constantly in front of the battle and subject to more intense fire from the Union guns. They stood near Bledsoe's Battery during the cannonade and were among the last to give up the chase of Sigel's retreating federals. They faced the blistering barrage unleashed by the Union guns when the federal troops fled Carthage. It was in this final attack that

Private Albert Withers, the Clay County boy from Liberty, died. Close to where Private Withers fell, another young rebel soldier felt the sting of Union grapeshot. Twenty-one-year-old David Rice Atchison, Jr., who fought with Hughes' First Infantry Regiment, wound up in the care of a private physician at Carthage and survived his wound much to the pride and relief of his famous father. The less well-connected remained anonymous. Several hundred unidentified Missourians never got into battle because they had no weapons. Great numbers of unarmed Missourians followed at a distance. More than a third of them watched the action from a vantage point back of the army waiting for a chance to fight. There were stories that the retreating federals dropped numerous muskets, which the Missourians picked up and immediately distributed to their unarmed comrades. Freshly armed men showed up in the battle line unknown to their commanders. More than once, a newcomer fell, leaving no record of who he was or where he came from. After the battle, some Missourians went back home, less enthused about the prospect of war and less convinced about the self-evident truth of the rebel cause, leaving their commanders to ponder their disappearance.[18]

Meanwhile on the Union side, the retreating federals tried to identify their losses, but stories about the Union dead likewise left names in doubt. For example, W. H. King of the State Guard claimed he shot Captain Bertrand, an officer in Sigel's Third Regiment, before the Union captain could shoot him. However, no mention is made of Captain Bertrand in any official records. Either King made up a story, or Captain Bertrand went to his grave anonymously. One eyewitness said that the federals abandoned some of the fallen in their haste to withdraw and that the Missourians buried many Union soldiers left dead on the field. Others left in rebel hospitals became prisoners. Reconstructed lists would show later that Sigel's tallies were badly understated and did not count at least 17 men taken by the rebels as prisoners. Five of the Union wounded remained at the Carthage courthouse. Several of the State Guard commanders also reported taking prisoners on the battlefield, and a year later in court-martial testimony, a captain in General Parsons' division revealed that he had turned over prisoners to Governor Jackson's staff. None of these losses were mentioned in Sigel's after-action report. He likewise accounted for none of the volunteers who joined his ranks along the march from Springfield. For instance, Jim Ross and his son-in-law Jim Alsup of Polk County wound up in unmarked graves in Jasper County, as probably did many more like them, but they never appeared on a Union casualty list. Union reports likewise made no mention of Owen Nichols, whom comrades left for dead beside the road. The omission of Nichols was particularly noticeable because he was supposedly Sigel's color bearer. Sigel appears to have ignored casualties except where there was a muster record for a Union soldier. Private Nichols' unit was Gatton's Company F of the Lawrence County Home Guard, the company that joined Sigel at Mount Vernon as a guard detail. This company and possibly other units of the Lawrence County Guard probably played a role in the Battle of Carthage. From the time of its formation in May 1861 to August 1861, the regiment lost an officer and 14 men killed and an unknown number wounded. The regiment disbanded on August 10 when General Lyon refused to accept an offer of the regiment to accompany him to Wilson's Creek. Therefore, it is likely that the Battle of Carthage accounts for some if not most of the casualties suffered by the Lawrence County Home Guard during its relatively brief period of existence.[19]

Colonel Sigel also glossed over his loss of war materials. Instead of losing his entire supply train, which the rebels threatened at one point, only a couple of baggage wagons were lost. He claimed that only one was lost, and that one in Carthage because there were no horses left to move it out of town. General Slack of the State Guard was very specific, however, in his claim that he captured two baggage wagons filled with supplies, one filled with buffalo robes. At the same time, Sigel made no mention of the supply wagons lost at Neosho with the capture of Captain Conrad's company.[20]

Many animals died in the shelling. Accountability for livestock and weapons got special scrutiny during the war. Commanders tried to offset their own losses of cannon, for example, with entries about arms and equipment captured from the other side. Sigel claimed to his superiors that two pieces of rebel artillery were disabled, including one that someone reported to have seen burst. Neither claim had validity. A keg of powder exploded in Bledsoe's Battery but the gun stayed in action. Another story said that rather than risk capture, Sigel buried two of his fieldpieces on an island in the middle of Spring River. Battlefield reports do not confirm this, and subsequent placement of the Union guns at Carthage seems to indicate that Sigel escaped with all eight of his guns, although there is room to consider the possibility that Sigel lost two guns somewhere. The various narratives on the placement of artillery at the last Union defense across Seminary Street speak only of six guns. The assumption is that two pieces retired up the Sarcoxie road to cover the withdrawing federals; however, the record is not clear on this. It makes sense that Sigel would not mention the loss of the two guns in his report because he published the report in the newspapers almost immediately after the battle, which would have made it easy for the rebels to retrieve the guns. The story of Sigel's buried guns found its way into the folklore of the battle, whether true or not. Long after peace returned, General Sigel revisited Carthage and the scenes of his campaigns of 1861. He allegedly drove over the road from Dry Fork Creek along the battle route into Carthage. Stopping at Spring River, he told his local escort that he had dismounted two brass field guns and had them buried in the river at the northern point of a small island. He inspected the river from the Spring River crossing to the railroad looking for the site, supposedly about halfway between the ford and the railroad. Some hired laborers dug but were unable to locate the guns where Sigel said he had buried them. Spring River shifts its course from time to time, and the guns may be there yet.[21]

The measurement of the intensity of a battle is in the number of those who fell. By such a scale, the Battle of Carthage, or Dry Fork Creek, does not compare with the carnage of succeeding Civil War engagements. In barely more than two weeks after the Battle of Carthage, the armies of the North and South, each 18,000 strong, met at Bull Run, not far from Manassas Junction, in Virginia. There along the banks of Young's Branch, on Henry House Hill, and along Chinn's Ridge, the Civil War revealed itself in its ugliest form. Almost 5,000 men fell, 847 killed, in one of the bloodiest battles of the war. The violence and carnage sobered both sides. The Confederate victory told the North that this was no mere political squabble and that a much longer and bloodier war was ahead than anyone had anticipated. The clamor of the Northern citizenry for punitive military action against the upstart South suddenly fell silent and became much less imperial than before.[22]

The bombardment of Fort Sumter opened the War between the States. After the attack in Charleston Harbor, opposing forces met several times at various places in the country in isolated skirmishes, so called for their brevity and the small size of the forces involved. Although important to the early development of the Civil War, these light engagements generally did not merit distinction as battles. The standard definition of a battle is a sustained fight between large, organized armed forces. Whether the Battle of Carthage rises to the classification of a battle may rest on the interpretation of this definition. Without question, Carthage was a sustained fight, lasting more than 12 hours. While one may argue about the poor status of organization, particularly among the Missouri State Guard divisions, the two sides nevertheless formed lines of battle and engaged in deadly armed exchanges, each side suffering numerous casualties. Some will argue that Carthage was not a battle because the opposing forces were not large enough and the number of casualties did not satisfy the definition of a battle when compared to later, bloodier outcomes of the Civil War. To say that the Battle of Carthage was unimportant because so few men died dismisses the real consequence of war. The Battle of Carthage rose to the same size and intensity of more than one battle of the Revolutionary War. For example, the Battle of Springfield, in Union County, New Jersey, June 23, 1780, had eerie similarities in size and casualties to the Battle of Carthage, and no one questioned that that was a battle. Fought almost on the same day as the Battle of Carthage 81 years before, 1,500 American Continentals — supported by an undetermined number of militia — met 6,000 British and Hessian troops. Thirteen Continentals died with 49 wounded, very close to Sigel's reported number of Union casualties at Carthage. The other side lost 25 killed and 234 wounded.

If Carthage was a battle, where then does it fit in the lineage of Civil War battles? It came before both Bull Run and Wilson's Creek, but after Big Bethel. Given the brevity of Bethel and the lack of full battlefield engagement, one begins to conclude that the Battle of Carthage is of singular importance in the lineage of the war. Put into political context — as the battle immediately following President Lincoln's proclamation of war against the Confederate States — the Battle of Carthage, Missouri, arguably has the distinction of being the first battle of the American Civil War.

Notes

Chapter 1

1. Connelley, *Standard History*, 299–300; Webb, *Battles and Biographies*, 298; Phillips, *Missouri's Confederate*, 170–172; Carr, *Missouri*, 220–240; Harvey, "Missouri," 23–26; Shoemaker, "Missouri: Heir of Southern Tradition," 435–446.

2. Carr, *Missouri*, 139–148; Axelrod, *Civil War*, 26.

3. Oates, *To Purge This Land*, 82–138; Carr, *Missouri*, 241–266; Harvey, "Missouri," 30–31.

4. Washburn, *Issues*, 8–10; *Leslie's Illustrated Newspaper*, 27 June 1857, 50.

5. Bordewich, "Day of Reckoning," 62–69; Axelrod, *Civil War*, 27–29.

6. Herndon and Weik, *Herndon's Lincoln*, 466–468.

7. Kirkpatrick, "Missouri on the Eve," 99.

8. Catton, *Coming Fury*, 370; Missouri General Assembly, House, *Missouri State Convention,* 132; Carr, *Missouri*, 267–290; Kirkpatrick, "Missouri on the Eve," 104. The State Convention met at Jefferson City and St. Louis in 19 sessions over a period of 23 days, beginning February 28, 1861, in Jefferson City. On the third day, March 4, 1861, it moved to the Mercantile Library Hall in St. Louis and concluded there in the afternoon of March 22, 1861.

9. Grant to Colonel H. K. Craig, 3 May 1861.

10. Snead, *Fight for Missouri,* 129; Carr, *Missouri*, 291–323; Blum, "Political and Military Activities," 118.

11. Woodward, *Life of General Lyon*, 221; *Review of Life of General Lyon*, 151.

12. Blair, "Testimony," 156–161; Wurthman, "Frank Blair," 263–287; Blum, "Political and Military Activities," 115; Snead, *Fight for Missouri*, 99; Anderson, *Story of a Border City*, 63–85; Harvey, "Missouri," 31–37.

13. Peckham, *Nathaniel Lyon*, 138; Harvey, "Missouri," 39.

14. Blum, "Political and Military Activities," 107–108; *Wöchentlicher Anzeiger des Westens* [St. Louis], 21 July 1854; Dunson, "Germans on Slavery," 355–366.

15. Primm, *Lion of the Valley*, 250; Rombauer, *Union Cause*, 226; Pollard, *First Year of the War*, 126–131; Leland, "War between Freedom and Slavery," 369–381, 405–413; Lyon, "No. 1, Report," 4–6; Covington, "Camp Jackson," 204–209; Harvey, "Missouri," 40; *Missouri's Sons of the South*, 707–710, 725.

16. *History of Carroll County,* 290–296.

17. United States, Record and Pension Office, *Organization and Status of Missouri Troops*, 246–320; Missouri General Assembly, House, *Missouri State Convention*, 54–56.

18. Nicolay, *Outbreak of Rebellion*, 115–125; Webb, *Battles and Biographies*, 7–71; Mark Twain quoted in Nevin, *Civil War*, 8; Pearce, "Memoir," 1.

19. Snead, *Fight for Missouri*, 193–210. Thomas Snead attended the meeting at the Planter's House hotel and wrote a firsthand account of it.

20. McElroy, *Struggle for Missouri*, 109–118; Davis, *Rise and Fall*, 401.

21. Heidler, et al., *Encyclopedia*, 1055; Grover, "Civil War in Missouri," 17; *History of Carroll County*, 298; Duncan, *John T. Hughes*, 76.

22. Catton, *Coming Fury*, 387; Lyon, "Engagement at Boonville," 11; Rorvig, "Significant Skirmish," 127–148.

23. Pollard, *First Year of the War*, 126–131; "Domestic Intelligence," *Harper's Weekly*, 13 July 1861, 419; Payne, "Fighting in Missouri," 913.

24. Blair, "Testimony," 160; Phillips, *Damned Yankee*, 215–216.

25. *History of Cole County*, 418, 493–496.

26. Owens, *Hier snackt wi Plattdutsch*, chapter 16; "Fight at Cole Camp," *New York Times*, 7 July 1861; Pollard, *First Year of the War*, 126–131.

Chapter 2

1. Harding, "Old Missouri State Guard," 5–6, 9, 25; Harding, *Service with the Missouri State Guard*, 12; Webb, *Battles and Biographies*, 69; *History of Saline*

County, 280–281; Young, *History of Lafayette County,* 85.

2. Holcombe, *History of Greene County,* 284.

3. Fairbanks and Tuck, *Past and Present,* 242; Holcombe, *History of Greene County,* 284.

4. Escott, *History and Directory,* 90; Holcombe, *History of Greene County,* 285–286; United States, *Organization and Status of Missouri Troops,* 146–164; Pinkney, "Souvenir," 9–11.

5. Conrad, *Encyclopedia,* 108–109; *Pictorial and Genealogical Record,* 55–57; Sixth District Congressional Election, 6 August 1860; VanGilder, *Jasper County,* 61; Cravens to Walter B. Douglas, 16 February 1914.

6. Conrad, *Encyclopedia,* 108; Holcombe, *History of Greene County,* 285, 289; Fairbanks and Tuck, *Past and Present,* 244–245; Pinkney, "Souvenir," 9–11. The Phelps Regiment of Home Guards was the same as the Greene and Christian County Home Guards.

7. Orr to Abraham Lincoln, 21 November 1861; Kirkpatrick, "Missouri on the Eve," 99.

8. Holcombe, *History of Greene County,* 286.

9. Ibid; Pinkney, "Souvenir," 11.

10. Escott, *History and Directory,* 88; Ihrig, *First One Hundred Years,* 11; Pinkney, "Souvenir," 11.

11. Holcombe, *History of Greene County,* 287; Escott, *History and Directory,* 102.

12. Escott, *History and Directory,* 102–103.

13. Holcombe, *History of Greene County,* 287.

14. Ibid.

15. Ihrig, *First One Hundred Years,* 7.

Chapter 3

1. Knox, *Camp-Fire and Cotton-Field,* 56.

2. For general coverage of the German Civil War service, see Rosengarten, *German Soldier.* For coverage specific to St. Louis, see Rombauer, *Union Cause,* 188–212, and Scharf, *History of Saint Louis,* 390–400.

3. Goodrich, "Gottfried Duden," 131–146.

4. Harvey, "Missouri," 31–40.

5. McPherson, *Battle Cry of Freedom,* 230; Carr, *Missouri,* 291–323; Blum, "Political and Military Activities," 127.

6. Angus, *Down the Wire Road,* 3; Escott, *History and Directory,* 88.

7. Holcombe, *History of Greene County,* 288.

8. Knox, *Camp-Fire and Cotton-Field,* 59; Voelkner, "Letters, 1861–1862."

9. Missouri General Assembly, *Appendix to the House Journal,* 196; Holcombe, *History of Greene County,* 294; Peckham, *Nathaniel Lyon,* 294; Crumpler, "Yankee Avenger," 47–51. Holcombe attributed the mutiny incident to Sigel; however, Crumpler said it was General Sweeny and not Sigel that put down the rebellion at Lebanon. Peckham identified the disgruntled company as part of the Third Regiment Reserve Corps, Missouri Home Guards.

10. Buegel, "Civil War Diary," 311. Corporal John T. Buegel was in Company F of Franz Sigel's Third Regiment U.S. Missouri Volunteers. His diary provides personal glimpses of the men in the Third; however, dates given by Buegel of regiment movements are generally unreliable.

11. Holcombe, *History of Greene County,* 739;

Plum, "Southwest Early in the War," 109, 112; Greene, *900 Miles,* 179.

12. Ihrig, *First One Hundred Years,* 13.

13. Knox, *Camp-Fire and Cotton-Field,* 61.

14. Holcombe, *History of Greene County,* 288; Engle, *Yankee Dutchman,* 56–57; Pinkney, "Souvenirs," 12–13.

15. Holcombe, *History of Greene County,* 288; Hinze and Farnham, *Battle of Carthage,* 63, citing *Springfield Mirror,* 28 June 1861.

16. Sheppard, "Confederate Girlhood," 9.

17. Escott, *History and Directory,* 103; Holcombe, *History of Greene County,* 288–289; Pinkney, "Souvenirs," 13.

18. Holcombe, *History of Greene County,* 288.

19. Sheppard, "Confederate Girlhood," 9–10; 1860 U.S. Census, M653 Roll 621, p. 168.

20. Sheppard, "Confederate Girlhood," 10.

21. Escott, *History and Directory,* 102.

22. Sheppard, "Confederate Girlhood," 10.

23. Ibid.

24. Conrad, *Encyclopedia,* 48; Escott, *History and Directory,* 86–88; McGregor, *Biographical Record,* 67–68; Fairbanks and Tuck, *Past and Present,* 967; Hood, "Carthage Man's Story," *Carthage Evening Press,* 3 July 1911.

25. Holcombe, *History of Greene County,* 294.

26. Sigel, "No. 2, Report," 16.

27. VanGilder, "Centennial History," *Carthage Evening Press,* 8 June 1961, A9; Holcombe, *History of Greene County,* 292; Missouri, *Appendix to the House Journal,* 196.

28. Sigel, "No. 2, Report," 16; *Fort Scott Democrat,* 7 July 1861.

Chapter 4

1. Howison, "History of the War," 336; Guernsey and Alden, *Harper's Pictorial History,* 139.

2. Cheavens, "Journal," 16.

3. Howison, "History of the War," 336; Cheavens, "Journal," 16; Ihrig, *First One Hundred Years,* 6, 10; Ware, *Lyon Campaign,* 181.

4. Howison, "History of the War," 336; Cheavens, "Journal," 16.

5. Livingston, *History of Jasper County,* 53.

6. Snead, *Fight for Missouri,* 238–239; Ingenthron and Van Buskirk, *Borderland Rebellion,* 45; Lademann, "Battle of Carthage," 134; Livingston, *History of Jasper County,* 53; Adamson, *Rebellion in Missouri,* 132.

7. Lindberg, "Semblance of a Weapon," 308–312; Lademann, "Battle of Carthage," 131; Weed, "Battle of Carthage," 392.

8. Ware, *Lyon Campaign,* 7.

9. Miles, *Bitter Ground,* 72.

10. Patrick, "Remembering the Missouri Campaign," 31; Duncan, *John T. Hughes,* 98; Harding, "Old Missouri State Guard," 10, 43–44.

11. McNamara, "Historical Sketch," A309; Pollard, *First Year of the Year,* 120.

12. Diggs, "Hazardous Trip," 464; 1860 U.S. Census, M653 Roll 613, p. 73.

13. Castel, *Sterling Price,* 30; United States, *Organization and Status of Missouri Troops,* 285–286.

14. Pillow to L. P. Walker, 703–705; Pearce, "Memoir," 4.

15. Perkins, "Jefferson Davis and Sterling Price," 399.

16. Cheavens, "Journal," 16.

17. Webb, *Battles and Biographies*, 68; Snead, *Fight for Missouri*, 217; Index of Service Records, Confederate; Hinze and Farnham, *Battle of Carthage*, 83; Boughan, "No. 7, Report," 29; Brophy, *Three Hundred Years*, 140; Weed, "Battle of Carthage," 392. Thomas Snead was aide-de-camp to Governor Jackson and later adjutant general of the Missouri State Guard. He went on to serve as an officer in the Confederate Army of the West and in the Confederate Congress. He became custodian of General Sterling Price's private and personal papers.

18. Castel, *Sterling Price*, 27–30; Snead, *Fight for Missouri*, 218.

19. Snead, *Fight for Missouri*, 218; 1860 U.S. Census, M653 Roll 607, p. 41. The story of Gil Roup is in Conrad, *Encyclopedia*, 170.

20. Hinze and Farnham, *Battle of Carthage*, 87–88, 104, 106; Cheavens, "Journal," 16; VanGilder, *Story of Barton County*, 11. An alternate historic name of the location of the State Guard camp is Muddy Petty Bottoms, a reference to the bottoms of Petty Creek. The property of Allen Petty, one of the founders of Lamar, lay south of Lamar and probably marked the second encampment of the State Guard at Murray Corners.

Chapter 5

1. Sweeny, "No. 1, Report," 15; Peckham, *Nathaniel Lyon*, 284.

2. Ware, *Lyon Campaign*, 165; Britton, *Civil War on the Border*, 70–71; Peckham, *Nathaniel Lyon*, 279; Lademann, "Battle of Carthage," 133; Du Bois, "Civil War Journal," 448. Du Bois served as an artillery captain in Major Sturgis' command.

3. "Departure of General Lyon," *Harper's Weekly*, 27 July 1861, 466.

4. Adamson, *Rebellion in Missouri*, 138, 143; Review of *Life of Nathaniel Lyon*, 151.

5. Duyckinck, *National History*, 514; Review of *Life of Nathaniel Lyon*, 151.

6. Ware, *Lyon Campaign*, 161.

7. Ibid., 106.

8. Ibid., 140.

9. Ibid., 155.

10. Wurthman, "Frank Blair," 266–267; Crumpler, "Yankee Avenger," 47–48; Ware, *Lyon Campaign*, 152.

11. Phillips, "Court Martial of Nathaniel Lyon," 296–308.

12. Ward, *Slaves' War*, 7.

13. The Great Comet of 1861 was widely covered by the press. Numerous scientific articles described its unusual appearance and the effect it had on the population.

Chapter 6

1. Nicolay and Hay, "Abraham Lincoln," 295. Nicolay and Hay were private secretaries to President Lincoln.

2. Adamson, *Rebellion in Missouri*, 138; Phillips, *Damned Yankee*, 225.

3. Adamson, *Rebellion in Missouri*, 141; Nicolay and Hay, "Abraham Lincoln," 292–294.

4. Britton, *Civil War on the Border*, 70; North, *History of Jasper County*, 228.

5. Peckham, *Nathaniel Lyon*, 278; Adamson, *Rebellion in Missouri*, 138.

6. Ware, *Lyon Campaign*, 159.

7. Ibid., 167; Adamson, *Rebellion in Missouri*, 138.

8. Kansas Adjutant General's Office, "Military History," 4; Du Bois, "Civil War Journal," 448.

9. Ware, *Lyon Campaign*, 163.

10. Grover, "Civil War in Missouri," 17–18.

11. Harding, "Old Missouri State Guard," 17, 21.

12. Britton, *Civil War on the Border*, 51–68; Snead, *Fight for Missouri*, 229–230; Shalhope, *Sterling Price*, 167; McCulloch, "Report to Hon. L. P. Walker," 606. Harding, "Old Missouri State Guard," 17; Harding, *Service with the Missouri State Guard*, 34; Adamson, *Rebellion in Missouri*, 133. Accounts vary as to how many troops arrived with Price at Cowskin Prairie. Estimates ran from a low of 1,000 to upwards of 2,000. General Ben McCulloch estimated the number at 1,700. James Harding, State Guard Quartermaster-General, who accompanied Price from Lexington, said there were 1,200 men with them by the time they reached Cowskin prairie, which is generally the settled number.

13. Trickett, "Civil War in the Indian Territory," 383.

14. Pearce, "Memoir," 1.

15. Moore, "Missouri," 50–63; Shalhope, *Sterling Price*, 167; Harding, *Service with the Missouri State Guard*, 35; Harding, "Old Missouri State Guard," 18; Adamson, *Rebellion in Missouri*, 133; Webb, *Battles and Biographies*, 68; Pearce, "Memoir," 2–3. The number of arms furnished by General Pearce varies from 600 to 1,000. Pearce claimed he loaned 1,000; Webb put the number at 615. James Harding who was General Price's quartermaster and was at Cowskin prairie with him said he went to Pearce's camp with the State Guard soldiers and receipted "some 600" flintlock muskets. He claimed Price did not return them to Pearce's Arkansas militia.

16. Moore, "Missouri," 51.

17. Bearss, "Fort Smith Serves General McCulloch," 322–328.

18. Stirman to Rebecca Stirman, 4 July 1861.

19. Ibid.

20. McCulloch quoted in Miller, "General Mosby M. Parsons," 44; McCulloch, "Report to Hon. L. P. Walker," 606; Bearss, "Fort Smith Serves General McCulloch," 328; Nevin, *Civil War*, 21.

Chapter 7

1. Dark and Dark, *Springfield*, 45; Hinze and Farnham, *Battle of Carthage*, 96.

2. Goodspeed, *Lawrence County*, 68–69, 88; Carl, "Military History of Lawrence County," 342; Missouri, *Appendix to the House Journal*, 225.

3. VanGilder, "Centennial History," A9.

4. *Atlas of Jasper County*, 11; Schrantz, *Jasper County*, 10–11.

5. VanGilder, "Centennial History," A10; Schrantz, *Jasper County*, 241; McMahan, *Reluctant Cannoneer*, 62.

6. Livingston, *History of Jasper County*, 39.

7. *Atlas of Jasper County*, 11.

8. Sigel, "No. 2, Report," 16.

9. Ibid.; "Battle at Carthage," *New York Times*, 21 July 1861. Sigel furnished his report to the *New York Times* in which he rendered a full description of the battle in German. His translated account included details of troop movements.

10. d'Orléans Paris, *History of the Civil War*, 322.

11. "Battle at Carthage," *New York Times*, 21 July 1861.

12. Sigel, "No. 2, Report," 16–17.

13. McCulloch, "Report to Hon. L. P. Walker," 39.

14. Holcombe, *History of Greene County*, 290; Giffen, "Strange Story," 408.

15. Giffen, "Strange Story," 408.

16. Sweeny, "No. 1, Report," 15; Sigel to Thomas L. Snead, 5 April 1886.

17. VanGilder, "Centennial History," A9; Holcombe, *History of Greene County*, 271; Wright, *Southern Girl in '61*, 164; Schrader, "Reminiscences."

18. VanGilder, "Centennial History," A10.

19. Ibid., A16; *McDonald and Newton Counties*, 247, 404; Atkins, Correspondence, 8 April 1862.

20. Richardson, *Secret Service*, 196; Ware, *Lyon Campaign*, 336; Engle, *Yankee Dutchman*, 3; Buegel, "Civil War Diary," 316; Zucker, *Forty-Eighters*, 46; Wilson and Fiske, "Sigel," 524; *Fort Scott Democrat*, 7 July 1861, republished "Great Battle in Missouri," *New York Times*, 11 July 1861; "Franz Sigel Dead," *New York Times*, 22 August 1902.

21. Lademann, "Battle of Carthage," 138; Crawford to His Parents, n. d.

22. Richardson, *Secret Service*, 197; VanGilder, "Centennial History," A9; Engle, *Yankee Dutchman*, 160.

23. Missouri, *Appendix to the House Journal*, 194–196, 361; Sigel, "No. 2, Report," 16; "Battle at Carthage," *New York Times*, 21 July 1861. The name of Captain Joseph Indest appears variously as Judest and Judes in military records.

24. Lademann, "Battle of Carthage," 131–139; Missouri, *Appendix to the House Journal*, 199–200; "Battle at Carthage," *New York Times*, 21 July 1861; Sigel, "No. 2, Report," 16; Sigel to Thomas L. Snead, 5 April 1886.

25. Sigel to Thomas L. Snead, 5 April 1886.

Chapter 8

1. John H. Bell, "Price's Missouri Campaign," 271; Mudd, "What I Saw," 91; Howison, "History of the War," 321–338; VanGilder, *Story of Barton County*, 7–8.

2. Cheavens, "Journal," 16; VanGilder, "Centennial History," A14; VanGilder, *Story of Barton County*, 7–8.

3. VanGilder, "Centennial History," A10; Pollard, *First Year of the War*, 131; VanGilder, *Story of Barton County*, 11; Pearce, "Memoir," 2–3.

4. Jackson, "General Orders, No. 16," 705; Rombauer, *Union Cause*, 280; Pollard, *First Year of the War*,
141; Bevier, *History of the First and Second Missouri*, 35; Snead, "First Year of the War," 268; Harding, "Old Missouri State Guard," 10; John H. Bell, "Price's Missouri Campaign," 271.

5. Jackson, "General Orders, No. 17," 705–706.

6. Jackson, "General Orders, No. 16," 705; Cheavens, "Journal," 17; Jackson, "General Orders, No. 17," 706; Patrick, "Remembering the Missouri Campaign," 31; Pollard, *First Year of the War*, 131; Taylor, "Our Jefferson City Correspondence," *New York Times*, 8 October 1861.

7. Hughes to R. H. Miller, 7 July 1861; Hughes, "Battle of Carthage," *New York Times*, 24 July 1861; *Liberty Tribune* [Mo.], 6 July 1861; *Charleston Courier* [Mo.], 26 July 1861; Cheavens, "Journal," 16; Bevier, *History of the First and Second Missouri*, 35; Davis, *Rise and Fall*, 365; Howison, "History of the War," 336; Holcombe, *History of Greene County*, 291; Bearss, "Fort Smith Serves General McCulloch," 328; Snead, *Fight for Missouri*, 218; Young, *History of Dade County*, 40; Young, *Truman's Birthplace*, 28.

8. Jackson, "General Orders, No. 16," 705; Pollard, *First Year of the War*, 131; Mudd, "What I Saw," 92; Cheavens, "Journal," 17; Jackson, "General Orders, No. 17," 705–706; Taylor, "Our Jefferson City Correspondence," *New York Times*, 8 October 1861; VanGilder, *Jasper County*, 71; North, *History of Jasper County*, 229; *Fort Scott Democrat*, 7 July 1861; "Great Battle in Missouri," *New York Times*, 11 July 1861; Shoemaker, *Missouri and Missourians*, 844–845; *Sacramento Daily Union*, 22 July 1861; VanGilder, *Story of Barton County*, 11.

9. Pollard, *First Year of the War*, 141; Shoemaker, *Missouri and Missourians*, 845; Rombauer, *Union Cause*, 280; Bevier, *History of the First and Second Missouri*, 35; Snead, "First Year of the War," 268; Schrantz, *Jasper County*, 32–33; Schrantz, "Battle of Carthage," 143; Violette, *History of Missouri*, 358–359; Denny and Bradbury, *Civil War's First Blood*, 41–44.

10. "Great Battle in Missouri," *New York Times*, 11 July 1861.

11. Boon to His Father, 7 July 1861; Pollard, *First Year of the War*, 131; Rains, "No. 3, Report," 20–22; Giffen, "Strange Story," 408; Miller, "Mosby M. Parsons," 36; Catton, *Coming Fury*, 371; *History of Carroll County*, 298.

12. Sigel, "No. 2, Report," 16; "Battle at Carthage," *New York Times*, 21 July 1861; Missouri, *Appendix to the House Journal*, 196; Snead, "First Year of the War," 262.

13. VanGilder, "Centennial History," A10; Hood, "Carthage Man's Story," *Carthage Evening Press*, 3 July 1911.

14. Ihrig, *First One Hundred Years*, 6–12; Britton, *Civil War on the Border*, 48–50.

15. Ware, *Lyon Campaign*, 165–166; Du Bois, "Civil War Journal," 448.

Chapter 9

1. *Atlas of Jasper County*, 6–7; Ihrig, *First One Hundred Years*, 6.

2. Tomes and Smith, *War with the South*, 429; Aeshle, "Mining Boom," 9; *Atlas of Jasper County*, 3.

3. *Atlas of Jasper County*, 7.
4. Cottrell, *Battle of Carthage*, 5; Schrantz, *Jasper County*, 241; North, *History of Jasper County*, 226; *Carthage Evening Press*, 8 June 1961, B2; Hood, "Carthage Man's Story," *Carthage Evening Press*, 3 July 1911; *Missouri State Gazetteer*, 48. The population of Carthage was 281 in 1860.
5. Knox, *Camp-Fire and Cotton-Field*, 58.
6. *Carthage Evening Press*, 8 June 1961, B2.
7. North, *History of Jasper County*, 221–228; VanGilder, *Jasper County*, 51.
8. VanGilder, *Jasper County*, 59–78.
9. McGregor, *Biographical Record*, 17; Livingston, *History of Jasper County*, 19.
10. *Carthage Evening Press*, 8 June 1961, B4; Schrantz, *Jasper County*, 26; Hood, "Carthage Man's Story," *Carthage Evening Press*, 3 July 1911; "Courthouse Destroyed," *Carthage Evening Press*, 15 October 1938.
11. Shirley, *Belle Starr*, 38; Lackmann, *Women of the Western Frontier*, 5–6.
12. *Atlas of Jasper County*, 2–11; Livingston, *History of Jasper County*, 16; Hood, "Carthage Man's Story," 3 *Carthage Evening Press*, 3 July 1911.
13. *Carthage Evening Press*, 8 June 1961, B2–7. L. L. Aldrich was a clerk in Linn's general store and later moved to Cauker City, Kansas, to edit the *Cauker City Public Record*. He wrote a detailed description of the city of Carthage as it appeared shortly before the Battle of Carthage. The *Carthage Evening Press* published Aldrich's description January 28, 1886, and again in 1961. Additional descriptions of the city come from interviews published in the "Centennial Edition," *Carthage Evening Press*, 28 June 1961, and VanGilder, *Jasper County*, 68–69.
14. Livingston, *History of Jasper County*, 38–39, 221; Schrantz, *Jasper County*, 24, 44; VanGilder, "Centennial History," A12.
15. *Official Register of the Officers and Cadets*, 16; United States, War Department, *87 Orders of General Court Martial*; Harrison, *Settlers*, 493; 1860 U.S. Census, M653 Roll 624, pp. 794, 827 and Roll 636, p. 876.
16. Lackmann, *Women of the Western Frontier*, 5–6; *Carthage Evening Press*, 8 June 1961, B2.
17. Livingston, *History of Jasper County*, 31.

Chapter 10

1. *Carthage Evening Press*, 8 June 1961, B4; Hood, "Carthage Man's Story," *Carthage Evening Press*, 3 July 1911.
2. *Carthage Evening Press*, 8 June, 1961, B4; "St. Louisan Recalls Days," *St. Louis Star*, 30 January 1922; United States, "Slave Schedules"; "Courthouse Destroyed," *Carthage Evening Press*, 15 October 1938.
3. Wright, *Southern Girl in '61*, 15.
4. North, *History of Jasper County*, 235–237; Livingston, *History of Jasper County*, 35–36; Frazier, *Slavery and Crime*, 264. The story of Colley and Bart, the two slaves burned alive on July 30, 1853, appeared in several Missouri newspapers of the time including *The Sentinel*, 4 August 1853; *Jefferson Examiner*, 9 August 1853; *The Carthage Banner* and *Springfield Advertiser*, *Weekly Statesman*, 12 August 1853; and twice in the

Liberty Tribune, 5 August and 19 August 1853, subsequently reported in *Freemen's Manual*, 92.
5. Flanigan, "First One Hundred Years," 3.
6. Schrantz, *Jasper County*, 249; VanGilder, "Centennial History," A9.
7. Ihrig, *First One Hundred Years*, 13; Christie, "Memoirs," 10 May 2011.
8. Jasper County, Missouri, Deed Record Book E, 91–120; McGregor, *Biographical Record*, 19; Hood, *Thomas Hood Family*, 19; Schrantz, *Jasper County*, 25, 51–52; *History of Cole County*, 418.
9. McGregor, *Biographical Record*, 20; Schrantz, *Jasper County*, 243–250; *Atlas of Jasper County*, 7; Jasper County, Missouri, Jasper County vs. Chenault; Schrantz, *Jasper County*, 241; Cottrell, *Battle of Carthage*, 5; "Courthouse Destroyed," *Carthage Evening Press*, 15 October 1938.
10. Snead, *Fight for Missouri*, 279; Sneed, "Curtis Wright House," 13; Buegel, "Civil War Diary," 314.

Chapter 11

1. Parsons, "No. 11, Report," 34–37; VanGilder, "Centennial History," A10; Adamson, *Rebellion in Missouri*, 145.
2. VanGilder, "Centennial History," A11.
3. Ibid., A9, A11.
4. North, *History of Jasper County*, 229. The local people knew the big spring on the outskirts of Carthage as James Spring. It later became known as Carter's Spring when Dr. John A. Carter moved to Carthage at the close of the Civil War and subsequently made a gift of the land to the city. The Battle of Carthage State Historic Site is located here.
5. VanGilder, "Centennial History," A12; Maxwell, "Knights of Knights Station"; "George Knight Writes," *Carthage Evening Press*, 10 July 1917.
6. Livingston, *History of Jasper County*, 49; Schrantz, *Jasper County*, 27–28; McGregor, *Biographical Record*, 139–141.
7. Schrantz, *Jasper County*, 30; VanGilder, "Centennial History," A11; Flanigan, "First One Hundred Years," 3. John Richardson's vote for Abraham Lincoln in the 1860 presidential election demonstrated his unyielding support of the Union. Only eleven people in Jasper County, including Richardson, voted for Lincoln.
8. VanGilder, "Centennial History," A11; Conrad, *Encyclopedia*, 516; Livingston, *History of Jasper County*, 53; North, *History of Jasper County*, 229.
9. Moore, *Rebellion Record*, 276; Richardson, *Compilation of the Messages and Papers*, 104–105.
10. Lincoln, *Collected Works*, 331–332, 338–339; United States, Supreme Court, "The Protector," 79 U.S. 700; United States, Record and Pension Office, *Organization and Status of Missouri Troops*, 11–12; "Proceedings of Congress," *New York Times*, 6 July 1861.
11. *Atlas of Jasper County*, 5–6; Livingston, *History of Jasper County*, 55; Schrantz, *Jasper County*, 47–48; McGregor, *Biographical Record*, 61–62; St. Louis Public Schools, *Official Report*, 590; *History of Cole County*, 418; Duncan, *John T. Hughes*, 130; Hood, "Carthage Man's Story," *Carthage Evening Press*, 3 July 1911.
12. VanGilder, "Centennial History," A11; Hood,

"Carthage Man's Story," *Carthage Evening Press*, 3 July 1911.

Chapter 12

1. Holcombe, *History of Greene County*, 290–291.
2. McCulloch, "Report to Hon. L. P. Walker," 606–607.
3. Harding, *Service with the Missouri State Guard*, 36; McCulloch, "Report to Hon. L. P. Walker," 606; Pearce, "Memoir," 2.
4. Denny and Bradbury, *Civil War's First Blood*, 45; McCulloch, "Report to Hon. L. P. Walker," 606.
5. McCulloch, "No. 2, Report," 39; Bearss, "Fort Smith Serves General McCulloch," 329; Harding, "Old Missouri State Guard," 18.
6. VanGilder, "Centennial History," A10.
7. Schrantz, "Battle of Carthage," 141; Shoemaker, *Missouri and Missourians*, 845; VanGilder, "Centennial History," A10; Adamson, *Rebellion in Missouri*, 149; Hinze and Farnham, *Battle of Carthage*, 103; VanGilder, *Jasper County*, 73–75.
8. Taylor, "Our Jefferson City Correspondence," *New York Times*, 8 October 1861; Parsons, "No. 11, Report," 34; Snead, *Fight for Missouri*, 223.
9. Parsons, "No. 11, Report," 34–37.
10. Webb, *Battles and Biographies*, 67.
11. Miller, "Mosby M. Parsons," 33–39.
12. Parsons, "No. 11, Report," 34–37; Jackson, "General Orders, No. 16," 706; Price, "General Orders, No. 10," 712–713.

Chapter 13

1. VanGilder, "Centennial History," A12, A19; John H. Bell, "Price's Missouri Campaign," 271.
2. Clark, "No. 8, Report," 30.
3. Thomas, "Battle of Carthage"; Hughes to R. H. Miller, 7 July 1861; Hughes, "Battle of Carthage," *New York Times*, 24 July 1861; Anderson, *Memoirs*, 49; Castel, *Sterling Price*, 29; Lindberg, "Semblance of a Weapon," 312; William H. McCown quoted in North, *History of Jasper County*, 232; Moore, *Rebellion Record*, 77; Harding, "Old Missouri State Guard," 26.
4. North, *History of Jasper County*, 985; VanGilder, "Centennial History," A14. The village of Coon Creek straddled the Barton-Jasper County line half way between Lamar and Carthage. The name changed to Midway, then Dublin in 1876.
5. VanGilder, "Centennial History," A12.
6. "George Knight Writes," *Carthage Evening Press*, 10 July 1917.
7. "Post Office Department Reports"; Map of the Battle of Dry Fork Creek, National Archives; "Jasper County Relinquishments"; United States, Surveyor General, "Missouri Plats," vol. 34, 7; "George Knight Writes," *Carthage Evening Press*, 10 July 1917.
8. "Battle at Carthage, *New York Times*, 21 July 1861; Sigel, "No. 2, Report," 16.
9. Switzler, et al., *Illustrated History*, 366; Conrad, *Encyclopedia*, 516; Neumann, et al., *Civil War Campaigns*, 3; 1860 U.S. Census, M653 Roll 624, p. 853; North, *History of Jasper County*, 229; Taylor, "Our Jef-

ferson City Correspondence," *New York Times*, 8 October 1861; Sigel, "No. 2, Report," 16; Schrantz, "Battle of Carthage," 144; Shoemaker, *Missouri and Missourians*, 845; VanGilder, "Centennial History," A12; Thomas, "Battle of Carthage." Lieutenant Max Tosk, Colonel Sigel's adjutant, reported that a scouting party operating two miles from Carthage encountered at five o'clock a rebel picket guard, who the federal party attacked and took prisoner. This was a probable version of the encounter at the Vincent Gray house. Other claims that Sigel's advance guard met the State Guard pickets at the Gray farm around 9 A.M. were not plausible. Meanwhile, Sigel implied in his report that the first exchange of shots came not at the Gray house but just after the federals crossed Dry Fork Creek. It is feasible that there was a brief encounter at the Gray house and then another when Shelby's men came forward at Dry Fork to check the Union advance prior to the full engagement of the two sides. State Guard Surgeon General George W. Taylor confirmed an early engagement of the pickets and understood that it came after the Dry Fork crossing. He reported that a State Guard soldier received a flesh wound in the right arm. The wounded soldier returned the fire, he said, killing the adjutant of Colonel Salomon's regiment. These are similar to the casualties associated with the contact at Vincent Gray's house, as well as those reported for the skirmish at the Carthage mills the previous evening. This leads to the conclusion that witnesses confused these separate incidents. There is no confirmation, by the way, of the death of Salomon's adjutant.
10. Webb, *Battles and Biographies*, 305–311; Edwards, *Shelby and His Men*, 24–27; Rains, "No. 3, Report," 20–22; Schrantz, "Battle of Carthage," 143.
11. Sigel, "No. 2, Report," 16.
12. Snead, "First Year of the War," 268.
13. Peyton, "No. 6, Report," 27; North, *History of Jasper County*, 229. North confirms the disposition of the two forces. His assertion, however, that Sigel left his supply wagons at the top of the hill about one-quarter mile beyond the Spring River crossing appears to contradict Sigel's account of his advance with his wagons toward the State Guard line.
14. Taylor, "Our Jefferson City Correspondence," *New York Times*, 8 October 1861; Thomas, "Battle of Carthage"; Clark, "No. 8, Report," 30; Rains, "No. 3, Report," 20–22.
15. Bronaugh, *Younger's Fight for Freedom*, 372.
16. Rains, "No. 3, Report," 20–22; Carr, *Missouri*, 315; Harding, "Old Missouri State Guard," 5, 9–10, 27.
17. VanGilder, "Centennial History," A12; Thomas, "Battle of Carthage."

Chapter 14

1. Hughes to R. H. Miller, 7 July 1861; Hughes, "Battle of Carthage," *New York Times*, 24 July 1861.
2. Rains, "No. 3, Report," 20–22; Slack, "No. 9, Report," 32–33; Clark, "No. 8, Report," 30; Rombauer, *Union Cause*, 280; Livingston, *History of Jasper County*, 53–54; Schrantz, *Jasper County*, 31–32; VanGilder, *Jasper County*, 75; Schrantz, "Battle of Carthage," 143.

3. Edwards, *Shelby and His Men*, 24–27.
4. Rains, "No. 3, Report," 20–22; Taylor, "Our Jefferson City Correspondence," *New York Times*, 8 October 1861; VanGilder, "Centennial History," A13; Rains, "No. 3, Report," 20–22; Peyton, "No. 6, Report," 27.
5. Hinze and Farnham, *Battle of Carthage*, 266; Price, "General Orders No. 3," 710–711.
6. Boughan, "No. 7, Report," 29.
7. Weightman, "No. 4, Report," 22–25.
8. Wilson, "Bledsoe of Missouri," 316–322; Shoemaker, *Missouri, Day by Day*, 284; Hughes, et al., *Doniphan's Expedition*, 539–540.
9. Rains, "No. 3, Report," 20–22; Owens, *Hier snackt wi Plattdutsch*, chapter 16; Young, *History of Lafayette County*, 87. Young said Colonel Graves was not actively engaged in the battle; however, he seems to be alone in this claim.
10. Weightman, "No. 4, Report," 22–25.
11. Rains, "No. 3, Report," 20–22; Slack, "No. 9, Report," 32–33.
12. Ford, "Civil War Reminiscences," 1–46.
13. *History of Carroll County*, 290–297; Cheavens, "Journal," 12–25; Cheavens, "Missouri Confederate," 17.
14. *History of Caldwell and Livingston Counties*, 1169–1173; Shoemaker, *Missouri, Day by Day*, 65–66; Bridges, "Confederate Hero," 234; Warner, *Generals in Gray*, 278; Harding, "Old Missouri State Guard," 37; "Obituary of Gen. W. Y. Slack," *Memphis Avalanche*, 8 May 1862.
15. Jackson, "General Orders, No. 16," 705; Jackson, "General Orders, No. 17," 706.

Chapter 15

1. Parsons, "No. 11, Report," 35; Clark, "No. 8, Report," 30.
2. Parsons, "Papers, 1847–1869;" Warner, *Generals in Gray*, 228–229; "Obituary of Mosby Monroe Parsons, *Jefferson City Missouri State Times*, 29 September 1865.
3. Parsons, "No. 11, Report," 35; VanGilder, "Centennial History," A14; Patrick, "Remembering the Missouri Campaign," 30–31.
4. Lindberg, "Semblance of a Weapon," 312; VanDiver, "Reminiscences of General Clark," 223–235.
5. Parsons, "No. 11, Report," 34–37; Ingenthron and Van Buskirk, *Borderland Rebellion*, 50.
6. Hinze and Farnham, *Battle of Carthage*, 119–121; Rains, "No. 3, Report," 20; Parsons, "No. 11, Report," 34; Weightman, "No.4, Report," 22; Clark, "No. 8, Report," 30; Slack, "No.9, Report," 32; Snead, *Fight for Missouri*, 224–225; Switzler, et al., *Illustrated History*, 266; Sigel, "No. 3, Report," 16; J. P. Bell, "Price's Missouri Campaign," 493.
7. Parsons, "No. 11, Report," 34–37; Weightman, "No. 4, Report," 23; Sigel, "No. 2, Report," 16; Switzler, et al., *Illustrated History*, 266; Taylor, "Our Jefferson City Correspondence," *New York Times*, 8 October 1861.
8. VanGilder, "Centennial History," A12; North, *History of Jasper County*, 169, 229; 1860 U.S. Census,

M653 Roll 624, pp. 820, 822; Map of the Battle of Dry Fork Creek, National Archives; see also Sweeny, Map of The Battle of Dry Fork Creek, Plate 33, Map 6.
9. VanGilder, "Centennial History," A12; VanGilder, *Jasper County*, 63.
10. VanGilder, "Centennial History," A12.
11. Snead, "First Year of the War," 269; Pollard, *First Year of the War*, 132; Ford, "Civil War Reminiscences," 1–46; Patrick, "Remembering the Missouri Campaign," 31–32; Neely, *Border Between Them*, 98–103.
12. "Our St. Louis Correspondence," *New York Times*, 15 July 1861; Price, "General Order No. 8."

Chapter 16

1. Sigel, "No. 2, Report," 16; Schrantz, "Battle of Carthage," 144; Lademann, "Battle of Carthage," 131–139; Rombauer, *Union Cause*, 272; United States, *Organization and Status of Missouri Troops*, 222; Adamson, *Rebellion in Missouri*, 120, 143; Harding, *Adjutant Generals Report*, 1–9. The identity of Captain Foerster unfortunately is unknown. Lademann, who served in Sigel's command, named him as a member of the Third Regiment; however, records extant to the period do not identify a Captain Foerster. A Captain John Diederich Voerster headed a 120-man company of pioneers in General Nathaniel Lyon's army, but that Captain Voerster was at Boonville with Lyon and not at Carthage with Sigel. Another Captain A. Voerster commanded a 106-man pioneer company, according to a Missouri Adjutant General's report. Possibly his pioneers accompanied Sigel to southwest Missouri, although there is no mention of his service at the Battle of Carthage. Captain A. Voerster's name appears in other records as Captain Anton Gerster.
2. Rains, "No. 3, Report," 20–22; Sigel, "No. 2, Report," 16; Taylor, "Our Jefferson City Correspondence," *New York Times*, 8 October 1861; VanGilder, "Centennial History," A12; Shoemaker, *Missouri and Missourians*, 845; Neumann, et al., *Civil War Campaigns*, 3; Larkin, *Missouri Heritage*, 86; Maxwell, "Knights of Knights Station"; "George Knight Writes," *Carthage Evening Press*, 10 July 1917.
3. North, *History of Jasper County*, 229; Missouri, *Appendix to the House Journal*, 200.
4. Sigel, "No. 2, Report," 16; Buegel, "Civil War Diary," 311; Adamson, *Rebellion in Missouri*, 150; Missouri, *Appendix to the House Journal*, 196; Switzer, et al., *Illustrated History*, 366; "Battle at Carthage," *New York Times*, 21 July 1861; VanGilder, "Centennial History," A12; Lademann, "Battle of Carthage," 131–139; Snead, "First Year of the War," 268–269; Schrantz, "Battle of Carthage," 141; Shoemaker, *Missouri and Missourians*, 843–845.
5. Missouri, *Adjutant General's Report*, 6.
6. VanGilder, "Centennial History," A12; Lademann, "Battle of Carthage," 131–139.
7. VanGilder, "Centennial History," A11; Patrick, "Remembering the Missouri Campaign," 34; Lindsey, "Cowskin Prairie and Wilson's Creek," *Missouri Republican*, 12 March 1886.
8. Switzler, et al., *Illustrated History*, 366; Rains,

"No. 3, Report," 20; Weightman, "No. 4, Report," 22; Sigel, "No. 2, Report," 16.

9. John H. Bell, "Price's Missouri Campaign," 271.

10. Buegel, "Civil War Diary," 316, 324–325; Van-Gilder, "Centennial History," A19.

11. VanGilder, "Centennial History," A12.

12. Neumann, et al., *Civil War Campaigns*, 4; Adamson, *Rebellion in Missouri*, 150; North, *History of Jasper County*, 229.

13. Heidler, *Encyclopedia*, 368; *New York Times*, 15 July 1861; *Atlas of Jasper County*, 5; Schrantz, "Battle of Carthage," 140; "Courthouse Destroyed," *Carthage Evening Press*, 15 October 1938.

14. Lademann, "The Battle of Carthage," 131–139; Lindberg, "Semblance of a Weapon," 311.

15. VanGilder, "Centennial History," A12.

16. Barlow, "Guibor's Battery," *Daily Missouri Republican*, 1 August 1885; Patrick, "Remembering the Missouri Campaign," 31.

Chapter 17

1. Harding, "Old Missouri State Guard," 2–5, 9, 12; Harding, *Service with the Missouri State Guard*, 6–10, 29; Lindberg, "Semblance of a Weapon," 308; *History of Cole County*, 254; Covington, "Camp Jackson," 211; Hughes, et al., *Doniphan's Expedition*, 434; "Guns of Carthage," *Carthage Evening Press*, 5 July 1938; Barlow, "Guibor's Battery," *Daily Missouri Republican*, 1 August 1885; Buegel, "Civil War Diary," 311. Doniphan's forces captured several cannons at the Battle of Sacramento, near Chihuahua City, Mexico. Ten ended up as trophies stored at various places in Missouri. The captured guns included two nine-, two eight-, four six-, and two four-pounders. Some of these guns formed the core of the Missouri State Guard batteries at the Battle of Carthage. Harding gives a complete return of ordinance stores before and after the Union capture of State Guard troops at Camp Jackson.

2. Grant, "Seizure of U.S. Arsenal," 649; Harding, *Service with the Missouri State Guard*, 10, 29; Grant to Colonel H. K. Craig, 3 May 1861; "Guns of Carthage," *Carthage Evening Press*, 5 July 1938. The list of arms and munitions taken from the Liberty Depot included 16 field guns of various descriptions: three brass six-pounder cannon, twelve iron six-pounders, and one three-pounder iron gun.

3. Patrick, "Remembering the Missouri Campaign," 27–30, 53 n18, 42, citing Major Nathaniel Grant to Colonel H. K. Craig, 3 May 1861; Harding, "Old Missouri State Guard," 9, 25. Harding mistakenly assigned four brass six-pounders from the Liberty Depot to Parsons' division when there were only three. The Guibor Battery did not have four guns until after the Battle of Wilson's Creek, and later fielded six pieces.

4. Patrick, "Remembering the Missouri Campaign," 29; Larkin, *Missouri Heritage*, 154; Harding, *Service with the Missouri State Guard*, 6–10, 29; Webb, *Battles and Biographies*, 66; Paxton, *Annals of Platte County*, 1070; Hughes, et al., *Doniphan's Expedition*, 539–542; Young, *History of Lafayette County*, 80–87; VanGilder, "Centennial History," A14; Blackmar,

Kansas, 617–618; Stevens, *Centennial History of Missouri*, 757; Conrad, *Encyclopedia*, 45; Livingston, "History of Jasper County," 53; Moore, "Missouri," 48; Courtney, "Old Sacramento," 381; Courtney, "Old Sacramento," 652–653; "Bledsoe's Battery," 650; Payne, "Fighting in Missouri," 913; Weed, "Battle of Carthage," 392; Clark, "Epic March of Doniphan's Missourians," 153; Wilson, "Bledsoe of Missouri," 102; Duncan, *John T. Hughes*, 71–84. Sacramento Creek is the same a Sacramento River. Veterans of the battle called it Sacramento Creek, or Sacramento Hill.

5. Wilson, "Bledsoe of Missouri," 101–103; *Osawattomie Herald* quoted in *Daily Times* [Kans.], 31 July 1861; "Guns of Carthage," *Carthage Evening Press*, 5 July 1938.

6. Wilson. "Bledsoe of Missouri," 101–103; Harding, "Old Missouri State Guard," 2. Harding claimed that Old Sacramento fired her last shot at the Battle of Pea Ridge, Arkansas, afterwards recast at Selma, Alabama.

7. Wilson, "Bledsoe of Missouri," 102–103; Harding, "Old Missouri State Guard," 2–3; "Guns of Carthage," *Carthage Evening Press*, 5 July 1938.

8. "Guns of Carthage," *Carthage Evening Press*, 5 July 1938; Taylor, "Our Jefferson City Correspondence," *New York Times*, 8 October 1861. Surgeon General Taylor, of the Missouri State Guard Eighth Military District, who was at the battle, gives a different description of the sizes of the guns at Carthage. He said the Missourians had five six-pounders and one twelve-pounder. The federals, he said, opened fire with one eighteen-, three twelve-, and four six-pounders, throwing shell, round shot, grape and canister. While there is agreement on his report of the artillery of the Missourians, most sources do not agree on his estimate of the sizes of the Union guns. Various reports say Sigel had anywhere from one to six twelve-pounder guns. It is unclear whether any of the eight federal guns were rifled or smooth bore.

9. VanGilder, "Centennial History," A12; Sigel, "No. 2, Report," 16; Edwards, *Shelby and His Men*, 24–27.

10. Rains, "No. 3, Report," 20–22; Barlow, "Guibor's Battery," *Daily Missouri Republican*, 1 August 1885; Parsons, "No. 11, Report," 34–37; Patrick, "Remembering the Missouri Campaign," 31.

Chapter 18

1. Taylor, "Our Jefferson City Correspondence," *New York Times*, 8 October 1861; Slack, "No. 9, Report," 32–33; Clark, "No. 8, Report," 30.

2. William H. McCown quoted in North, *History of Jasper County*, 232; VanGilder, "Centennial History," A14; VanGilder, *Jasper County*, 74.

3. Clark, "No. 8, Report," 30; Buegel, "Civil War Diary," 311; "War in Missouri," *New York Times*, 14 July 1861; "Our St. Louis Correspondence," *New York Times*, 15 July 1861.

4. "A brief history of Company H" — apparently written by Captain Indest, in Missouri, *Appendix to the House Journal*, 196.

5. Adamson, *Rebellion in Missouri*, 150; Buegel, "Civil War Diary," 311; North, *History of Jasper County*,

229; VanGilder, *Jasper County*, 75; Larkin, *Missouri Heritage*, 86; Switzler, et al., *Illustrated History*, 266; Clark, "No. 8, Report," 30; "War in Missouri," *New York Times*, 14 July 1861; "Our St. Louis Correspondence," *New York Times*, 15 July 1861.

6. Barlow, "Guibor's Battery," *Daily Missouri Republican*, 1 August 1885; Parsons, "No. 11, Report," 37; Patrick, "Remembering the Missouri Campaign," 31.

7. Barlow, "Guibor's Battery," *Daily Missouri Republican*, 1 August 1885; Patrick, "Remembering the Missouri Campaign," 31.

8. J. P. Bell, "Price's Missouri Campaign," 493; "Death of Hiram Bledsoe," 95; Rains, "No. 3, Report," 20–22; Weightman, "No. 4, Report," 22–25.

9. Richardson, *Secret Service*, 156; VanGilder, "Centennial History," A15; John H. Bell, "Price's Missouri Campaign," 271.

10. Patrick, "Remembering the Missouri Campaign," 29–30; Wilson, "Bledsoe of Missouri," 102.

11. Rains, "No. 3, Report," 20–22; Barlow, "Guibor's Battery," *Daily Missouri Republican*, 1 August 1885; Patrick, "Remembering the Missouri Campaign," 32.

12. Sigel, "No. 2, Report," 16; Edwards, *Shelby and His Men*, 24–27; Mudd, *With Porter in North Missouri*, 325–326.

13. Boon to His Father, 7 July 1861; Clark, "No. 8, Report," 30; Wallace, "Gen. E. W. Price," 208.

14. Rains, "No. 3, Report," 20–22.

15. Hughes, et al., *Doniphan's Expedition*, 549; Edwards, *Shelby and His Men*, 26–27; Barlow, "Guibor's Battery," *Daily Missouri Republican*, 1 August 1885; Patrick, "Remembering the Missouri Campaign," 32; Hughes to R. H. Miller, 7 July 1861; Hughes, "Battle of Carthage," *New York Times*, 24 July 1861.

16. Edwards, *Shelby and His Men*, 24–27; Patrick, "Remembering the Missouri Campaign," 31; "Guns of Carthage," *Carthage Evening Press*, 5 July 1938; "Incident at Cowskin Prairie," 22.

17. Bevier, *History of the First and Second Missouri*, 132; Wilson, "Bledsoe of Missouri," 102.

18. Thomas, "Battle of Carthage"; "Incident of War," *New York Times*, 24 July 1861.

19. Lademann, "Battle of Carthage," 134.

20. VanGilder, "Centennial History," A14; *Daily Times* [Kans.], 25 July 1861; Wilson, "Bledsoe of Missouri," 103; "Guns of Carthage," *Carthage Evening Press*, 5 July 1938.

21. VanGilder, "Centennial History," A14.

22. Ibid.; Cottrell, *Battle of Carthage*, 13; Larkin, *Missouri Heritage*, 21.

23. VanGilder, "Centennial History," A14.

24. Ibid.; Hood, "Carthage Man's Story," *Carthage Evening Press*, 3 July 1911.

25. Parsons, "No. 11, Report," 34–37; Clark, "No. 8, Report," 30.

26. Weightman, "No. 4, Report," 22–25.

Chapter 19

1. Nevin, *Civil War*, 20; Rives, "No. 10, Report," 34; Colonel Rives called Dry Fork Creek Bear Creek. Some of the Missouri officers and chroniclers of the battle also mistakenly called it Coon Creek. One un-

informed historian wrote it up as the Battle of Corn Creek, perhaps because of its cornfield setting.

2. Slack, "No. 9, Report," 32–33.

3. Parsons, "No. 11, Report," 34–37; Cheavens, "Journal," 12–25; Hughes to R. H. Miller, 7 July 1861; Hughes, "Battle of Carthage," *New York Times*, 24 July 1861; *History of Caldwell and Livingston Counties*, 762.

4. Rains, "No. 3, Report," 20–22.

5. Peyton, "No. 6, Report," 27.

6. McCown, "No. 5, Report," 25–26.

7. Boughan, "No. 7, Report," 29; Peyton, "No. 6, Report," 27; McCown, "No. 5, Report," 25–26.

8. McCown, "No. 5, Report," 25–26

9. Boughan, "No. 7, Report," 29.

10. Rains, "No. 3, Report," 20–22.

11. "Battle at Carthage," *New York Times*, 21 July 1861; Sigel, "No. 2, Report," 16; Patrick, "Remembering the Missouri Campaign," 32.

12. Thomas, "Battle of Carthage"; Clark, "No. 8, Report," 30; Hughes to R. H. Miller, 7 July 1861; Hughes, "Battle of Carthage," *New York Times*, 24 July 1861; Buegel, "Civil War Diary," 311; Slack, "No. 9, Report," 32–33.

13. Clark, "No. 8, Report," 30.

14. Rains, "No. 3, Report," 20–22; Clark, "No. 8, Report," 30.

15. Clark, "Epic March of Doniphan's Missourians," 152; Du Bois, "Civil War Journal," 446–447; *History of Cole County*, 492; Payne, "Early Days of War," 926; Weightman, *To the Congress of the United States*, 22.

16. Rains, "No. 3, Report," 20–22; Boon to His Father, 7 July 1861.

17. Parsons, "No. 11, Report," 34–37.

18. Clark, "No. 8, Report," 30.

19. Taylor, "Our Jefferson City Correspondence," *New York Times*, 8 October 1861; *Sacramento Daily Union*, 22 July 1861; North, *History of Jasper County*, 230.

20. *McDonald and Newton Counties*, 247; Taylor, "Our Jefferson City Correspondence," *New York Times*, 8 October 1861.

21. John H. Bell, "Price's Missouri Campaign," 272.

22. Patrick, "Remembering the Missouri Campaign," 31; "Great Battle in Missouri," *New York Times*, 11 July 1861; *Sacramento Daily Union*, 22 July 1861; Clark, "No. 8, Report," 31.

23. Rains, "No. 3, Report," 20–22; Peyton, "No. 6, Report," 27.

24. Rains, "No. 3, Report," 20–22.

Chapter 20

1. VanGilder, "Centennial History," A14; Conrad, "No. 1, Report," 38.

2. Denny and Bradbury, *Civil War's First Blood*, 44; McIntosh, "No. 3, Report," 39–40; Conrad, "No. 1, Report," 38; Pearce, "Memoir," 2.

3. Steele and Cottrell, *Civil War in the Ozarks*, 31; Ingenthron and Van Buskirk, *Borderland Rebellion*, 49; Cutrer, *McCulloch*, 210–212; McCulloch, "No. 2, Report," 39; McCulloch, "Report to Hon. L. P. Walker,"

607; Sigel, "No. 2, Report," 16; Boon to His Father, 7 July 1861; "Great Battle in Missouri," *New York Times*, 11 July 1861; Cheavens, "Journal," 19. General McCulloch said at first that McIntosh captured 80 men but later amended that to 137. He put the number of arms taken at 150, although Captain McIntosh who led the raid reported that he found only 100 rifles. Sigel, meanwhile, reported only 94 men captured. Private H. L. Boon, in a letter to his father, said McCulloch captured 100 Dutch and their arms. A story that ran in an Eastern newspaper based on reports out of Kansas City put the number of prisoners at Neosho at 200. Private Cheavens, who later witnessed McCulloch's parole of the Union prisoners, set the number at 125. The difference between the 137 prisoners in McCulloch's final report and the 125 Cheavens saw paroled may be twelve Union men who refused to take an oath to the Confederacy. There is no explanation for the twelve recalcitrant prisoners or how Major McIntosh miscounted by 57 men.

4. *Goodspeed's History of Newton*, 248.
5. Conrad, "No. 1, Report," 38.
6. Sigel, "No. 2, Report," 16; Lademann, "Battle of Carthage," 131–139.
7. Schrantz, *Jasper County*, 37; VanGilder, "Centennial History," A15; Sigel, "No. 2, Report," 16.
8. Slack, "No. 9, Report," 32–33.
9. Taylor, "Our Jefferson City Correspondence," *New York Times*, 8 October 1861.
10. Peyton, "No. 6, Report," 27.
11. Weightman, "No. 4, Report," 22–25.
12. Parsons, "No. 11, Report," 34–37.
13. "Brave Old Confederate Died," *Fayetteville Observer* [N.C.], 3 June 1897, from the *Atlanta Constitution*; Rosser to J. Marshall McCue; 1860 U.S. Census, M653 Roll 625, p. 124; Weightman, "No. 4, Report," 22–25.
14. Livingston, *History of Jasper County*, 53; Weightman, "No. 4, Report," 22–25; Rains, "No. 3, Report," 20–22.
15. Parsons, "No. 11, Report," 34–37.
16. Edwards, *Shelby and His Men*, 26–27; Barlow, "Guibor's Battery," *Daily Missouri Republican*, 1 August 1885; Patrick, "Remembering the Missouri Campaign," 32.
17. Thomas, "Battle of Carthage"; North, *History of Jasper County*, 230.
18. John H. Bell, "Price's Missouri Campaign, 1861," 271–272.
19. Ibid.
20. Ibid.
21. Hughes to R. H. Miller, 7 July 1861; Hughes, "Battle of Carthage," *New York Times*, 24 July 1861; VanGilder, "Centennial History," A15; Weightman, "No. 4, Report," 22–25; Clark, "No. 8, Report," 31.
22. VanGilder, *Jasper County*, 75; Taylor, "Our Jefferson City Correspondence," *New York Times*, 8 October 1861; Sweeny, Map of the Battle of Dry Fork Creek," Plate 33, Map 6; Dyer, *Compendium of the War*, 1313, 1324; VanGilder, "Centennial History," A15.
23. Clark, "No. 8, Report," 31.
24. Weightman, "No. 4, Report," 22–25; Slack, "No. 9, Report," 32–33.
25. Rives, "No. 10, Report," 34.

Chapter 21

1. Bevier, *History of the First and Second Missouri*, 38; VanGilder, "Centennial History," A13; VanGilder, *Jasper County*, 75.
2. Sigel to Thomas L. Snead, 5 April 1886; "The Battle at Carthage," *New York Times*, 21 July 1861.
3. Taylor, "Our Jefferson City Correspondence," *New York Times*, 8 October 1861; "Battle in Missouri," *New York Times*, 12 July 1861; *Sacramento Daily Union*, 22 July 1861; Clark, "No. 8, Report," 30–32; Sigel to Thomas L. Snead, 5 April 1886.
4. Steele and Cottrell, *Civil War in the Ozarks*, 26; Sigel, "No. 2, Report," 16.
5. Parsons, "No. 11, Report," 34–37.
6. Sigel, "No. 2, Report," 16; Slack, "No. 9, Report," 32–33.
7. Sigel to Thomas L. Snead, 5 April 1886.
8. Weightman, "No. 4, Report," 22–25.
9. Ibid.
10. North, *History of Jasper County*, 230; Peyton, "No. 6, Report," 27.
11. Boughan, "No. 7, Report," 29; VanGilder, "Centennial History," A13, A16; Bronaugh, *Younger's Fight for Freedom*, 372; VanGilder, *Jasper County*, 76; North, *History of Jasper County*, 232.
12. "Our St. Louis Correspondence," *New York Times*, 15 July 1861; "Battle of Carthage," *Harper's Weekly*, 3 August 1861, 487; "War in Missouri," *New York Times*, 14 July 1861; "Battle in Missouri," *New York Times*, 12 July 1861.
13. Livingston, *History of Jasper County*, 53; Adamson, *Rebellion in Missouri*, 151.
14. "The Battle of Carthage," *Harper's Weekly*, 3 August 1861, 487; Lademann, "Battle of Carthage," 134–135.
15. Lademann, "Battle of Carthage," 131–139.
16. VanGilder, "Centennial History," A12; Weightman, "No. 4, Report," 22–25; Sigel, "No. 2, Report," 16; Lademann, "Battle of Carthage," 131–139.
17. Lademann, "Battle of Carthage," 131–139; Taylor, "Our Jefferson City Correspondence," *New York Times*, 8 October 1861.
18. John H. Bell, "Price's Missouri Campaign," 271.
19. Clark, "No. 8, Report," 31; Boughan, "No. 7, Report," 29; Peyton, "No. 6, Report," 27; Rains, "No. 3, Report," 20–22.

Chapter 22

1. Parsons, "No. 11, Report," 34–37.
2. VanGilder, "Centennial History," A16; McCown, "No. 5, Report," 25–26; General Index Cards, M380, Roll 2. Index rolls list Private John Byler as John Byter, Missouri State Guard Eighth Division.
3. VanGilder, "Centennial History," A16; North, *History of Jasper County*, 232; Grover, "Civil War in Missouri," 14; King, "Early Experiences," 502.
4. VanGilder, "Centennial History," A13; Sigel, "No. 2, Report," 16; Taylor, "Our Jefferson City Correspondence," *New York Times*, 8 October 1861.

5. VanGilder, "Centennial History," A13, 16.
6. Wilkie, *Missouri in 1861*, 107–114; VanGilder, "Centennial History," A16.
7. VanGilder, "Centennial History," A17; Van-Gilder, *Jasper County*, 76; Hood, "Carthage Man's Story," *Carthage Evening Press*, 3 July 1911.
8. Sigel, "No. 2, Report," 16; VanGilder, "Centennial History," A17; Thomas, "Battle of Carthage."
9. Sigel, "No. 2, Report," 16; *Atlas of Jasper County*, 5; North, *History of Jasper County*, 231.
10. Cheavens, "Journal," 12–25.
11. Clark, "No. 8, Report," 31.
12. Parsons, "No. 11, Report," 34–37; VanGilder, "Centennial History," A13, A16.

Chapter 23

1. Schrantz, *Jasper County*, 41.
2. Weightman, "No. 4, Report," 22–25; Van-Gilder, "Centennial History," A17; Ostmeyer, "Carthage," *Joplin Globe*, 25 April 2011.
3. VanGilder, "Centennial History," A18; Ostmeyer, "Carthage," *Joplin Globe*, 25 April 2011; North, *History of Jasper County*, 231; 1860 U.S. Census, M653 Roll 624, p. 832; Hood, "Carthage Man's Story," *Carthage Evening Press*, 3 July 1911.
4. *Atlas of Jasper County*, 5; King, "Early Experiences," 503; Duncan, *John T. Hughes*, 1, 71–84; Bundschu, "Address," 11 August 1963.
5. Slack, "No. 9, Report," 32–33; Thomas, "Battle of Carthage," (n. d.).
6. Slack, "No. 9, Report," 32–33; North, *History of Jasper County*, 231.
7. VanGilder, "Centennial History," A16; North, *History of Jasper County*, 231.
8. VanGilder, "Centennial History," A17; Weightman, "No. 4, Report," 22–25; King, "Early Experiences," 503.
9. Slack, "No. 9, Report," 32–33; VanGilder, "Centennial History," A17; Conrad, *Encyclopedia*, 516; *Fort Scott Democrat*, 7 July 1861; Hughes to R. H. Miller, 7 July 1861; Hughes, "Battle of Carthage," *New York Times*, 24 July 1861; Clark, "No. 8, Report," 31.
10. Slack, "No. 9, Report," 32–33; Bevier, *History of the First and Second Missouri*, 38; Confederate States Army Casualties Lists; Thomas, "Battle of Carthage." The "Battle of Carthage" manuscript of Archie Thomas is unsigned and undated; however, contextual evidence suggests that the author was A. Thomas of Captain Blackwell's Carroll County Company. The Confederate States Army Casualties Lists confirms A. Thomas as slightly wounded.
11. Thomas, "Battle of Carthage."
12. Hood, "Carthage Man's Story," *Carthage Evening Press*, 3 July 1911; "Courthouse Destroyed," *Carthage Evening Press*, 15 October 1938.
13. Hood, "Carthage Man's Story," *Carthage Evening Press*, 3 July 1911.
14. VanGilder, "Centennial History," A17, A20; *Atlas of Jasper County*, 22; Ostmeyer, "Carthage," *Joplin Globe*, 25 April 2011; McGregor, *Biographical Record*, 92–96; Hood, "Carthage Man's Story," *Carthage Evening Press*, 3 July 1911.

Chapter 24

1. Parsons, "No. 11, Report," 34–37.
2. Rives, "No. 10, Report," 34.
3. McCown, "No. 5, Report," 25–26; Peyton, "No. 6, Report," 27; Rains, "No. 3, Report," 20–22; Hood, "Carthage Man's Story," *Carthage Evening Press*, 3 July 1911.
4. Rives, "No. 10, Report," 34; Sigel, "No. 2, Report," 16, Slack, "No. 9, Report," 33; Hughes to R. H. Miller, 7 July 1861; Hughes, "Battle of Carthage," *New York Times*, 24 July 1861. Various participants in the battle dispute the number of supply wagons that changed hands. Sigel said he lost but one wagon; General Slack claimed capture of two wagons loaded with tents and other quartermaster's stores; and Colonel Hughes wrote of the capture of several baggage wagons. In making his report, Sigel failed to mention the seven wagons lost at Neosho with the capture of Captain Conrad's company.
5. Conrad, *Encyclopedia*, 516; Schrantz, "The Battle of Carthage," 147; VanGilder, "Centennial History," A16; VanGilder, *Jasper County*, 76; Maxwell, "Knights of Knights Station"; "George Knight Writes," *Carthage Evening Press*, 10 July 1917. The attack on Sigel's wagons at Carthage remains one of the anonymities of the battle. George Knight vividly recalled the attack more than fifty years after the battle and wrote in 1917, "When the head of the column was nearing Carthage, the wagons and artillery were about from where the Baptist church now stands to where the Mo. Pacific freight house is situated. The confederate cavalry came dashing from the west. The infantry that was marching beside the wagons was right faced and there was rapid firing from both sides for a short time, at the end of which the confederates were disappearing to the south and the federals moved on through Carthage and out southeast to a little east of River street on the low ridge south where the stone stands at the southwest corner of Carter's park." George Taylor, writing to the *New York Times*, described contact between the rebel and Union forces operating between Spring River and Carthage. However, he portrayed the State Guard forces as sharpshooters and not cavalry. Whether the two men spoke of the same sequence of events is not clear. If the attack occurred as the Union wagons entered Carthage, as George Knight remembered, one of the minor mysteries of the confrontation is where the rebel attackers came from. The State Guard cavalry at the time was struggling to cross Spring River and the rebel infantry lagged some distance behind Sigel's retreating federals. This may be an instance of local secessionist squads preempting the fighting that later took place inside Carthage.
6. Edwards, *Shelby and His Men*, 26–27; Switzler, et al., *Illustrated History*, 367.
7. Lademann, "Battle of Carthage," 136–137; Hood, "Carthage Man's Story," *Carthage Evening Press*, 3 July 1911.
8. George Knight quoted in VanGilder, "Centennial History," A17; Sigel, "No. 2, Report," 18; Slack, "No. 9, Report," 33; Hughes to R. H. Miller, 7 July 1861; Hughes, "Battle of Carthage," *New York Times*, 24 July 1861; Parsons, "No. 11, Report," 36; *Atlas of*

Jasper County, 5; North, *History of Jasper County*, 231; Lademann, "Battle of Carthage," 136–137; "George Knight Writes," *Carthage Evening Press*, 10 July 1917; Maxwell, "Knights of Knights Station"; Hood, "Carthage Man's Story, " *Carthage Evening Press*, 3 July 1911. A description of the first Union defense appeared in an 1876 Jasper County atlas. It described the placement of the two guns Sigel first sent to the eastern heights and went on to tell in some detail of the disposition of the Union artillery and infantry. The report said Sigel withdrew up the State road "leaving two pieces of artillery in position near where the windmill, east of the square now is, supported by a company of infantry, while the main force fell back, without stopping, into the hollow, near the spring, which he had left in the morning. He planted his remaining six pieces of artillery on the elevation just west of the railroad crossing southwest of the spring, and marched his infantry across the spring branch and over the hill, halting them in the road south of the house now occupied by Mr. Hubbard." An 1883 history of Jasper County rendered a description of Sigel's defense identical to the *Atlas of Jasper County* description, except to update it from Mr. Hubbard's house to a place on the road "south of the house on the Wilbur [*sic*] farm." The K. L Wilber farm was located in Township 28N Range 31W Section 3. The 1876 reference to the railroad crossing was to orient the reader because at the time of the battle, there was no railroad. However, the State road generally followed the path later taken by the railroad.

9. VanGilder, "Centennial History," A14, A18.

10. Parsons, "No. 11, Report," 34–37; Weightman, "No. 4, Report," 22–25; *Sacramento Daily Union*, 22 July 1861.

11. "Our St. Louis Correspondence," *New York Times*, 15 July 1861; Switzler, et al., *Illustrated History*, 366–368; Hughes to R. H. Miller, 7 July 1861; Hughes, "Battle of Carthage," *New York Times*, 24 July 1861; Parsons, "No. 11, Report," 34–37.

12. Parsons, "No. 11, Report," 34–37; Slack, "No. 9, Report," 32–33.

13. Lademann, "Battle of Carthage," 131–139.

14. Slack, "No. 9, Report," 32–33; Rives, "No. 10, Report," 34.

15. Hughes to R. H. Miller, 7 July 1861; Hughes, "Battle of Carthage," *New York Times*, 24 July 1861; Conrad, *Encyclopedia*, 516; *Atlas of Jasper County*, 5; Sigel, "No. 2, Report," 18; Slack, "No. 9, Report," 32–33; North, *History of Jasper County*, 231; Lademann, "Battle of Carthage," 137; Schrantz, *Jasper County*, 40; VanGilder, "Centennial History," A18; VanGilder, *Jasper County*, 73; Weightman, "No. 4, Report," 22–25; Edwards, *Shelby and His Men*, 26–27; Hughes to R. H. Miller, 7 July 1861; Hughes, "Battle of Carthage," *New York Times*, 24 July 1861; Hood, "Carthage Man's Story," *Carthage Evening Press*, 3 July 1911. Schrantz said that Sigel made another short stand at the edge of the timber two miles farther on from the first defense. VanGilder noted that the final State Guard attack came at the future site of Knight's station when a detail of Rain's cavalry drew a hail of poorly aimed Union bullets, just a smattering of musket fire.

16. Lademann, "Battle of Carthage," 131–139.

17. Cheavens, "Journal," 12–25.

18. VanGilder, "Centennial History," A20.

19. Ibid., A9.

Chapter 25

1. Parsons, "No. 11, Report," 34–37.

2. Patrick, "Remembering the Missouri Campaign," 31–32.

3. Weightman, "No. 4, Report," 22–25; King, "Early Experiences," 503; James, "Battle of Oak Hills," 72.

4. J. P. Bell, "Price's Missouri Campaign," 492.

5. "Full Particulars of the Battle," *Morning Herald*, 16 July 1861; Hood, "Carthage Man's Story," *Carthage Evening Press*, 3 July 1911.

6. Younger, *Confessions of a Missouri Guerrilla*, 11, 97; Settle, *Jesse James*, 20; Woodson, *History of Clay County*, 250; Hughes to R. H. Miller, 7 July 1861; Hughes, "Battle of Carthage," *New York Times*, 24 July 1861; Slack, "No. 9, Report," 32–33; Connelley, *Quantrill*, 200. Connelley maintained that Quantrill was in Texas at the time of the Battle of Carthage; however, he seems to have been an exception in that opinion.

7. VanGilder, "Centennial History," A20.

8. VanGilder, "Centennial History," A20; McGregor, *Biographical Record*, 61; Jasper County, Missouri, Jasper County vs. Chenault; Hood, "Carthage Man's Story," *Carthage Evening Press*, 3 July 1911; "Courthouse Destroyed," *Carthage Evening Press*, 15 October 1938. The Hood family went to Kansas. Mrs. Hood died there the following year, in 1862, leaving nine children. One of the Hood sons died at Stockton, Missouri, in 1864, while serving as a Union scout. One courageous act of Norris Hood links the Hood family forever to the history of Jasper County. He became something of a celebrity after the war for saving the county records. When hostilities first flared up, Judge John R. Chenault conspired with County Clerk Stanfield Ross to move the county records from the courthouse to the Newton county jail in Neosho. Upon learning that secessionist partisans had removed the records, Hood took a wagon and a small escort of Union cavalrymen from Fort Scott, Kansas, to Neosho and recovered them. He moved his family and the county records to Fort Scott, where he remained for the duration of the war, and then returned to Carthage sometime later. Jasper County officials later filed the modern equivalent of a million dollar lawsuit against Southern sympathizers, accusing Judge Chenault and other defendants of causing the destruction of the courthouse, the Carthage jail, and the Seminary building, as well as the circuit court records. They did not know at the time that the records were safe with Norris Hood at Fort Scott.

9. VanGilder, "Centennial History," A20; McGregor, *Biographical Record*, 61; "News from South-Western Missouri," *Daily Times* [Kans.], 23 July 1861; Maxwell, "Knights of Knights Station"; "George Knight Writes," *Carthage Evening Press*, 10 July 1917.

10. Thomas, "Battle of Carthage"; Harding, "Old Missouri State Guard," 21–22.

11. Boon to His Father, 7 July 1861; Hood, "Carthage Man's Story," *Carthage Evening Press*, 3 July 1911.

12. Hughes to R. H. Miller, 7 July 1861; Hughes, "Battle of Carthage," *New York Times*, 24 July 1861.

13. Boon to His Father, 7 July 1861; "Death of Albert Withers," *Liberty Tribune* [Mo.], 19 July 1861; Hughes to R. H. Miller, 7 July 1861; Hughes, "Battle of Carthage," *New York Times*, 24 July 1861; Confederate States Army Casualties Lists.

14. Boon to His Father, 7 July 1861.

15. Slack, "No. 9, Report," 32–33; Boon to His Father, 7 July 1861; Pollard, *First Year of the War*, 133.

16. Hughes to R. H. Miller, 7 July 1861; Hughes, "Battle of Carthage," *New York Times*, 24 July 1861.

Chapter 26

1. Cutrer, *McCulloch*, 212.

2. Ibid.; McCulloch, "No. 2, Report," 39; McCulloch, "Report to Hon. L. P. Walker," 606. Cutrer said McCulloch's troops met Jackson's State Guard "before midnight," at Cassville. This seems unlikely because Cassville was in the opposite direction. Moreover, McCulloch wrote in his report from Neosho on July 5 that he intended to push forward tomorrow. He later wrote that hearing of heavy cannonading to the north, he reached Neosho before morning (July 6), rested briefly, and then marched 20 miles to meet Jackson. This would appear to coincide with most reports that he reached the State Guard troops late on the morning of July 6.

3. McCulloch, "Report to Hon. L. P. Walker," 606; Shoemaker, *Missouri and Missourians*, 845; Adamson, *Rebellion in Missouri*, 136. Shoemaker calculated the total number of troops in the confederate vanguard on July 6 at 6,000 men. Adamson estimated 2,700 men in McCulloch's mounted rifles; Pearce, he said, fielded 2,200 infantry, cavalry, and artillery; and Price had about 1,200 men at Cowskin prairie for 6,100 troops in the McCulloch command at that point.

4. Maxwell, "Knights of Knights Station"; "George Knight Writes," *Carthage Evening Press*, 10 July 1917.

5. VanGilder, "Centennial History," 18; Lademann, "Battle of Carthage," 131–139.

6. Lademann, "Battle of Carthage," 131–139; Hood, "Carthage Man's Story," *Carthage Evening Press*, 3 July 1911.

7. Lademann, "Battle of Carthage," 131–139.

8. Hood, "Carthage Man's Story," *Carthage Evening Press*, 3 July 1911.

9. Ibid.

10. VanGilder, "Centennial History," A17, 20; Ostmeyer, "Carthage," *Joplin Globe*, 25 April 2011; Hood, "Carthage Man's Story," *Carthage Evening Press*, 3 July 1911.

11. McCulloch, "Report to Hon. L. P. Walker," 607; *Atlas of Jasper County*, 5; North, *History of Jasper County*, 231–232; Patrick, "Remembering the Missouri Campaign," 31.

12. VanGilder, "Centennial History," A12; Thomas, "Battle of Carthage."

13. Lindberg, "Semblance of a Weapon," 312; VanGilder, "Centennial History," A11; Shalhope, *Sterling Price*, 171; Adamson, *Rebellion in Missouri*, 134; Boon to His Father, 7 July 1861.

14. Boon to His Father, 7 July 1861.

15. Lademann, "Battle of Carthage," 131–139; Snyder to Thomas L. Snead, 2 June 1886; McCulloch, "Report to Hon. L. P. Walker," 606–607; Kirkpatrick, "Missouri in the Early Months," 262, 266; Castel, *Sterling Price*, 30; Cutrer, *McCulloch*, 206; McCulloch, "Report to Hon. L. P. Walker," 606–607; Pearce, "Memoir," 4.

16. Thomas, "Battle of Carthage"; VanGilder, "Centennial History," A19; Jasper County, Missouri, Deed Record Book E, 680.

17. "War in Missouri," *New York Times*, 14 July 1861; "Great Battle in Missouri," *New York Times*, 11 July 1861; Cheavens, "Journal," 19; Conrad, "No. 1, Report," 38.

18. McCulloch, "Report to Hon. L. P. Walker," 606–607.

19. Mudd, "What I Saw," 92.

20. Weightman, "No. 4, Report," 22–25.

21. Stirman to Rebecca Stirman, 10 July 1861.

22. Clark, "No. 8, Report," 31; Hughes to R. H. Miller, 7 July 1861; Hughes, "Battle of Carthage," *New York Times*, 24 July 1861; McCulloch, "Report to Hon. L. P. Walker," 607–608.

23. McCulloch, "Report to Hon. L. P. Walker," 607–608.

Chapter 27

1. Lademann, "Battle of Carthage," 131–139.

2. Ibid.

3. Sweeny, "No. 1, Report," 15–16; Ingenthron and Van Buskirk, *Borderland Rebellion*, 51; Wilkie, *Missouri in 1861*, 91–101; Du Bois, "Civil War Journal," 448–449; *Sacramento Daily Union*, 22 July 1861; Adamson, *Rebellion in Missouri*, 151.

4. Switzler, et al., *Illustrated History*, 366.

5. Sweeny, "No. 1, Report," 15–16.

6. Wilkie, *Missouri in 1861*, 112; Cheavens, "Journal," 19; "War in Missouri," *New York Times*, 22 July 1861; "Our St. Louis Correspondence," *New York Times*, 15 July 1861; *Sacramento Daily Union*, 22 July 1861; "General Franz Sigel Dead," *New York Times*, 22 August 1902; "Battle of Carthage," *Harper's Weekly*, 3 August 1861, 487; Ware, *Lyon Campaign*, 336; Blair, "Testimony," 204.

7. Adjutant General's Office, "Hospital Registers."

8. Wright, *Southern Girl in '61*, 151.

9. Ibid., 216–217.

10. Sheppard, "Confederate Girlhood," 10.

11. Sweeny, "No. 1, Report," 15–16.

12. Adamson, *Rebellion in Missouri*, 151; Ware, *Lyon Campaign*, 179–190.

13. Lyon to Colonel Sigel, 10 July 1861.

14. Wilkie, *Missouri in 1861*, 191–200; Du Bois, "Civil War Journal," 449–450.

15. "War in Missouri," *New York Times*, 14 July 1861.

16. Du Bois, "Civil War Journal," 450–456.

17. "Political and Military Activities," 128–129.

18. Sweeny to General Lyon, 11 July 1861.

19. "War in Missouri," *New York Times*, 14 July 1861.

20. Carr, *Missouri*, 324; Nevin, *Civil War*, 8; Review of *Nathaniel Lyon*, 152.

21. Stirman to Rebecca Stirman, 10 July 1861.

Postscript

1. King, "Early Experiences," 502; Duncan, *John T. Hughes*, 127; Harding, "Old Missouri State Guard," 39.

2. Grover, "Civil War in Missouri," 5–6.

3. Congress of the Confederate States, "Act to Give Aid," 6 August 1861, 721; Jackson to Major General Price, in *Official Records*, 722–723.

Appendix

1. Thomas, "Battle of Carthage."

2. "Full Particulars of the Battle," *Morning Herald* [St. Louis], 16 July 1861.

3. "Battle in Missouri," *New York Times*, 12 July 1861; Switzler, et al., *Illustrated History*, 366–368; Estimates of casualties come primarily from battlefield reports published in the *Official Records*, the National Park Service estimate of casualties, and various publications and newspaper accounts of the battle. See also "Casualties at the Battle of Dry Fork and Carthage"; email correspondence, National Archives, 15 June 2011; Sigel, "No. 2, Report," 19; and Du Bois, "Civil War Journal," 454.

4. Hughes to R. H. Miller, 7 July 1861; Hughes, "Battle of Carthage," *New York Times*, 24 July 1861; *Fort Scott Democrat*, 7 July 1861; "Great Battle in Missouri," *New York Times*, 11 July 1861.

5. "Reported Battles in Missouri," *New York Times*, 11 July 1861; *Fort Scott Democrat*, 7 July 1861; Cottrell, *Battle of Carthage*, 13; "Reported Death of Gen. Rains," *New York Times*, 12 July 1861.

6. "News from South-Western Missouri," *Daily Times* [Kans.], 23 July 1861.

7. Cheavens, "Journal," 19; Ostmeyer, "Carthage," *Joplin Globe*, 25 April 2011.

8. Rains, "No. 3, Report," 22; *Fort Scott Democrat*, 7 July 1861; "Great Battle in Missouri," *New York Times*, 11 July 1861.

9. Clark, "No. 8, Report," 30; VanGilder, *Jasper County*, 75; Steele and Cottrell, *Civil War in the Ozarks*, 28; *Fort Scott Democrat*, 7 July 1861; *Sacramento Daily Union*, 22 July 1961.

10. *Sacramento Daily Union*, 22 July 1861; Taylor, "Our Jefferson City Correspondence," *New York Times*, 8 October 1861.

11. Confederate States Army Casualties Lists; *Atlas of Jasper County*, 5.

12. Bevier, *History of the First and Second Missouri*, 38; Davis, *Rise and Fall*, 365; North, *History of Jasper County*, 232; Campbell, *Rebellion Register*, 49; Blankenbecker, "Pioneer Life," 139.

13. Dyer, *Compendium of the War*, 587, 797; *Atlas to Accompany the Official Records*.

14. Schrantz, *Jasper County*, 40; Shoemaker, *Missouri Day by Day*, 16.

15. Shoemaker, *Missouri and Missourians*, 845.

16. Cheavens, "Journal," 19, n29. Easley does not give the source of her information; VanGilder, "Centennial History," A9; Ingenthron and Van Buskirk, *Borderland Rebellion*, 49; Adjutant General's Office, "Hospital Registers," MR 929.3 U; Hinze and Farnham, *Battle of Carthage*, 205, 278 n2, citing federal muster rolls of the Third and Fifth Missouri Volunteers housed in the National Archives.

17. Blair, "Testimony," 160.

18. Boon to His Father, 7 July 1861; "Death of Albert Withers," *Liberty Tribune* [Mo.], 19 July 1861; Hughes to R. H. Miller, 7 July 1861; Hughes, "Battle of Carthage," *New York Times*, 24 July 1861; Confederate States Army Casualties Lists; Peyton, "No. 6, Report," 27; *History of Carroll County*, 309.

19. Boon to His Father, 7 July 1861; Sigel, "No. 2, Report," 16; VanGilder, "Centennial History," A9, A19; Goodspeed, *Lawrence County*, 69; King, "Early Experiences," 502.

20. Lindberg, "Semblance of a Weapon," 311; Steele and Cottrell, *Civil War in the Ozarks*, 26; Slack, "No. 9, Report," 32–33.

21. VanGilder, "Centennial History," A16; *Carthage Evening Press*, 3 June 1933, cited in "Guns of Carthage," *Carthage Evening Press*, 5 July 1938.

22. Herndon and Weik, *Herndon's Lincoln*, 539–549.

Bibliography

This book makes extensive use of the United States, War Department, *War of the Rebellion: A Compilation of the Official Records of the Union and Confederate Armies*, 70 volumes in four series, Washington, D.C.: Government Printing Office, 1880–1901, hereafter cited as *Official Records*.

Adamson, Hans Christian. *Rebellion in Missouri.* New York: Chilton, 1961.

Adjutant General's Office. "Hospital Registers; Springfield, Mo, 1861–1863." United States National Archives. Springfield, Mo.: Library Center, 1988. Microfilm MR 929.3 U.

Aeshle, Edwin H. "Mining Boom of the 1890s." *White River Valley Historical Quarterly* 2 (1965): 9–15.

Anderson, Ephraim. *Memoirs: Historical and Personal.* St. Louis: Times, 1868.

Anderson, Galusha. *The Story of a Border City During the Civil War.* Boston: Little, Brown, 1908.

Angus, Fern. *Down the Wire Road in the Missouri Ozarks.* Marionville, Mo.: Fern Angus, 1992.

Atkins, Charles H. Correspondence, 8 April 1862. Charles H. Atkins Collection, MSS 03-27. Little Rock: Butler Center for Arkansas Studies, 1862.

Atlas of Jasper County, Missouri. Heritage County Atlas Reprints, vol. 6., Greene County Archives Bulletin No. 43. Springfield, Mo.: Greene County Archives and Records Center, [1876] 1999.

Atlas to Accompany the Official Records of the Union and Confederate Armies: House Miscellaneous Documents, series 1, vol. 40, pt. 1. Washington, D.C.: Government Printing Office, 1892.

Axelrod, Alan. *The Civil War,* 3d ed. New York: Penguin, 2011.

Barlow, William P. "Guibor's Battery in 1861." *Daily Missouri Republican* [St. Louis], 1 August 1885.

Bartels, Carolyn. *The Forgotten Men: Missouri State Guard.* Independence, Mo.: Two Trails, 1995.

"Battle at Carthage, Missouri; Official Report of Colonel Sigel." *New York Times,* 21 July 1861.

"Battle in Missouri, Particulars of the Recent Action Near Carthage." *New York Times,* 12 July 1861.

"Battle of Carthage." *Harper's Weekly,* 3 August 1861.

"Battle of Carthage." *New York Illustrated News,* 22 July 1861.

Bearss, Edwin C. "Fort Smith Serves General McCulloch as a Supply Depot." *Arkansas Historical Quarterly* 24 (1965): 315–347.

Bell, J. P. "Price's Missouri Campaign of 1861." In *Missouri's Sons of the South,* vol. 2, 492–494. St. Louis: Missouri Division Sons of Confederate Veterans, 1998.

Bell, John H. "Price's Missouri Campaign, 1861." *Confederate Veteran* 22 (1914): 271–272.

Bevier, Robert S. *History of the First and Second Missouri Confederate Brigades: 1861–1865. And, from Wakarusa to Appomattox, a Military Anagraph.* St. Louis: Bryan, Brand, 1879.

Blackmar, Frank W., ed. *Kansas: A Cyclopedia of State History,* vol. 2. Chicago: Standard, 1912.

Blair, Frank P. "Testimony, 7 February 1862." In United States. Congress. Joint Committee on the Conduct of the War. *Report of the Joint Committee on the Conduct of the War: Department of the West.* Washington, D.C.: Government Printing Office, 1863.

Blankenbecker, C. C. "Pioneer Life in Bates County." In *Old Settlers' History of Bates County, Mo.—*

from its first Settlement to the First Day of January, 1900. Amsterdam, Mo.: Tathwell & Maxey, 1897.

"Bledsoe's Battery." In *Missouri's Sons of the South*, vol. 2, 650. St. Louis: Missouri Division Sons of Confederate Veterans, 1998.

Blum, Virgil C. "The Political and Military Activities of the German Element in St. Louis, 1859–1861." *Missouri Historical Review* 42 (1948): 103–129.

Boon, H. L. Correspondence to His Father, 7 July 1861. *Glasgow Weekly Times* [Mo.], 18 July 1861.

Bordewich, Fergus M. "Day of Reckoning." *Smithsonian* (October 2009): 62–69.

Boughan, Richard A. "No. 7, Report of Lieutenant Colonel Boughan." In *Official Records*, series 1, vol. 3, 29–30. Washington, D.C., 1881.

"Brave Old Confederate Died." *Fayetteville Observer* [N.C.], 3 June 1897.

Bridges, Hal. "A Confederate Hero: General William Y. Slack." *The Arkansas Historical Quarterly* 10 (1951): 233–237.

Britton, Wiley. *The Civil War on the Border*, vol. 1. New York: G. P. Putnam's Sons, 1890.

Bronaugh, Warren Carter. *The Younger's Fight for Freedom: A Southern Soldier's Twenty Years' Campaign to Open Northern Prison Doors—with Anecdotes of War Days.* Columbia, Mo.: Warren Carter Bronaugh & E. W. Stephens, 1906.

Brophy, Patrick. *Fire and Sword: A Missouri County in the Civil War.* Nevada, Mo.: Bushwhacker, 2008.

_____. *Three Hundred Years: Historical Highlights of Nevada and Vernon County, Missouri.* Boulder, Colo.: Donna G. Logan, 1993.

Buegel, John T. "The Civil War Diary of John T. Buegel, Union Soldier, Part1." Translated by William G. Bek. *Missouri Historical Review* 40 (1946): 307–329.

Bundschu, Henry A. "Address." Hughes Monument Dedication Papers, 11 August 1963 (C3494). Manuscripts Division, State Historical Society of Missouri, Columbia.

Campbell, Robert Allen. *The Rebellion Register: A History of the Principal Persons and Places, Important Dates, Documents and Statistics, Military and Political.* Indianapolis: Robert Douglass, [1866] 1887.

Carl, Eugene H. "Military History of Lawrence County." In *Lawrence County, Missouri, History.* Mt. Vernon, Mo.: Lawrence County Historical Society, 1974.

Carr, Lucien. *Missouri, a Bone of Contention.* Boston: Houghton, Mifflin, 1888.

"Carthage During the War." *Carthage Evening Press* [Mo.], 30 June 1917.

Castel, Albert. *General Sterling Price and the Civil War in the West.* Baton Rouge: Louisiana State University Press, 1993.

Casualties at the Battle of Dry Fork and Carthage. Record Group 94, Records of the Adjutant General's Office, entry 652, Regimental Casualty Lists, Civil War. Washington, D.C.: National Archives.

Catton, Bruce. *The Coming Fury.* Centennial History of the Civil War Series, vol. 1. Garden City, N.Y.: Doubleday, 1961.

"Centennial Edition." *Carthage Evening Press*, 28 June 1961.

Cheavens, Henry Martyn. "Journal of the Civil War in Missouri: 1861, Henry Martyn Cheavens." Edited by Virginia Easley. *Missouri Historical Review* 56 (1961): 12–25.

_____. "A Missouri Confederate in the Civil War. The Journal of Henry Martyn Cheavens, 1862–1863." Edited by James E. Moss. *Missouri Historical Review* 57 (1962): 16–52.

Christie, Robert J. "The Memoirs of Dr. Robert J. Christie, June 17, 1831- July 27, 1909." Edited by Michael Flanagan. Accessed May 10, 2011, http://flanaganfamily.net/genealo/memoirs.htm#chVI.

Clark, John B. "No. 8, Report of Brig. Gen. John B. Clark." In *Official Records*, series 1, vol. 3, 30–31. Washington, D.C., 1881.

Clark, Kimball. "The Epic March of Doniphan's Missourians." *Missouri Historical Review* 80 (1986): 134–155.

Confederate States Army Casualties Lists and Narrative Reports 1861–1865. Washington, D.C.: National Archives, 1970. Microfilm M836 Roll 3.

Congress of the Confederate States. "An Act to Give Aid to the People and State of Missouri, August 6, 1861." In *Official Records*, series 1, vol. 53, 721. Washington, D.C., 1898.

Connelley, William E. *Quantrill and the Border Wars.* Cedar Rapids: Torch, 1910.

_____. *A Standard History of Kansas and Kansans*, vol. 1. New York: Lewis, 1918.

Conrad, Howard Louis. *Encyclopedia of the History of Missouri: A Compendium of History and Biography for Ready Reference.* New York: Southern History, 1901.

Conrad, Joseph. "No. 1, Report of Capt. Joseph Conrad." In *Official Records*, series 1, vol. 3, 38. Washington, D.C., 1881.

Cottrell, Steve. *The Battle of Carthage and Carthage in the Civil War.* n. p., 1990.

"Courthouse Destroyed in Civil War." *Carthage Evening Press*, 15 October 1938.

Courtney, W. J. "Old Sacramento, the Silver-Tongued Cannon." *Confederate Veteran* 28 (1920): 381.

_____. "Old Sacramento, the Silver-Tongued Cannon." In *Missouri's Sons of the South*, vol. 2,

652–653. St. Louis: Missouri Division Sons of Confederate Veterans, 1998.

Covington, James W. "The Camp Jackson Affair, 1861." *Missouri Historical Review* 55 (1961): 197–212.

Cravens, William M. Correspondence to Walter B. Douglas, 16 February 1914. Carthage, Mo.: Jasper County Records Center.

Crawford, William H. Correspondence to His Parents, n. d. "Henry Clay Crawford and William H. Crawford, Letters, 1857–1865" (C0239). State Historical Society of Missouri, Columbia.

Crumpler, Hugh. "Yankee Avenger: Gen. Nathaniel Lyon, Union Commander at the Battle of Wilson's Creek." *Ozarks Watch*, vol. 4, no. 4 (Spring 1991), 47–51.

Cutrer, Thomas W. *Ben McCulloch and the Frontier Military Tradition*. Chapel Hill: University of North Carolina Press, 1993.

Dark, Harris Edward, and Phyllis Dark. *Springfield of the Ozarks: An Illustrated History*. Woodland Hills, Calif.: Windsor, 1981.

Davis, Jefferson. *The Rise and Fall of the Confederate Government*, vol. 1. Richmond: Garrett & Massie, 1881.

"Death of Albert Withers, Esq." *Liberty Tribune* [Mo.], 19 July 1861.

"Death of Hiram Bledsoe." In *Missouri's Sons of the South*, vol. 1, 95. St. Louis: Missouri Division Sons of Confederate Veterans, 1998.

Denny, James, and John Bradbury. *The Civil War's First Blood: Missouri, 1854–1861*. Boonville, Mo.: Missouri Life, 2007.

"Departure of General Lyon from Boonville." *Harper's Weekly*, 27 July 1861.

Diggs, Lorena. "Hazardous Trip in War Days: Reminiscences of Mrs. P. H. Haggard, 1908." *Confederate Veteran* 39 (1931): 463–465, 475.

"Domestic Intelligence, The Battle of Boonville." *Harper's Weekly*, 13 July, 1861.

d'Orléans Paris, Louis-Philippe-Albert, Louis Fitzgerald Tasistro, et al. *History of the Civil War in America*, vol. 1. Philadelphia: J.H. Coates, 1875.

Du Bois, John Van Duesen. "The Civil War Journal and Letters of Colonel John Van Deusen Du Bois." Edited by Jared C. Lobdell. *Missouri Historical Review* 60 (1966): 436–459.

Duncan, Charles V., Jr. *John T. Hughes, from His Pen*. Independence, Mo.: Two Trails [1991] 2002.

Dunson, A. A. "Notes on the Missouri Germans on Slavery." *Missouri Historical Review* 59 (1965): 355–366.

Duyckinck, Evert A. *National History of the War for the Union: Civil, Military and Naval*, vol. 1. New York: Johnson, Fry, 1861.

Dyer, Frederick H., *A Compendium of the War of the Rebellion*, vol. 2. Des Moines: Dyer, 1908.

Edwards, John N. *Shelby and His Men; or, the War in the West*. Kansas City: Hudson-Kimberly, 1897.

Engle, Stephen D. *Yankee Dutchman: The Life of Franz Sigel*. Baton Rouge: Louisiana State University Press, 1999.

Escott, George S. *History and Directory of Springfield and North Springfield*. Springfield, Mo.: George S. Escott, 1878.

"Events of the Civil War in Jasper County." *Carthage Evening Press*, 1 September 1921.

Fairbanks, Jonathan, and Clyde Edwin Tuck. *Past and Present of Greene County, Missouri*, vol. 2. Indianapolis: A. W. Bowen, 1915.

"Fight at Cole Camp." *New York Times*, 7 July 1861.

Flanigan, John H. The First One Hundred Years of the Jasper County Circuit Court, Address before the Jasper County Bar Association, 1 March 1941. Carthage, Mo.: Jasper County Records Center.

Ford, Salem Holland. Civil War Reminiscences. Collection B194. St. Louis: Missouri Historical Society, 1909.

Frazier, Harriet C. *Slavery and Crime in Missouri, 1773–1865*. Jefferson, N.C.: McFarland, 2001.

Freemen's Manual, vol. 1. Columbus, Ohio: L.L. Rice, 1853.

"Full Particulars of the Battle in South-West Missouri." *Morning Herald* [St. Louis], 16 July 1861.

"General Franz Sigel Dead." *New York Times*, 22 August 1902.

General Index Cards, Compiled Military Service Records. Washington, D.C.: National Archives. Microfilm M380 Roll 2.

"George Knight Writes of the Battle of Carthage." *Carthage Evening Press*, 10 July 1917.

Giffen, Lawrence E. "The Strange Story of Major General Franz Sigel: Leader and Retreater." *Missouri Historical Review* 84 (1990): 404–427.

Goodrich, James W. "Gottfried Duden: A Nineteenth Century Missouri Promoter." *Missouri Historical Review* 74 (1981): 131–146.

Goodspeed. *Lawrence County Section of Goodspeed's Newton, Lawrence, Barry and McDonald Counties History*. Cassville, Mo.: Litho [1888] 1973.

Goodspeed's History of Newton, Lawrence, Barry, and McDonald Counties, Missouri. Chicago: Goodspeed, 1888.

Goodspeed's History of Phelps County, Missouri. Rolla, Mo.: Missouri School of Mines, [1889] 1943.

Grant, Nathaniel. Correspondence to Colonel H. K. Craig. 3 May 1861. Record Group 156, Records of the Office of the Chief of Ordinance, Letters Received, 1812–1894 (entry 21). Washington, D.C.: National Archives.

_____. "Seizure of U.S. Arsenal at Liberty, Missouri." In *Official Records*, series 1, vol. 1, 649. Washington, D.C., 1881.

"Great Battle in Missouri." *New York Times*, 11 July 1861.

Greene, A. C. *900 Miles on the Butterfield Trail.* Denton: University of North Texas Press, 1994.

Grover, George S. "Civil War in Missouri." *Missouri Historical Review* 8 (1913): 1–28.

Guernsey, Alfred H., and Henry M. Alden, eds. *Harper's Pictorial History of the Great Rebellion*, vol. 1. Chicago: Star, [1866] 1894.

"Guns of Carthage." *Carthage Evening Press*, 5 July 1938.

Harding, Chester. *Adjutant Generals Report of Missouri State Militia for the Year of 1861.* St. Louis: George Knaps, 1862.

Harding, James. "Old Missouri State Guard. General James Harding Gives Personal Reminiscences of Service in Its Ranks." Carthage, Mo.: Jasper County Records Center, n. d. Manuscript.

——. *Service with the Missouri State Guard: The Memoir of Brigadier General James Harding.* Edited by James E. McGhee. Springfield, Mo.: Oak Hills, [1885] 2000.

Hargett, Janet L. *List of Selected Maps of States and Territories.* Washington, D.C.: National Archives, 1971.

Harrison, John Houston. *Settlers by the Long Grey Trail: Some Pioneers to Old Augusta County.* Baltimore: Genealogical, 1935.

Harvey, Charles M. "Missouri from 1849–1861." *Missouri Historical Review* 2 (1907): 23–40.

Heidler, David Stephen, Jeanne T. Heidler, David J. Coles, eds. *Encyclopedia of the American Civil War: A Political, Social, and Military History.* New York: W. W. Norton, 2002.

Herndon, William H., and Jesse William Weik. *Herndon's Lincoln; the True Story of a Great Life; the History and Personal Recollections of Abraham Lincoln.* Chicago: Belford, Clarke, 1889.

Hinze, David, and Karen Farnham. *The Battle of Carthage: Border War in Southwest Missouri, July 5, 1861*, 3d ed. Gretna, La.: Pelican, [1997] 2004.

History of Caldwell and Livingston Counties, Missouri. St. Louis: National Historical, 1886.

History of Carroll County, Missouri. St. Louis: Missouri Historical, 1881.

History of Cole, Moniteau, Benton, Miller, Maries and Osage Counties, Missouri. Chicago: Goodspeed, 1889.

History of Saline County, Missouri. St. Louis: Missouri Historical, 1881.

Holcombe, R. I. *History of Marion County, Missouri.* Reprint. Marceline, Mo.: Walsworth, [1884] 1979.

——, ed. *History of Greene County, Missouri.* St. Louis: Western Historical, 1883.

Hood, Clyde B., III. *The Thomas Hood Family.* Bountiful, Utah: Family History, 1994.

Hood, Thomas C. "Carthage Man's Story of Battle of Carthage." *Carthage Evening Press*, 3 July 1911.

Howison, Robert R. "History of the War." *Southern Literary Messenger* 37 (1863): 321–338.

Hughes, John Taylor. "The Battle of Carthage: The Rebel Account, July 6, 1861." *New York Times*, 24 July 1861.

——. Correspondence to Mr. R. H. Miller, 7 July 1861. "Military Papers, Missouri State Guard (Confederate) Battle Descriptions." Clarence W. Alvord and Idress Head Collection (C0970, f.213). Manuscripts Division, State Historical Society of Missouri, Columbia.

Hughes, John Taylor, William Elsey Connelley, Dewitt Clinton Allen, and Charles R. Morehead. *Doniphan's Expedition and the Conquest of New Mexico and California.* Reprint. Topeka: William E. Connelley, [1848] 1907.

Ihrig, B.B., ed. *The First One Hundred Years, a History of the City of Sedalia, Missouri, 1860–1960.* Sedalia, Mo.: Centennial History, 1960.

"Incident at Cowskin Prairie in Story, Literature, and History." *Ozarks Watch*, vol. 8, no. 3 (1995), 20–25.

"Incident of War." *New York Times*, 24 July 1861.

Index of service records, Confederate, 1861–1865. Box 107 Reel s735. Jefferson City, Mo.: Office of Adjutant General.

Ingenthron, Elmo, and Kathleen Van Buskirk. *Borderland Rebellion: A History of the Civil War on the Missouri-Arkansas Border.* Branson, Mo.: Ozarks Mountaineer, 1980.

Jackson, C. F. [Claiborne]. Correspondence to Major General Price. In *Official Records*, series 1, vol. 53, 721–723. Washington, D.C., 1898.

Jackson, Claiborne. "General Orders, No. 16." In *Official Records*, series 1, vol. 53, 705. Washington, D.C., 1898.

——. "General Orders, No. 17." In *Official Records*, series 1, vol. 53, 705–706. Washington, D.C., 1898.

James, J. W. "Battle of Oak Hills." *Confederate Veteran* 24 (1916): 72.

Jasper County Relinquishments, State Roads, 1851. #7 Box 60. Jefferson City, Mo.: Missouri State Archives.

Jasper County, Missouri. Deed Record Book E, 551/1-2-1860. In *Black Families of the Ozarks*, vol. 1, 91–120, Greene County Archives Bulletin No. 45. Springfield, Mo.: Greene County Archives and Records Center, n. d.

Jasper County, Missouri. Jasper County vs. Chenault, John R., et al. Box 23 Folder 117. Carthage, Mo.: Jasper County Records, 25 July 1865.

Jobe, Sybil, ed. *Centennial History of Newton County, Missouri.* Reprint. Neosho, Mo.: Newton County Historical Society, [1876] 1976.

Johnson, Wes. "Artifacts Reminder of Carthage Battle," *Springfield News-Leader*, 4 July 2011.

Kansas Adjutant General's Office. "Military History of Kansas Regiments." In *Report of the Adjutant General of the State of Kansas, 1861–1865*. Topeka: Kansas State Print, 1896.

King, W. H. "Early Experiences in Missouri." *Confederate Veteran* 17 (1909): 502–503.

Kirkpatrick, Arthur Roy. "Missouri in the Early Months of the Civil War." *Missouri Historical Review* 55 (1961): 235–266.

———. "Missouri on the Eve of the Civil War." *Missouri Historical Review* 55 (1961): 99–108.

Knox, Thomas W. *Camp-Fire and Cotton-Field: Southern Adventure in Time of War. Life with the Union Armies, and Residence on a Louisiana Plantation.* New York: Blelock, 1865.

Lackmann, Ronald W. *Women of the Western Frontier in Fact, Fiction, and Film.* Jefferson, N.C.: McFarland, 1997.

Lademann, Otto C. "The Battle of Carthage, Mo., Friday, July 5, 1861." In *War Papers Read before the Commandery of the State of Wisconsin, Military Order of the Loyal Legion of the United States*, vol. 4. Milwaukee: Burdick & Allen, [1907] 1914.

Larkin, Lew. *Missouri Heritage.* Columbia, Mo.: American, 1968.

Leland, Charles Godfrey. "The War between Freedom and Slavery in Missouri." *Continental Monthly* 1 (April 1862): 369–381, 405–413.

Leser, Frederick. *In Memoriam. Franz Hassendeubel, Colonel 17th Regiment, Miss. Volunteer Infantry. "Western Turner Rifles." 1861.* Philadelphia: n. p., 1899.

Lincoln, Abraham. *The Collected Works of Abraham Lincoln*, vol. 4. Edited by Roy P. Basler. New Brunswick: Rutgers University Press, 1953.

Lindberg, Kip A. "The Semblance of a Weapon: Arms and Equipment of the Missouri State Guard." In *Sterling Price's Lieutenants: A Guide to the Officers and Organization of the Missouri State Guard, 1861–1865*. By Richard C. Peterson, James E. McGhee, Kip A. Lindberg, and Keith I. Daleen, 308–312. Shawnee Mission, Kans.: Two Trails, 1995.

Lindsey, Flavius J. "Cowskin Prairie and Wilson's Creek." *Missouri Republican* [St. Louis], 12 March 1886.

Livingston, Joel Thomas. *A History of Jasper County, Missouri, and Its People*, vol. 1. Chicago: Lewis, 1912.

Lyon, Nathaniel. Correspondence to Colonel Sigel, 10 July 1861. "Lyon Correspondence to Sigel, Huffman's Crossing of Osage River, Just Above Mouth of Sack [*sic*] River" (C0470). State Historical Society of Missouri, Columbia.

———. "Engagement at Boonville, Report of Brig. Gen. Nathaniel Lyon." In *Official Records*, series 1, vol. 3, 11–12. Washington, D.C., 1881.

———. "No. 1, Report of Captain Nathaniel Lyon." In *Official Records*, series 1, vol. 3, 4–5. Washington, D.C. 1881.

Map of the Battle of Dry Fork Creek, Mo., Accompanying Report of Capt. T. W. Sweeny, 2nd U.S. Infantry. Records of the Adjutant General's Office, Record Group 94, Cartographic Section. Washington, D.C.: National Archives.

Matthews, Robert Pinkney. "Souvenir of the Holland Co. Home Guards and Phelps Regiment Mo. Volunteer Inf." (C1160), n. d., n. p. State Historical Society of Missouri, Columbia.

Maxwell, Lena Knight. "Knights of Knights Station." Carthage, Mo.: Jasper County Records Center, 1980. Manuscript.

McCown, James. "No. 5, Report of Col. James McCown." In *Official Records*, series 1, vol. 3, 25–26. Washington, D.C., 1881.

McCulloch, Ben. "No. 2, Report of Brig. Gen. Ben McCulloch. In, *Official Records*, series 1, vol. 3, 39. Washington, D.C., 1881.

———. "Report to Hon. L. P. Walker, Camp Jackson, Ark." In *Official Records*, series 1, vol. 3, 606–608. Washington, D.C., 1881.

McDonald and Newton Counties Sections of Goodspeed's History of Newton, Lawrence, Barry, and McDonald Counties, Missouri. Reprint. Chicago: Goodspeed, [1888] 1972.

McElroy, John. *The Struggle for Missouri.* Washington, D.C.: National Tribune, 1909.

McGregor, Malcolm G. *The Biographical Record of Jasper County, Missouri.* Chicago: Lewis, 1901.

McIntosh, James. "No. 3, Report of Capt. James McIntosh." In *Official Records*, series 1, vol. 3, 39–40. Washington, D.C., 1881.

McMahan, Robert T. *Reluctant Cannoneer: The Diary of the Twenty-Fifth Independent Light Ohio Artillery.* Edited by Michael E. Banasik. Iowa City: Camp Pope, 2000.

McNamara, J. H. "An Historical Sketch of the Sixth Division, Missouri State Guard, from Its Organization in 1861," A309. Mosby Monroe Parsons Collection. St. Louis: Missouri Historical Society.

McPherson, James M. *Battle Cry of Freedom: The Civil War Era.* New York: Oxford University Press, 2003.

Miles, Kathleen White. *Bitter Ground: The Civil War in Missouri's Golden Valley.* Warsaw, Mo.: Printery, 1971.

Miller, Robert E. "General Mosby M. Parsons: Missouri's Secessionist General." *Missouri Historical Review* 80 (1985): 33–57.

Missouri. *Adjutant General's Report of the State Militia for 1861.* Jefferson City: n. p., 1864.

Missouri General Assembly. House of Representatives. *Missouri State Convention, 1861–1863; Journal of the House of the State of Missouri at the Twenty-First Session of the Missouri General Assembly.* Jefferson City: W. G. Cheeney, 1861.

_____. House of Representatives. *Appendix to the House Journal of the Adjourned Session of the Twenty-Second General Assembly of Missouri.* Jefferson City: J. P. Ament, 1863.

Missouri's Sons of the South, vol. 2. St. Louis: Missouri Division Sons of Confederate Veterans, 1998.

Missouri State Gazetteer and Business Directory. St. Louis: Sutherland & McEvoy, 1860.

Monaghan, Jay. *Civil War on the Western Border 1854–1865.* Boston: Little, Brown, 1955.

Moore, Frank. *The Rebellion Record: A Diary of American Events,* vol. 1. New York: G. P. Putnam, 1862.

Moore, John C. "Missouri." In *Confederate Military History,* vol. 9. Edited by Clement A. Evans. Atlanta: Confederate, 1899.

Mudd, Joseph A. "What I Saw at Wilson's Creek." *Missouri Historical Review* 7 (1912): 89–105.

_____. *With Porter in North Missouri: A Chapter in the History of the War Between the States.* Washington, D.C.: National, 1909.

Neely, Jeremy. *The Border between Them: Violence and Reconciliation on the Kansas-Missouri Line.* Columbia: University of Missouri Press, 2007.

"Negroes Burnt at Carthage." *Weekly Statesman* [Mo.], 12 August 1853.

Neumann, Robert, James Joplin, Richard W. Hatcher III, and Mary Markey. *Civil War Campaigns in the Ozarks.* n. p., 1980.

Nevin, David. *The Civil War: The Road to Shiloh — Early Battles in the West.* Alexandria, Va.: Time-Life, 1983.

"News from South-Western Missouri," *Daily Times* [Leavenworth, Kans.], 23 July 1861.

Nicolay, John G. *The Outbreak of Rebellion.* New York: Charles Scribner's Sons, 1881.

Nicolay, John G., and John Hay. "Abraham Lincoln: A History." *The Century Magazine* 36 (1888): 281–305.

North, F. A., ed. *History of Jasper County, Missouri, Including a Condensed History of the State, a Complete History of Carthage and Joplin, etc.* Des Moines: Mills, 1883.

Oates, Stephen B. *To Purge This Land with Blood: A Biography of John Brown.* New York: Harper & Row, 1970.

"Obituary Mosby Monroe Parsons, Camargo, Nuevo Leon, Mexico, 15 Aug. 1865." *Jefferson City Missouri State Times,* 29 September 1865.

"Obituary of Gen. W. Y. Slack, *Memphis Avalanche,* 8 May 1862." In "Sketch of General W. Y. Slack, of Missouri." *The Land We Love,* 6 (March 1869): 357–360.

Official Register of the Officers and Cadets of the U.S. Military Academy, West Point, New York. Washington, D.C.: U.S. Government, June 1850.

Orr, Sample. Telegram to Abraham Lincoln, 21 November 1861. In *The Abraham Lincoln Papers,* Series 1, General Correspondence. Washington, D.C.: Library of Congress, 1833–1916.

Ostmeyer, Andy. "Carthage Considered Site of First Major Land Battle of Civil War." *The Joplin Globe* [Mo.], 25 April 2011.

"Our St. Louis Correspondence: Authentic Description of the Battle of Carthage." *New York Times,* 15 July, 1861.

Owens, Robert. *Hier snackt wi Plattdutsch* [Here We Speak Low German]. Cole Camp, Mo.: City of Cole Camp, 1989.

Parsons, M. M. "No. 11, Report of Brig. Gen. Monroe M. [*sic*] Parsons." In *Official Records,* series 1, vol. 3, 34–37. Washington, D.C., 1881.

Parsons, Mosby Monroe. Papers, 1847–1869. St. Louis: Missouri Historical Society.

Patrick, Jeffrey L., ed. "Remembering the Missouri Campaign of 1861: The Memoirs of Lieutenant William P. Barlow, Guibor's Battery, Missouri State Guard." *Civil War Regiments: A Journal of the American Civil War* 5 (1997): 21–60.

Paxton, William McClung. *Annals of Platte County, Missouri, from Its Exploration Down to June 1, 1897.* Kansas City: Hudson-Kimberly, 1897.

Payne, James A. "Early Days of War in Missouri." In *Missouri's Sons of the South,* vol. 2, 925–928. St. Louis: Missouri Division Sons of Confederate Veterans, 1998.

_____. "Fighting in Missouri." In *Missouri's Sons of the South,* vol. 2, 913–915. St. Louis: Missouri Division Sons of Confederate Veterans, 1998.

Pearce, N. B. "Nicholas Bartlett Pearce Memoir, 1892." Manuscript Resources of the Civil War. Fayetteville: University of Arkansas Special Collections. Microfilm 124.

Peckham, James. *General Nathaniel Lyon and Missouri in 1861. A Monograph of the Great Rebellion.* New York: American News, 1866.

Perkins, J. R. "Jefferson Davis and General Sterling Price." In *Missouri's Sons of the South,* vol. 1, 399–406. St. Louis: Missouri Division Sons of Confederate Veterans, 1998.

Peyton, R. L. Y. "No. 6, Report of Col. R. L. Y. Peyton." In *Official Records,* series 1, vol. 3, 27–28. Washington, D.C., 1881.

Phillips, Christopher. *Damned Yankee: A Life of General Nathaniel Lyon.* Columbia: University of Missouri Press, 1990.

Phillips, Christopher. *Missouri's Confederate: Claiborne Fox Jackson and the Creation of Southern Identity in the Border West,* Missouri Biography Series. Edited by William E. Foley. Columbia: University of Missouri Press, 2000.

Phillips, Christopher W. "The Court Martial of Lieutenant Nathaniel Lyon." *Missouri Historical Review* 81 (1987): 296–308.

Pictorial and Genealogical Record of Greene County, Missouri: Together with Bibliographies of Prominent Men of Other Portions of the State, Both Living and Dead. Chicago: Goodspeed, 1893.

Pillow, Gideon J. "Correspondence with L. P. Walker, June 28 to July 2, 1861." In *Official Records*, series 1, vol. 53, 703–705. Washington, D.C., 1898.

Piston, William Garrett, and Thomas P. Sweeney. *Portraits of Conflict: A Photographic History of Missouri in the Civil War.* Fayetteville: University of Arkansas Press, 2009.

Plum, William R. "The Southwest Early in the War." In *The Military Telegraph during the Civil War in the United States*, vol. 1, 108–126. Chicago: Jansen, McClurg, 1882.

Pollard, Edward Alfred. *The First Year of the War.* New York: C. B. Richardson, 1863.

Pompey, Sherman Lee. *Muster Lists of the Missouri Confederates*, vol. 4. Independence, Calif.: Historical & Genealogical, 1965.

Post Office Department Reports of Site Locations, 1837–1950: Missouri, Jasper County. Kansas City: National Archives at Kansas City, 1866. Microfilm M1126 Roll 232.

Price, Sterling. "General Orders No. 3." In *Official Records*, series 1, vol. 53, 710–711. Washington, D.C., 1898.

Price, Sterling. "General Order No. 8." General Orders, 1861 (C1494). Manuscripts Division. State Historical Society of Missouri, Columbia.

Price, Sterling. "General Orders, No. 10." In *Official Records*, series 1, vol. 53, 712–713. Washington, D.C., 1898.

Price, Sterling. Proclamation. "*Standard Extra*, Columbia, Missouri, 1861 (SUNP0886)." State Historical Society of Missouri, Columbia.

Primm, James Neal. *Lion of the Valley: St. Louis Missouri, 1764–1980*, 3d ed. St. Louis: Missouri Historical Society, 1998.

"Proceedings of Congress. Senate. Afternoon Session. The Message. National Affairs." *New York Times*, 6 July 1861.

Rains, James S. "No. 3, Report of Brig. Gen. James S. Rains." In *Official Records*, series 1, vol. 3, 20–22. Washington, D.C., 1881.

"Reported Battles in Missouri." *New York Times*, 11 July 1861.

"Reported Death of Gen. Rains." *New York Times*, 12 July 1861.

Review of *The Life of General Nathaniel Lyon*, by Ashbel Woodward. *New Englander and Yale Review* 22 (1863): 149–153.

Richardson, Albert D. *The Secret Service, the Field, the Dungeon, the Escape.* Hartford, Conn.: American, 1865.

Richardson, James D. *A Compilation of the Messages and Papers of the Confederacy, Including the Diplomatic Correspondence, 1861–1865*, vol. 1. Nashville: United States, 1905.

Rives, B. A. "No. 10, Report of Col. B. A. Rives. In *Official Records*, series 1, vol. 3, 34. Washington, D.C., 1881.

Rombauer, Robert J. *The Union Cause in St. Louis in 1861: An Historical Sketch.* St. Louis: Nixon-Jones, 1909.

Rorvig, Paul. "The Significant Skirmish: The Battle of Boonville, June 17, 1861." *Missouri Historical Review* 86 (1992): 127–148.

Rosengarten, Joseph George. *The German Soldier in the Wars of the United* States, 2d ed. Philadelphia: J.B. Lippincott, 1890.

Rosser, Thomas H. Correspondence to J. Marshall McCue, Leavenworth County [Kans.] Historical Society & Museum, 1886.

St. Louis Public Schools. *Official Report*, vol. 7, 1889–1892. Saint Louis: Board of Education, 1892.

"St. Louisan Recalls Days when Slaves were Sold at Auction at Entrance to the Court House." *St. Louis Star*, 30 January 1922.

Scharf, J. Thomas, *History of Saint Louis City and County*, vol. 1. Philadelphia: L. H. Everts, 1883.

Schrader, William Henry. "Reminiscences," n. d. (C1519). Manuscripts Division, State Historical Society of Missouri, Columbia.

Schrantz, Ward L. "The Battle of Carthage." *Missouri Historical Review* 31 (1936): 140–149.

Schrantz, Ward L. *Jasper County, Missouri, in the Civil War.* Carthage, Mo.: Carthage Press, 1923.

Settle, William A. *Jesse James Was His Name.* Lincoln: University of Nebraska Press, 1977.

Shalhope, Robert E. *Sterling Price: Portrait of a Southerner.* Columbia: University of Missouri Press, 1971.

Sheppard, Louisa Cheairs McKenny. "A Confederate Girlhood: The Memoirs of Louisa Cheairs McKenny Sheppard." Campbell-McCammon Collection, Acc. #92-72.1. Box 2 Folder 4. Springfield, Mo.: History Museum for Springfield-Greene County, 1892. Manuscript.

Shirley, Glenn. *Belle Starr and Her Times: The Literature, the Facts, and the Legends.* Norman: University of Oklahoma Press, 1990.

Shoemaker, Floyd C. *Missouri and Missourians: Land of Contrasts and People of Achievements*, vol. 1. Chicago: Lewis, 1943.

_____. "Missouri: Heir of Southern Tradition and Individuality." *Missouri Historical Review* 36 (1942): 435–446.

_____, ed. *Missouri, Day by Day*, vols. 1 and 2. Columbia, Mo.: State Historical Society of Missouri, 1942–1943.

Sigel, Franz. Correspondence to Thomas L. Snead.

April 5, 1886. WICR 31022 Cab. 30, Dwr. D, Box 1. Republic, Mo.: Wilson's Creek National Battlefield Museum.

_____. "No. 2, Report of the Battle of Carthage." In *Official Records*, series 1, vol. 3, 16–19. Washington, D.C., 1881.

Sixth District Congressional Election Results. 6 August 1860. Jefferson City, Mo.: Missouri State Archives.

Slack, W. Y. "No. 9, Report of William Y. Slack." In *Official Records*, series 1, vol. 3, 32–33. Washington, D.C., 1881.

Snead, Thomas L. *The Fight for Missouri, from the Election of Lincoln to the Death of Lyon.* New York: C. Scribner's Sons, 1886.

_____. "The First Year of the War in Missouri." In *Battles and Leaders of the Civil War*, vol. 1, Centennial War Series, 262–277. Edited by Robert Underwood Johnson and Clarence Clough Buehl. Secaucus, N.J.: Castle, 1887.

Sneed, Nancy Jane. "The Curtis Wright House." *Ozarks Watch*, Summer 1988.

Snyder, John F. Correspondence to Thomas L. Snead, June 2, 1886. WICR 31022 Cab. 30, Dwr. D, Box 1. Republic, Mo: Wilson's Creek National Battlefield Museum.

Steele, Philip W., and Steve Cottrell. *Civil War in the Ozarks.* Gretna, La.: Pelican, 2009.

Stevens, Walter B. *Centennial History of Missouri (The Center State): One Hundred Years in the Union, 1820–1921*, vol. 1. St. Louis: S. J. Clarke, 1921.

Stirman, Erasmus. Correspondence to Rebecca Stirman. Rebecca Stirman Davidson Family Papers. Fayetteville: University of Arkansas Special Collections Manuscript Collection MC541.

Sturges, J. A., ed. *Illustrated History of McDonald County, Missouri.* Pineville, Mo.: J. A. Sturges, 1897.

Sweeny, Thomas W. Correspondence to General Lyon, July 11, 1861. Wilson's Creek National Battlefield.

_____. Map of the Battle of Dry Fork Creek. In *Atlas to Accompany the Official Records of the Union and Confederate Armies: House Miscellaneous Documents*, series 1, vol. 40, pt. 1. Washington, D.C.: Government Printing Office, 1892.

_____. "No. 1, Report of Captain Thomas W. Sweeny." In *Official Records*, series 1, vol. 3, 15–16. Washington, D.C., 1881.

Switzler, W. F., C. R. Barns, R. A. Campbell, Alban Jasper Conant, and G. C. Swallow. *Switzler's Illustrated History of Missouri, from 1541 to 1877.* St. Louis: C.R. Barns, 1879.

Taylor, George W. "Our Jefferson City Correspondence." *New York Times*, 8 October 1861.

Thomas, Archie. "Battle of Carthage, Jasper County, Missouri, 5 July 1861." Rolla: Western Historical

Manuscript Collection, University of Missouri-Rolla, n. d.

Tomes, Robert, and Benjamin G. Smith. *The War with the South: A History of the Late Rebellion*, vol. 1. New York: Virtue & Yorston, 1862–1867.

Tracy, Albert. "Journal, 1861" (C1273). State Historical Society of Missouri, Columbia.

Trickett, Dean. "The Civil War in the Indian Territory." *Chronicles of Oklahoma* 19 (1941): 383.

"Union Forever." *New York Times*, 21 April 1861.

United States. "Census of Missouri Slave Schedules," Jasper County, 1860. Springfield, Mo.: Library Center, n. d. Microfilm #46 T7-146.

United States. Record and Pension Office. *Organization and Status of Missouri Troops (Union and Confederate) in Service during the Civil War.* Washington, D.C.: Government Printing Office, 1902.

United States. Surveyor General, "Missouri Plats," vol. 34. Jefferson City, Mo.: Missouri State Archives. Microfilm F400.

United States. War Department. *87 Orders of General Court Martial, Courts of Inquiries and Letters Commenting on Said Courts 1838–1852.* Washington, D.C.: Government Printing Office, 1838.

VanDiver, W. D. "Reminiscences of General John B. Clark." *Missouri Historical Review* 20 (1926): 223–235.

VanGilder, Marvin L. "A Centennial History of the Battle of Carthage." *Carthage Evening Press*, 8 June 1961.

_____. *Jasper County: The First Two Hundred Years.* Carthage, Mo.: Jasper County Commission, 1995.

_____. *The Story of Barton County; a Complete History: 1855–1872.* Lamar, Mo.: A. Reiley, 1972.

Violette, E. M. *History of Missouri.* Reprint. Cape Girardeau, Mo.: Ramfire, [1918] 1951.

Voelkner, Henry. Letters, 1861–1862, (C0436). State Historical Society of Missouri, Columbia.

Wallace, J. C. "Gen. E. W. Price." In *Missouri's Sons of the South*, vol. 1. St. Louis: Missouri Division Sons of Confederate Veterans, 1998.

"War in Missouri, further Particulars of the Battle of Carthage." *New York Times*, 14 July 1861.

"War in Missouri, Our Springfield Correspondence." *New York Times*, 22 July, 1861.

Ward, Andrew. *The Slaves' War: The Civil War in the Words of Former Slaves.* Boston: Houghton Mifflin, 2008.

Ware, Eugene Fitch. *The Lyon Campaign in Missouri: Being a History of the First Iowa Infantry.* Topeka: Crane, 1907.

Warner, Ezra J. *Generals in Gray, Lives of the Confederate Commanders.* Baton Rouge: Louisiana State University Press, [1959] 2006.

Washburn, Israel. *The Issues: The Dred Scott Deci-*

sion: The Parties. Washington, D.C.: Congressional Republican Committee, 1860.

Webb, William L. Battles and Biographies of Missourians, or, the Civil War Period of Our State. Kansas City: Hudson-Kimberly, 1900.

Weed, F. F. "In the Battle of Carthage." Confederate Veteran 26 (1918): 392.

Weightman, R. H. "No. 4, Report of Col. Richard H. Weightman." In Official Records, series 1, vol. 3, 22–24. Washington, D.C., 1881.

Weightman, Richard Hanson. To the Congress of the United States,: by R. H. Weightman, Senator-elect, State of New Mexico. Requesting the Passage of a Bill Declaring New Mexico One of the United States of America on Certain Conditions. Washington, D.C.: Gideon, 1851.

Wilkie, Franc Bangs. Missouri in 1861: The Civil War Letters of Franc B. Wilkie, Newspaper Correspondent. Edited by Michael E. Banasik. Iowa City: Camp Pope, 2001.

Wilson, James Grant, and John Fiske, eds. "Sigel." In Appleton's Cyclopedia of American Biography, vol. 5. New York: D. Appleton, 1888.

Wilson, Joseph A. "Bledsoe of Missouri." In Battles and Biographies of Missourians, Or, the Civil War Period of Our State. Edited by William L. Webb. Kansas City: Hudson-Kimberly, 1900.

_____. "Bledsoe of Missouri." In Missouri's Sons of the South, vol. 1, 101–103. St. Louis: Missouri Division Sons of Confederate Veterans, 1998.

Woodson, William H. History of Clay County Missouri. Topeka: Historical, 1920.

Woodward, Ashbel. The Life of General Nathaniel Lyon. Hartford, Conn.: Case, Lockwood, 1862.

Wright, Louise Wigfall. A Southern Girl in '61: The War-Time Memories of a Confederate Senator's Daughter. New York: Doubleday, Page, 1905.

Wurthman, Leonard B., Jr. "Frank Blair: Lincoln's Congressional Spokesman." Missouri Historical Review 64 (1970): 263–287.

Young, A. J., ed. History of Dade County and Her People from the Date of the Earliest Settlements to the Present Time. Greenfield, Mo.: Pioneer Historical, 1917.

Young, Reba. Truman's Birthplace. Gretna, La.: Pelican, 2004.

Young, William. Young's History of Lafayette County, vol. 1. Indianapolis: B. F. Bowen, 1910.

Younger, Cole. Confessions of a Missouri Guerrilla: The Autobiography of Cole Younger. New York: Fireship, 2008.

Zucker, A. E., ed. The Forty-Eighters, Political Refugees of the German Revolution of 1848. New York: Columbia University Press, 1950.

Index

Numbers in **bold italics** indicate pages with photographs.

219